CW01465677

The Pathologies of Power

The foreign policy of the United States is guided by deeply held beliefs, few of which are recognized, much less subjected to rational analysis, Christopher J. Fettweis writes in this, his third book. He identifies the foundations of those beliefs – fear, honor, glory, and hubris – and explains how they have inspired poor strategic decisions in Washington. He then proceeds to discuss their origins. The author analyzes recent foreign policy mistakes, including the Bay of Pigs invasion, the Vietnam war, and the Iraq war, and he considers the decision-making process behind them, as well as the beliefs inspiring those decisions. The American government's strategic performance, Professor Fettweis argues, can be improved if these pathological beliefs are acknowledged and eliminated.

Christopher J. Fettweis is an associate professor of political science at Tulane University. He is the author of *Dangerous Times?: The International Politics of Great Power Peace* (2010) and *Losing Hurts Twice as Bad: The Four Stages to Moving Beyond Iraq* (2008).

The Pathologies of Power

Fear, Honor, Glory, and Hubris in U.S. Foreign Policy

CHRISTOPHER J. FETTWEIS

Tulane University

CAMBRIDGE
UNIVERSITY PRESS

CAMBRIDGE
UNIVERSITY PRESS

32 Avenue of the Americas, New York, NY 10013-2473, USA

Cambridge University Press is part of the University of Cambridge.

It furthers the University's mission by disseminating knowledge in the pursuit
of education, learning, and research at the highest international levels of excellence.

www.cambridge.org
Information on this title: www.cambridge.org/9781107682719

© Christopher J. Fettweis 2013

This publication is in copyright. Subject to statutory exception
and to the provisions of relevant collective licensing agreements,
no reproduction of any part may take place without the written
permission of Cambridge University Press.

First published 2013

Printed in the United States of America

A catalog record for this publication is available from the British Library.

Library of Congress Cataloging in Publication data
The pathologies of power : fear, honor, glory, and hubris in U.S. foreign policy /
Christopher J. Fettweis, Tulane University.
pages cm
Includes bibliographical references and index.
ISBN 978-1-107-04110-3 (hardback) –
ISBN 978-1-107-68271-9 (pbk.)
1. United States – Foreign relations.   2. United States – Foreign relations –
Psychological aspects.   3. Political psychology – United States.   4. International
relations – Psychological aspects.   5. International relations – Decision
making.   I. Fettweis, Christopher J.
JZ1480.P368   2013
327.73–dc23   2013012171

ISBN 978-1-107-04110-3 Hardback
ISBN 978-1-107-68271-9 Paperback

Cambridge University Press has no responsibility for the persistence or accuracy of
URLs for external or third-party Internet Web sites referred to in this publication
and does not guarantee that any content on such Web sites is, or will remain,
accurate or appropriate.

For Kimberly Deborah

Contents

Preface and Acknowledgments

Collective amnesia descends upon society following foreign policy disasters. People everywhere seem to exhibit symptoms of short-term memory loss; at the very least, few appear particularly eager to discuss what just occurred. Enterprising journalists might undertake first drafts of history, but for the most part the event barely registers in the popular imagination. For a certain period of time, one whose length is directly related to the magnitude of the disaster, the embarrassment and shame generated by national mistakes make them too raw for people to confront in any real depth. Lessons, if there are any, have to wait.

Vietnam was all but ignored by the media for quite some time following the fall of Saigon, for example, and was hardly mentioned at all during the presidential campaign of 1976.[1] Popular culture was equally reticent: no major film dealt with the reality of the war until 1979, and then not again until 1986. The uninformed newcomer to the United States in the mid-1970s could have been forgiven for being unaware that any tragic, unnecessary war had just been fought in Southeast Asia.

It is in these periods, however, that beliefs about such events solidify and narratives coalesce, if in private. Few people ever change the positions at which they subconsciously arrive during these seemingly

---

[1] George C. Herring, *America's Longest War: The United States and Vietnam, 1950–1975* (New York: Knopf, 1979), p. 273.

somnambulant times. These brief respites are not merely efforts at mass denial, in other words, but crucial phases in society's long-term interpretation, in the process of coming to terms with what just occurred, or with what its country just did.

This book was written during such a period. The war in Iraq has officially ended, and hardly anyone wants to talk about it. The only consensus, if unspoken, is that mistakes were made. What they were, why they happened, or how they can be avoided in the future are questions few seem ready to confront. But whether the public is ready for it or not, the interpretation of Iraq cannot – and certainly should not – be postponed indefinitely. The opening of the George W. Bush Library in April 2013 offered apologists the opportunity to fire off the first round of revisionist history and to suggest that an utterly unrepentant Bush deserves praise since, after all, he tried his best. And he loves America so darn much.

That narrative cannot be allowed to take hold. No society – especially not the American society – likes to admit mistakes, but Iraq cannot be thought of otherwise. The war was the greatest catastrophe in post–Cold War U.S. foreign policy, one that has led to the deaths of untold tens of thousands and has left behind a chaotic, violent, sectarian mess. On the same day that two bombs killed three spectators of the Boston Marathon, a series of blasts in Iraq killed thirty-three people and wounded hundreds. Americans don't even hear such news anymore; it has become the norm in post-Saddam, George Bush Iraq, too commonplace to notice.

This book has been written to help us understand why the invasion of Iraq and other U.S. foreign policy mistakes occurred, going beyond surface explanations in search of deeper roots, in the ultimate hope of helping to prevent the next national disaster.

Like all others, this book was not written by its author alone. Special thanks go to Peter Burns, Brian Brox, Patrick Egan, Martin Mendoza, John Mueller, Joseph Parent, Aaron Schneider, Mark Vail, Dana Zartner, and a particularly thorough reviewer. I presented portions of this book a number of times over the last couple of years, including at a variety of conferences, the U.S. Naval War College, and the Mershon Center for International Security at Ohio State, and I received very helpful ideas and feedback in each instance. I am also thankful to the Army Corps of Engineers, who proved temporarily competent enough to keep Lake Pontchartrain out of uptown New Orleans for seven years in a row, allowing me to finish the book. Most of all, I want to thank my girls – Celeste, Lucy, and Kimberly – who give me a reason to get out of bed in the morning.

Introduction

Pathological Beliefs and U.S. Foreign Policy

There have been occasions throughout history when war was thrust upon an unwilling and unprepared United States. Those times have been exceptions rather than the rule, however; most of the time when Washington has used force, it has done so by choice rather than necessity, following a period of extensive rumination and debate. No decision was more obviously on the horizon or more widely discussed, for example, than the 2003 invasion of Iraq. For months leading up to the invasion, talking-head programs and op-ed pages were filled with the views of people with all manner of foreign policy qualifications and lack thereof. The possibility of regime change in Baghdad was easily the top issue on the political agenda in 2002. Whatever can be said of the ultimate wisdom of that venture (and much deserves to be, and will be, said), it was not under-considered.

This national debate should have produced a good outcome, at least in theory. In the "marketplace of ideas," or arena of debate in a free society, the strongest arguments should rise to the surface on the basis of superior logic and evidence, while those built on weaker foundations should sink into oblivion. As John Stuart Mill argued centuries ago, vigorous public debate ought to be the ally of truth and wisdom, producing the best policy outcomes.[1] Why, then, did the final decisions regarding Iraq go so terribly wrong?

---

[1] John Stuart Mill, *On Liberty* (New York: Cambridge University Press, 1989), part 2. See also Jack Snyder and Karen Ballentine, "Nationalism and the Marketplace of Ideas," *International Security*, Vol. 21, No. 2 (Autumn 1996), pp. 5–40.

Foreign policy blunders are usually not too difficult to explain. Once historians have had a chance to dig into archives and see what policy makers thought and believed at the time, mistakes usually become at least understandable, if perhaps never entirely forgivable. States are typically led into disasters by leaders convinced they were making correct, even necessary choices and who were doing their best under impossibly difficult circumstances. George W. Bush believed that Saddam Hussein posed a real threat to the United States and thought that removing him would be rather simple. A generation earlier, Lyndon Johnson believed that it was important to preserve U.S. credibility in Vietnam, and certainly did not want to be remembered as the first president to lose a war. His predecessor believed that the Castro regime was not only a threat but fundamentally fragile, vulnerable to collapse with the slightest superpower push.

Foreign policies, like all other human actions, are motivated by beliefs. Without a basic conception of how the world works, what is important and what is not, and ultimately about the nature of people, decisions would be impossible to make. The key to understanding foreign policy failures, therefore, lies not in the actions themselves but in the beliefs that gave rise to them. Where do incorrect – pathologically incorrect – foreign policy beliefs come from? Or, to be blunt, why do so many American leaders hold underexamined views of the world that inspire foolish, counterproductive actions?

A series of underlying, often unstated, and certainly unsupported beliefs lies at the root of U.S. foreign policy. Even before September 11, Americans considered the world to be a dangerous place where the enemies of freedom and liberty lurked in many corners. Victory over our adversaries would be impossible without their respect; when the United States lacks credibility, many believe, policy making becomes infinitely more difficult. Furthermore, Americans worry that their nation's status as the world's leader may be about to come to an end. But in the final analysis, since there is nothing this country cannot do once its mind is made up, Americans know the United States will persevere and rise again.

The ancients would recognize these beliefs and place them into familiar categories: fear, honor, glory, and hubris. Modern leaders may be reluctant to acknowledge that they are susceptible to such basic, primal atavisms, but often their differences with the Caesars are more in style than substance. This book is about these and other beliefs prevalent in both popular and leadership circles in the United States, which are simultaneously pervasive, influential, and underexamined. They help account for some of the worst foreign policy decisions the United States has made in recent years, from the Bay of Pigs to Vietnam to Iraq, and they will cause many more in years to come if they are not recognized and corrected. If this country is to learn from its disastrous experience in Iraq rather than merely shrug it off as another in a long series of inevitable blunders, then it needs to take a moment to analyze the roots of its actions. Though their origins may be ancient, these categories of pathological belief are not omnipotent. While it may never be possible to eliminate fear, honor, glory, or hubris from foreign policy making, their detrimental effects on behavior can at the very least be minimized.

To improve the quality of their foreign policy choices, leaders should periodically examine the underlying beliefs that motivate their behavior, with the goal of minimizing the influence of the ones that have a high probability of producing low-quality results, which are usually those based on thin reasoning and evidence. Consistently strong foreign policy cannot be built on an irrational foundation; indeed rationality in decision making should be thought of as a minimum requirement for sagacious policy makers, for their own good as well as that of their countries and of the international system as a whole. The sixteen-month-long debate leading up to Iraq exposed just how deeply a number of pathological beliefs are imbedded in the minds of many Americans. Inertia guarantees they will remain there unless acted upon by a force.

PATHOLOGICAL BELIEFS AND INTERNATIONAL RELATIONS

At any given time, society is home to a number of ideas, beliefs, and ideologies that compete with one another to form the foundation for policy making. In mature democracies, the weaker of these should not persist for too long in the marketplace of ideas. Unfortunately, this weeding-out process does not always function in practice as it does in theory; all too often, the fittest ideas do not survive. The victors are just as likely to be weaker beliefs, ones that proved essentially

impervious to alteration by exposure to reason and fact.[2] The odds in
the marketplace are stacked against many ideas, irrespective of their
wisdom, before the competition begins. In reality societal debates
are not detached intellectual evaluations of evidence where victory
goes to the most logical, but passionate, emotional struggles where
entrenched assumptions fight one another for control over decisions
(and decision makers), and where the outcome is always uncertain.
Rather than a marketplace of ideas, in other words, foreign policy
debates more closely resemble a battlefield of beliefs.

It is on this battlefield that policy is formed. To explain the behavior of the individual, examine his or her beliefs; similarly, to understand the foreign policy actions of a state, collective beliefs are a good
place to begin. The triumphs of the United States as well as its various
mistakes all have their origins in the assumptions that provide the
justification for action by shaping the cost-benefit analyses performed
prior to decisions. When pathological beliefs defeat more rational
ones, states march toward disaster.

Given their manifest importance in explaining state behavior, it is
somewhat surprising how little attention is paid to beliefs as a causal
variable in the study of international politics.[3] Scholars have spent
time describing U.S. foreign policy ideologies in elites and masses,
but rarely have they examined their genesis, evolution, or effects.[4]
Little effort has been made to evaluate particular beliefs, to assess

[2] Chaim Kaufmann, "Threat Inflation and the Failure of the Marketplace of Ideas:
The Selling of the Iraq War," *International Security*, Vol. 29, No. 1 (Summer 2004),
pp. 5–48.
[3] Exceptions include Douglas W. Blum, "The Soviet Foreign Policy Belief System:
Beliefs, Politics, and Foreign Policy Outcomes," *International Studies Quarterly*, Vol. 37,
No. 4 (December 1993), pp. 373–94; Richard J. Payne, *The Clash with Distant Cultures:
Values, Interests, and Force in American Foreign Policy* (Albany: State University of New York
Press, 1995); Robert Jervis, "Understanding Beliefs," *Political Psychology*, Vol. 27, No.
5 (October 2006), pp. 641–63; and those discussed later. The relationship between
attitudes and behavior is a much studied subject in sociology; for a review of the
basic concepts and early scholarship, see Howard Schuman and Michael P. Johnson,
"Attitudes and Behavior," *Annual Review of Sociology*, Vol. 2 (1976), pp. 161–207.
[4] Ole R. Holsti and James N. Rosenau have been tracking elite opinion and ideology for decades. See their "The Domestic and Foreign Policy Beliefs of American
Leaders," *Journal of Conflict Resolution*, Vol. 32, No. 2 (June 1988), pp. 248–94; and
"Liberals, Populists, Libertarians, and Conservatives: The Link between Domestic
and International Affairs," *International Political Science Review*, Vol. 17, No. 1 (January
1996), pp. 29–54. See also Charles W. Kegley, Jr., "Assumptions and Dilemmas in the
Study of Americans' Foreign Policy Beliefs: A Caveat," *International Studies Quarterly*,

both their empirical justification and importance in development of policy.[5] Normative questions about their utility or wisdom are even more rarely addressed, as if such assessments are outside the scope (or capability) of scholarship. There are many good reasons for these omissions, because the study of beliefs immediately encounters a number of significant methodological and epistemological challenges. However, no model that entirely omits their influence can hope to explain behavior in the international system. As long as people run countries, beliefs will explain behavior of states.

Rather than ask why unsupportable ideas survive to impoverish foreign policy debates, perhaps scholars should wonder how pathological beliefs rise to become such prominent fixtures in the first place and what might be done to correct them, or perhaps to aid more rational beliefs. A few definitions might provide a good starting point for such an effort.[6]

On Beliefs, Pathological and Otherwise

The person who decides to take a big risk because of astrological advice in the morning's horoscope can benefit from baseless superstition if the risk pays off. Probability and luck suggest that successful policies can sometimes be based on incorrect beliefs. Far more often, however, poor intellectual foundations lead to suboptimal or even disastrous outcomes. It is only when they lead to bad policies that

Vol. 30, No. 4 (December 1986), pp. 447–71; Leslie A. Hayduk, Pamela A. Ratner, Joy L. Johnson, and Joan L. Bottorff, "Attitudes, Ideology and the Factor Model," *Political Psychology*, Vol. 16, No. 3 (September 1995), pp. 479–507; William O. Chittick, Keith R. Billingsly, and Rick Travis, "A Three-Dimensional Model of American Foreign Policy Beliefs," *International Studies Quarterly*, Vol. 39, No. 3 (September 1995), pp. 313–31; and Edwin Eloy Aguilar, Benjamin O. Fordham, and G. Patrick Lynch, "The Foreign Policy Beliefs of Political Campaign Contributors," *International Studies Quarterly*, Vol. 41, No. 2 (June 1997), pp. 355–65.

[5] An exception is Paul R. Brewer and Marco R. Steenbergen, "All Against All: How Beliefs about Human Nature Shape Foreign Policy Opinions," *Political Psychology*, Vol. 23, No. 1 (March 2002), pp. 39–58. See also Evan Luard, *War in International Society: A Study in International Sociology* (London: I. B. Taurus, 1986).

[6] It should be noted up front that this volume deals with a number of concepts whose meanings have, in some cases, been the subject of thousands of years of debate. For the most part, it will make a conscious decision to recognize, but *not* to engage, the minutiae of these discussions. Emphasis will be placed on clarity rather than comprehensiveness.

beliefs become pathological and subjects for this analysis. The United States, unfortunately, suffers from a number.

In their simplest form, beliefs are *ideas that have become internalized and accepted as true*, often without much further analysis.[7] They are the assumptions we all work into our lives, the foundation for the prisms through which actors perceive and interpret their surroundings. Beliefs essentially shape the set of behavioral options, acting as heuristic devices for those seeking to organize and interpret new information and respond appropriately.[8] People are not born with beliefs; the origins of beliefs are in nurture rather than nature, and they become accepted, not because of rational analysis but trust in those who relay them. People do not choose their religious beliefs, for example, based on a review of the evidence. Secular beliefs are also sustained by faith as much as fact, and are thus distinguished from knowledge (classically, "justified true belief") by the absence of any stringent requirement for justification. Although they almost always have some basis in reality, beliefs need not pass rigorous tests to prove that they match it. No amount of evidence can convince some people that vaccines do not cause autism, for example, or that the climate is changing because of human activity. Ultimately, as Robert Jervis explains, "we often believe as much in the face of evidence as because of it."[9]

Beliefs are more than mere perceptions or intellectual interpretations of the external world. Once internalized, they can quickly become central to an actor's identity structure or basic sense of self. Beliefs are *visceral as much as intellectual*, in other words, connected to emotion rather than reason, and as such are nearly impervious to alteration by new information.[10] Tolstoy memorably observed that

7 Many different definitions of beliefs exist. For one of the most commonly used, see Martin Fishbein and Icek Ajzen, *Belief, Attitude, Intention and Behavior: An Introduction to Theory and Research* (Reading, MA: Addison-Wesley Publishing Co., 1975).

8 Payne, *Clash with Distant Cultures*, p. 10; and Blum, "The Soviet Foreign Policy Belief System," pp. 373–94. Beliefs are functionally similar to what Ted Hopf called "habits," which cause "an infinitude of behaviors [to be] effectively deleted from the available repertoire of possible actions." "The Logic of Habit in International Relations," *European Journal of International Relations*, Vol. 16, No. 4 (December 2010), p. 541.

9 Robert Jervis, "Understanding Beliefs and Threat Inflation," in A. Trevor Thrall and Jane K. Cramer, *American Foreign Policy and the Politics of Fear: Threat Inflation Since 9/11* (New York: Routledge, 2009), p. 18.

10 A good deal of experimental evidence exists to support the assertion that beliefs are nearly impervious to disconfirmation. See Craig A. Anderson, Mark R. Lepper,

even the most intelligent people "can very seldom discern even the simplest and most obvious truth if it be such as to oblige them to admit the falsity of conclusions they have formed, perhaps with much difficulty – conclusions of which they are proud, which they have taught to others, and on which they have built their lives."[11] Indeed part of the reason our beliefs are so resistant to change is because they shape the way new information is interpreted and filter out that which appears contradictory.[12]

Indeed beliefs often become so central to identity that substantial anxiety can be generated when new information calls them into question. It is far easier to fit new evidence into previously constructed cognitive frameworks, or to simply ignore it altogether, than to subject deeply held sub-rational assumptions to reexamination and risk destabilization of the sense of self. The mind constructs intricate and powerful defenses to prevent such destabilization and to bolster what psychologists refer to as "ontological security."[13] Those who suggest that our beliefs are incorrect are often greeted with the most passionate of denunciations. Furthermore, evidence suggests the beliefs of political experts – especially extremely negative views of adversaries – may well be even more resistant to change than those of other people.[14] In practice, this means the arena of foreign policy debate is dominated by people likely to disagree vehemently and emotionally

and Lee Ross, "Perseverance of Social Theories: The Role of Explanation in the Persistence of Discredited Information," *Journal of Personality and Social Psychology* Vol. 39, No. 6 (December 1980), pp. 1037–49; Charles G. Lord, Lee Ross, and Mark. R. Lepper, "Biased Assimilation and Attitude Polarization: The Effects of Prior Theories on Subsequently Considered Evidence," *Journal of Personality and Social Psychology*, Vol. 37, No. 11 (November 1979), pp. 2098–109; and Krystyna Rojahn and Thomas F. Pettigrew, "Memory for Schema-Relevant Information: A Meta-Analytic Resolution," *British Journal of Social Psychology*, Vol. 31, No. 2 (June 1992), pp. 81–109. See also Dan Reiter, *Crucible of Beliefs: Learning, Alliance, and World Wars* (Ithaca, NY: Cornell University Press, 1996).

[11] Leo Tolstoy, *What is Art?* (New York: Funk and Wagnalls Company, 1904), p. 143.

[12] Paul Slovic, *The Perception of Risk* (London: Earthscan, 2000), p. 222.

[13] Jennifer Mitzen adapted this psychological concept for international politics in "Ontological Security in World Politics: State Identity and the Security Dilemma," *European Journal of International Relations*, Vol. 12, No. 3 (September 2006), pp. 341–70.

[14] Mark Peffley and John Hurwitz, "International Events and Foreign Policy Beliefs: Public Response to Changing Soviet-U.S. Relations," *American Journal of Political Science*, Vol. 36, No. 2 (May 1992), pp. 431–61.

when their beliefs come into conflict, as they so often do. Facts may change, but beliefs stay the same.

Once enough members of a group have internalized a belief it can affect collective behavior, becoming part of the conventional wisdom of widely shared assumptions that, because everybody knows, nobody really considers.[15] Collective beliefs tend to be even more resistant to change than those of the individual because they are continually fortified by broader society. During the Cold War, people did not need to know much about communism to believe that it was antithetical to U.S. values, for example. What everyone knows must be true. By coloring interpretation of new information and framing the options for action in groups, collective beliefs create their own reality, which may or may not match the material world. Once embedded in what Robert Lane called the "cultural matrix of behavior and expectation," a belief can be "so persuasive and dense that one mistakes it for the natural environment."[16]

Perhaps because beliefs do not generally demand close examination or evaluation, they can be held quite strongly by people from all across the spectrum of cognitive complexity. What separates modern people from those of the Middle Ages is not intelligence, as even a cursory examination of castle construction reveals, but beliefs. The brilliance of medieval architects was combined with the belief in witches, succubi, and the validity of trial by ordeal. Germany in the 1930s was simultaneously the most scientifically advanced country in Europe and the most backward in its basic beliefs regarding races, the sanctity of rural life, and the importance of *lebensraum*. That these and other Nazi beliefs were never subjected to close intellectual examination might help explain the extremes of behavior they inspired.

Beliefs are rarely held in isolation. People tend to construct tightly connected, interrelated sets that provide a certain level of consistency to their interpretation of the outside world. When so constructed, sets of beliefs can be said to constitute *belief systems* or *ideologies*, which

---

[15] Jervis, "Understanding Beliefs and Threat Inflation," p. 19.
[16] Robert E. Lane, *Political Thinking and Consciousness: The Private Life of the Political Mind* (Chicago, IL: Markham Publishing, 1969), p. 315.

form the foundation of many core elements of identity, from political orientation to religion to sense of national purpose.[17] Belief systems reinforce the staying power of their component elements, making each even more immune to change. "Coherent and internally consistent belief systems tend to be self-perpetuating," noted Holsti and Rosenau, and soon come to shape the way actors interpret new information.[18] Belief systems also tend to generate "disbelief systems," or the corresponding broad set of information actors reject as false without much consideration. Disbelief systems are usually better described as a series of unrelated subsets rather than a unified whole, as coming chapters discuss. Conflating disbelief systems, and assuming that all falsehoods are related, seems to be a natural human tendency.[19]

Although beliefs drive foreign policy, they are not determinative, even among relatively homogenous populations. Indeed, although beliefs change far more slowly than ideas, they can and do evolve over time as people learn from events as well as from their own experiences. Few people still believe that the earth is at the center of the universe, for instance, or that insults to honor must be answered by a duel to the death. It is also possible, if somewhat less common, for ideologies to change if enough of their component beliefs are drawn into question. Political scientists have studied cognitive evolution in foreign policy for two decades, and have generally reached the conclusion that learning – sometimes significant learning – regularly takes place.[20] It is possible, therefore, to hope for more rationality in policy making. Indeed rational foreign policy decisions might be a rather

[17] Philip E. Converse, "The Nature of Belief Systems in Mass Publics," in David E. Apter, ed., *Ideology and Discontent* (New York: Macmillan, 1964), pp. 206–61. Converse employed the two terms interchangeably, explaining that, although his subject was *belief systems*, he would use *ideologies* "for aesthetic relief where it seems most appropriate" (p. 209). See also Paul A. Dawson, "The Formation and Structure of Political Belief Systems," *Political Behavior*, Vol. 1, No. 2 (Summer 1979), pp. 99–122.
[18] Ole R. Holsti and James Rosenau, "Vietnam, Consensus, and the Belief Systems of American Leaders," *World Politics*, Vol. 32, No. 1 (October 1979), p. 56. See also Richard Nisbett and Lee Ross, *Human Inference: Strategies and Shortcomings of Social Judgment* (Englewood Cliffs, NJ: Prentice-Hall, 1980).
[19] See Milton Rokeach, *The Open and Closed Mind: Investigations into the Nature of Belief Systems and Personality Systems* (New York: Basic Books, 1960), esp. p. 33.
[20] For discussions of learning in foreign policy, see George Modelski, "Is World Politics Evolutionary Learning?" *International Organization*, Vol. 44, No. 1 (Winter 1990), pp. 1–24; George W. Breslauer and Philip E. Tetlock, eds., *Learning in U.S.*

uncontroversial, widely shared goal, if only there were a common understanding of what exactly rationality is.

Rationality

For many social scientists, rationality is an assumption to be employed or rejected rather than a goal to which decision makers should aspire. In the study of international politics, rational choice theory is generally employed *descriptively* as part of the attempt to explain the behavior of states.[21] The assumption of rationality in behavior is ubiquitous in international relations theory and foreign policy analysis as well.[22] Using a weak definition, sometimes referred to as *instrumental* rationality, virtually anything people or states do can be considered rational, in the sense that decisions are goal oriented and the actor can usually explain what that goal is.[23] However, most conceptions of rationality go beyond this basic, rather low bar. Those who employ *procedural* rationality suggest policy makers select (or should select) from a set of options after a process of reflection and evaluation.[24] One of the few aspects common to these and other conceptions of rationality is the value judgment that its opposite is undesirable.[25] Irrationality is not merely purposeless, insane action, according to many political scientists, but rather those choices based on incorrect assumptions

and Soviet Foreign Policy (Boulder, CO: Westview Press, 1991); Sarah E. Mendelson, "Internal Battles and External Wars: Politics, Learning, and the Soviet Withdrawal from Afghanistan," *World Politics*, Vol. 45, No. 3 (April 1993), pp. 327–60; Jack S. Levy, "Learning and Foreign Policy: Sweeping a Conceptual Minefield," *International Organization*, Vol. 48, No. 2 (Spring 1994), pp. 279–312; and Reiter, *Crucible of Beliefs.*

[21] Many consider rational choice theory to have begun with Anthony Downes, *An Economic Theory of Democracy* (New York: Harper and Rowe, 1957).

[22] Neta C. Crawford, "The Passion of World Politics: Propositions on Emotion and Emotional Relationships," *International Security*, Vol. 24, No. 4 (Spring 2000), pp. 116–17; Stephen G. Walker and Akan Malici, *U.S. Presidents and Foreign Policy Mistakes* (Palo Alto, CA: Stanford University Press, 2011), p. 16.

[23] Herbert A. Simon, "Rationality in Political Behavior," *Political Psychology*, Vol. 16, No. 1 (March 1995), esp. pp. 45–46.

[24] On instrumental and procedural rationality, see Frank C. Zagare, "Rationality and Deterrence," *World Politics*, Vol. 42, No. 2 (January 1990), pp. 238–60.

[25] Irrationality does have its place, especially in strategy. See Robert Mandel, "The Desirability of Irrationality in Foreign Policy Making: A Preliminary Theoretical Analysis," *Political Psychology*, Vol. 5, No. 4 (December 1984), pp. 643–60.

that lead to negative outcomes.[26] Decisions are irrational, in other words, if other options existed for the policy maker that would have had foreseeable and preferable consequences.[27] History inevitably passes such judgments, however unfairly.

While this book has an important descriptive element, it is also *prescriptive*: it seeks both to explain foreign policy behavior and evaluate it, in the hope that by doing so improvements can be made. The target is both foreign policy scholarship and that battlefield of beliefs, the sphere of debate from which decisions arise. Rationality in this instance will be treated as an ideal, therefore, as a difficult and lofty goal for policy makers rather than an assumption about how actors behave.

For our purposes, rational beliefs are those based on valid, demonstrably true foundations. They employ, in Jervis's words, "those ways of interpreting evidence that conform to the generally accepted rules of drawing inferences" and stand the greatest chance of leading to productive foreign policy decisions.[28] Successful policies are by no means guaranteed, since target actors will make strategic choices of their own, but rational beliefs surely make the best foundation for policy making. Irrationality can sometimes produce good decisions, but its batting average is likely to be comparatively low.

Determining the rationality of beliefs is no small challenge. Jervis dealt with a similar dilemma in judging the accuracy of perceptions, which he addressed by focusing not on whether the perception was "correct" but on how it was derived from the available information. Jack Levy went further, arguing that "the concept of misperception is meaningful only if there exists in principle a correct perception." In the same way, there can be no irrational beliefs without corresponding, stronger, rational ones. Misperception, to Levy, "involves a discrepancy between the psychological environment

---

[26] Herbert A. Simon, *Reason in Human Affairs* (Stanford, CA: Stanford University Press, 1983).

[27] Nigel Howard, *Paradoxes of Rationality: Games, Metagames, and Political Behavior* (Cambridge, MA: MIT Press, 1971), p. 6. This book is essentially adopting what economists refer to as an *instrumental* approach to rationality; see Bernard Walliser, "Instrumental Rationality and Cognitive Rationality," *Theory and Decision*, Vol. 27, Nos. 1–2 (July 1989), pp. 7–36.

[28] Robert Jervis, *Perception and Misperception in International Politics* (Princeton, NJ: Princeton University Press, 1976), p. 119.

of the decision makers and the operational environment of the 'real world.'"[29] Irrational belief involves a similar discrepancy, but includes both the psychological and the emotional environment of the decision maker.

In its ideal form, rational foreign policy maximizes benefits while minimizing costs. Whether or not any single act can be said to meet that standard is often quite difficult to determine. At least four major problems arise immediately during any attempt to separate rational actions from irrational, at least in the way undertaken here. First of all, as Herbert Simon pointed out more than a half century ago, because all rationality is bounded by time and space, future costs and benefits are unknowable a priori.[30] Decision makers necessarily operate with incomplete information and in ignorance of potential consequences. Any judgment of action must take into account the reality that leaders do not have access to crystal balls when they try to set the best course for their states. What seems irrational in retrospect may well have looked quite logical to those making decisions in the stress of the moment, without the benefit of hindsight.

Second, the most important political costs and benefits are unmeasurable. Unlike economists, foreign policy analysts have no objective metrics with which to judge actions. Who is to say, for instance, just how many human lives a state should be willing to sacrifice in the pursuit of a particular goal? Not only do value judgments affect the evaluation of every foreign policy decision, but outcomes are often ambiguous and controversial. Even separating success from failure is not always a straightforward exercise.[31] No universally accepted, clear criteria for the assessment of rationality in security policy exist.[32]

[29] Jack Levy, "Misperception and the Causes of War: Theoretical Linkages and Analytical Problems," *World Politics*, Vol. 36, No. 1 (October 1983), pp. 76–99, esp. p. 79. See also Harold and Margaret Sprout, *The Ecological Perspective on Human Affairs* (Princeton, NJ: Princeton University Press, 1965).

[30] Herbert Simon, *Models of Man: Social and Rational* (New York: John Wiley & Sons, 1957). For a good review and discussion of the concept's first fifty years, see Gerd Gigerenzer and Reinhard Selten, *Bounded Rationality: The Adaptive Toolbox* (Cambridge, MA: MIT Press, 2002).

[31] Dominic D. P. Johnson and Dominic Tierney, *Failing to Win: Perceptions of Victory and Defeat in International Politics* (Cambridge, MA: Harvard University Press, 2006).

[32] Nancy Kanwisher, "Cognitive Heuristics and American Security Policy," *Journal of Conflict Resolution*, Vol. 33, No. 4 (December 1989), p. 653.

Third, state behavior may not always reflect the decisions, rational or not, of leaders. By the time a choice has been affected by infighting bureaucracies, interest groups, congress, political parties, and the media, output might not resemble initial input. Even if leaders were rational, in other words, politics might prevent the construction of good foreign policy. It can be difficult for outsiders to separate decisions caused by irrational beliefs from those that are the result of dysfunctional policy-making processes. Napoleon famously (and perhaps apocryphally) warned any would-be analyst to never ascribe to malice that which is adequately explained by incompetence; by replacing "malice" with "irrationality" one can neatly capture a limitation of any desire to apply a minimum standard for rationality to policy making.

Finally, foreign policy situations are usually quite complex. The motivations of policy makers and the factors they were compelled to take into consideration often remain unknown to outsiders. Leaders must often juggle multiple goals simultaneously, some of which appear to pull them in opposite directions. Those who would judge decisions after the fact cannot possibly be familiar with the full range of considerations decision makers had to weigh. One should be somewhat modest, therefore, when partaking in post-hoc criticism.

These objections (and others, no doubt) are difficult to overcome for any study hoping to assess the rationality of foreign policy behavior. They do not, however, preclude examination of the beliefs that help give rise to actions. Even if one remains unconvinced that there can be a basis with which to judge rationality in choices, the process of discussion and evaluation would still be a worthwhile exercise. Self-examination would force policy makers to explain to their constituents (and to themselves) the rationale behind the choices they make. By aspiring to be rational in thought and action, by making dispassionate assessment a virtue, decision makers could improve their performance. Rational people – and rational states – try to remain alert to the biases in their analysis, according to Robert Nozick, and "take steps to correct those biases."[33] They attempt to base their choices on the best available evidence and remain open to the suggestion that their preconceptions may be mistaken. Recognizing and eliminating

[33] Robert Nozick, *The Nature of Rationality* (Princeton, NJ: Princeton University Press, 1993), p. 75.

common pathologies, or obstacles to rationality, would be a good first step in that effort.

The Effect of Pathological Beliefs

The importance of foreign policy beliefs goes far beyond the academy, since they affect real-world decisions in consistent, predictable, and occasionally destructive ways. Because collective beliefs tend to create their own reality, those societies that devote little attention to foreign affairs to begin with, whose members seek short cuts and slogans to help make sense of the world – in other words, those like the United States – can be particularly vulnerable to their influence.[34] Those examined in this volume tend to have two other effects, each of which can prove quite counterproductive or pathological for the long-term U.S. interest.

First and foremost, the pathological beliefs (or simply "pathologies") considered here almost always lend support to the most hawkish, belligerent position in any foreign policy debate.[35] Fear, honor, glory, and hubris rarely convince leaders to cooperate with rivals or foes; these categories of belief expand the set of *casus belli* far more widely than any rational calculation would support. Furthermore, those wars based on irrational foundations are most likely to lead to national disaster. Iraq is the most obvious recent example of this heightened bellicosity, but it is hardly alone. As coming chapters explain, honor compelled U.S. participation in the First World War and Vietnam more than any other single factor. Were it not for a fear of communism, the strength of which puzzled our allies, the United States would never have found itself engaged in Korea, Cambodia, Central America, or a host of other Cold War battles in geopolitically irrelevant backwaters. And throughout it all, hubris greased the gears of war by assuring leaders that not only were they in the right, but that the goals were always attainable. Together these factors account for

---

[34] See George W. Ball, "Slogans and Realities," *Foreign Affairs*, Vol. 47, No. 4 (July 1969), pp. 623–41.

[35] In this way, they resemble biases, which also tend to push states in hawkish directions. See Daniel Kahneman and Jonathan Renshon, "Hawkish Biases," in A. Trevor Thrall and Jane K. Cramer, *American Foreign Policy and the Politics of Fear: Threat Inflation Since 9/11* (New York: Routledge, 2009), pp. 79–96.

the empirically supportable impression that, comparatively speaking, the United States is (in Stephen Rosen's words) "an unusually warlike people."[36]

Thus pathological beliefs are related to misperceptions, which have received a good deal more attention from scholars, but a couple of important distinctions should be made.[37] Perception is intellectual and ideational, for one thing, while belief is emotional, visceral, and connected much more deeply to identity. A functional distinction exists as well: whereas many common misperceptions make *others* appear more belligerent than they are, pathological beliefs make *us* more belligerent than we otherwise would be. If unchecked, both can push states in the direction of conflict.

Second, pathologies often help policy makers justify action at times when no vital, tangible interests are otherwise at stake. When pathology defines reality, policies become the opposite of what rational analyses of the national interest would suggest is appropriate. As a general rule, the more leaders have to explain the motivation for an action, the less important it probably is. No explanation of the rationale behind the war in Afghanistan was necessary, for instance, or for the entry into World War II. But Wilson had to explain to the American public why he brought the United States into World War I, and there was no shortage of complex rationales provided for Vietnam and Iraq. When war is truly necessary, it does not generally require justification or reference to often ill-considered beliefs.

This is therefore not merely a theoretical exercise. This volume proceeds with a value-based, if seemingly logical, assumption: Strategic performance can be improved if pathological beliefs are recognized and eliminated. Chances will drop for major blunders or folly, better serving the overall security, prosperity, and liberty of the United States. Improvements in policy would result from a dispassionate, rational analysis of material costs and benefits of any proposed action. In other words, although the United States does not always act rationally, it would usually be better off if it did. Taking a moment to consider the possibility that some of our deepest beliefs just might

---

[36] Stephen Peter Rosen, "Blood Brothers: The Dual Origins of American Bellicosity," *The American Interest*, Vol. 4, No. 6 (July/August 2009), p. 21.

[37] See especially Robert Jervis, *Perception and Misperception in International Politics* and Levy, "Misperception and the Causes of War."

be pathological would improve the quality of U.S. foreign policy decisions, and perhaps even prevent the next tragic blunder.

Although pathology is not unique to the United States, this book nonetheless concentrates its efforts on U.S. policy, which is a decision not driven merely by parochialism. The actions of the strongest members of any system are the most consequential; when the United States errs, many suffer, and conversely more would benefit from improvement in its decisions. For good or ill, the strong have a disproportionate influence on the weak. Furthermore, the United States is the most interesting case for this kind of investigation in one important way: as the system's most powerful member, it retains the highest degree of strategic flexibility. The world's preeminent state can control its own destiny, and has a wider array of choices than any other country in history. While this makes for interesting foreign policy debates, it also implies that Uncle Sam's blunders are often self-inflicted, and all the more egregious, since other, wiser options always exist. Finally, any discussion of pathological foreign policy beliefs must begin with the United States because, by virtue of a number of compounding factors, it is particularly susceptible to so many.

Two and a half decades ago, historian Barbara Tuchman wondered if it is even possible for a country to protect itself from "stupidity in policy-making," or if governments can be educated in any real sense.[38] If such a thing is possible, the protection will come from an improvement of beliefs, following a long process of consideration, calculation, and debate.

PATHOGENESIS

"To what extent are we in ignorance of our own motives," wondered Harold Lasswell a half-century ago, "and accustomed to improvise merely plausible explanations of and to ourselves?"[39] Even patients who are aware of their irrationalities often cannot explain how their

---

[38] Barbara Tuchman, *The March of Folly: From Troy to Vietnam* (New York: Ballantine Books, 1984), p. 384.

[39] Harold D. Lasswell, *Psychopathology and Politics*, new ed. (New York: Viking Press, 1960), p. 20. See also Timothy D. Wilson, *Strangers to Ourselves: Discovering the Adaptive Unconscious* (Cambridge, MA: Harvard University Press, 2002).

problems arose. An important step toward cure, for individuals as well as states, is understanding the genesis of pathologies.

Insights into pathogenesis can be found on all three of Kenneth Waltz's well-known levels of analysis.[40] The first, usually referred to as the *individual* level or image, focuses on the impact people, alone and in groups, have on international politics. As Waltz explained, according to this way of thinking, "the most important causes of political arrangements and acts are found in the nature and behavior of man."[41] While the factors influencing U.S. foreign policy from this level will not be unique to the American experience, they can nonetheless be important in aiding our understanding of the genesis of its pathological beliefs.

"Since everything is related to human nature," explained Waltz, "to explain anything one must consider more than human nature."[42] His next level of analysis – the *state* – examines factors at work inside countries. Such factors can include the type of regime that runs the affairs of state (democracy, autocracy, theocracy, etc.); the organization and interaction of bureaucratic actors within those regimes; the shared history, culture, and religion of its people; and special interest groups of all stripes, from lobbyist groups to the media to big business and the military-industrial complex. It is in this second image that we begin to examine factors that are, if not unique to, perhaps more prevalent in American society, a number of which are examined repeatedly in the chapters to come.

The final level, commonly referred to as the *system*, considers the structure of international politics and how it affects the decisions of each member country. The three most important features of that structure are the background condition of anarchy, or absence of a central authority that can make and enforce rules, the resulting "self-help imperative," and the specific polarity of the system. Because of anarchy, each state must live with a certain degree of danger and the

---

[40] Kenneth N. Waltz, *Man, the State and War: A Theoretical Analysis* (New York: Columbia University Press, 1959). Other scholars have made modifications to Waltz's framework over the years, adding levels and/or altering their definitions, but none significantly improved upon the original, at least in any way that would improve this analysis.

[41] Waltz, *Man, the State and War*, p. 42.

[42] Waltz, *Man, the State and War*, p. 80.

knowledge that nothing would prevent its neighbors from attacking should they decide to do so. Members must therefore take action to ensure their own security, or help themselves. "Polarity" refers to the distribution of power among members of the system. As explained in more detail in the next chapter, the current system is demonstrably "unipolar" in that it contains one dominant state. The United States is by far the strongest actor in the post–Cold War world, towering over the other members in every tangible and intangible category of power. Unipolarity, as we will see, can have both positive and negative effects on decision making.

"So fundamental are man, the state, and the system in any attempt to understand international relations that seldom does an analyst, however wedded to one image, entirely overlook the other two," argued Waltz.[43] Indeed, and unfortunately for political scientists who prefer parsimonious models of complex phenomena, it will probably never be possible to disentangle the precise importance of the factors from each level of analysis. Few are mutually exclusive and all contribute to the development of pathological beliefs to some degree. While historians are by training and temperament comfortable with multicausality, political scientists are rarely satisfied with explanations that list important variables and imply that "everything matters."[44] Although it will prove possible to make some determinations about the relative explanatory power of the variables under consideration, in the final analysis demystifying the precise genesis of pathology is probably not as urgent a task as problem recognition, treatment, and cure. Even if the origin of pathologies prove understandable, they will never be excusable. The only utility of an attempt to come to terms with the genesis of counterproductive, incorrect beliefs is a process of exorcising them from the U.S. collective unconscious. At its best the study of political psychology not only helps explain foreign policy mistakes but attempts to help prevent them.[45] This study is an attempt to both.

[43] Waltz, *Man, the State and War*, p. 162.
[44] See the essays in Colin and Miriam Fendius Elman, eds., *Bridges and Boundaries: Historians, Political Scientists, and the Study of International Relations* (Cambridge, MA: MIT Press, 2001).
[45] Jonathan Mercer, "Rationality and Psychology in International Politics," *International Organization*, Vol. 59, No. 1 (Winter 2005), p. 99.

OUTLINE AND THEMES

What are the origins of the pathological forces that drive U.S. foreign policy? Where do irrational, counterproductive, or simply false beliefs come from? The chapters to come examine many aspects of some of the major categories of pathology beliefs that most commonly affect U.S. foreign policy, seeking to establish their existence and speculate about their origins. Some are unique to the United States while others are the result of human psychological imperfection and are therefore common to all countries, if more obviously so in the unipolar power. Some have affected the post–Cold War world with special virulence, while others have been part of this nation's decision making from its founding. All, however, are in need of closer examination and recognition if U.S. foreign policy decision making is to be improved.

The first chapter examines what may be the most important category of pathology in U.S. foreign policy: fear. Beginning with the end of the Second World War, the United States adopted the roles of the world's premier power *and* its supreme worrier. It has consistently detected more danger in faraway corners of the world than any other state, including its closest allies. Accordingly, Washington could find little support for its contention that the vital interests of the West were at stake in Southeast Asia in the 1960s, for example, or in Central America two decades later. The threat from international communism went away, but that heightened perception of threat lingered: Since the end of the Cold War, fear has inspired a belief that the world is a fundamentally dangerous place – which it is not, as this chapter explains, compared to any previous era – and obviously made possible the tragically unnecessary intervention in Iraq. The fears of the United States are quite unfounded, irrational, and, since they inspire so much unnecessary action, pathological. This chapter is unavoidably the book's longest, since it introduces a number of themes and concepts that will be relevant to all that follow, such as unipolarity, neoconservatism, and the liberal tradition.

Few modern leaders worry about the status of their honor, at least in public. They do worry, at times obsessively, about their credibility. The second chapter examines the continuing importance of honor, albeit in its current form, for U.S. foreign policy. As with many of the other pathologies under consideration, the beliefs inspired by honor drive states to become belligerent and uncooperative. The chapter first discusses the traditional importance of honor in international and interpersonal politics, and then explains the central role it plays in the construction of security in any system that lacks a central authority. It examines what an "honor culture" is and how in such a culture aggressive action is deterred. Where aggression is unlikely, as in today's international system, the imperative to maintain a healthy reputation for honor deters nothing of consequence, and can instead be destructively irrational. The chapter then speculates about the genesis of the honor pathology, which is today manifest in the "credibility imperative," and why it continues to have such salience in the new century. Honor as a motivation for action seems as anachronistic today as horse-drawn carriages, alchemy, and the duel. But it persists, if under different guises; and to the extent that it persists, it pathologizes. William Wohlforth has argued that "we do not have a body of scholarship that tells us with certainty that appeals to honor, prestige, or reputation are necessarily disingenuous or wrong."[46] This chapter hopes to lay the foundation for just such a body.

Chapter 3 deals with another classic motivation for war. Like honor, glory is not a word twenty-first-century leaders often mention to their civilized, liberal constituents. But it too persists under a new name, arousing much the same type of responses in modern states as it did in the time of Thucydides. Although states might no longer speak of glory, they continue to place a high premium on their prestige, for reasons that are as pathological as they are ancient and primal. They compete for status in big ways and small, often seemingly without regard for cost or benefit. The United States puts a particularly high value on being number one, not just for understandable security reasons but also at least in part simply out of desire to be the best. It is the world's most competitive – perhaps "hypercompetitive" – state. Since relative U.S. power may well wane over the course of the coming century, it is certainly worthwhile to determine just how important it is to stand atop the list of countries in so many categories, as well as what is and what is not worth doing to remain there. Sharing the title

---

[46] William Wohlforth, "Honor as Interest in Russian Decisions for War, 1600–1995," in Elliot Abrams, ed., *Honor among Nations: Intangible Interests and Foreign Policy* (Washington, DC: Ethics and Public Policy Center, 1998), p. 43.

of champion might be distasteful for any country, but when it begins to arouse great concern and counterproductive action it becomes dangerously pathological.

Hubris is the subject of Chapter 4. The United States is certainly not the first to have suffered from its effects, but today no state displays its influence more clearly. No other country believes that it is the "indispensible nation" established by God to bring freedom, democracy, and open trading systems to the rest of the world. The rhetoric of the exceptionalism narrative sells with the public, and is a *sine qua non* for high leadership posts. If hubris only led to an inflated sense of self-worth, it would not be pathological; unfortunately, it has counterproductive effects on behavior. Leaders under its spell tend to overestimate their capabilities and those of their country. The well-known "can-do" spirit of the United States, where everything is possible if we only work hard enough, is a direct descendent of the belief that this nation was founded by God to do His work. Hubris also interferes with the ability to understand and relate to others, which often leads to unpleasant surprises when they do not respond to our actions as we anticipated. Overall, American hubris leads to faulty estimations of costs that confuse anyone trying to make rational decisions.

The specific beliefs that fall into the categories that will provide the structure for the coming chapters are summarized in the table below.

Category	Associated Beliefs
Fear	• The world is a very dangerous place. • The United States will always be the target of evil actors.
Honor	• Healthy credibility makes the achievement of foreign policy goals easier. • Our actions today can shape the future actions of others. • States can, through their actions, control the perceptions of others. • Cooperation is weakness that encourages challenges from other states.
Glory	• Competition, among people and states, is healthy and always leads to the best possible outcomes. • In international affairs, it is important to be the best.
Hubris	• The United States is a unique, exceptional country. • The people of the United States can accomplish almost anything they set their mind to.

Each chapter follows the same rough pattern: it first attempts to establish the existence of the beliefs as powerful, if not always dominant, forces in the U.S. foreign policy marketplace of ideas. It then lays out the evidence to support the contention that the beliefs in question are pathological or profoundly counterproductive. Insights are drawn from a variety of disciplines, including psychology, sociology, anthropology, economics, history, philosophy, and biology. The rest of each chapter examines the genesis of these pathologies, considering explanatory factors from each level of analysis.

To summarize, then: at times the United States is inspired to act because it is frightened of the dangers that seem to lurk behind the world's every corner. It struggles hard to maintain credibility because it believes that by doing so it will be able to affect the decisions of its many enemies. Whatever it does, however, the United States is secure in the knowledge that it is a unique country, blessed by God to bring about a better world by spreading freedom and fighting the evil of tyranny. As part of its mission, it is also important for the United States to remain not only the world's moral paragon but also its political, military, economic, scientific, educational, and cultural leader. Fortunately, pursuit of its lofty goals is easier than it would be for other countries, since it is blindingly obvious to all that the United States can be trusted, for, even if it errs at times, at least its intentions are beyond reproach.

Every one of these common beliefs is demonstrably pathological. In the past they have worked together to bring about disaster after disaster in U.S. foreign policy. If uncorrected, they will certainly do so again. The concluding chapter offers thoughts about how such a correction could take place.

"Perhaps the most widely held assumption in any society is, ultimately, that of its own sanity," wrote Brent Rutherford a half-century ago. "Some individuals do suffer more or less from some forms of mental illness, but there is little doubt as to the general level of societal mental health."[47] The suggestion that the people of the United States share a number of group psychological pathologies will not be easy to

---

[47] Brent M. Rutherford, "Psychopathology, Decision-Making, and Political Involvement," *Journal of Conflict Resolution*, Vol. 10, No. 4 (December 1966), p. 392.

accept. The evidence needs to be especially convincing, the reasoning logical, and the benefits clear to convince any society that a problem exists and to make the case for change sufficiently compelling.

"We need to take beliefs seriously," argued Jervis, "even – or especially – when we find them flawed."[48] If indeed foreign policy is a product of beliefs, then presumably better policy is made when they are accurate. Our most basic assumptions are by their nature resistant to change, but change is not impossible; it occurs slowly, glacially at times, but it does happen. Few people alter their ideologies based on the cases made by others, no matter how powerful and logical. Strong, rational arguments can, however, plant nagging doubts that over time can lead people to abandon pathological beliefs. Like a piece of popcorn stuck between teeth, reasoned analysis can sometimes be impossible to ignore, and eventually has to be addressed.

Or at least that is the hope that motivates this book.

[48] Robert Jervis, "Understanding Beliefs and Threat Inflation," p. 33.

1

Fear

The Power of Nightmares in a Safe Society

In politics, what begins in fear usually ends up in folly.
Samuel Taylor Coleridge[1]

In so far as we feel ourselves in any heightened trouble at the present moment, that feeling is largely of our own making.
George F. Kennan[2]

British civil servant Cyril Northcote Parkinson began a 1955 essay in *The Economist* by observing that "work expands so as to fill the time available for its completion."[3] "Parkinson's Law," as it has become known, is commonly shortened to read that *work expands along with time.* International politics has its own version, according to Karl Deutsch: *insecurity expands along with power.*[4] As states get stronger, they identify more interests, and the number of threats they perceive tends to grow. Consequently, the stronger countries are, the more insecure they often feel. Logic might suggest that the opposite should be true, that power and security ought to be directly related, that as state

---

[1] Quoted by Barry Glassner, *The Culture of Fear: Why Americans are Afraid of the Wrong Things* (New York: Basic Books, 1999), p. xxviii.
[2] Quoted by Samuel F. Wells, Jr., "Sounding the Tocsin: NSC 68 and the Soviet Threat," *International Security*, Vol. 4, No. 2 (Autumn 1979), p. 128.
[3] Cyril Northcote Parkinson, *Parkinson's Law: The Pursuit of Progress* (London: John Murray, 1958).
[4] Karl W. Deutsch, *The Analysis of International Relations* (Englewood Cliffs, NJ: Prentice-Hall, 1968), p. 88.

power grows, so too should security. Presumably potential challengers should be emboldened by weakness and deterred by strength. Why, then, do strong states seem to worry more, often about seemingly trivial matters? The tendency for insecurity to expand with power is not merely paradoxical, it is pathological because it is based on an irrational belief that often inspires counterproductive behavior.

Even though by any reasonable measure the United States is the safest country in the history of the world, it does not usually act that way. For many analysts of U.S. foreign policy, one belief has remained constant since at least World War II: *we are living in dangerous times.* Many of those who make and/or comment on U.S. foreign policy maintain that the world is full of enemies and evil, so this (whenever *this* is) is no time to relax. Former Speaker of the House Newt Gingrich is hardly alone in his oft-expressed, unshakeable belief that the world is a "fundamentally dangerous place," one to which our current leaders (whoever they are) are underreacting, irresponsibly leaving the people vulnerable.[5] Constant repetition of this idea has over time generated genuine belief in leaders and followers alike, and substantial, sometimes amorphous fear. A 2009 poll found that nearly 60 percent of the public – and fully half of the membership of the Council on Foreign Relations (CFR) – considered the world more dangerous than it was during the Cold War.[6] Though the source of that danger has evolved over the years, from communist spies to Soviet missiles to Japanese industrialists to Islamic terrorists, the United States has always detected threats in the system more serious than other countries realize. The world might have seemed much safer after the Cold War came to an end, but Americans knew better.

Although great insecurity has often accompanied great power, this need not be the case. Presumably better policy would arise from a rational, realistic assessment of threat. Insecurity, whether

[5] Gingrich has made this argument throughout his long career. See his *To Renew America* (New York: Harper Collins, 1995), p. 185, as well as virtually any speech or talk.
[6] Another quarter (and a fifth of CFR members) consider the dangers equivalent. Pew Center for the People and the Press, "America's Place in the World in 2009: An Investigation of Public and Leadership Opinion about International Affairs," December 2009, available at http://www.people-press.org/files/legacy-pdf/569.pdf. See also Micah Zenko and Michael A. Cohen, "Clear and Present Safety: The United States is More Secure than Washington Thinks," *Foreign Affairs*, Vol. 91, No. 2 (March/April 2012), pp. 79–93.

real or imagined, leads to expansive, internationalist, interventionist grand strategies; the more danger a state perceives, the greater its willingness to go abroad in search of monsters to destroy. The "preventive" war in Iraq is the most obvious consequence of the inflated U.S. perception of threat, but it is hardly the only one. This particularly American pathology is in need of diagnosis and cure, lest Iraq be not a singular debacle but a harbinger of other disasters to come.

THE INSECURITY PATHOLOGY IN THE UNITED STATES

Fear is a natural and often useful emotion for individuals and states alike. Without it, after all, homo sapiens would probably not have survived long in the prehistoric environment. Modern states inhabiting an anarchic system must always remain wary of their neighbors, whose intentions are not fully knowable. A certain amount of fear has historically been healthy for states seeking to anticipate attacks or to survive them if they occurred.[7] It is when fear is generated in great quantities, when it is out of proportion to extant threats, that it can lead to unhealthy paranoia and counterproductive policies.

Despite its manifest and widely acknowledged importance, fear is not often studied by scholars of international relations.[8] The line between healthy fear and pathological paranoia, for instance, remains elusive even for those who have spent years examining the subject. Psychologists Robert Robins and Jerrold Post wrote that political paranoia is so difficult to define and understand because "it begins as a distortion of an appropriate political response but far overshoots the mark."[9] Paranoia really only becomes manifest through action

---

[7] Ioannis Evrigenis, *Fear of Enemies and Collective Action* (New York: Cambridge University Press, 2008), esp. p. xii. For a discussion of the relationship between fear and the theories of international relations, see Shiping Tang, "Fear in International Politics: Two Positions," *International Studies Review*, Vol. 10, No. 3 (September 2008), pp. 451–71.

[8] Neta C. Crawford, "The Passion of World Politics: Propositions on Emotion and Emotional Relationships," *International Security*, Vol. 24, No. 4 (Spring 2000), p. 118.

[9] Robert S. Robins and Jerrold M. Post, *Political Paranoia: The Psychopolitics of Hatred* (New Haven, CT: Yale University Press, 1997), p. 5.

that is disproportionate to the objective risks. It is at that point that it becomes pathological for the state as well.

When excessive, fear cannot help but distort the decision-making process by making unlikely events seem possible or even probable. As Edmund Burke observed a century and a half ago, "No passion so effectively robs the mind of all its powers of acting and reasoning as fear."[10] In practice, states that exhibit unwarranted fear, because they sense danger and enemies everywhere, are far more likely to lash out in what they perceive as self-defense. Perhaps unsurprisingly, publics that sense danger are far more likely to support active self-defense in the hopes of erring on the side of caution.[11] They are prone to support actions that reason would suggest are unnecessary and often end up doing more harm than good to their objective self-interest. Most basically, they are unlikely to weigh accurately the pros and cons of decisions, raising the danger of blunders and folly.

Those suffering from paranoia exhibit a number of traits, at least three of which can have pathological political effects. First, they often harbor extreme suspicion of, and hostility toward, those around them. One of the reasons for this is because paranoid individuals tend to project their own mindset onto others, believing that their opponents think and act as they do. Stalin, for instance, assumed everyone around him was secretly plotting his destruction because that is what he would have been doing were he in their shoes.[12] He slaughtered thousands of his best military officers as a result, seriously weakening the Soviet Union's defenses in the process. Second, paranoid people tend to exhibit "centrality," or the assumption that they are the root cause of all that goes on around them. Finally, political paranoia

[10] Quoted by David L. Altheide, *Creating Fear: News and the Construction of Crisis* (New York: Aldine de Gruyter, 2002), p. 59.
[11] See Leonie Huddy, Stanley Feldman, Charles Taber, and Gallya Lahav, "Threat, Anxiety, and Support of Antiterrorism Policies," *American Journal of Political Science*, Vol. 49, No. 3 (July 2005), pp. 593–608; Richard K. Herrmann, Philip E. Tetlock, and Penny S. Visser, "Mass Public Decisions to Go to War: A Cognitive-Interactionist Framework," *American Political Science Review*, Vol. 93, No. 3 (September 1999), pp. 553–73; and Bruce W. Jentleson, "The Pretty Prudent Public: Post-Vietnam American Opinion on the Use of Force," *International Studies Quarterly*, Vol. 36, No. 1 (March 1992), pp. 49–74.
[12] See Robert C. Tucker, "The Dictator and Totalitarianism," *World Politics*, Vol. 17, No. 4 (July 1965), pp. 555–83.

routinely generates what to outsiders appears to be delusional thinking, the most significant manifestation of which is a grandiose sense of
self.[13] Taken together, these effects can lead to a warped, inaccurate
view of the world, and eventually to counterproductive foreign policy
decisions.

Paranoia need not affect all aspects of life to be important in
some. People may be perfectly rational about their own personal
safety, for instance, but harbor unreasoning fear for their country. In
other words, perceptions of individual and collective safety might not
be consistent. In fact, paranoia is probably more common in groups
than it is in individuals. People "go mad in herds," wrote Charles
Mackay in 1852, "while they only recover their senses only slowly, and
one by one."[14] One consistent finding of post-9/11 polling is that
people seem more worried about terrorist attacks in general than
in their own communities – in other words, personal threat is not as
dire as national threat.[15] People need not be paranoid for themselves
to be so for their country, once they have become part of the group.
And as a group, Americans detect more danger in the world than
do others.

In international politics, Robert Jervis reminds us, "it is always difficult to tell how paranoid you should be."[16] Threats and enemies
exist. The line between reasonable skepticism and pathological fear
can be a fine one at times, and its outline is often difficult to determine for those imbedded within stressful foreign policy situations.
It is therefore no small challenge for leaders to stay on the healthy
side, to assess risks correctly and craft policies accordingly. Doing
so is only possible following a thorough, reasonable consideration
of the threats society faces. From its founding, however, leaders of
the United States have not proven terribly sagacious at making such
assessments.

---

[13] For more, see Robins and Post, *Political Paranoia*, p. 7.

[14] Charles Mackay, *Extraordinary Popular Delusions and the Madness of Crowds* (Boston, MA: L. C. Page and Company, 1932), p. xx.

[15] Leonie Huddy, Stanley Feldman, Theresa Capelos, and Colin Provost, "The Consequences of Terrorism: Disentangling the Effects of Personal and National Threat," *Political Psychology*, Vol. 23, No. 3 (September 2002), pp. 485–509.

[16] Thierry Balzacq and Robert Jervis, "Logics of Mind and International System: A Journey with Robert Jervis," *Review of International Studies*, Vol. 30, No. 4 (October 2004), p. 569.

Fear and U.S. Foreign Policy

The first great threat the United States perceived, the one that dominated its first century, emanated from Great Britain. London's malicious influence seemed visible everywhere, from the high seas to the Caribbean to the financial markets.[17] Though the British were the first existential threat the United States faced, they were hardly the last, replaced as time went on by Germans, Bolsheviks, anarchists, Japanese, and others. By the 1950s, communism had generated a level of national fear that eclipsed all previous records, inspiring the United States to raise and maintain an enormous peacetime military for the first time in its history, an action that would have surely horrified its founding generation. The Cold War ended but the high perception of threat lived on. Rogue states, terrorism, and proliferation filled the void left by the Soviet Union, giving the American people no respite from anxiety. September 11 merely put a face on the danger many already knew existed. When it came to fear, at least, Robert Kagan was correct when he noted that "America did not change on September 11," but "only became more itself."[18]

Insecurity is not limited to U.S. leaders. Opinion polls throughout the 1990s revealed high levels of anxiety in the American public on a host of issues.[19] Although the U.S. public is not quite as concerned about terrorism as it was in the immediate aftermath of 9/11, between a quarter to a third of Americans consistently tell pollsters they are "very" or "somewhat" worried that they or their families will be victims of terrorist violence.[20] In April 2007, 82 percent of Americans told pollsters the world was a more dangerous place than it used to be and that it was getting worse. One year later, the same poll found a "significant majority" of Americans were anxious about U.S. security, demonstrating that in

[17] James Chace and Caleb Carr, *America Invulnerable: The Quest for Absolute Security from 1812 to Star Wars* (New York: Summit Books, 1988), p. 38.
[18] Robert Kagan, *Of Paradise and Power: America and Europe in the New World Order* (New York: Knopf, 2003), p. 85.
[19] Frank Furedi, *Culture of Fear: Risk-Taking and the Morality of Low Expectation* (London: Cassell, 1997), p. 61.
[20] Polls reviewed by Daniel Gardner, *The Science of Fear: How the Culture of Fear Manipulates Your Brain* (New York: Plume, 2008), pp. 248–50; and Yaeli Bloch-Elkon, "Public Perceptions and the Threat of International Terrorism after 9/11," *Public Opinion Quarterly*, Vol. 75, No. 2 (Summer 2011), pp. 366–92.

the United States, "anxiety remains steady over time." Only 15 percent
reported being not worried about "the way things are going for the
United States in world affairs."[21] Six in ten Americans apparently think
a third world war is "likely to occur" in their lifetime; others, including
influential opinion makers, believe it has already begun.[22] A 2010 Pew/
Smithsonian poll echoed this finding, with 58 percent of respondents
expecting to see a major war before 2050.[23]

    This level of anxiety is striking when compared to that of other
states. More than one observer has noted that the United States routinely perceives threats to be far more dire and immediate than do
other great powers.[24] Whether the issue is Islamic fundamentalist terrorism or rogue actors like Saddam Hussein and Hugo Chavez, the
United States detects higher levels of danger than any other state.
Steven Everts observed that while Europeans who debate foreign policy tend to focus on "challenges," Americans discuss "threats," a significant selection of terms.[25] During the Cold War, the pattern was the
same: the United States feared an attack by the Warsaw Pact far more
than did its West European allies, who presumably had more to lose if
such an event occurred; it worried about the influence of communist
China more than South Korea, Japan, and the ASEAN states; and it

---

[21] Scott Bittle and Jonathan Rochkind, "Anxious Public Pulling Back from Use of
Force," *Confidence in U.S. Foreign Policy Index*, Vol. 4 (Spring 2007) and "Energy,
Economy New Focal Points for Anxiety over U.S. Foreign Policy," *Confidence in U.S.
Foreign Policy Index*, Vol. 6 (Spring 2008), both available at http://www.publicagenda.
org/foreignpolicy/index.htm, accessed December 10, 2012.

[22] Will Lester, "Poll: Americans Say World War III Likely," *Washington Post*, July 24,
2005. Norman Podhoretz, *World War IV: The Long Struggle Against Islamofascism* (New
York: Doubleday, 2007).

[23] Pew Research Center for People and the Press, "Public Sees a Future Full of Promise
and Peril," June 22, 2010, available at http://people-press.org/2010/06/22/
public-sees-a-future-full-of-promise-and-peril/, accessed December 10, 2012.

[24] George F. Kennan, *The Cloud of Danger: Current Realities of American Foreign Policy*
(Boston: Little, Brown & Co., 1977); Chace and Carr, *America Invulnerable*; John
A. Thompson, "The Exaggeration of American Vulnerability: The Anatomy of a
Tradition," *Diplomatic History*, Vol. 16, No. 1 (Winter 1992), pp. 23–43; Dana H.
Allin, *Cold War Illusions: America, Europe and Soviet Power, 1969–1989* (New York: St.
Martin's Press, 1994); and Robert H. Johnson, *Improbable Dangers: U.S. Conceptions of
Threat in the Cold War and After* (New York: St. Martin's Press, 1994).

[25] Steven Everts, "Unilateral America, Lightweight Europe? Managing Divergence in
Transatlantic Foreign Policy," Centre for European Reform Working Paper, No. 9
(February 2001), p. 3, available at http://www.cer.org.uk/sites/default/files/publi-
cations/attachments/pdf/2011/cerwp9-2788.pdf, accessed December 10, 2012.

obsessed over the potential pernicious influence of Castro and the Sandinistas more than did the smaller states of the region.[26] Despite the fact that the other states in the system are all demonstrably weaker than the United States and are therefore presumably more vulnerable to a variety of threats, they do not seem to worry about their safety nearly as much as does Uncle Sam.

Clearly fear played a key role in inspiring many people to support the invasion of Iraq – fear of weapons of mass destruction (WMD), of Saddam's potential links to Al Qaeda, and of his general evil irrationality. The Bush administration warned inaction was fraught with great peril, conjuring images of catastrophic terrorist attacks and mushroom clouds. "There is no doubt that Saddam Hussein now has weapons of mass destruction," warned Vice President Cheney. "There is no doubt he is amassing them to use against our friends, against our allies, and against us."[27] Few outside of the United States seemed to agree. Even the other members of the "Coalition of the Willing" tended to have a much harder time selling the war to their publics; the American people always feared more than did the British, for example.[28] "After the Cold War, and even after 9/11, Europeans felt relatively secure," Kagan observed. "Only the Americans were frightened."[29]

Anxious actors take steps to protect themselves. A good secondary measure of the degree of insecurity a state feels, therefore, is the size of its military. While almost the entire industrialized world has cut back on defense spending since the Cold War, the United States has been an outlier, spending more today in real terms than ever before, and 70 percent more in 2010 than in 2000 (not including war supplementals).[30] No military-industrial complex can take full credit for the

[26] See Eric A. Nordlinger, *Isolationism Reconfigured: American Foreign Policy for a New Century* (Princeton, NJ: Princeton University Press, 1995), pp. 269–70.
[27] Dick Cheney, Address to the Veterans of Foreign Wars, Nashville, TN, August 26, 2002, in John Ehrenberg, J. Patrice McSherry, Jose Ramon Sanchez, and Caroleen Marji Sayej, eds., *The Iraq Papers* (New York: Oxford University Press, 2009), p. 75.
[28] See Philip H. Gordon and Jeremy Shapiro, *Allies at War: America, Europe, and the Crisis over Iraq* (New York: McGraw Hill, 2004).
[29] Robert Kagan, "The September 12 Paradigm: America, the World, and George W. Bush," *Foreign Affairs*, Vol. 87, No. 5 (September–October 2008), p. 31.
[30] Daniel Wirls, *Irrational Security: The Politics of Defense from Reagan to Obama* (Baltimore, MD: Johns Hopkins University Press, 2010), p. 1.

strong, consistent support for an enormous military. It is the belief about the dangers inherent in the world that keeps the public so concerned about the strength of its defense and so supportive of its warriors.

Fear is an ever-present element in U.S. domestic life as well. The United States is the world's most heavily armed industrialized society in large part because its people fear being victimized, by criminals, terrorists, and/or their own government, to a far greater degree than those of other countries. The latter threat boggles minds abroad like few other issues; people of other lands are invariably baffled at the degree to which a nontrivial number of Americans are convinced private citizens need to arm themselves to keep Washington's fascist tendencies in check. In January 2013, 53 percent of respondents told Pew pollsters the federal government was a threat to their "rights and freedoms."[31] Paranoid elements may be present in every society, but the proportion of Americans who harbor fears utterly disconnected from reality is troublingly, uniquely high.[32]

While the people of the United States may not be the only or even the most paranoid in the world, their fear is the least justified. By some measure some Middle Eastern societies exhibit stronger symptoms, sometimes in debilitating ways, but the people of that region have understandable historical (and current) reasons to be fearful because they have long memories of mistreatment at the hands of outsiders and their own leaders.[33] They are also relatively weak. The paranoia of the powerless can be explained and forgiven more readily than that of the strongest country the world has ever known. The dangers that lurk in the international system, or the "security environment," must be quite extreme to justify such a high level of fear in the United States.

---

[31] Pew Research Center for People and the Press, "Majority Says the Federal Government Threatens Their Personal Rights," January 31, 2013, available at http://www.people-press.org/2013/01/31/majority-says-the-federal-government-threatens-their-personal-rights/.

[32] A review of relevant comparative data regarding fear can be found in Peter N. Stearns, *American Fear: The Causes and Consequence of High Anxiety* (New York: Routledge, 2006).

[33] Robert S. Robins and Jerrold M. Post, *Political Paranoia: The Psychopolitics of Hatred* (New Haven, CT: Yale University Press, 1997), p. 53.

THE SECURITY ENVIRONMENT

Does the level of fear in the United States accurately reflect the dangers in the twenty-first-century system, or is it a pathological, paranoid overestimation of threat? For a belief to be pathological – for fear to be paranoia – it must be based on an incorrect or irrational foundation. After all, as the old saying goes, just because you are paranoid does not mean there is no one out to get you. Modern states certainly face a number of possible dangers and threats; for the twenty-first-century United States, however, none is particularly dire either in the system in general or in its particulars. The following sections move from bigger picture to little.

General: Overview of the Twenty-First-Century International System

One of the most basic tenets of the study of international relations is that because there is no central world government, because the system is marked by a condition of anarchy, each state has to look out for its own security. None can be fully certain of the intentions of its neighbors, who all possess some level of offensive military capability. It is a dangerous world, in other words, in which state survival is never guaranteed.[34]

Apparently unbeknownst to many observers, the world has quietly, gradually evolved away from this Hobbesian, tragic, violent reality. In some very important ways, the system of the twenty-first century hardly resembles that of the sixteenth or seventeenth or even the early twentieth. The overall trends in conflict and violence in the world the United States inhabits today ought to give comfort to those who fear and puzzle those who believe the rules governing international politics never fundamentally change.

Ongoing conflicts in Syria, Afghanistan, the Congo, and elsewhere tend to obscure what is certainly the most important empirical reality in twenty-first-century international politics: there has never been a more peaceful, less violent period of time than the post–Cold War era.

---

[34] For an overview of this, see John J. Mearsheimer, *The Tragedy of International Politics* (New York: W. W. Norton, 2001).

The number and intensity of all kinds of conflict are at historically low levels: major war between great powers is so rare that a growing number of scholars suspect it may have become obsolete; interstate war has also become exceedingly uncommon, especially when compared to any previous era; and intrastate violence, such as ethnic conflicts, civil wars, and coups, is at its lowest level since scholars began to collect data about it.[35] Whether this decline in violence represents a fundamental change in the rules that govern state behavior or a temporary respite between cataclysms is not yet clear, but there is no doubt that the post–Cold War era has been more stable and peaceful than those that preceded it.

By now these trends are – or should be – familiar to anyone who studies international politics. Declining conflict numbers tell only part of the story, however, and do not by themselves fully describe the nature of the current system. Discrimination and repression against minority groups appears to have diminished worldwide, as have incidents of genocide and major violations of human rights (by as much as 90 percent).[36] Those wars that do break out are not as bloody as

---

[35] The empirical and theoretical literature on this phenomenon is immense and growing, as one would expect. For some of the most up-to-date data and evidence, see Monty G. Marshall and Benjamin R. Cole, *Global Report 2011: Conflict, Governance, and State Fragility* (Vienna, VA: Center for Systemic Peace, December 2011); and Human Security Report Project, *Human Security Report 2009/2010: The Causes of Peace and the Shrinking Costs of War* (New York: Oxford University Press, 2011). Summaries, extrapolations, explanations, and analyses can be found in Richard Rosecrance, *The Rise of the Virtual State: Wealth and Power in the Coming Century* (New York: Basic Books, 1999); John Mueller, *Retreat From Doomsday: The Obsolescence of Major War* (New York: Basic Books, 1989) and *The Remnants of War* (Ithaca, NY: Cornell University Press, 2004); James Lee Ray, "The Abolition of Slavery and the End of International War," *International Organization*, Vol. 43, No. 3 (Summer 1989), pp. 405–39; Robert Jervis, "Theories of War in an Era of Leading Power Peace," *American Political Science Review*, Vol. 96, No. 1 (March 2002), pp. 1–14; Raimo Väyrynen, *The Waning of Major War: Theories and Debates* (New York: Routledge, 2006); Christopher J. Fettweis, *Dangerous Times? The International Politics of Great Power Peace* (Washington, DC: Georgetown University Press, 2010); Richard Ned Lebow, *Why Nations Fight: Past and Future Motives for War* (New York: Cambridge University Press, 2010); Joshua S. Goldstein, *Winning the War on War: The Decline of Armed Conflict Worldwide* (New York: Penguin, 2011); and Steven Pinker, *The Better Angels of Our Nature: Why Violence has Declined* (New York: Viking, 2011).

[36] For data on discrimination and repression, see the data kept by the Minorities at Risk Project, *Minorities at Risk Dataset* (College Park, MD: Center for International Development and Conflict Management, 2012), http://www.cidcm.umd.edu/mar/. Genocide and mass slaughter numbers are contained in the report of the Human

they were in times past; the magnitude of warfare, defined by the average number of battle deaths per conflict per year, has steadily declined since the 1980s, as has the risk for the average person of dying in battle.[37] Peace settlements have proven more stable over time, and fewer new conflicts are breaking out than ever before.[38] Those conflicts that do persist have less support from outside actors; when third parties have intervened in neighboring conflicts, it has usually been in the attempt to bring a conflict to an end.[39] Twenty-first-century "power vacuums" repel rather than attract. Overall global military spending declined by one third in the first decade after the fall of the Berlin Wall.[40]

Today, for the first time in history, state survival is all but assured for even the smallest members of the international system. Since World War II, precisely *zero* UN members have been forcibly removed from the map (the only country to disappear against its will – South Vietnam – held only observer status). International borders have all but hardened; conquest is dead.[41] States of the twenty-first century

Security Centre, *Human Security Report 2005* (New York: Oxford University Press, 2005), p. 41, which analyzes the genocide dataset maintained by Barbara Harff.

[37] Andrew Mack, "Global Political Violence: Explaining the Post-Cold War Decline," Coping with Crisis Working Paper Series, International Peace Academy (March 2007), p. 7; Bethany Lacina, Nils Peter Gleditsch, and Bruce Russett, "The Declining Risk of Death in Battle," *International Studies Quarterly*, Vol. 50, No. 3 (September 2006), pp. 673–80; Monty G. Marshall and Benjamin R. Cole, *Global Report 2009: Conflict, Governance, and State Fragility* (Fairfax, VA: Center for Systemic Peace, December 2009), p. 4; and Erik Melander, Magnus Öberg, and Jonathan Hall, "Are 'New Wars' More Atrocious? Battle Severity, Civilians Killed and Forced Migration before and after the End of the Cold War," *European Journal of International Relations*, Vol. 15, No. 3 (September 2009), pp. 505–36.

[38] Nils Petter Gleditsch, "The Liberal Moment Fifteen Years On," *International Studies Quarterly*, Vol. 52, No. 4 (December 2008), p. 694.

[39] Lotta Harbom and Peter Wallensteen, "Armed Conflict and Its International Dimensions, 1946–2004," *Journal of Peace Research*, Vol. 42, No. 5 (September 2005), pp. 623–35; and Mark W. Zacher, "The Territorial Integrity Norm: International Boundaries and the Use of Force," *International Organization*, Vol. 55, No. 2 (Spring 2001), p. 242.

[40] See Mary Kaldor, "Beyond Militarism, Arms Races and Arms Control," essay prepared for the Social Science Research Council, December 8, 2001, available at http://www.ssrc.org/sept11/essays/kaldor_text_only.htm.

[41] Zacher, "The Territorial Integrity Norm: International Boundaries and the Use of Force," pp. 215–50; Anna Simons, "The Death of Conquest," *The National Interest*, No. 71 (Spring 2003), pp. 41–49; and Tanisha M. Fazal, *State Death: The Politics and Geography of Conquest, Occupation, and Annexation* (Princeton, NJ: Princeton University Press, 2007).

need not worry about annihilation or absorption by their neighbors. The stronger countries are even safer, and the strongest is the safest.

None of this is to suggest that the world is without problems, of course, or that war is completely absent or impossible. Warfare persists in a few parts of the globe and low-level violence continues in many more, even if it often more closely resembles criminal predation than traditional war.[42] Given the rapid increase in world population and number of countries (the League of Nations had 63 members at its peak between the wars, while the United Nations currently has 193), however, a pure extrapolation of historical trends might lead one to expect a great deal more warfare than there currently is. This unprecedented, exponential systemic and population growth has not resulted in the Malthusian clashes for resources that so many foresaw.[43] Despite a few minor wars and not-so-minor terrorist attacks, it seems clear that more citizens of the twenty-first century – both in terms of raw numbers and as a percentage of the overall global population – will lead mundane, peaceful lives than in any that came before, bothered perhaps by quiet desperation but not by the violence of war. That bears repeating: *today a far greater percentage of the world's population lives in peace than at any time before in history*, which is a non-trivial, curiously underreported and underappreciated statistic. It is not unreasonable to say the world is experiencing a golden age of peace and security, even if few people seem to notice.

While the empirical reality of these trends in international security is not in dispute, their underlying cause is.[44] Some scholars, primarily

---

[42] See Jeffrey Gettleman, "Africa's Forever Wars," *Foreign Policy*, No. 178 (March/April 2010), pp. 73–75. See also Mueller, *The Remnants of War*.

[43] See, for instance, John Orme, "The Utility of Force in a World of Scarcity," *International Security*, Vol. 22, No. 3 (Winter 1997/98), pp. 138–67; Thomas F. Homer-Dixon, *Environment, Scarcity and Conflict* (Princeton, NJ: Princeton University Press, 1999); Robert D. Kaplan, *The Coming Anarchy: Shattering the Dreams of the Post Cold War* (New York: Random House, 2000); Michael T. Klare, *Resource Wars: The New Landscape of Global Conflict* (New York: Metropolitan Books, 2001); and Colin H. Kahl, *States, Scarcity, and Civil Strife in the Developing World* (Princeton, NJ: Princeton University Press, 2006).

[44] One objection has actually been raised by the scholars at the Uppsala Conflict Data Program (UCDP), who have reported a recent up-tick in conflict levels. The difference lies in the definition they employ: these scholars reject the traditional definition of conflict, which has for four decades been marked by a minimum of one thousand battle deaths – see J. David Singer and Melvin Small, *The Wages of War, 1816–1965: A Statistical Handbook* (New York: John Wiley & Sons, 1972), p. 35 – preferring to set

realists, take the view that nuclear weapons have thrust peace upon the otherwise conflictual system.[45] Liberal explanations include the expanding number of democracies, multilateral institutions, and the deepening complexity of economic interdependence.[46] Constructivists do not necessarily deny the importance of any of these factors, but give primary credit to an evolution in ideas and norms in contemporary international society.[47]

All such explanations have one important factor in common: the change they describe is likely irreversible. Nuclear weapons cannot be uninvented, and no defense against their use is ever going to be completely foolproof. The pace of globalization and economic interdependence shows no sign of slowing. Democracy seems firmly embedded in the cultural fabric of many of the places in which it currently exists, and may well be in the process of spreading to the few places where it does not. Even the global economic crisis that began in the fall of 2008 has not had any impact on the level of external or internal conflict around the world.[48] Financial despair has not overwhelmed the

the mark instead at twenty-five. Therefore, they come to some unique conclusions about violence worldwide – including, for instance, that there was an active conflict in the United States in 2011 against Al Qaeda. See Lotta Themnér and Peter Wallensteen, "Armed Conflict, 1946–2011," *Journal of Peace Research*, Vol. 49, No. 4 (July 2012), pp. 565–75.

[45] Kenneth N. Waltz, "Nuclear Myths and Political Realities," *The American Political Science Review*, Vol. 84, No. 3 (September 1990), pp. 731–45; John Lewis Gaddis, "The Long Peace: Elements of Stability in the Postwar International System," *International Security*, Vol. 10, No. 4 (Spring 1986), pp. 99–142; Carl Kaysen, "Is War Obsolete? A Review Essay," *International Security*, Vol. 14, No. 4 (Spring 1990), pp. 42–64; and Robert Rauchhaus, "Evaluating the Nuclear Peace Hypothesis: A Quantitative Approach," *Journal of Conflict Resolution*, Vol. 53, No. 2 (April 2009), pp. 258–77.

[46] Richard Rosecrance, *The Rise of the Trading State: Commerce and Conquest in the Modern World* (New York: Basic Books, 1986); Stephen G. Brooks, *Producing Security: Multinational Corporations, Globalization, and the Changing Calculus of Conflict* (Princeton, NJ: Princeton University Press, 2005); Erik Gartzke, "The Capitalist Peace," *The American Journal of Political Science*, Vol. 51, No. 1 (January 2007), pp. 166–91; Gleditsch, "The Liberal Moment Fifteen Years On," pp. 691–712; and Erik Gartzke and J. Joseph Hewitt, "International Crises and the Capitalist Peace," *International Interactions*, Vol. 36, No. 2 (April 2010), pp. 115–45.

[47] Evan Luard, *War in International Society: A Study in International Sociology* (London: I. B. Taurus, 1986); Mueller, *The Remnants of War*; and Ray, "The Abolition of Slavery and the End of International War," pp. 405–39.

[48] A good list of past and current conflicts is maintained by Monty G. Marshall at the Center for Systemic Peace, "Major Episodes of Political Violence, 1946–2012," available at http://www.systemicpeace.org/warlist.htm, accessed December 10, 2012.

aversion to conflict. The United Nations, while oft criticized, shows no signs of disappearing. And finally, history contains precious few examples of the return of institutions deemed outmoded, barbaric, and/or futile by society.[49] In other words, *normative evolution is typically unidirectional.* Few would argue, for instance, that slavery or dueling are likely to reappear in this century. As long as science, technology, and economics do not take unprecedented steps backward, major war is unlikely to return, and minor wars will continue to be rare as weak states imitate the behavior of the strong. Illiberal normative recidivism is exceptionally rare.[50] While the future is unknowable, there is good reason to believe the current stability will prove to have a good deal of staying power. "Just as expectations of war can be self-fulfilling," observes Jervis, "so can expectations of peace."[51]

As a result of this, although perhaps a war against a "peer competitor" cannot be completely ruled out of the distant future, in the near term no such conflict appears plausible. And certainly the threat of direct attack, of actual invasion of the U.S. homeland, is utterly preposterous. In 1838, Lincoln made an observation that is even more true today: "Shall we expect some transatlantic military giant, to step the Ocean, and crush us at a blow? Never! All the armies of Europe, Asia and Africa combined, with all the treasure of the earth (our own excepted) in their military chest; with a Bonaparte for a commander, could not by force, take a drink from the Ohio, or make a track on the Blue Ridge, in a trial of a thousand years."[52] Today the Department of Defense is euphemistically named; nothing it does actually defends the United States, because no state considers attacking it.[53] There simply are no "existential" threats to the U.S. homeland.

That U.S. leaders have not recognized these peaceful trends should not be surprising. "Between the happening of a historical process

---

49 This point is made by Robert Jervis in "Theories of War in an Era of Leading Power Peace," p. 9; see also Alexander Wendt, *Social Theory of International Relations* (New York: Cambridge University Press, 1999), p. 312.
50 See Fettweis, *Dangerous Times?*
51 Robert Jervis, "Force in Our Times," *International Relations*, Vol. 25, No. 4 (December 2011), p. 413.
52 Roy P. Basler, ed., *Abraham Lincoln: His Speeches and Writings* (Cambridge, MA: Da Capo Press, 2001).
53 Andrew J. Bacevich makes this argument in *The Limits of Power: The End of American Exceptionalism* (New York: Metropolitan Books, 2008), p. 53.

and its recognition by rulers," wrote historian Barbara Tuchman, "a lag stretches, full of pitfalls."[54] It then falls to outside observers to point out that ours is not a particularly dangerous world, no matter how conventional is the wisdom to the contrary. The United States is a member of an extremely stable system, and as a result, it is an extremely safe, secure state.

Specifics, Part I: Terrorism

Few would consider conventional war, much less outright assault, the leading security challenge facing the United States today. Instead irregular or nonstate actors, especially terrorists, have topped the list of threats to the West since 9/11. Eleven years after the attacks, two-thirds of the American public still considered terrorism a "critical" threat to the United States.[55] The primary guiding principle of U.S. foreign policy making, for better or worse, is the continuing struggle against terrorism. The American people ought to take comfort from the knowledge that terrorists are their greatest security threat, since the danger they pose is relatively minor.

It is important to note up front that international terrorism is not on the rise, hype and fear notwithstanding. The number of worldwide incidents is far smaller than during the Cold War when there were sixty to seventy annually, most of which were bombings, in the United States alone.[56] As long as one classifies the wars in Iraq and Afghanistan guerrilla conflicts rather than sustained terrorist campaigns, the incidence of terrorist attacks would demonstrate a steady decline for two decades.[57] The peak of worldwide terrorist activity came during the early 1990s; there were 300 attacks in 1991 compared to 58 in 2005.[58]

---

[54] Barbara W. Tuchman, *A Distant Mirror: The Calamitous 14th Century* (New York: Knopf, 1978), p. 211.

[55] Dina Smeltz, *Foreign Policy in the New Millennium: Results of the 2012 Chicago Council Survey of American Public Opinion and U.S. Foreign Policy* (Chicago, IL: Chicago Council on Global Affairs, September 10, 2012).

[56] Brian Michael Jenkins, *Would-Be Warriors: Incidents of Jihadist Terrorist Radicalization in the United States since September 11, 2001* (Santa Monica, CA: RAND, 2010), pp. 8–9.

[57] Human Security Report Project, *Human Security Brief 2007* (Vancouver: Human Security Report Project, 2008).

[58] Terrorist incidents are tracked in the Global Terrorism Database by the National Consortium for the Study of Terrorism and the Responses to Terrorism at the University of Maryland. The data is accessible at http://www.start.umd.edu/gtd/ as

Despite the "war on terror" narrative so prevalent over the last decade, the small amount of terrorism that does exist is not particularly Islamic in character. The European Union counted 2,139 terrorist incidents in the five years from 2006 to 2010; of those, nine – or 0.4 percent – were perpetrated by Islamist groups.[59] Islamic terrorism has been all but absent in the United States in the decade following 9/11, with the gunman at Fort Hood and perhaps the Boston Marathon bombers providing the only substantial exceptions.[60] So-called homegrown terrorism has not proven particularly dangerous, nor is it becoming more frequent.[61] There is good evidence to believe, especially since the death of Osama bin Laden, that Islamic fundamentalist terrorism is in the process of essentially burning itself out.[62]

Today the specific risks posed by terrorists to any individual are extremely minor, smaller even than being struck by lightning.[63] National security officials tend to discount such statistics, at least in part because they conflict with their preexisting beliefs about the ubiquity and danger of the threat. As Ambassador Philip Wilcox, the State Department coordinator for counterterrorism, insisted irrationally and pathologically, when it comes to measuring terrorism "we shouldn't place too much emphasis on statistics."[64]

Obviously Islamic fundamentalist terrorists do pose some degree of danger to American citizens, at home and abroad. However, rational leaders would interpret this issue for what it is: a law enforcement

of August 7, 2009. See also J. Joseph Hewitt, Jonathan Wilkenfeld, and Ted Robert Gurr, eds., *Peace and Conflict, 2010: Executive Summary* (College Park, MD: Center for International Development and Conflict Management, 2010), p. 2.

[59] Data compiled from Europol's annual *TE-SATs* or *EU Terrorism Situation and Trend Reports* (The Hague, Netherlands: European Police Office, 2006–11), available online at the Europol website, https://www.europol.europa.eu/.

[60] John Mueller and Mark G. Stewart, "The Terrorism Delusion: America's Overwrought Response to September 11," *International Security*, Vol. 37, No. 1 (Summer 2012), pp. 81–110.

[61] Risa A. Brooks, "Muslim 'Homegrown' Terrorism in the United States: How Serious the Threat?" *International Security*, Vol. 36, No. 2 (Fall 2011), pp. 7–47.

[62] Steven Pinker reviews the evidence for this in *The Better Angels of Our Nature*, p. 358.

[63] John Mueller, *Overblown: How Politicians and the Terrorism Industry Inflate National Security Threats, and Why We Believe Them* (New York: Free Press, 2006); and John Mueller and Mark G. Stewart, *Terror, Security, and Money: Balancing the Risks, Benefits, and Costs of Homeland Security* (New York: Oxford University Press, 2011).

[64] Quoted by Andrew J. Bacevich, *American Empire: The Realities and Consequences of U.S. Diplomacy* (Cambridge, MA: Harvard University Press, 2002), p. 119.

challenge of the first order rather than an existential strategic threat. Fortunately, there is no meaningful dissent in the industrialized world about modern transnational problems like terrorism, weapons proliferation, human trafficking, drug smuggling, and piracy. Multilateral cooperation, coordination, and intelligence sharing to address such issues are in the interest of every state and occur at high, if often underreported, levels. Police action against terrorism is much less expensive than war, and is likely to be far more productive. The life expectancy of the international terrorist has plummeted drastically since 9/11.

President Bush repeatedly used the term "Islamic fascists" to describe the enemy that he reoriented the U.S. defense establishment to fight, portraying Al Qaeda not as a ragtag band of lunatics but as a threat to the American republic itself. It is not uncommon for even sober analysts to claim that Islamic terrorism represents an "existential threat" to the United States, especially if weapons of mass destruction were ever employed. Perhaps it is Parkinson's Law that inspires some analysts to compare Islamic fundamentalists with the great enemies of the past, from the Nazis to the communists, since no rational analysis of their destructive potential would arrive at such a conclusion. Threat is a function of capabilities and intent; even if Al Qaeda has the intent to threaten the existence of the United States, it certainly does not possess the capability to do so. As always, little analytical insight is gained from misplaced historical analogies.

Even terrorists equipped with weapons of mass destruction would be incapable of causing damage so cataclysmic that it would prove fatal to modern states. The United States absorbed the impact of 9/11 with little long-term macroeconomic damage, for instance. Within forty days the Dow Jones Industrial Average bounced back to the level at which it closed on September 10, 2001.[65] If terrorists could overcome substantial obstacles and use the most destructive weapons in a densely populated area, the outcome would obviously be terrible for those unfortunate enough to be nearby. We should not operate under the illusion, however, that doomsday would then arrive. Modern industrialized countries can cope with disasters, both natural

[65] Gardner, *The Science of Fear*, p. 259.

and manmade. As unpleasant as such highly unlikely events would be, they do not represent existential threats to the republic.

Biological and chemical weapons, though often lumped in with nuclear, may be somewhat easier to manufacture but kill far fewer people. While the prospect of terrorists obtaining and using such weapons is one of the most consistently terrifying of the new era, it is also highly unlikely and not nearly as dangerous as sometimes portrayed. As the very well-funded, well-staffed Aum Shinrikyo found out in the 1990s, workable forms of WMD are hard to purchase, harder still to synthesize without state help, and then quite challenging to use effectively. The group managed to kill a dozen people on the Tokyo subway system at rush hour. While tragic, the attack was hardly the stuff of apocalyptic nightmares. Superweapons are simply not easy for even the most sophisticated nonstate actors to employ.[66]

Nuclear weapons in particular are, for practical purposes, simply beyond the capability of terrorists. Presumably nonstate actors could obtain atomic weaponry in four ways: they could buy them, steal them, build them, or receive them from a nuclear state. The obstacles to all of these avenues have been dealt with at length elsewhere.[67] To summarize quickly, nuclear forensics makes it impossible for states to give or sell weapons to terrorists and then deny their actions plausibly afterward. Atomic explosions create "radiation signatures" that allow scientists to determine where the bomb came from.[68] Giving nuclear weapons away would be the functional equivalent of using them, and would therefore be subject to the same deterrent forces. Theft of nuclear weapons has never happened; if it did, the thieves would not be able to set off the bomb. The act of detonation is significantly more complicated than portrayed by

---

[66] For one of the best discussions of the Aum, including its motivations, actions, and ultimate failure, see Robert J. Lifton, *Destroying the World in Order to Save It: Aum Shinrikyo, Apocalyptic Violence, and the New Global Terrorism* (New York: Henry Holt, 1999).

[67] For details, see John Mueller, *Atomic Obsession: Nuclear Alarmism from Hiroshima to Al-Qaeda* (New York: Oxford University Press, 2009).

[68] For a review of the (unclassified) science behind nuclear forensics, see Kenton J. Moody, Ian D. Hutcheon, and Patrick M. Grant, *Nuclear Forensic Analysis* (New York: Taylor & Francis, 2005). The policy implications are discussed by Michael A. Levi, *On Nuclear Terrorism* (Cambridge, MA: Harvard University Press, 2007), pp. 127–33.

Hollywood. Modern weapons are typically equipped with the functional equivalent of self-destruct devices, nonnuclear explosives that detonate if the device is tampered with, rendering it useless. Even today's crudest weapons possess security features that would prove extremely difficult for all but the most expert – perhaps only a handful in the world – to defeat.[69]

Most unlikely of all is the construction of nuclear weapons, which, even for a terrorist group that has somehow obtained enough enriched uranium or plutonium, would be a virtual impossibility. The construction of a nuclear reaction requires the work of talented physicists, chemists, machinists, metallurgists, and engineers, at the very least. Prototypes must be tested, and failures will precede success. The Aum, by far the best funded and equipped terrorist group in history, assembled scientists from many disciplines with access to nearly unlimited resources before deciding that nuclear weapons were out of its reach. Many states struggle to develop them successfully. The suggestion that Al Qaeda or some similar group, whose members have failed to make operative shoe, underpants, and gasoline car bombs, could forge a workable atomic weapon is an example of paranoia in action. Analysts of risk have a term for danger so small it can effectively be considered zero: *de minimis.*[70] The threat from terrorists armed with nuclear weapons is clearly a *de minimis* risk.

For modern states, terrorism is a chronic rather than a life-threatening condition, one that causes problems and needs constant attention but will not prove fatal. Its practitioners can kill people and scare many more, but the localized damage they can cause is incapable of changing the character of Western civilization. Only the people of the West, largely through their own fear and overreaction, can accomplish that. While U.S. analysts spend time worrying about such events, it is worth recalling that the diplomats of any prior age would likely have been quite grateful to have our problems. Terrorism and other irregular threats of the early twenty-first century are in reality quite minor in comparison to those of eras that came before, and certainly do not threaten the existence of this or any other country.

---

[69] Mueller, *Atomic Obsession,* pp. 166–67. See also Stephen M. Younger, *The Bomb: A New History* (New York: Echo, 2009), pp. 153–54.

[70] Gardner, *The Science of Fear,* p. 187.

Specifics, Part II: Failed, Rogue, Bothersome States

Second only to terrorism on the list of things that have animated the post–Cold War United States are those countries that often operate outside of accepted behavioral norms, either because of illegitimate, tyrannical leaders or the complete breakdown of governance. The Clinton administration spoke of "rogue states," many of which would find themselves part of President Bush's "Axis of Evil" a few years later. Today, it is often said, the United States seems to be threatened not by the strength of its adversaries, but by their weakness. "Disorder breeds disorder," argued Frederick Kagan. "Just as disordered regions were a feeding ground for the Soviets during the Cold War, so now they are potential bases for the enemies of America and our way of life."[71] Those states that cannot control their borders or that are too weak to act against nonstate actors operating on their territory seem of primary concern to Washington. The 2002 *National Security Strategy* made the case on page one: "America is now threatened less by conquering states," it says (rather awkwardly), "than we are by failing ones."[72] "Of the world's more than 70 low-income nations," according to another analysis, "about 50 of them – excluding well-armed hostile nations such as North Korea – are weak in a way that threatens U.S. and international security" because of their general inability to control events on their soil.[73] After all, the thinking goes, Al Qaeda thrived in the chaos of post-Soviet Afghanistan.

One might think that such a revolutionary reconceptualization of the relationship between power and threat would have generated more controversy than it has. An acceptance of this new logic – which proposes that the weakest, most disorganized, and even pathetic regimes pose great danger to the strongest country in the history of the world – would demand an entirely new understanding of international relations. One suspects that Thucydides, Machiavelli, and Bismarck would respectfully disagree. More traditional thinking might suggest rogue

[71] Frederick W. Kagan, "Back to the Future: NSC-68 and the Right Course for America Today," *SAIS Review*, Vol. 19, No. 1 (Winter–Spring 1999), pp. 69–70.

[72] George W. Bush, *The National Security Strategy of the United States of America* (Washington, DC: Government Printing Office, 2002), p. 1.

[73] Stuart Eizenstat, John Edward Porter, and Jeremy M. Weinstein, "Rebuilding Weak States," *Foreign Affairs*, Vol. 84, No. 1 (January/February 2005), p. 136.

and failed states have weakness in common – in the case of the latter, profound weakness – and weak states have very limited ability to harm the strong. Observers from any past age might well be baffled at the suggestion that failed states present a more dire threat to great power interests than do successful ones, or that the United States is more endangered by Somalia, say, than by China. Threat has traditionally been directly, not indirectly, related to power. Weak countries, even those that are actively hostile, should worry rational observers far less than strong. Rogue states simply do not pose serious risks to the security of the United States.

Fears of "safe havens" arising in the chaos of state failure are equally misplaced. For one thing, the training a terrorist group needs is obviously rather minimal compared to that of a conventional army. Basic instruction on explosives is often the only necessary skill, and it is one that does not require a safe haven, as Palestinian groups have amply demonstrated over the years. A shed appears to be sufficient. Those drills displayed prominently on Al Qaeda propaganda videos, which feature recruits swinging from monkey bars and crawling under ropes for some reason, are of little utility in the kinds of attacks commonly perpetrated by modern terrorists, most of whom seem to have been able to function quite effectively without much training at all. The training Umar Farouk Abdulmutallab required before he shoved a bomb into his underpants and walked onto a plane was spiritual, not military.

Contrary to conventional wisdom, Al Qaeda did not flourish in a failed state. It was in fact sheltered by the most coherent government Afghanistan has had since at least the mid-1970s, which suggests that an ungoverned region was hardly necessary to carry out the 9/11 attacks. The cells that planned and perpetrated the hijackings could have presumably done so whether or not Osama was safe in Kandahar. Sanctuary for terrorists was also apparently not necessary to execute the multitude of attacks that have occurred since the deposition of the Taliban, from Madrid to Bali to London, nor was a safe haven a *sine qua non* for the daily attacks in Iraq. In fact, the vast majority of terrorist groups throughout history, from the IRA to the Basques to the anarchists a century ago, have been able to operate in hostile territory, without havens in which to train on monkey bars.

Finally, it is worth noting that the number of failed states is not increasing. In fact, the number of state failures remained nearly

constant over the course of the second half of the twentieth century, and has been actually declining since a brief surge during the
relative chaos following the immediate post-Soviet period.[74] It is
not the case that globalization is leading to major disruptions of
governance and that large swaths of the globe have become lawless
and anarchic, occasional perceptions to the contrary notwithstanding. The strongest countries have little to fear from the weak areas
of the world.

Specifics, Part III: Nuclear Proliferation

Fears that nuclear weapons will spread around the world date back
to at least the Kennedy administration. In 1963, the president worried that by the early 1970s more than twenty-five countries might
have the bomb; with the hindsight of a half century, it is clear his
concerns were misplaced. Still, that fear lives on. The more hands
with access to these weapons, the logic goes, the more likely they
will be used or fall into the wrong hands. Today, no one discusses
the dangers of nuclear proliferation and the attendant specter of
their use more than Graham Allison and his Managing the Atom
program at Harvard's Belfer Center, for whom the world is perpetually at the edge of a nuclear "tipping point" after which run-
away proliferation will occur. That such a point has never arrived
and shows no signs of doing so seems to offer little solace to those
sounding the most frightening tocsins regarding mushroom clouds
and fallout.

Fortunately, there is far more proliferation pressure in imagination than in reality. In fact, the post–Cold War era has experienced

---

[74] Marshall and Cole, *Global Report 2011: Conflict, Governance and State Fragility.* For his-
torical perspective, see Jack A. Goldstone, Ted Robert Gurr, Barbara Harff, Marc A.
Levy, Monty G. Marshall, Robert H. Bates, David L. Epstein, Colin H. Kahl, Pamela
T. Surko, John C. Ulfelder, Jr., and Alan N. Unger, *State Failure Task Force Report:
Phase III Findings* (McLean, VA: Science Applications International Corporation
[SAIC], September 30, 2000), available at http://globalpolicy.gmu.edu/pitf/
SFTF%20Phase%20III%20Report%20Final.pdf. See also Harold James, *The Roman
Predicament: How the Rules of International Order Create the Politics of Empire* (Princeton,
NJ: Princeton University Press, 2006), p. 111. Finally, *Foreign Policy* magazine pub-
lishes an annual analysis of state failure around the world; see its website for its
reports, www.foreignpolicy.com/failedstates.

Nuclear Weapons States, 1989 and 2012	
1989	2012
United States	United States
USSR	Russia
China	China
United Kingdom	United Kingdom
France	France
India	India
Pakistan	Pakistan
Israel	Israel
South Africa	North Korea

a slower pace of proliferation than any since World War II. In two decades the total number of countries with nuclear weapons has held steady, even if the membership in the "nuclear club" has changed a bit:

Two states founded the nuclear club in the 1940s (the United States and the USSR), one more joined in the 1950s (the United Kingdom), and two each in the sixties (France and China), seventies (India and Israel), and eighties (Pakistan and South Africa). In the 1990s, there were none. The overhyped nuclear tests on the Indian subcontinent in 1998 merely confirmed what had been widely known for years – both countries possessed nuclear arsenals. The nonproliferation regime suffered no consequences; no other state followed their lead. North Korea has been the only new nuclear weapons state to emerge since the end of the Cold War, and its test also did not inspire any other government to go down that route, despite many breathless warnings to the contrary. Allison had predicted that a North Korean test would "unleash a proliferation chain reaction, with South Korea and Japan building their own nuclear weapons by the end of the decade. Taiwan would seriously consider following suit."[75] None of his feared consequences occurred, in part because the United States was able to convince leaders in these countries that they were safe under the U.S. nuclear umbrella, and in part because they seem to have decided that

---

[75] Graham T. Allison, *Nuclear Terrorism: The Ultimate Preventable Catastrophe* (New York: Henry Holt, 2004), p. 166.

nuclear weapons have little practical utility. Proliferation "cascades" are the exception, not the rule.

Since the collapse of the USSR, trends in proliferation have actually been negative: three states that inherited part of the Soviet arsenal (Belarus, Ukraine, and Kazakhstan) peacefully surrendered the weapons to Russia, and South Africa decided to give up its weapons. Proliferation momentum has not only ground to a halt since the end of the Cold War, in other words, it has swung in the opposite direction. Allison's repeated warnings that "global trend lines in all things nuclear are worsening" simply fly in the face of the evidence.[76]

In fact, only one country seems intent on developing nuclear weapons today. Even if a package of sticks and carrots cannot be arranged to dissuade Iran from going down that road – and such an arrangement might well prove possible – there is little reason to believe that leaders in Tehran would act any less rationally with nuclear weapons than have all other members of the nuclear club. As discussed later in this chapter, the idea that *they* are fundamentally different and less rational than *we* are is a misperception common to the enemy image. Iranians would have to be suicidally irrational to use their weapons or give them to nonstate actors, and no state in history has ever committed suicide. One of the basic lessons of International Relations 101 is that the central, overarching goal of those in power is to stay in power, and no act would bring a regime down faster than using nuclear weapons. Overall, the United States could live with a nuclear Iran, if efforts to buy it off fail to stop its program.

No matter what Tehran does, few other countries appear interested in joining the nuclear club. Repeated warnings by Saudi Arabia, Egypt, and others that they will follow Iran down that route are taken at face value by a surprising number of people, as if such statements are not primarily made to pressure the United States to act. Washington would surely have options with which to affect the calculations of its allies if and when Iran tests its first bomb. It is certainly possible that the arrival of an Iranian nuclear weapon would pass with just as little long-term consequence as did the North Korean tests of 2006. The U.S.

[76] Graham T. Allison and Ernesto Zedillo, "The Fragility of the Global Nuclear Order," *Boston Globe*, September 30, 2008.

nuclear umbrella might prove sufficient to calm Saudi and Turkish fears. At the very least, it is hardly inevitable that a proliferation chain would occur.

None of this will prove comforting to nuclear alarmists like Allison, for whom warning lights are perpetually blinking in a world running out of time. He and his colleagues have provided the battlefield of beliefs with some of its most disquieting images, of nuclear-armed terrorists and irradiated major cities. That nothing of the kind has come close to occurring does not seem to sap their motivation to scare. Facts about risk rarely alter the deeply held beliefs of those convinced about the dangers involved in nuclear proliferation or any other of today's various bogeymen.

Specifics Part IV: Vague Dangers and Unknown Unknowns

"When I was coming up, it was a dangerous world, and you knew exactly who they were," George W. Bush told an Iowa audience in 2000. "It was us vs. them, and it was clear who them was. Today, we are not so sure who the 'they' are, but we know they're there."[77] Bush knew evil was out there, but was not quite clear on how or when it would strike. September 11 just confirmed his suspicions. Indeed, at times today's security debate seems driven less by actual threats than vague, unnamed dangers. "The real threat we now face," according to the 1992 National Military Strategy, "is the threat of the unknown, the uncertain."[78] Secretary of Defense Dick Cheney testified to Congress that "a proper appreciation of uncertainty" had to be a "critical part of any realistic defense strategy."[79] At a press conference ten years later, his successor, Donald Rumsfeld, warned about "unknown unknowns," the threats that "we don't know we don't know," which "tend to be the

[77] George W. Bush, Iowa Western Community College, January 21, 2000. Quoted by Kathleen J. Ferraro, "The Culture of Social Problems: Observations of the Third Reich, the Cold War, and Vietnam," *Social Problems*, Vol. 52, No. 1 (February 2005), p. 7.
[78] Colin Powell, *National Military Strategy of the United States* (Washington, DC: U.S. Government Printing Office, January 1992), p. 4.
[79] Quoted and discussed by Paul Wolfowitz in "Shaping the Future: Planning at the Pentagon, 1989–93," in Melvyn P. Leffler and Jeffrey W. Legro, *In Uncertain Times: American Foreign Policy after the Berlin Wall and 9/11* (Ithaca, NY: Cornell University Press, 2011), p. 58.

difficult ones."[80] Robert Kagan and William Kristol worry that if the United States fails to remain highly engaged, the system "is likely to yield very real external dangers, as threatening in their own way as the Soviet Union was a quarter century ago."[81] What exactly these dangers would be is left open to interpretation, and are almost beside the point. In the absence of identifiable threats, the unknown can provide us with an enemy, one whose power and danger is limited only by the imagination. It is what Benjamin Friedman and Harvey Sapolsky call "the threat of no threats," and is perhaps the most frightening of all.[82] Our imaginations can conjure demons far more frightening than any that exist in the real world.

Even if, as everyone schooled in folk wisdom knows, anything is possible, it is not the case that everything is plausible. Vague, generalized dangers should never be acceptable replacements for specific threats when crafting national policy. There is no limit on the potential dangers the human mind can manufacture, but there are very definite limits on the specific threats the system contains. "To make any thing very terrible, obscurity seems in general to be necessary," noted Edmund Burke. "When we know the full extent of any danger, when we can accustom our eyes to it, a great deal of the apprehension vanishes."[83] The full extent of today's dangers is not only knowable, but relatively minor.

For a bit of final perspective, consider this: in the summer of 2009, the officers studying at the U.S. Naval War College were, for the first time, given a "read ahead" book, one they were told to finish before they began their studies. The book chosen by their commandant was *World War Z: An Oral History of the Zombie War*. That semester the author, Max Brooks (who happens to be the son of Mel Brooks), was invited to the college to address the student body, sparking a discussion about how militaries could plan for and cope with new security

---

[80] "DoD News Briefing," February 12, 2002, www.defenselink.mil/transcripts/transcript.aspx?transcriptid=2636.

[81] Robert Kagan and William Kristol, eds., *Present Dangers: Crisis and Opportunity in American Foreign and Defense Policy* (San Francisco, CA: Encounter Books, 2000), p. 4.

[82] Benjamin Friedman and Harvey Sapolsky, "You Never Know(ism)," *Breakthroughs*, Vol. 15, No. 1 (Spring 2006), pp. 3–11.

[83] Quoted by Corey Robin in *Fear: The History of a Political Idea* (New York: Oxford University Press, 2004), p. 72.

challenges. One might suggest that if there were actual, dire security threats, the premier professional military education institution in the United States would not spend its time idly speculating about the best way to fight zombies.[84]

The United States has entered an age when conventional threats to its security are entirely absent and unconventional threats are relatively minor and rare. Even a global financial crisis has not led to an increase in interstate or terrorist violence; democracy has never been healthier – the number of states with elected leaders is higher than ever; prosperity is not threatened by anything other than the business cycle.[85] However, few seem to believe this to be the case. There is a disconnect between that low level of threat and high level of threat perception among leaders and the public alike. A foreign policy pathology is present, one with important, deleterious implications for the decisions made by the United States.

PATHOGENESIS

How can one account for this mismatch between perceptions of threat and reality that exists in the United States? Where does this political pathology come from? A number of potential explanations exist, drawn from factors of individual psychology, those unique to the American experience and structural features of the international system. As is often the case in international political psychology, these variables are not independent of one another, nor are they neatly measurable.[86] They are instead interdependent, additive, and mutually reinforcing. Recognition of the various compounding factors can

---

[84] In May 2011, the Centers for Disease Control and Prevention followed suit, listing on its website instructions to deal with a zombie outbreak. Ali S. Khan, "Preparedness 101: Zombie Apocalypse," Centers for Disease Control and Prevention, May 16, 2011, available at http://blogs.cdc.gov/publichealthmatters/2011/05/preparedness-101-zombie-apocalypse/. Theorists of international relations also have apparently had some extra time on their hands in a world without war: Daniel Drezner, *Theories of International Politics and Zombies* (Princeton, NJ: Princeton University Press, 2011).

[85] The Polity IV Project has tracked the number of democracies around the world for many years. See its most recent report, Marshall and Cole, *Global Report 2011: Conflict, Governance and State Fragility.*

[86] Janice Stein comments on the methodological difficulties inherent in state-level political psychology in "Building Politics into Psychology: The Misperception of Threat," *Political Psychology*, Vol. 9, No. 2 (June 1988), p. 248.

lead to the minimization of their effects and perhaps even a decrease in the pathological pressures of fear.

INDIVIDUAL LEVEL

Fear is hardwired into human nature.[87] Without the ability to recognize danger and react with self-preservation in mind, the species would not have survived for long. That heightened level of fear may have benefited cavemen, but it can prove counterproductive for moderns. Some scholars have recently suggested that neurological evolution may have essentially conditioned people to feel their group is fragile, as were hunter-gather groups.[88] In the modern world, this would mean that people may naturally tend to harbor greater fear for the fate of their state than for their own.

The explanation for the fear that exists in U.S. political discourse, therefore, should begin with an examination of human beings and their natural predilection for suspicion and occasional panic. The insecurity pathology ultimately resides within the minds of the leaders who design and implement policies, not in anthropomorphized states. While this level of analysis cannot explain pathological U.S. fear in its entirety, since American leaders as people are no different from those of other countries, it is nonetheless helpful to understand its cognitive foundations.

Those in power may be more susceptible to paranoia than the general public, for a number of reasons. First, modern leaders must bear the burden of protecting the people, a position that rewards suspicion and distrust of others. They also have access to more information, much of which is fairly frightening. There is no reason to doubt the sincerity of Dick Cheney, who professed feeling constant, unrelenting pressure to keep vigilant in the war against terrorists, for instance.[89]

---

[87] To be precise, it appears hardwired into the amygdala. Ten years of research on the neurobiological origins and effects of fear can be found in Mohammed R. Milad and Gregory J. Quirk, "Fear Extinction as a Model for Translational Neuroscience: Ten Years of Progress," *Annual Review of Psychology*, Vol. 63 (2012), pp. 129–51.

[88] Anthony C. Lopez, Rose McDermott, and Michael Bang Petersen, "States in Mind: Evolution, Coalitional Psychology, and International Politics," *International Security*, Vol. 36, No. 2 (Fall 2011), esp. pp. 67–72.

[89] Barton Gellman, *Angler: The Cheney Vice Presidency* (New York: Penguin, 2008).

Those who consider themselves the guardians manning the walls of civilization can never allow themselves to relax.

The political profession at times rewards a cautious, even paranoid approach to power. History contains no shortage of career paths exhibiting a direct correlation between personal insecurity and political achievement.[90] Time and time again people who behaved in borderline deranged manners have attracted followers, solidified bases, come to power, and remained there for extended periods of time across a wide variety of settings. Paranoia can at times be advantageous for the would-be leader, since enemies do exist and broad purges surely kill conspirators alongside innocents. U.S. leaders are not autocrats, obviously, but they do enjoy an unprecedented level of power, nearly unchecked – and certainly uncheckable – by the international system. Perhaps decision makers in the United States demonstrate some of the destabilizing effects of great power, if they never really reach the nearly debilitating paranoia of the dictator or cloistered king. The pathologies of leaders can only account for part of the fear present in today's American elite and broader society. Human nature plays an important role as well, especially because it contributes to some of the misperceptions common to foreign policy analysis. At least five are significant in helping to explain the genesis and persistence of fear in an otherwise safe United States: First, people are generally not good at judging risk, which is a necessary component of threat assessment. Most of the time, emotional reactions tend to precede, and then trump, rational analysis; people react to images faster than they do to numbers, and even when the risk is explained those images never fully recede. The ubiquitous videos from 9/11 generate visceral reactions far more powerful than any intellectual discussion of the individual's miniscule risk of falling victim. Overall, human beings are good with stories and bad with numbers.[91] It is quite difficult to conceive of 300 million people but easy to see the suffering of the few. As a result of this process, which psychologist Ralph White called the "non-rational inflation of anxiety," the risk of terrorism or any other such danger always seems much greater than it actually is.[92]

[90] Robins and Post, *Political Paranoia.*
[91] Gardner, *The Science of Fear*, p. 89.
[92] Ralph K. White, *Nobody Wanted War* (New York: Doubleday, 1968), p. 128.

Second, in what might be considered the consistency fallacy, people often assume that causes need to be as dramatic as results.[93] Big events cannot be produced by luck, accident, or blunder; they must have big inputs too, to appear logically consistent. People seem to derive a certain amount of psychological comfort in the notion that there is some order to the universe, which consistency in cause and effect helps to maintain. For example, many people find it hard to accept those explanations for the 9/11 terrorist attacks that focus on the actions of a miserable ragtag group of malcontents spearheaded by nineteen individuals who were fortunate not to have been detected. Many insist (and still insist) that a state had to be behind the attacks, or that Al Qaeda is filled with a new breed of super genius. People routinely overestimate the size and power of their enemies, and terrorists have been no exception.[94] It appears human to want to minimize capricious or arbitrary aspects of life, even when it is frightening to do so. A dangerous world is easier to live in than a chaotic, arbitrary one.

Third, policy makers tend to learn more from events as opposed to nonevents. War in particular teaches more than peace. President Bush's world view was dramatically altered by 9/11, for example, and President Carter is said to have learned about the nature of the Soviet Union from the invasion of Afghanistan rather than the cooperative détente era. Acts of violence have particularly powerful, sometimes disproportionate influences on the development of beliefs compared to what Jervis called "negative outcomes," like "aggression that does not occur, crises that are avoided, quiet compromises, and slow, peaceful transformations."[95] Like the modern media, the human brain tends to focus on dramatic events at the expense of what might be considered a more balanced evaluation of reality. As a result, recent research suggests that people seem to have more confidence in studies that report danger than they do in those that show low risk.[96]

---

[93] Robert Jervis discusses this in his classic work on misperception, *Perception and Misperception in International Politics* (Princeton, NJ: Princeton University Press, 1976), pp. 230–31.

[94] Robins and Post, *Political Paranoia*, p. 12.

[95] Jervis, *Perception and Misperception in International Politics*, p. 235.

[96] Gardner, *The Science of Fear*, p. 174.

The fourth source of misperception that leads to unwarranted fear is what psychologists refer to as the "negativity bias." Describing what the authors argued is "a general principle or law of psychological phenomena," a review of this literature explained that not all stimuli affect people the same way. "Bad emotions, bad parents, and bad feedback have more impact than good ones," they explain. "And bad information is processed more thoroughly than good.... Bad impressions and bad stereotypes are quicker to form and more resistant to disconfirmation than good ones."[97] Hundreds of studies across fields have supported this contention, confirming that in a wide variety of areas people seem predisposed to concentrate on bad news and events more than on good. As many professors can attest, one critical comment on evaluations is often more memorable than dozens of supportive ones. Negative experiences make a more lasting impression on our lives than do positive.

While this bias may have understandable evolutionary origins – focusing on the negative could well have aided the survival of prehistoric people – its implications for modern foreign policy are uniformly poisonous.[98] Unless they are conscious of this bias and vigilant against its effects, leaders will tend to focus on the bad events and form more negative impressions of others than a neutral examination of the evidence would warrant. Dominic Johnson and Dominic Tierney have shown how the negativity bias affected U.S. perceptions of events in Vietnam and helped shape responses to them. Throughout the conflict, U.S. leaders were highly sensitive to information that appeared threatening, which affected their decisions far more than positive news.[99] Today, Iran's Holocaust denial and foiled plots to assassinate Saudi ambassadors generate deeper, more lasting impressions of the regime than do its numerous offers to cooperate against Al Qaeda

---

[97] Roy F. Baumeister, Ellen Bratslavsky, Catrin Finkenauer, and Kathleen D. Vohs, "Bad is Stronger than Good," *Review of General Psychology*, Vol. 5, No. 4 (December 2001), p. 323.

[98] A variety of potential explanations for the negativity bias is reviewed in Paul Rozin and Edward B. Roysman, "Negativity Bias, Negativity Dominance, and Contagion," *Personality and Social Psychology Review*, Vol. 5, No. 4 (November 2001), pp. 296–320.

[99] Dominic Johnson and Dominic Tierney, "Bad World: The Negativity Bias and International Politics," Paper Presented at the International Studies Association Conference, San Diego, CA, April 1–4, 2012.

and the Taliban.[100] Negative impressions of others quite naturally lead not just to loathing, but to fear.

Finally, one of the most common and most pernicious misperceptions is the seemingly ubiquitous human need to identify an enemy or a force against which to struggle. George Kennan once observed that "it sometimes seems to me that people have a need for the externalization of evil. They have the need to think that there is, somewhere, an enemy boundlessly evil, because this makes them feel boundlessly good."[101] The "enemy image" has been the subject of a considerable amount of scholarship, and there can be little doubt that at times it can lead to the development of pathological beliefs.[102] "As long as there is an enemy," argued one of the classic works on the subject, "needs which some men have for scapegoats are fulfilled, and they can hate them with impunity and even, at times, with public approbation."[103] Since many people appear to need enemies for their own self-image – it is meaningless to be the "good guy" if there is no corresponding "bad guy" – evil will always be discovered, even where none exists. In the absence of clear rivals, foreign policy tends to flounder, rudderless, as critics accused U.S. foreign policy of doing in the 1990s. The attacks of 9/11 merely confirmed what many already believed: our enemies are massing against us. But our psychological need to have opponents does not make danger real.

Psychologists and political scientists are split over whether all people need enemies or whether certain personality types are more in need of adversaries than others.[104] Murray and Meyers found consistent differences among American elites about the identification of enemies: those who were most suspicious about the Soviet Union were among

---

[100] Ambassador James Dobbins gives a firsthand account of the Iranian offers of cooperation following 9/11 in *After the Taliban: Nation-Building in Afghanistan* (Washington, DC: Potomac Books, 2008).

[101] Nicholas Thompson, *The Hawk and the Dove: Paul Nitze, George Kennan, and the History of the Cold War* (New York: Henry Holt and Co., 2009), p. 271.

[102] See Vamik D. Volkan, *The Need to Have Enemies and Allies: From Clinical Practice to International Relationships* (Northvale, NJ: Jason Aronson, Inc., 1988).

[103] David J. Finlay, Ole R. Holsti, and Richard R. Fagen, *Enemies in Politics* (Chicago, IL: Rand McNally, 1967), p. 8.

[104] For a good review of both positions, see Shoon Kathleen Murray and Jason Meyers, "Do People Need Foreign Enemies? American Leaders' Beliefs after the Soviet Demise," *Journal of Conflict Resolution*, Vol. 43, No. 5 (October 1999), pp. 555–69.

the quickest to identify new enemies after its collapse.[105] Intense cold warriors were more likely to believe that Russia continued to pose a threat and that China soon would too, and that high levels of defense spending remained prudent. It appears likely that some people from certain ideological backgrounds are more prone to perceive enemies and danger in the system than are others.

American political leaders may be especially prone to misperceiving enemies, since they are conditioned by a two-party political system that encourages competitive thinking and rewards those who defeat their rivals. Furthermore, as discussed later in this volume, many argue that the United States was born as a civic religion or ideology, and ideologies are by nature expansive. States are rarely content to practice them at home and not attempt to spread them across their borders. In doing so, they tend to confront those who hold different belief systems. Ideology provides another basis upon which to define enemies, which in this case would be those who resist the truth and the proliferation of our beliefs. Therefore, it is generally true that states whose identity is based on ideology rather than nationality tend to identify internal and external enemies with even greater consistency.[106]

Enemy images are not always irrational, of course. There are sometimes forces that are indeed working to do us serious harm. The enemy image becomes pathological only when levels of hostility are misperceived or incorrect. Unfortunately, intentions of the other are often only fully evident in retrospect, as archives become opened to historians. But this does not mean that policy makers are wise to err on the side of caution at all times; being right is surely more important. True safety does not come through constant worst-case-scenario planning, since that often leads to counterproductive policies. Actions made to maximize safety can end up putting states in greater danger. Fortunately, there is a recognizable pattern to misperceived enemy images – international, domestic, or interpersonal – to which policy makers can refer as they try to determine the true level of hostility in

[105] Murray and Meyers, "Do People Need Foreign Enemies?" p. 566.
[106] Finlay, Holsti, and Fagen argued that "in groups with an overriding ideological orientation, enemies are an integral part of the organization's immediate and long-range problems of survival, maintenance of group solidarity, and fulfillment of plans." Finlay, Holsti, and Fagen, *Enemies in Politics*, p. 10.

the other. Beliefs that act as indicators of the existence of the enemy image include, but are not limited to, the following:

- We are trustworthy and peace loving, but we cannot be too sure about them.
- We have *principles*; they have an *agenda*.
- Our side is heterogeneous and disorganized; theirs is unified and strategic.
- They are clever, devious, and patient, and unlike us they plan many steps into the future. We play checkers, in other words, but they play chess.
- When we speak, we say what we mean. For political and/or selfish purposes, they often hide their true intentions, hoping to appear more moderate and reasonable than they are.
- Since they are fundamentally different from us in outlook and desires, our very existence constitutes a threat to them. They will never accept coexistence.
- Their followers are probably open to persuasion, since they are basically good people misled by their leaders. We need to appeal to the common people and present our case more clearly.
- Overall they cannot succeed unless aided by moral failures on our side.
- There is one language they understand: force.
- And for a variety of reasons, they do not value human life like we do.

When policy makers find themselves thinking along similar lines, they would be well served to be cognizant of the possibility that misperception may be at work, and that the hostility of the other is probably exaggerated. This is not to say harmony is an option, just that differences might not be as intractable as they appear. Not all enemies are existential. Many can be mollified, or even simply be monitored and resisted without ever succumbing to the kind of pathological fear some of them probably hope to create.

The salient argument about these effects of misperception is that they all tend to point in the same direction, leading actors to overestimate the hostility of the other and raising levels of threat.[107] If they

---

[107] Jervis, *Perception and Misperception in International Politics*, p. 424.

are not aware of the probability that they are misperceiving others, many leaders will form beliefs based on an incorrect assessment of their malevolence. All of us would be well advised to realize that the world is probably a bit less hostile than we initially perceive it to be, and that it is natural to overestimate its dangers.

As mentioned in the introduction, misperceptions make others appear more belligerent than they are; pathological beliefs make us more belligerent than we otherwise would be. If unchecked, both can push states in the direction of conflict.

STATE LEVEL

A number of factors unique to the American experience may help explain the existence of the insecurity pathology, ones that make it more likely the United States would detect great danger where little exists. Exceptionalism, a strong feature of the U.S. political culture that is dealt with at some length in coming chapters, has been directly linked with elevated perceptions of threat by scholars who have studied the issue.[108] Furthermore, high levels of religiosity make Americans susceptible to Manichean explanations of international affairs and accustom them to accepting beliefs on faith rather than evidence; certain domestic political ideologies, especially neoconservatism, detect higher levels of danger than others; its unique geography and history may have made the United States especially prone to overreaction; and the media, with their "entertainment logic," have an interest in keeping fear levels high, as do government officials.

Religiosity and Evil

Every major religion contains some concept of evil, usually as a tangible reality that poses a great threat to the righteous. On his famous tour of the young United States, French aristocrat Alexis de Tocqueville may have been the first to note that no country was more religious than the United States; anthropologist Margaret Mead believed that of all the groups she studied over the course of her career, none "think of

---

[108] K.J. Holsti, "Exceptionalism in American Foreign Policy: Is It Exceptional?" *European Journal of International Relations*, Vol. 17, No. 3 (September 2011), pp. 381–404.

life in as habitually moral terms as do Americans."[109] Contemporary evidence suggests these observations remain true, that American religiosity is higher than that of any industrialized county. A 2002 Pew survey found that the people of poor nations place more importance on religion than do those of wealthy countries – with the exception of the United States, a stark outlier in the global north.[110] For the last sixty years, around 95 percent of Americans report a belief in God, compared to about half of Europeans and Japanese.[111] Survey data have been fairly consistent on this point for some time.[112]

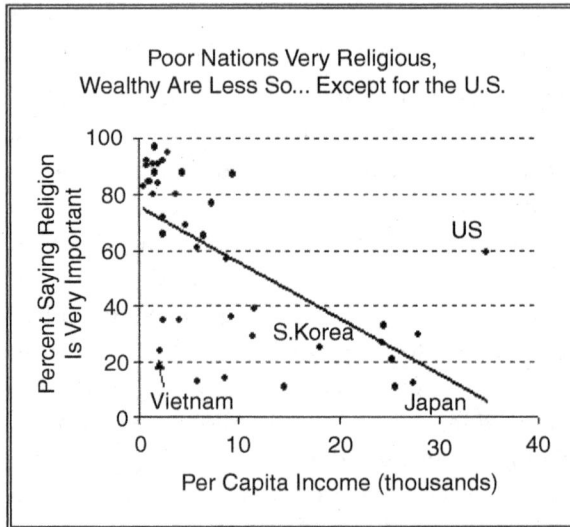

The overwhelming majority of Americans subscribe to one of the various forms of Christianity, some of which appear more likely to generate fear than others. The political power of the religious right in particular has grown enormously over the course of the past generation. Between 1971 and 1990 evangelical churches gained 6 million members while

[109] Margaret Mead, *And Keep Your Powder Dry: An Anthropologist Looks at America* (New York: William Morrow and Company, 1943), p. 11.
[110] "Among Wealthy Nations: U.S. Stands Alone in its Embrace of Religion," Pew Center for People and the Press, December 19, 2002, available at http://pew-global.org/2002/12/19/among-wealthy-nations/, accessed November 2, 2010. Figure reproduced by permission of the Pew Center for People and the Press.
[111] Lebow, *Why Nations Fight*, p. 220.
[112] See Pippa Norris and Ronald Inglehart, *Sacred and Secular: Religion and Politics Worldwide* (New York: Cambridge University Press, 2009).

"mainline" Protestant faiths lost 2.6 million.[113] According to a March 2004 Pew Poll, 40 percent of Americans believe in the literal truth, or inerrancy, of the Bible.[114] Nowhere else in the West is evolution, or prayer in schools, or the right to post the Ten Commandments in state houses controversial. Europeans do not turn books on the rapture into best sellers. Not only are the people of the United States more religious, therefore, they are more conservative and fundamentalist in their faith than anywhere else in Christendom.

Religiosity in the United States is not merely a popular or regional phenomenon but one that extends to the highest offices and affects decision making at all levels. Few other world leaders would have been comfortable speaking about religion as openly and consistently as did George W. Bush, for example, who once said he had "a calling from beyond the stars to stand for freedom."[115] In the United States, Christian faith is a de facto prerequisite for higher office in many areas of the country. And, as sociologist Robert Bellah argued a half century ago, Americans are much more comfortable mixing religious imagery and belief with their politics than are most other people around the world. "The separation of church and state," he wrote, "has not denied the political realm a religious dimension."[116] Religiosity affects all areas of private and public life, and foreign policy is hardly immune.[117]

This high level of religious belief has a few concrete consequences that help explain the persistence of underlying pathological fear in the United States. First, religion affects the way other beliefs are formed. Since religious faith is by nature unprovable, those who profess it have in effect been trained to accept new information without

[113] See Sarah Diamond, *Not by Politics Alone: The Enduring Influence of the Christian Right* (New York: Guilford Press, 1998), pp. 9–10.
[114] Cited by Anatol Lieven, *America Right or Wrong: An Anatomy of American Nationalism* (New York: Oxford University Press, 2004), p. 140.
[115] Stefan Halper and Jonathan Clarke, *The Silence of the Rational Center: Why American Foreign Policy is Failing* (New York: Basic Books, 2007), p. 9.
[116] Robert N. Bellah, "Civil Religion in America," *Daedalus*, Vol. 96, No. 1 (Winter), p. 4. See also Michael Angrosino, "Civil Religion Redux," *Anthropological Quarterly*, Vol. 75, No. 2 (Spring 2000), pp. 239–67.
[117] Stephen R. Rock, *Faith and Foreign Policy: The Views and Influence of U.S. Christians and Christian Organizations* (New York: Continuum, 2011). See also Madeleine Albright, *The Mighty and the Almighty: Reflections on America, God, and World Affairs* (New York: Harper Collins, 2006).

much support. They can be perhaps expected to demand a lower standard of evidence during the formation of their nonreligious beliefs as well, since a core component of their identities has developed without any material proof. Furthermore, religious people have grown accustomed to disregard new evidence that might threaten their beliefs. In other words, those with unshakable religious faiths may well be more likely to have other beliefs that make few demands for evidence and that resist change.

Second, fundamentalist Christians in particular tend to view themselves in perpetual combat for the soul of the United States.[118] Many fervent believers of all religions feel their faith is under siege in an age of secularism, science, and reason, but the persecution Christians feel in the United States has been exceptional, fueling outrage at those times when the boundaries between church and state appear strengthened. Some make it an article of faith that the United States is a "Judeo-Christian nation," bending the beliefs of their secular saints – the founding fathers – as evidence when necessary.[119] The suffering of the early believers at the hands of the Romans is an essential part of Christian teaching, which contributes to a central aspect of fundamentalist identity: the image of a small community of the faithful in perpetual struggle against a hostile society. The fact that Christians constitute the overwhelming majority in the United States and dominate all levels of government matters little. Many Christians feel that their faith is under siege and that they must wage culture wars against society's various infidels, or Satan himself. Extrapolation from domestic enemies to foreign is not a great leap.

Finally, and most important, the religiosity of the United States and rise of fundamentalists vis-à-vis mainline sects has helped to forge a Manichean world view in the United States, the belief that in most cases there is wrong and right, black and white, evil and good.[120]

---

[118] Clyde Wilcox and Carin Robinson, *Onward Christian Soldiers? The Religious Right in American Politics*, 4th ed. (Boulder, CO: Westview Press, 2010).

[119] David Barton is one of the most prominent. See his *The Jefferson Lies: Exposing the Myths You've Always Believed about Thomas Jefferson* (Nashville, TN: WallBuilder Press, 2012).

[120] Walter Russell Mead, "God's Country?" *Foreign Affairs*, Vol. 85, No. 5 (September–October 2006), pp. 24–43; Paul Froese and F. Carson Mencken, "A U.S. Holy War? The Effects of Religion on Iraq War Attitudes," *Social Science Quarterly*, Vol. 90, No. 1 (March 2009), pp. 103–16.

America is not just a state pursuing its interests in anarchy but God's agent on earth, the leader of the forces of light in their perpetual struggle against darkness. The people of the United States have long been more comfortable with the notion of evil as a tangible reality than their more secular counterparts in Europe. Seven in ten Americans believe in the personal existence of the devil, compared to half that number of Britons.[121] President Bush used "evil" as much as a noun as an adjective, pitting his administration against it wherever it reared its head. "We are in a conflict between good and evil," he explained in 2002. "America will call evil by its name.... And we will lead the world in opposing it."[122] Throughout its history, America's enemies, from the Redcoats to the Kaiser to Iran, have not just been rivals but manifestations of malevolence. Decision makers with Manichean world views are more susceptible to the misperceptions discussed earlier in this chapter, more likely to interpret the actions of others as hostile, and less likely to compromise with those they see as the forces of darkness.

Manicheans tend to group all their enemies together, assuming there is coordination among the forces of darkness. The inability – or unwillingness – to distinguish between rivals is a hallmark of what social psychologist Milton Rokeach famously labeled a "closed belief system."[123] People with such a personality tend to group all their "disbelief systems," or those beliefs they automatically and unthinkingly reject, into one category of evil. It becomes natural for such people to conflate Islam with fascism ("Islamofascism"), or Osama bin Laden with Saddam Hussein, or communists with Nazis ("Communazis") as was not uncommon during the Cold War.[124] For these purposes, it is most significant to note that Rokeach and his colleagues found that cor-

---

[121] Americans: Frank Newport, "Americans More Likely to Believe in God Than the Devil, Heaven More Than Hell," Gallup News Service, June 2007, available at http://www.gallup.com/poll/27877/americans-more-likely-believe-god-than-devil-heaven-more-than-hell.aspx, accessed December 10, 2012. Britons: Lieven, *America Right or Wrong*, p. 8.

[122] George Bush, Graduation Speech at West Point, June 1, 2002.

[123] Milton Rokeach, *The Open and Closed Mind: Investigations into the Nature of Belief Systems and Personality Systems* (New York: Basic Books, 1960), p. 38.

[124] Alexander Stephan, *Communazis: FBI Surveillance of German Émigrê Writers* (New Haven, CT: Yale University Press, 2000).

relations between closed belief systems and anxiety are always positive. The world such people inhabit is a perpetually dangerous one.[125]

Manichaeism is evident in the eager embrace of the war on terror by religious fundamentalists, and the high level of antipathy held by many of its leaders toward Islam itself. Franklin Graham, son of the extremely influential Billy, has repeatedly called Islam "very evil and wicked"; to Pat Robertson, it is a "monumental scam." Jerry Falwell said on *60 Minutes* that Mohammed was "a terrorist."[126] Islamic fundamentalists, these people and others argue, harbor hatred for the United States not based on what it has *done*, but on what it *is*: the world's leading voice for freedom, democracy, and modernity.[127] "Bible-believing Christians" were the largest supporters of the war in Iraq, "by far," according to *Newsweek's* Howard Fineman.[128] A number of studies have connected fundamentalist, evangelical faith – specifically the belief in an inerrant Bible – to militaristic foreign policy preferences.[129] The religious views of some people encourage the belief that the world is full of enemies who need to be destroyed in the name of God. The United States contains many such people, some of whom are in influential positions of moral, intellectual, and even military and political leadership.

"Protestant-inspired moralism," argued Seymour Martin Lipset, "has determined the American style in foreign relations generally."[130] The belief in the inherent goodness of our cause and evil of the other continues to affect the tone of U.S. diplomatic relations, making casualties of realism and rationality. "The world of the paranoid admits no

---

[125] Rokeach, *The Open and Closed Mind*, pp. 56, 403.

[126] Quoted by Fareed Zakaria, "Time to Take on America's Haters," *Newsweek*, October 21, 2002.

[127] Bernard Lewis, "The Roots of Muslim Rage," *The Atlantic Monthly*, Vol. 266, No. 3 (September 1990), pp. 47–60; and David Frum and Richard Perle, *An End to Evil: How to Win the War on Terror* (New York: Random House, 2003).

[128] Howard Fineman, "Bush and God," *Newsweek*, March 10, 2003. See also Ira Chernus, *Monsters to Destroy: The Neoconservative War on Terror and Sin* (London: Paradigm Publishers, 2006).

[129] David C. Barker, Jon Hurwitz, and Traci L. Nelson, "Of Crusades and Culture Wars: 'Messianic' Militarism and Political Conflict in the United States," *Journal of Politics*, Vol. 70, No. 2 (April), pp. 307–22; Ted G. Jelen, "Religion and Foreign Policy Attitudes," *American Politics Research*, Vol. 22, No. 3 (July 1994), pp. 382–400; Corwin E. Smidt, "Religion and American Attitudes toward Islam and an Invasion of Iraq," *Sociology of Religion*, Vol. 66, No. 3 (Autumn 2005), pp. 243–61.

[130] Quoted in Seymour Martin Lipset, *American Exceptionalism: A Double-Edged Sword* (New York: W. W. Norton, 1996), p. 20.

shades of gray," wrote Robins and Post. "There is no room for uncertainty."[131] It is little wonder, then, that paranoia and religious faith seem to fit together so well in the United States.

Neoconservatism

World views are strongly linked to risk perceptions. People who profess allegiance to some ideological positions have a greater predisposition to believe that the world is a dangerous place than do others.[132] Across the world, right-wing political parties always sense more danger than their competitors, and those of the United States are no exception. Indeed suspicion of outsiders and paranoid politics is so central to right-wing populism, from the National Front in France to the Danish People's Party, that it can justifiably be considered one of the defining features of the movement.

In the American political spectrum, no group fears as much as do the so-called neoconservatives, who consistently detect higher levels of threat in the system than most other analysts.[133] Few political ideologies generate as much controversy, for and against. There is little demand for yet another lengthy discussion of the influence of "neocons" on foreign policy, since so many already exist. And it is only fair to point out up front that pathology is hardly unique to neoconservatives; many different leaders and strategists throughout American history from all across the political spectrum have acted based on the kinds of incorrect or underexamined beliefs at issue here. Still, since members of the movement will play a rather prominent role in this chapter and in those to come – and since this is a book primarily about the battlefield of beliefs, upon which the neocons play a quite prominent role – a brief discussion is in order.

Neoconservatism was born as a response to the 1960s, as a group of left-leaning intellectuals split with the mainstream of the Democratic Party over a variety of domestic and foreign issues. Many of the most prominent members of that group – including Irving Kristol, Daniel

---

[131] Robins and Post, *Political Paranoia*, p. 8.
[132] Paul Slovic, *The Perception of Risk* (London: Earthscan, 2000).
[133] For a discussion of neoconservatism and its exceptionally high perceptions of threat, see Stefan Halper and Jonathan Clarke, *America Alone: The Neo-Conservatives and the Global Order* (New York: Cambridge University Press, 2005).

Patrick Moynihan, Daniel Bell, Seymour Martin Lipset, and others – were primarily concerned with domestic matters, but the movement also had a foreign policy component heavily critical of the liberalism epitomized by George McGovern and of détente and cooperation with the Soviets.[134] In Cold War matters, neoconservatives were the intellectual heirs to James Burnham, Paul Nitze, and other hardliners who favored a strategy of rolling back communism over merely containing it where it existed.

One might have expected the end of the Cold War to elevate the domestic policy concerns of neocons over the foreign. Quite the opposite is true; in fact, the current incarnation of neoconservatism has little to say about domestic matters. The movement has also lost its home in the Democratic Party, having migrated to become the dominant foreign policy force within the GOP. Its core tenets have been so often mischaracterized or presented as caricature that it is easy to lose sight of what neoconservatism is: a robust, uniquely American foreign policy ideology likely to have enormous influence over U.S. action for some years to come, no matter which party controls the White House.

Although critics have characterized neoconservatism in many ways over the years, the most useful definitions of the world view are supplied by those who have embraced the label with enthusiasm. At its core, according to Robert Kagan, neoconservatism has six main components: a "patent moralism and idealism in world affairs," a belief in the potentially beneficial role of U.S. power in promoting liberty and democracy, support for continued U.S. primacy, confidence in U.S. military power in achieving its objectives, suspicion of international institutions, and a "tendency toward unilateralism."[135] Like all ideologies, neoconservatism has few pure members. Many intellectuals and analysts accept some tenets and not others; there is no point in

---

[134] Good discussions of the evolution of the movement include Irving Kristol, *Neoconservatism: The Autobiography of an Idea* (New York: Simon and Schuster, 1995); Irwin Stelzer, ed., *The Neocon Reader* (New York: Grove Press, 2004); Michael C. Williams, "What is the National Interest? The Neoconservative Challenge in IR Theory," *European Journal of International Relations*, Vol. 11, No. 3 (September 2005), pp. 307–37; and Jacob Heilbrunn, *They Knew They Were Right: The Rise of the Neocons* (New York: Doubleday, 2008).

[135] Robert Kagan, "Neocon Nation: Neoconservatism, c. 1776," *World Affairs*, Vol. 170, No. 4 (Spring 2008), pp. 13–35. See also Irving Kristol, "The Neoconservative Persuasion: What It Was, and What It Is," *The Weekly Standard*, Vol. 8, No. 47 (August 25, 2003).

joining tendentious debates over who is and who is not a "neocon." Whether Dick Cheney, Donald Rumsfeld, John McCain, or anyone else should be considered members of the club, for instance, is far less important than analyzing how closely their foreign policy recommendations match its ideology. Neoconservatism as a world view, rather than its specific membership, is at issue.

Neoconservatism makes a number of consistent, demonstrably pathological contributions to the marketplace of ideas that have over time greatly affected the U.S. view of the outside world and of its role. Among the common, interrelated beliefs that help define the faith are the following:

1) The world is a very dangerous place, far more dangerous than most Americans realize.

First and foremost, neoconservatives and their predecessors have been consistent in their belief that the world is a very dangerous place, seeing themselves as modern Paul Reveres warning their naïve countrymen of the dangers closing in on the American public from a variety of angles. A heightened threat perception is part of the common understanding of neoconservatism for many observers, and separates the ideology from more traditional conservatism.[136] "Particulars might change," argued a prominent critic, "but for neoconservatives crisis is a permanent condition. The situation is always urgent, the alternatives stark, the need for action compelling, the implications of delay or inaction certain to be severe."[137] The people of the United States need to be constantly reminded of the threats they face, the thinking goes, since they tend to assume the best in people and drift toward complacency. What critics see as fear mongering, therefore, is to neoconservatives an honest description of a dangerous world. Thus Secretary of Defense James Forrestal, an intellectual forerunner of today's neoconservatives, was completely sincere in 1947 when he observed that "there is no method, there is no way except the meth-

---

[136] See Halper and Clarke, *America Alone*; and Coral Bell, *The Reagan Paradox: American Foreign Policy in the 1980s* (New Brunswick, NJ: Rutgers University Press, 1989), pp. 11–13.
[137] Andrew J. Bacevich, *The New American Militarism: How Americans are Seduced by War* (New York: Oxford University Press, 2005), p. 77.

ods of worry, of constant concern, and of unceasing energy that will give us our security."[138]

To the extent that neoconservatism affects national anxiety levels, therefore, it does so in a uniform direction. Its members manned the parapets during the Cold War, warning against relaxation and/ or accommodation, and after the fall of the Berlin Wall argued that Americans could not let their guard down without rogue states, terrorists, and generalized chaos taking advantage. Former Speaker of the House Newt Gingrich may be the most prominent offender, stating with steadfast consistency for two decades that the United States faces far more hazards than most of its citizens realize, but he is hardly alone. Indeed one need look no further than the titles of some of the major recent neoconservative works – *Present Dangers, World War IV, The War against the Terror Masters, Against All Evil, Why We Fight, Surrender is Not an Option*, and so forth – to come away with the impression that the world is a very dangerous place where freedom is under continual assault.[139] What may appear to others to be rather minor challenges are often elevated by neocons to threats of the first order. This occurred most famously in 2003, when many in the movement argued Iraq was not a greatly degraded regional power but "a threat like no other," about which "we have every reason to assume the worst."[140] "After September 11, Saddam's weapons of mass destruction pose a kind of danger to us that we hadn't fully grasped before," wrote Kagan and Kristol in early 2002. "It is a tough and dangerous decision to send American soldiers to fight and possibly die in Iraq," they admitted. "But it is more horrible to watch men and women leap to their deaths from flaming skyscrapers."[141]

Since the dangers of which they warn tend to be at odds with objective reality, neoconservative tocsins tend to be stated rather than

---

[138] Thompson, *The Hawk and the Dove*, p. 87.

[139] Kagan and Kristol, *Present Dangers*; Podhoretz, *World War IV*; Michael Ledeen, *The War against the Terror Masters* (New York: St. Martin's Press, 2002); Frum and Perle, *An End to Evil*; William J. Bennett, *Why We Fight: Moral Clarity and the War on Terrorism* (New York: Doubleday, 2003); and John Bolton, *Surrender is Not an Option: Defending America at the United Nations* (New York: Simon and Schuster, 2007).

[140] Lawrence F. Kaplan and William Kristol, *The War over Iraq: Saddam's Tyranny and America's Mission* (San Francisco, CA: Encounter Books, 2003), p. 73.

[141] Robert Kagan and William Kristol, "What to Do about Iraq," *The Weekly Standard*, January 21, 2002.

demonstrated, or supported with evidence that is anecdotal rather than analytical. To cite one typical example, Frederick Kagan begins a piece with a liberal hawk coauthor by stating that "we live at a time when wars not only rage in nearly every region but threaten to erupt in many places where the current relative calm is tenuous."[142] That they overlook important empirical information – such as that there is far less warfare than ever before, and that every region is more stable than at any time in recorded history – should be unsurprising, since the belief of dangers is based on faith rather than fact. It does not seem to bother neoconservatives at all that this belief does not match the evidence. When Perle and Frum write that "there is no middle way for Americans: It is victory or holocaust," they do so knowing they will never be challenged about how exactly the second alternative would come about.[143] Any identifiable or imaginable danger is to neoconservatives evidence of tremendous threat.

Not only does danger exist, but security conditions are constantly deteriorating, and as a result today is always more dangerous than yesterday. Even in 1947, according to James Burnham, the world political situation was "immeasurably worse" than it had been a decade prior.[144] Though the Cold War threat was apparently much more dire than that posed by the Axis, the collapse of the Soviet Union did not reduce the danger. "Islamofascists," according to Norman Podhoretz, "are even more dangerous and difficult to beat than their totalitarian predecessors of World War II and World War III."[145] Donald and Frederick Kagan even argued that the Soviet Union had in fact become a "force for stability," which was quite the opposite of what they and other neoconservatives were saying while it existed.[146] The notion that the Cold War was a time of relative stability when the United States faced a predictable foe is now commonplace in neoconservative writing, usually

---

[142] Frederick Kagan and Michael O'Hanlon, "The Case for Larger Ground Forces," Stanley Foundation, Bridging the Foreign Policy Divide Project, April 2007, available at http://www.stanleyfdn.org/publications/other/Kagan_OHanlon_07.pdf, p. 1.

[143] Frum and Perle, *An End to Evil*, p. 9.

[144] James Burnham, *The Struggle for the World* (New York: The John Day Company, Inc., 1947), p. 159.

[145] Podhoretz, *World War IV*, p. 13.

[146] Donald Kagan and Frederick W. Kagan, *While America Sleeps: Self-Delusion, Military Weakness, and the Threat to Peace Today* (New York: St. Martin's Press, 2000), p. 269.

offered without a hint of irony, as if these were not the very people who had spent a generation crafting the case that the Soviets were evil, irrational, and fundamentally unpredictable.

It is also worth noting that this heightened sense of threat has in recent years come into conflict with the support for democracy among neoconservatives. The most obvious fissure developed over the implications of the Arab Spring, with one camp optimistic over the potential for the spread of freedom, and the other pessimistic and concerned that fundamentalists could take charge in Egypt and elsewhere.[147] It was not the first time this had happened, however. The 2006 U.S. decision to support the elections in the Palestinian territories created a major split along the same lines, between what might be thought of as the democracy and fear camps. "There were severe fissures among neoconservatives over this," Cheney's former advisor David Wurmser has said. "We were ripping each other to pieces."[148] Such divisions can be confusing for outsiders who mistakenly consider neoconservatism a tightly unified, monolithic ideology. There is in fact a healthy degree of debate inside the movement, which ought to give pause to those seeking to determine precisely who is and who is not a true member.

2) Our enemies are fundamentally unlike us – they are irrational, implacable, even suicidal

Neoconservatism is a moral absolutist ideology.[149] Its members tend to accept on faith the notion that the United States is the primary force for good in the world, and are equally convinced that its enemies must be evil. Neocons are particularly susceptible, therefore, to the distortions generated by enemy images. Those countries that oppose the United States cannot be expected to behave rationally, much less peacefully; they are internally unified, clever, mendacious, devious, and eternally patient.[150]

---

[147] See the debate between Raul Marc Gerecht and Daniel Pipes over whether it is better to have "elected Islamists or dictators," sponsored by Intelligence Squared, New York, NY, October 4, 2012, available at http://www.intelligencesquaredus.org/iq2-tv/item/763-better-elected-islamists-than-dictators.

[148] David Rose, "The Gaza Bombshell," *Vanity Fair*, April 2008.

[149] J. Peter Scoblic argues conservatives are as a group generally comfortable with moral absolutes, in *U.S. vs. Them: Conservatism in the Age of Nuclear Terror* (New York: Penguin, 2008).

[150] *NSC-68*, which at times reads like a parody of the enemy image, refers throughout to U.S. "principles" but Soviet "designs." S. Nelson Drew, ed., *NSC-68: Forging the Strategy of Containment* (Washington, DC: National Defense University, 1996).

For decades the center of all the world's evil was Moscow. "The Soviet Union, unlike previous aspirants to hegemony," warned *NSC-68*, "is animated by a new fanatic faith."[151] It was this faith that made the USSR fundamentally different from, and antithetical to, the United States, deterrable only with a decisive strategic advantage. If the Soviets were ever to surpass the power of the United States they might be tempted to attack, in part because they had to know that because of their economic weakness such an advantage would be temporary. This fear was repeated by hardliners and proto-neocons like *NSC-68*'s principal author, Paul Nitze, throughout the Cold War: the Soviets might well be tempted to attack immediately upon achieving superiority, irrespective of the political situation.[152] Relaxations of tension were illusory and dangerous, therefore, since Moscow would never actually relax. The Soviets did not desire stability – they did not even have an equivalent Russian word for "deterrence" – and sought instead to overthrow freedom and democracy everywhere. Nuclear weapons were just a means to that ultimate end. Richard Pipes was typical when he warned that the danger arose because "we consider nuclear war unfeasible and suicidal for both, and our chief adversary views it as feasible and winnable for himself."[153]

Two decades of releases from the Soviet archives, as well as recently declassified studies commissioned by the Pentagon, paint a picture of a Kremlin much different than the one the neocons imagined.[154]

[151] Drew, *NSC-68*, p. 38.
[152] Drew, *NSC-68*, p. 70; H. Rowan Geither, Jr., "Deterrence and Survival in the Nuclear Age," Report of the Security Resources Panel of the Science Advisory Committee, November 7, 1957; Albert Wohlstetter, "The Delicate Balance of Terror," *Foreign Affairs*, Vol. 37, No. 2 (January 1959), pp. 211–34; James Burnham, *The War We Are In: The Last Decade and the Next* (New Rochelle, NY: Arlington House, 1967), p. 23; Norman Podhoretz, *The Present Danger* (New York: Simon and Schuster, 1980), esp. p. 55; Edward N. Luttwak, *On the Meaning of Victory: Essays on Strategy* (New York: Simon and Schuster, 1986), p. 265. See also Bruce Kuklick, *Blind Oracles: Intellectuals and War from Kennan to Kissinger* (Princeton, NJ: Princeton University Press, 2006), p. 68. Specific rebuttals to the "window of opportunity" arguments can be found in Robert H. Johnson, "Periods of Peril: The Window of Vulnerability and Other Myths," *Foreign Affairs*, Vol. 61, No. 4 (Spring 1983), pp. 950–70; and Richard Ned Lebow, "Windows of Opportunity: Do States Jump Through Them?" *International Security*, Vol. 9, No. 1 (Summer 1984), pp. 147–86.
[153] Richard Pipes, "Why the Soviet Union Thinks It Could Fight and Win a Nuclear War," *Commentary*, Vol. 64, No. 1 (July 1977), p. 34.
[154] The Pentagon study was commissioned by Andrew Marshall, longtime head of the Office of Net Assessment, and declassified in 2009: John G. Hines, Ellis M. Mishulovich, and John F. Shull, *Soviet Intentions 1965–1985, Volume I: An Analytical*

There is no evidence that Moscow ever thought nuclear war was "winnable," or that it considered a first strike if and when it ever reached parity with the United States. Rather than having been warped by a fanatical ideology, the strategic thinking of Soviet planners greatly resembled that of their U.S. counterparts, except in a position of inferiority. They were much more like us than the neoconservatives believed, and just eager to avoid world war.. As for "deterrence," they had adopted the English word into their language and the concept into their strategic thinking.[155] *NSC-68* had misperceived Soviet intentions quite badly.

Like all the central components of the ideology, the enemy image in neoconservative thinking survived the end of the Cold War intact. The label has changed – communists have been replaced by Islamofascists – but the basic assumptions of evil and irrationality remain the same.[156] Whoever the enemy happens to be, neoconservatives warn, they cannot be trusted to be as rational as the United States. Eternal vigilance and struggle is necessary to defeat, not merely contain, their malevolence. As a result, neoconservative perceptions of danger today are even less accurate than they were in 1950, since the objective level of threat is so much lower.

3) Neoconservatives are uniquely positioned to understand
the dangers posed by the enemy

Many early neoconservatives were converts from Trotskyism, which they claimed granted them unique insight into communism's inherent evils. To understand why the Soviet mind was fundamentally different from the American, one needed to study its seemingly obscure antecedents. Thus a generation of Cold Warriors were urged to read not only Marx and Lenin but Kropotkin; today, the sagacious warrior on terror must consult not only bin Laden but Qutb and a variety of other precursor texts to understand the true nature of the enemy, which is by definition much different than us. Pipes, a Sovietologist

Comparison of U.S.-Soviet Assessments during the Cold War (McLean, VA: BDM Federal, Inc., September 22, 1995).

155　See Richard K. Betts, "The Concept of Deterrence in the Postwar Era," *Security Studies*, Vol. 1, No. 1 (Autumn 1991), pp. 25–36.

156　Kaplan and Kristol wrote of Saddam Hussein's "supreme irrationality" because of which deterrence would not work. Kaplan and Kristol, *The War Over Iraq*, p. 82.

of Polish extraction, was one of those capable of decoding Moscow's intentions. "Soviet military literature, like all Soviet literature on politics broadly defined, is written in an elaborate code language," he wrote. "Buried in the flood of seemingly meaningless verbiage, nuggets of precious information on Soviet perceptions and intentions can more often than not be unearthed by a trained reader."[157] Similarly, a host of "experts" on Islam popped up after September 11 to explain the evils of that religion to the uninitiated.[158]

Their specialized knowledge gives neocons confidence to proclaim that the danger level is greater than the current administration – whichever it is – is willing to admit. The State Department is always particularly culpable in underestimating threats, as is the CIA. At times neoconservatives have managed to persuade presidents to allow outside teams to examine raw intelligence to demonstrate the extent of the CIA naiveté, all of which determined that the United States was in far more danger than anyone realized. The first such episode occurred in the 1970s, when President Ford was persuaded to allow a few groups of outside "experts" to do independent assessments of the threat posed by the Soviet Union. The most important of these was dominated by leading neoconservatives, such as Richard Pipes (the chair), Paul Nitze, and Paul Wolfowitz. The conclusions of these "Team Bs" (all of which suggested that the Soviet Union posed a far greater threat than the CIA realized) were preordained and leaked widely to the press. The impact of this unofficial group on the marketplace of ideas was therefore rather substantial, since the professional intelligence officers tended to keep better secrets.

We know now that the various Team Bs were correct, in a sense: the CIA had indeed been misjudging Soviet capabilities. The U.S. intelligence community had been routinely *overestimating* Soviet strength, however, not underestimating. Team B's analyses were even less accurate, and wildly so. "Wherever Team B looked at 'hard' data," wrote one scholar two decades later, "it saw the worst possible case."

[157] Richard Pipes, "Why the Soviet Union Thinks It Could Fight and Win a Nuclear War," *Commentary*, Vol. 64, No. 1 (July 1977), p. 27.
[158] These experts are described, if tendentiously, by Wajahat Ali, Eli Clifton, Matthew Duss, Lee Fang, Scott Keyes, and Faiz Shakir in *Fear, Inc.: The Roots of the Islamophobia Network in America* (Washington, DC: Center for American Progress, August 2011), available at http://www.americanprogress.org/issues/2011/08/pdf/islamophobia.pdf, accessed December 10, 2012.

Consistent with the enemy image, Team B "assumed that Murphy's Law was not operative in the Soviet Union," and that all their best aspirations and plans would work to the maximum degree possible.[159] Both sets of analysts seemed to miss what should have been a rather central observation, that the ossified Soviet system was beginning a process of collapse.

The same neoconservative rereading of raw intelligence occurred in the lead-up to the invasion of Iraq, with even more disastrous results. The so-called Policy Counter Terrorism Evaluation Group led by Undersecretary of Defense (and proud neoconservative) Douglas Feith was given access to all information regarding Saddam Hussein and Al Qaeda.[160] Feith's group, which consciously regarded itself as a reincarnation of the older Team B, unsurprisingly found more links than the professional intelligence analysts and fed its conclusions directly to the Office of the Vice President.[161] Its biggest supporter injected that interpretation into the national conversation, just as Pipes's group had done a generation before.

These alternate readings of intelligence should be viewed as expressions of true belief about dangers in the international system as much as exercises in political manipulation. They are an example of the methods with which neoconservatives project their beliefs into national debates, beliefs that raise the levels of threat beyond what any rational standard would support. The intelligent, effective promotion of ideas has always been a hallmark of the movement.

4) As a result of all the above, the United States underspends on defense
The final constant of neoconservative thinking is the belief that the United States must increase the share of its resources devoted to the struggle against evil in order to be safe. The level of spending, whatever it might be (and however it is measured, either in raw terms or by the stupefyingly astrategic "percentage of GDP"), is never enough.

---

[159] Anne Hessing Cahn, *Killing Détente: The Right Attacks the CIA* (University Park: Pennsylvania State University Press, 1998), p. 166.

[160] The group is often confused with Feith's "Office of Special Plans," which was a somewhat different entity. His memoirs explain the difference and defend his actions: Douglas J. Feith, *War and Decision: Inside the Pentagon at the Dawn of the War on Terrorism* (New York: HarperCollins, 2008).

[161] Scoblic, *U.S. vs. Them*, p. 220.

Peace dividends are illusory, since danger is constant. *NSC-68* called for a trebling of U.S. defense spending; to Frederick Kagan, its recommendations are somehow "more important today than it was while the Soviet Union was alive."[162]

To concentrate minds, neoconservatives have often given the United States deadlines for its rearmament. For the authors of *NSC-68*, 1954 was likely to be a year of tremendous danger without major U.S. action, since it was the year the Soviets would otherwise achieve parity and be tempted to attack.[163] The Gaither Report of 1957, which was also written principally by Nitze, suggested the year of maximum danger was 1959, for the same reason.[164] Though the year changed, the threat persisted; during the Reagan years, the Soviet window of opportunity was said to open in 1984, if not before.[165] Today the threat stems from Iranian nuclear weapons, which if developed will be used immediately by that irrational regime. Action must always be taken quickly to avert disaster.

Deadline or no, neoconservatives believe there is a direct relationship between military spending and safety. Since no level of safety is ever fully sufficient in a world of enemies, defense capabilities can never be too high, or even high enough.

One final observation about neoconservatism is in order, especially for these purposes: it is and has always been a distinctly American ideology. Not only were its original and current members all Americans, but no comparable world view is nearly as influential in the politics of any other state. Though hawks exist in every country and at every time – and to repeat, neocons have no monopoly on counterproductive, irrational belief – no other ideological group advocates quite the same mixture of evangelical faith in democracy and pathological fear of the other. No cabal of neocon advisors whispers in the ear of any other leader, and no *Weekly Standards* exist elsewhere to promote its beliefs. To Irving Kristol, neoconservatism's unique Americaness was "beyond doubt."[166] For those seeking reasons why pathological fear

---

[162] Kagan, "Back to the Future," p. 56.
[163] Drew, *NSC-68*, p. 92.
[164] Cahn, *Killing Détente*, p. 4.
[165] Podhoretz, *The Present Danger*, p. 55.
[166] Irving Kristol argued that neoconservatism's unique Americaness was "beyond doubt." See his "The Neoconservative Persuasion: What It Was, and What It Is."

persists in U.S. foreign policy debates, therefore, the possible influence of neoconservatism might be a good place to start.

Media and Society

The United States is served – or held hostage – by a twenty-four-hour news cycle that thrives on conflict and danger. Fear is an essential component of the business model of both CNN and Fox, a necessary tool to keep fingers away from remote controls during commercial breaks. Voices of reason tend to spoil the fun and may inspire people to seek excitement elsewhere. News outlets win by being more frightening, angrier, and simpler than their competitors, not by supplying historical perspective, statistics, or reassurance. If no danger exists it must be created, or at least creatively implied.

Sensationalism in the media is nothing new. More than a century has passed since William Randolph Hearst told his reporters to furnish pictures of atrocities in Cuba so he could furnish the war that would save his papers.[167] Today the wide choice of outlets creates competition for viewers much more intense than that the media faced during the Cold War. The public now has multiple round-the-clock national news channels that somehow manage to produce less analysis than the networks did in their nightly half-hour broadcasts a generation ago. More than ever before, the media operates according to a "logic of entertainment" at least as much as information and analysis.[168]

The imperatives of that logic are amplified even further now that media messages are beyond the control of professionals. The sensationalist instincts of the "mainstream media" are miniscule compared to those of the Internet-based "new media," where fairness or accuracy often appear to be afterthoughts, not goals. Many beliefs that are pervasive in the United States, such as those of the "truthers" who think the United States was behind the 9/11 attacks or the "birthers" who doubt the birthplace of Barack Obama, were never championed by mainstream media outlets. The very thing that makes the new media so attractive to so many – the absence of the gate-keeping mechanisms of professional journalism – also renders it susceptible to

---

[167] Evan Thomas, *The War Lovers: Roosevelt, Lodge, Hearst, and the Rush to Empire, 1898* (New York: Little, Brown and Company, 2010), p. 161.

[168] David L. Altheide discusses this in *Creating Fear*, p. 177.

unchecked misinformation, much of which can affect the formation of beliefs.[169]

That logic leads it to stoke fear, often unintentionally, by offering compelling entertainment in the competition for ratings. The effect is not always so accidental, however; indeed some media figures have built careers on creating the impression that the United States is constantly on the verge of catastrophe. The country is in a death spiral, they warn, and the only thing that can possibly save it is their advice. Radio and television host Glenn Beck, who regularly trembles with passion and fear, is perhaps the most obvious example. It is too bad that Richard Hofstadter did not live long enough to hear Beck's show, since it would have given him more evidence for his justly famous essay on the paranoid style in American politics. "The paranoid spokesman sees the fate of conspiracy in apocalyptic terms," Hofstadter wrote. "He traffics in the birth and death of whole worlds, whole political orders, whole systems of human values. He is always manning the barricades of civilization. He constantly lives at a turning point."[170] Beck inhabits such a point, or so he believes, and he passes on that belief to his audience on a daily basis. Millions listen to his daily review of the evidence for the coming revolution, one purportedly concocted by a nefarious secret alliance of socialists, anti-Zionists, George Soros, service employee unions, Islamists, and members of the Obama administration. The conspiracy reaches all the way to the top, where at the head of the CIA sits an "operative" of the Muslim Brotherhood.[171]

Beck might be alone in detecting secret communist plots to undermine our freedoms (can it be a coincidence, for example, that President Obama chose to hold his first official rally of the 2012 campaign on May 5, which happens to be Karl Marx's birthday?!), but he shares visions of UN schemes to force internationalist values upon us with many on the right, including prominent political commentators.[172] He repeatedly tells his listeners that he does not know when the revolution will

---

[169] See Stephan Lewandowsky, Ullrich K. H. Ecker, Colleen M. Seifert, Norbert Schwartz, and John Cook, "Misinformation and Its Correction: Continued Influence and Successful Debiasing," *Psychological Science in the Public Interest*, Vol. 13, No. 3 (September 2012), pp. 106–31.

[170] Richard Hofstadter, "The Paranoid Style in American Politics," *Harper's Magazine*, Vol. 229, No. 1374 (November 1964), p. 82.

[171] Beck made the claim about George Brennan on March 11, 2013.

[172] Dick Morris and Eileen McGann, *Here Come the Black Helicopters! UN Global Governance and the Loss of Freedom* (New York: Broadside Books, 2012).

occur – Beck admits he is not good at "timing" – but that it is indeed coming and everyone needs to prepare. And pray, of course. Beck's audience, like that of Fox News in general, not only has its anxieties regularly confirmed and intensified but finds out about entirely new threats to its security with which it was previously unfamiliar.

One cannot dismiss Beck as merely an opportunistic showman who spins wild conspiracy theories to profit from insecure times. There is little evidence of insincerity in his paranoia: Beck appears preoccupied with dangers posed by personal enemies as well, warding them off at public events with bulletproof vests and at home with a six-foot barrier that surrounded his Connecticut estate.[173] Still, there are many entrepreneurs who have cynically arisen to profit from the national anxiety, creating a virtual fear industry that has been a natural sponsor of, and partner with, Fox News. To take but one example, the "Vivos Group," which manufactures custom-built, high-end bomb shelters for those hoping to ride out the apocalypse in comfort and style, has been an advertiser on and a subject of Fox News reports. Beck, Sean Hannity and other talk radio hosts endlessly peddle gold and "food insurance" as tools with which listeners can provide for their families through the coming dark age. As is often the case, satirist Stephen Colbert captured this spirit best: "Nothing moves product like the hot stink of fear."[174]

Representations of society in the entertainment media are, if anything, worse. The people of the United States watch more television than any other, and the world they are exposed to on their sets is far more violent and dangerous than reality. According to one widely cited study, the typical American adolescent in the late 1980s witnessed upward of thirty thousand violent acts and eight thousand murders on television; today those numbers must be much higher.[175] People turn to fiction in part to escape their humdrum, boring lives, of course, and most are quite capable of separating reality from fantasy. However, the effect of continued, consistent exposure to hyper violent shows and

[173] Mark Leibovich, "Being Glenn Beck," *New York Times Magazine*, October 3, 2010, p. 37.
[174] Stephen Colbert, *The Colbert Report*, March 10, 2010.
[175] Harry M. Hoberman, "Study Group Report on the Impact of Television Violence on Adolescents," *Journal of Adolescent Health Care*, Vol. 11, No. 1 (January 1990), pp. 45–49.

films on threat perceptions will vary from individual to individual; over time, their cumulative power should not be underestimated. Indeed a good deal of experimental evidence suggests that belief formation can be profoundly affected by fictional representations of reality.[176] Indeed research on the effects of fictional violence on various aspects of society goes back decades.[177] Although almost none of it directly examines the relationship of fiction to the national perception of risk, many sociologists mark the beginning of the obsession with threats and danger in Western societies to the 1970s, which is also when the real exponential growth of the media began.[178] When people turn on their televisions – or their computers or phones – they are exposed to a world more frightening than the one they inhabit. "The more you read and watch," according to journalist Daniel Gardner, "the more you fear."[179] Despite the fact that violent crime has steadily declined all across the country for more than two decades, popular concern for it has not waned apace, as is clear from surveys and behavior, such as the rise of gated communities in many cities.[180]

Perhaps the media receives too much blame for the many ills in American society. It is everybody's whipping post, the go-to scapegoat for politicians looking to deflect public ire away from themselves or moralists hoping to rid society of sin. Its power should not be exaggerated. Although the media can manufacture panics, and though it certainly can magnify the threats its consumers perceive on a daily basis, it cannot generate fear in audiences that are not somewhat predisposed to that reaction. If society did not already contain a sense of inherent risk, or a susceptibility to believing in present dangers, it would not react to the media's provocations. If the American public

---

[176] Elizabeth J. Marsh, Michelle L. Meade, and Henry L. Roediger, "Learning Facts from Fiction," *Journal of Memory and Language*, Vol. 49, No. 4 (November 2003), pp. 519–36; and Elizabeth J. Marsh and Lisa K. Fazio, "Learning Errors from Fiction: Difficulties in Reducing Reliance on Fictional Stories," *Memory & Cognition*, Vol. 34, No. 5 (July 2006), pp. 1140–49.

[177] For a review of the history of the study of violence in the media, see Glenn G. Sparks and Cheri W. Sparks, "The Effects of Media Violence," and the other essays in Jennings Bryant and Dolf Zillmann, eds., *Media Effects: Advances in Theory and Research* (London: Routledge, 2002), pp. 269–86. See also Glassner, *The Culture of Fear*.

[178] For a review, see Gardner, *The Science of Fear*, pp. 57–58.

[179] Gardner, *The Science of Fear*, p. 196.

[180] Pinker, *The Better Angels of Our Nature*.

were not predisposed to buying threats, in other words, the media would not be effective in selling them.[181] One cannot fan a flame that is not there. As always, the media is as much effect as cause of trends in any society.

George Kennan once observed that truth is a poor competitor in the marketplace of ideas. "The counsels of impatience and hatred can always be supported by the crudest and cheapest symbols," he wrote. "For the counsels of moderation, the reasons are often intricate, rather than emotional, and difficult to explain. And so the chauvinists of all times and places go their appointed way: plucking the easy fruits, reaping the little triumphs of the day at the expense of someone else tomorrow, deluging in noise and filth anyone who gets in their way, dancing their reckless dance on the prospects for human progress."[182] While they probably receive more than their share of the blame for the various ills of society, it remains the case that the noise and filth produced by the American media is louder and thicker than in any other state.

Pearl Harbor, 9/11, and Strategic Surprise

Perhaps the most obvious cause of the pervasive sense of fear in the United States, at least over the course of the last decade, was the terrorism of September 11. Not only were the attacks horrifying beyond the imagination of compassionate people everywhere, but they also tapped into a deep, shared historical concern of the American people that magnified their effect in ways the terrorists could not have anticipated.

Arnold Wolfers observed decades ago that "nations tend to be most sensitive to threats that have either experienced attacks in the recent past or, having passed through a prolonged period of an exceptionally high degree of security, suddenly find themselves thrust into a situation of danger."[183] The oceans that had created "free security" for America's first 150 years no longer seemed to offer the same

---

[181] Sociologist Frank Furedi makes this point in *Culture of Fear*, esp. p. 52.

[182] George Kennan, *American Diplomacy, 1900–1950* (New York: Mentor, 1951), p. 56.

[183] Arnold Wolfers, *Discord and Collaboration: Essays on International Politics* (Baltimore, MD: Johns Hopkins University Press, 1962), p. 151.

protection as the twentieth century wore on.[184] The geography that afforded the American people the luxury to forget about the problems of the world for a while helped to generate greater-than-average shock, and the preconditions for overreaction, following those times when its presumed safety is violated. Since the attacks of 9/11 were an enormous shock, perhaps it should be unsurprising that the United States has reacted more strongly than other states might have.

Many observers have argued that the United States is unusually concerned with the possibility of surprise attack.[185] Pearl Harbor trained many American strategists to worry that surprise attack might come when they least expected it, a fear that seemed confirmed by September 11. It was the type of "psychological hammer blow" Brent Rutherford described in 1966 as those that lead actors to "adopt several adaptive or maladaptive behaviors. The selection of these behaviors is based on the learning and internalization of these methods early in life, and is largely unconscious."[186] The terrorist attacks had a greater impact on the United States than they may have had elsewhere, and not just in the metaphorical, macro sense: Depression and anxiety disorders were exceptionally common in their initial aftermath.[187] People became fixated on the possibility of another attack, waiting for the "other shoe to drop," a shoe that many worried would be even worse. "Worry about terrorism did not decline as time passed and the threatened onslaught failed to materialize," as Gardner has noted. "Instead, it slowly rose."[188] Periods of apparent calm are not comforting to societies who believe surprise attacks can materialize

[184] C. Vann Woodward, "The Age of Reinterpretation," *The American Historical Review*, Vol. 66, No. 1 (October 1960), pp. 1–19.
[185] The literature is quite extensive. Good places to start include Richard K. Betts, *Surprise Attack: Lessons for Defense Planning* (Washington, DC: The Brookings Institution Press, 1982); John Lewis Gaddis, *Surprise, Security, and the American Experience* (Cambridge, MA: Harvard University Press, 2004); and Charles F. Parker and Eric K. Stern, "Blindsided? September 11 and the Origins of Strategic Surprise," *Political Psychology*, Vol. 23, No. 3 (September 2002), pp. 601–30.
[186] Brent M. Rutherford, "Psychopathology, Decision-Making, and Political Involvement," *Journal of Conflict Resolution*, Vol. 10, No. 4 (December 1966), p. 403.
[187] Mark A. Schuster, Bradley D. Stein, Lisa H. Jaycox, Rebecca L. Collins, Grant N. Marshall, Marc N. Elliott, Annie Jie Zhou, David E. Kanouse, Janina L. Morrison, and Sandra H. Berry, "A National Survey of Stress Reactions after the September 11, 2001 Terrorist Attacks," *New England Journal of Medicine*, Vol. 345, No. 20 (November 15, 2001), pp. 1507–12.
[188] Gardner, *The Science of Fear*, p. 249.

out of nowhere, without warning. In the fall of 2007, *New York Times* columnist Thomas Friedman argued that "9/11 has made us stupid ... our reaction to 9/11 – mine included – has knocked America completely out of balance."[189]

That the fear of surprise attack is understandable does not make it rational. A nation focused on the potential for unprovoked attack will never feel safe and will be perpetually vulnerable to folly. Perhaps it would help to focus on the odds of such attacks, and the potential damage one could cause, both of which are relatively minor for the world's strongest state. Small states have every reason to fear surprise attack; big states, however, do not.

Government and the Politics of Fear

In his memoirs, Douglas MacArthur observed that, throughout his lifetime, "our government kept us in a perpetual state of fear," in a "continual stampede of patriotic fervor – with a cry of a grave national emergency. Always there has been some terrible evil at home or some monstrous foreign power that was going to gobble us up."[190] No discussion of fear would be complete without acknowledgment that on occasion it can be politically useful to scare the public. Politicians cannot help but notice that their poll numbers rise when the populace is afraid, and it would be surprising if they did not take advantage on occasion. Fearful people seek protection and "rally 'round the flag."[191] This is hardly a new phenomenon; H. L. Mencken observed that, prior to the U.S. entry into World War I, Woodrow Wilson and other liberals realized that "the only way to make the mob fight was to scare it half to death."[192] More recently, the U.S. public showed little enthusiasm for the first Gulf war until President George H. W. Bush began injecting the threat of Iraqi nuclear weapons into his justification speeches.[193] The next Bush administration built support for its

---

[189] Thomas L. Friedman, "9/11 is Over," *New York Times*, September 30, 2007, p. 12.
[190] Quoted by David P. Barash, *Beloved Enemies: Our Need for Opponents* (Amherst, NY: Prometheus Books, 1994), p. 21.
[191] John E. Mueller, "Presidential Popularity from Truman to Johnson," *American Political Science Review*, Vol. 64, No. 1 (March 1970), pp. 18–34.
[192] H. L. Mencken, *Prejudices: A Selection* (New York: Vintage Books, 1958), p. 114.
[193] John Mueller, *Policy and Opinion in the Gulf War* (Chicago, IL: University of Chicago Press, 1994).

war against Saddam by warning that the alternative was likely to be nuclear attacks on the United States, smoking guns in the form of mushroom clouds. When faced with such choices, the American people understandably go along. Manipulation of popular perceptions by leaders, therefore, surely contributes to the national pathology.

The peculiarities of American electoral politics provide few incentives for rational security discourse. In 1960, Senator John Kennedy rode fears of a "missile gap," which he knew was fictional, into the White House. Since then, Republicans have more frequently suggested that electing their opponents would leave the country vulnerable to a variety of bears in the woods. Democrats have responded by attempting to sound tough on security matters, which usually implies the exaggeration of threats where necessary.[194] In a striking contrast to 1933, when it was in Franklin Roosevelt's political interest to assure Americans that the greatest danger was "fear itself," in 2004 it was in George W. Bush's political interest to do the opposite.[195] In 2006, Vice President Cheney campaigned on behalf of Republican congressional candidates by repeatedly warning of the "mass death" that would occur if the Democrats took over.[196] One study found that in the United States, unlike in the United Kingdom and elsewhere, voters respond quite directly and positively to the politics of fear.[197] In American politics, fear wins debates and votes, while appeals to reason can seem to indicate a lack of seriousness regarding the threat *du jour*. There is evidently little political downside to frightening people and keeping them good and scared.

The political establishment in the United States has been united in the seriousness of the terrorist threat and totally misleading about the risks.[198] While he was secretary of defense, Donald Rumsfeld wrote a series of internal memos instructing his subordinates to remind the public of how much danger they were in, to "keep elevating the

[194] Zenko and Cohen, "Clear and Present Safety," pp. 79–93.
[195] Gardner, *The Science of Fear*, p. 266.
[196] Peter Baker, "Cheney Back Delivering the Grim Campaign Speech," *Washington Post*, October 8, 2006.
[197] Russian voters seem to act much like American ones when it comes to responding to fear stimuli. Sarah Oates, Lynda Lee Kaid, and Mike Berry, *Terrorism, Elections, and Democracy: Political Campaigns in the United States, Great Britain, and Russia* (New York: Palgrave Macmillan, 2009).
[198] Gardner, *The Science of Fear*, p. 269.

threat," and to "talk about Somalia, the Philippines, etc. Make the American people realize they are surrounded in the world by violent extremists."[199] The Department of Homeland Security (DHS) has been a particularly egregious institutional offender. Rather than conceive of its role as a voice of reason in the fight against terror, or fear itself, the department has often sought to increase national anxiety in the name of battling complacency. Over the course of its nine-year lifespan, the color-coded terrorism alert system was raised to "high" a number of times (including for three straight weeks in February 2003, the month before the invasion of Iraq), despite the fact that the average person could do nothing in response. Rather than provide statistics about the true risk of the terrorist threat, DHS leaders have preferred to report "gut feelings" about impending attacks and advise the public to stockpile duct tape and plastic sheeting.[200] Homeland Security courses and departments have popped up around the country, all with public funding, spreading the fear gospel under the guise of scholarship. Without fear, after all, support for the department would collapse. Overall, Osama had no better ally in his attempt to frighten the American people. "There is America, full of fear from north to south, from west to east," he said in one of his occasional rambling videos, "and Thank God for that."[201] He also could have thanked DHS.

Fear is not generated merely for the sake of bolstering the popularity of whatever administration is generating it. For U.S. policy makers, part of the inspiration to consistently inflate dangers is the imperative to beat back the isolationist bogeyman so many of them assume lurks in the American public and in Congress. The real "present danger," according to Kagan and Kristol, "is that the United States, the world's dominant power on whom the maintenance of international peace and the support of liberal democratic principles depends, will shirk its responsibilities and – in a fit of absentmindedness, or parsimony, or indifference – allow the international

---

[199] Robin Wright, "From the Desk of Donald Rumsfeld...," *Washington Post*, November 1, 2007.

[200] "Chertoff's Gut," *Chicago Tribune*, July 12, 2007.

[201] Quoted in Brigitte Lebens Nacos, *Mass-Mediated Terrorism: The Central Role of the Media in Terrorism and Counterterrorism* (New York: Rowman & Littlefield, 2007), p. 50.

order that it created and sustains to collapse."[202] Without constant reminders of the dangers lurking in the system, the United States could return to a "September 10th mentality." To many in the U.S. national security establishment, the greatest weapon against the prime domestic enemy – that desire on part of the American people to mind their own business – is fear.

None of this is to imply that leaders are always, or even usually, insincere when they issue warnings about the present dangers. People are quite capable of aligning their political interests with their beliefs about security and danger. "Humans are compulsive rationalizers," wrote Gardner. "Self-interest and sincere belief seldom part company."[203] Rumsfeld believed that people needed to be reminded of threats; Chertoff's gut actually told him to expect attacks; Cheney "believed in his bones that the risks were mortal and real," according to the most authoritative review of his term.[204] For these purposes, it is important to note that even initially disingenuous motivations quickly become the truth, as a result of every human being's desire to be internally consistent. No matter what President Bush's initial calculations were regarding Iraq, for example, there is little doubt that today he truly believes Saddam represented a clear and present danger and that removing him was the right thing to do. To believe otherwise would be cognitively unacceptable for almost anyone in his position. When necessary, the mind creates beliefs where none existed before.

In the final analysis, the sincerity of scaremongering political leaders does not much matter. After all, as Kennan wrote, "history does not forgive us our national mistakes because they are explicable in terms of domestic politics."[205] Stoking pathological fires not only has effects for the short term by gathering support for otherwise unnecessary action, but it tends to do long-term damage as well. Once lit, such fires are very hard to extinguish. Fear and

---

[202] Robert Kagan and William Kristol, "National Interest and Global Responsibility," in Robert Kagan and William Kristol, eds., *Present Dangers: Crisis and Opportunity in American Foreign and Defense Policy* (San Francisco, CA: Encounter Books, 2000), p. 4.

[203] Gardner, *The Science of Fear*, p. 139.

[204] Gellman, *Angler: The Cheney Vice Presidency*, p. 227.

[205] Kennan, *American Diplomacy*, p. 65.

anxiety persist long after they are useful and continue to drive decisions, becoming at times beyond the power of more responsible
leaders to control.

Politicians surely understand what will resonate with their constituents and what will not; like the media, they are reflections of the
society from which they arise. If the public were not susceptible to
pathologies a priori, then leaders would not make reference to them
as part of their campaign or governing strategies. Not all societies are
going to prove receptive to fear mongering, for instance, at least not
regarding all subjects. Only in a deeply pathological society is reason
a synonym for weakness. Sagacious leaders who refer to pathological beliefs to advance a decision arrived at for other reasons must
first know the society they are trying to manipulate. "Anxiety about
terrorism," wrote John Mueller and Mark Stewart, "seems substantially to be a bottom-up phenomenon rather than one inspired by
policymakers, risk entrepreneurs, politicians, and members of the
media, who seem more nearly to be responding to the fears (and
exacerbating them) than creating them."[206] That U.S. politicians
realize scaring the public generates advantages at the ballot box says
as much about America as it does about its leaders. Societies cannot
be frightened if they are not predisposed to fear. Perhaps sixty years
of threat inflation from official circles have had long-term, deeply
pathological consequences. Large portions of the public may have
developed beliefs about dangers and enemies that will take generations to change.

There are also a number of important actors within the U.S. government whose institutional interests prevent any recognition that
the United States is safe. The budget and overall *raison d'être* of the
military, for instance, would be called into question in a safe world.
The intelligence services issue regular assessments of the security
environment that conveniently fail to mention the proliferation
of peace. As a result, its members dismiss the evidence. Fear has a
number of institutional constituencies beyond DHS, in other words,
who are professionally inclined to detect danger whether or not it
exists. "It is difficult to get a man to understand something," Upton

---

[206] Mueller and Stewart, "The Terrorism Delusion," p. 110.

Sinclair famously noted, "when his salary depends upon his not understanding it."[207]

Even when these actors are aware of the evidence of stability, they explain it away or discount it. General Martin Dempsey, President Obama's chairman of the Joint Chiefs of Staff, gave an address in April 2012 in which he gave a depressingly stark example of this and confirmed Sinclair's observation. "We should always be willing to re-examine our assumptions and to follow the evidence where it leads," the general began. Inertia can prevent us from seeing "the new truths standing right before our eyes," he argued, and "our preconceived notions can obscure the weak signals of impending change" because of the tendency to "resist new and uncomfortable observations." Dempsey then went on to discuss Steven Pinker's brilliant book reviewing the worldwide decline of violence ... and how its findings, although indisputable, are actually irrelevant. Reexamination of the evidence led Dempsey to argue that although the world "seems less dangerous," it is "actually more dangerous." This "security paradox," as he called it, was due to the proliferation of destructive technologies like ballistic missiles, exploding fertilizer, and computer viruses. "More people have the ability to harm us or deny us the ability to act than at any point of my life," he argued.[208] So while these technologies have yet to affect U.S. security or international politics in any meaningful way, the general believed catastrophe was right around the corner. Danger still existed, and no one should relax.

The United States may well have a number of built-in historical, political, and cultural factors that make it more prone to pathological fear than other countries. But those factors alone, even when combined with the typical human traits from the individual level, would not have been ignited into such high levels of fear if the United States had not been blessed – or cursed – with tremendous relative power. Its

[207] Upton Sinclair, Jr., *I, Candidate for Governor: And How I Got Licked* (Berkeley, CA: University of California Press, 1935), p. 109.

[208] Martin E. Dempsey, "Chairman's Remarks," John F. Kennedy Jr. Forum, Harvard University, Boston, MA, April 12, 2012, available at http://www.jcs.mil/speech. aspx?id=1690. See also Greg Jaffe, "The World is Safer, But No One Will Say So," *Washington Post*, November 4, 2012, p. B1.

fears might have remained dormant had it not been for the peculiar structure of power in the international system.

SYSTEM LEVEL

The United States currently towers over all other states in all traditional measures of power, especially regarding its military and economy, notwithstanding the financial crisis that began in 2008. The truly remarkable aspect of the current era, as Stephen Brooks and William Wohlforth have pointed out, is the across-the-board dominance of the United States.[209] If this is not *unipolarity*, or a system marked by one state with no real peers in terms of power and influence, then such a condition has never – and probably will never – exist. Still, not every scholar agrees that the system is unipolar or that it will remain so for long.[210] It should not be controversial, however, that the United States remains the primary military and economic power in the world today, and possesses tremendous capability across the spectrum of power. The insecurity pathology finds at least some of its inspiration in the position the United States occupies in the imbalanced post–Cold War international system, whether everyone can agree that it is truly unipolar or not.

Since great powers have broader interests than do smaller, one might expect a "hyperpower" to have the broadest interests of all.[211] With great power comes both flexibility to pursue a wide variety of goals and responsibility to affect the progression of events. "Most countries are primarily concerned with what happens in their neighborhoods," as Jervis has explained, "but the world is the unipole's neighborhood."[212] As interests expand, new threats appear, which, if states are not careful, can soon take on an inflated importance and

---

[209] Stephen G. Brooks and William C. Wohlforth, "American Primacy in Perspective," *Foreign Affairs*, Vol. 81, No. 4 (July/August 2002), pp. 20–33; their view remains the same in their most recent work, *World out of Balance: International Relations and the Challenge of American Primacy* (Princeton, NJ: Princeton University Press, 2008). See also Robert Jervis, "Unipolarity: A Structural Perspective," *World Politics*, Vol. 61, No. 1 (January 2009), pp. 188–213.

[210] Samuel P. Huntington, "The Lonely Superpower," *Foreign Affairs*, Vol. 78, No. 2 (March/April 1999), pp. 35–49; and John J. Mearsheimer, *The Tragedy of Great Power Politics* (New York: W. W. Norton, 2001), p. 381.

[211] French Foreign Minister Hubert Védrine is widely credited with popularizing the term "hyperpower" to describe the United States.

[212] Jervis, "Unipolarity," p. 200.

inspire unnecessary action. Threats to secondary interests can rapidly be misinterpreted as significant dangers if not kept in perspective by a constant, conscious process of evaluation. Interest inflation, the central tenet of Parkinson's Law for international relations, is a common but avoidable contributor to this foreign policy pathology.

Unipoles tend to be status quo powers, hoping above all to retain their position in the international hierarchy. Instability and conflict anywhere can appear to be the first steps toward chaos and unpredictable systemic shake-ups. The unipolar power, therefore, tends to perceive threats where other powers do not and is more tempted to get involved in far-off turbulence that it can imagine would have the potential to threaten its hard-won international order. Its insecurity has no natural limits, and if not kept in check can easily lead to over-expansion, overspending, and decline.[213]

As a general rule, the greater its power, the harder it is for a state is to disconnect vital interests from peripheral. As expansion occurs, new dangers are perceived that seem to require action, leading to further expansion and subsequent identification of new threats. Jack Snyder has explained that for history's great powers, "the preventive pacification of one turbulent frontier usually led to the creation of another one, adjacent to the first."[214] Examples are not difficult to find. Two millennia after its collapse, it is easy to forget that insecurity inspired the growth of the Roman Empire. As historians have argued for centuries, its most prominent conquests, from Gaul to Dacia to Iberia, were driven not only by the desire for glory but also by the sincere belief that any untamed populations along its widening periphery could represent a threat to the empire.[215] Cicero explained that many Romans felt expansion was thrust upon them as part of a project to rid themselves of "frightening neighbors."[216] The fact that most of

[213] This is the process Jack Snyder first discussed in *Myths of Empire: Domestic Politics and International Ambition* (Ithaca, NY: Cornell University Press, 1991).

[214] Jack Snyder, "Imperial Myths and Threat Inflation," in A. Trevor Thrall and Jane K. Cramer, eds., *American Foreign Policy and the Politics of Fear: Threat Inflation since 9/11* (New York: Routledge, 2009), p. 41.

[215] For good reviews, see Robert M. Errington, *The Dawn of Empire: Rome's Rise to Power* (London: Hamish Hamilton Ltd., 1971); and Erich S. Gruen, *The Hellenistic World and the Coming of Rome* (Berkeley, CA: University of California Press, 1986).

[216] William V. Harris, *War and Imperialism in Republican Rome, 327–70 B.C.* (Oxford: Clarendon Press, 1985), p. 164.

these neighbors were manifestly weaker did not matter; as its power grew, so too did Rome's insecurity. On this, Joseph Schumpeter is probably unsurpassable:

There was no corner of the known world where some interest was not alleged to be in danger or under actual attack.... Rome was always being attacked by evil-minded neighbors, always fighting for a breathing space. The whole world was pervaded by a host of enemies, and it was manifestly Rome's duty to guard against their indubitably aggressive designs. They were enemies only waiting to fall on the Roman people.[217]

Even Rome's most ardent defenders stop short of claiming its expansion could be fully explained by virtuous, defensive motives; Roman leaders, especially those before Augustus, were rarely shy about their desire for the glory that can only come through conquest. There should be no doubt, however, that its strategists were not wholly motivated by increasing Roman prestige.[218] The most powerful, and in many ways safest, society in the ancient world was unconvinced that its security was assured as long as it had neighbors. Their mere existence always constituted a potential threat.

Similar fears haunted the great European empires of the premodern and modern eras. The enormous size of the Spanish Empire, which at its height encompassed a quarter of the earth's land area, meant its leaders could always detect a threat lurking somewhere. In 1626, King Philip IV was said to have lamented that "with as many kingdoms and lordships as have been linked to this crown, it is impossible to be without war in some area, either to defend what we have acquired or to divert our enemies."[219] Madrid spent itself into decline trying to address its many dangers, real and imagined.[220] Great Britain also exhibited a high level of insecurity throughout the eighteenth and nineteenth centuries. As the boundaries of the empire expanded,

[217] Joseph A. Schumpeter, "The Sociology of Imperialisms," in Joseph A. Schumpeter, *Imperialism and Social Classes* (Oxford: Basil Blackwell, 1951), p. 65.

[218] P. A. Brunt, *Roman Imperial Themes* (Oxford: Clarendon Press, 1990), p. 102.

[219] Quoted by Geoffrey Parker in "The Making of Strategy in Hapsburg Spain: Philip II's 'Bid for Mastery,' 1559–1598," in Williamson Murray, MacGregor Knox, and Alvin Bernstein, eds., *The Making of Strategy: Rulers, States, and War* (New York: Cambridge University Press, 1994), p. 119.

[220] J. H. Elliott, "Managing Decline: Olivares and the Grand Strategy of Imperial Spain," in Paul Kennedy, ed., *Grand Strategies in War and Peace* (New Haven, CT: Yale University Press, 1991), pp. 87–104.

new dangers consistently appeared just over the horizon. British politicians and strategists felt turbulence on colonial borders "pulled them toward expansion," in the words of a prominent historian of the era.[221] The notion that the empire could never be safe until all potential threats were addressed encouraged unnecessary forays into places that sapped Britain's strength, like Afghanistan, Uganda, Zululand, and the Crimea.

There is little doubt that these and other empires of the past did have enemies, in the forms of strong rival powers and various barbarian peoples, that could have been the cause of genuine security concerns. Insecurity is only pathological when elevated to disproportionate, irrational levels. The lack of existential enemies is but one of the many ways the United States does not resemble the unipoles of the past. Its dominance is far greater, as is the strength of its pathology. While its heightened perception of threat may well be a common reaction to overwhelming relative power, nothing in the structure of the system suggests this is a necessary, unavoidable outcome. Human decisions still matter. System-level factors may help explain the insecurity pathology, but they do not make it inevitable, much less defensible.

Overall, imbalances of power sometimes create anxiety, even in the strongest states. The United States is not the only example. More than one observer has been puzzled by the insecurity and fear displayed by Israel, despite the fact that it has never been stronger compared to its neighbors than it is now. Although Israel is currently much safer than at any time in its brief history, "it wallows in a sense of existential threat that has only grown with time," according to an editorial in the liberal newspaper *Haaretz*.[222] The malaise and anxiety extend to the right wing as well.[223] "To enter Israel is to pass through a hall of mirrors," writes *New York Times* columnist Roger Cohen. "A nation exerting complete military dominance in the West Bank becomes one that, under

[221] John S. Galbraith, "The 'Turbulent Frontier' as a Factor in British Expansion," *Comparative Studies in Society and History*, Vol. 2, No. 2 (January 1960), p. 168. See also Ronald Robinson and John Gallagher, *Africa and the Victorians: The Official Mind of Imperialism* (London: Page, 1961).

[222] "In its 62nd year, Israel Is in a Diplomatic, Security and Moral Limbo," *Haaretz*, April 19, 2010, available at http://www.haaretz.com/print-edition/opinion/in-its-62nd-year-israel-is-in-a-diplomatic-security-and-moral-limbo-1.284517.

[223] Ethan Bronner, "Mood Is Dark as Israel Marks Its 62nd Year as a Nation," *New York Times*, April 20, 2010.

an almost unimaginable peace accord, might be menaced from there. A nation whose army and arsenal are without rival in the Middle East becomes one facing daily existential threat. A nation whose power has grown steadily over decades relative to its scattered enemies becomes one whose future is somehow less secure than ever."[224] An enormous advantage in relative power has not made the Israelis feel safer, even if, objectively speaking, they certainly are.

Rich people worry a great deal about their security. They build tall fences, install motion detectors, and hire private security guards to protect themselves and their belongings from the throngs of have-nots they assume are plotting to take what is theirs. Wealth creates insecurity in individuals, and it seems to do so in states as well. Those who have more than what could be considered their fair share, perhaps bothered a bit by subconscious guilt, worry about losing what they have more than those who live in relative penury. In international politics, the United States has the most, and fears the most too. "America may be uniquely powerful in its global scope," Zbigniew Brzezinski believes, so as a result "its homeland is also uniquely insecure."[225] That kind of thinking has a certain amount of intuitive appeal, even if it is devoid of logic; if unchecked, it can lead to disaster.

The sense that the world is vastly more complex and dangerous after the Cold War is widespread. "Yes, we have slain a large dragon," James Woolsey said during his confirmation hearings prior to becoming director of central intelligence. "But we live now in a jungle filled with a bewildering variety of poisonous snakes. And in many ways, the dragon was easier to keep track of."[226] Secretary of State Madeleine Albright lamented that "we must plot our defense not against a single powerful threat, as during the Cold War, but against a viper's nest of perils."[227] A very senior military officer preferred this formulation a decade later: during the Cold War the United States was locked in a

[224] Roger Cohen, "Israeli Unassailable Might and Unyielding Angst," *New York Times*, April 23, 2010.
[225] Zbigniew Brzezinski, *The Choice: Global Domination or Global Leadership* (New York: Basic Books, 2004), p. ix.
[226] Douglas Jehl, "C.I.A. Nominee Wary of Budget Cuts," *New York Times*, February 3, 1993.
[227] Quoted in Bacevich, *American Empire*, p. 118.

room with a cobra, but now it has to deal with a limitless number of bees.[228] All such metaphors overlook the fact that there have always been snakes and bees in the world, but the United States notices them now only because the dragon/cobra is gone. Terrorism and other threats of the twenty-first century are not new; the only thing that has changed is the amount of time U.S. leaders have to devote to worrying about them. Background problems have today been moved to the foreground, elevated to replace what was a major threat emanating out of Moscow.[229] Nostalgia for the Cold War is the purview of those with highly selective memories. The world was a much more dangerous place then.

Many in this country simply refuse to believe the world is remarkably peaceful and that the United States is fundamentally safe, no matter how strong the evidence may be. Irrational fears should not be expected to wilt in the face of rational arguments. "The paranoid is too smart to be thrown off," argue Robins and Post. "The apparently contradictory facts only prove how clever and sinister his opponents are. He *knows* the danger is there."[230] Yet national security, like personal security, is never absolute. Americans have to learn to live with some risk, preferably before it inspires further counterproductive actions. They need not be pathological in their fear, even in economically uncertain times, which tend to "nourish belief in conspiracies of evil," according to historian Barbara Tuchman.[231] They just need to remain aware of the high probability that today's threats are in reality less dangerous then they first appear, and adjust their behavior accordingly.

Policy makers would be wise to beware of Parkinson's Law, the natural tendency to see more threats as power grows. Perhaps this tendency to identify more threats as power increases is one of the natural leveling forces of international politics; unless U.S. leaders wish to see the unipolar moment end sooner than it needs to, they need to recognize the United States is the safest country in the history of the world, even if it does not always act that way.

---

[228] From a not-for-attribution talk at the Naval War College, 2007.
[229] Daniel Wirls makes a similar point in *Irrational Security*, p. 42.
[230] Robins and Post, *Political Paranoia*, p. 8.
[231] Tuchman, *A Distant Mirror*, p. 542.

2

Honor

Credibility, Resolve, and Paper Tigers

Unlike in times past, honor is not central to the identity structure of citizens of modern, liberal, information-age nation-states. Any leader who would attempt to inspire twenty-first-century society with direct appeals to the national honor would likely be met with disdain and ridicule. The term has been out of fashion for generations, having become connected to outdated conceptions of masculinity more relevant to the Middle Ages than to today's international system. Honor might have compelled Louis XIV to wage wars against his neighbors and inspired foppish noblemen to meet at twenty paces, but such concerns are surely absent from modern, rational discourse. Or so we think.

However anachronistic the term might sound to modern ears, the remnants of honor linger on in today's international system, if under slightly different guises. The main evolution in the concept has been in how it is discussed, not its ultimate importance in explaining state behavior. Few leaders worry about the status of their honor; they do worry, at times obsessively, about their credibility. "Whatever course you follow," warned former Vice President Dick Cheney, "the essential thing is to keep commitments, and to leave no doubts about the credibility of your country's word."[1] The "credibility imperative," to use

---

[1] Dick Cheney, "Concerns about America's Foreign Policy Drift," Remarks at the Center for Security Policy, October 22, 2009, available at http://www.realclearpolitics.com/articles/2009/10/22/concerns_about_americas_foreign_policy_drift.html, accessed December 17, 2012.

94

historian Robert McMahon's phrase, has occupied a central position in every major U.S. foreign policy debate in the last sixty years, affecting discourse and decisions in predictable – and deeply pathological – ways.[2] To the extent that states act in pursuit or protection of their honor in its modern form, they usually do so in opposition to their actual, measurable, tangible interests.

While all states remain concerned to some degree with their reputations, no country today seems to take the imperative to remain credible as seriously as does the United States.[3] Scholars have not been able to detect equivalent levels of concern for credibility in any other state, even the Soviet Union, who presumably faced many of the same challenges during the Cold War without exhibiting similar influence of the imperative.[4]

This chapter examines the continuing importance of honor in modern U.S. foreign policy. It proceeds in four main sections: the first discusses the traditional importance of honor in international and interpersonal politics and explains the central role it plays in the construction of security in any system without a central authority. While modern leaders rarely speak of honor, this is more a change in vocabulary than behavior; today when they say credibility, others hear honor.[5] The second section describes the predictable, consistent effects honor has on state behavior in general and on U.S. foreign policy in particular. The third section argues that the lingering concern for honor is pathological, for a couple of reasons: There is

---

[2] Robert J. McMahon, "Credibility and World Power: Exploring the Psychological Dimension in Postwar American Diplomacy," *Diplomatic History*, Vol. 15, No. 4 (Fall 1991), p. 464. Stephen Walt prefers the "credibility fetish," which is a bit more expressive. "Why are U.S. Leaders so Obsessed with Credibility?" *Foreign Policy* Blog, September 11, 2012, available at http://walt.foreignpolicy.com/posts/2012/09/11/the_credibility_fetish.

[3] Richard Ned Lebow makes this point in *Why Nations Fight: Past and Future Motives for War* (New York: Cambridge University Press, 2010), p. 218.

[4] McMahon, "Credibility and World Power," p. 471. See also Franklin B. Weinstein, "The Concept of a Commitment in International Relations," *Journal of Conflict Resolution*, Vol. 13, No. 1 (March 1969), pp. 39–56; and Robert Jervis, "Perceiving and Coping with Threat," in Robert Jervis, Richard Ned Lebow, and Janice Stein, eds., *Psychology and Deterrence* (Baltimore, MD: Johns Hopkins University Press, 1985), pp. 13–33.

[5] See Barry O'Neill, *Honor, Symbols, and War* (Ann Arbor, MI: University of Michigan Press, 1999); and Kurt Walling, "Alexander Hamilton on Honor and American Foreign Policy," in Elliot Abrams, ed., *Honor among Nations: Intangible Interests and Foreign Policy* (Washington, DC: Ethics and Public Policy Center, 1998), p. 91.

no evidence that it helps states attain their goals, for instance, and it certainly has no relevance in those systems (like today's international) that contain no existential threats to member security. The chapter then speculates about the genesis of the honor pathology and why it continues to have such salience in the new century.

Honor as a motivation for action seems as obsolete today as horse-drawn carriages, alchemy, and the duel. But it persists, if in slightly different forms, and to the extent that it persists, it pathologizes.

HONOR, CREDIBILITY, AND WAR

Scholars of international politics since Thucydides seem to agree about the general importance of honor in explaining state behavior, but the concept remains vague, undertheorized, and underexamined.[6] Anthropologists, historians, and psychologists have paid it more attention to this point than have political scientists, but their understanding is hardly complete.[7] Indeed the term has been used in so many different contexts over the years in reference to so many concepts that it might at times seem to have no central meaning at all.[8] What exactly is "honor"? Where does it come from? How does

---

[6] The few works that specifically examine the importance of honor in international relations include Geoffrey Best, *Honour among Men and Nations: Transformation of an Idea* (Toronto: University of Toronto Press, 1982); Elliot Abrams, ed., *Honor among Nations: Intangible Interests and Foreign Policy* (Washington, DC: Ethics and Public Policy Center, 1998); O'Neill, *Honor, Symbols, and War*; and Michael Donelan, *Honor in Foreign Policy* (New York: Palgrave Macmillan, 2007).

[7] See, for instance, J. K. Campbell, *Honour, Family and Patronage* (Oxford: Clarendon Press, 1964); J. G. Peristiany, ed., *Honour and Shame: The Values of Mediterranean Society* (London: Weidenfeld and Nicolson, 1965); Bertram Wyatt-Brown, *Southern Honor: Ethics and Behavior in the Old South* (New York: Oxford University Press, 1982); William Ian Miller, *Bloodtaking and Peacemaking: Feud, Law and Society in Saga Iceland* (Chicago, IL: University of Chicago Press, 1990); and Richard E. Nisbett and Dov Cohen, *Culture of Honor: The Psychology of Violence in the South* (Boulder, CO: Westview Press, 1996).

[8] Frank Henderson Stewart, *Honor* (Chicago, IL: University of Chicago Press, 1994), p. 9. Richard Ned Lebow spent nearly 600 pages discussing honor in great depth recently without ever offering an explicit definition (*A Cultural Theory of International Relations* [New York: Cambridge University Press, 2008]). When this omission was pointed out in an online discussion of his work, Lebow protested, claiming to have "characterized" honor as "standing achieved in accordance with rules." That phrase, however, does not appear in the book. The closest Lebow comes to a definition is on page five, when he notes that honor "refers to the seemingly universal desire to stand out among one's peers, which is often achieved by selfless, sometimes even sacrificial,

it affect state behavior? What kinds of outcomes or policies does it encourage?

Honor's definition is better explored at book length, or at least nine long columns, which is what the *Oxford English Dictionary* devotes to it. In foreign affairs, and for the purposes of this book, honor can be said to be *the resolve to respond to provocation or insult*. What is considered a provocation, as well as the set of acceptable or expected responses, varies from society to society; the responses, however, must almost always contain at least the threat of violence. He who possesses honor must, in Geoffrey Best's words, demonstrate an "instant readiness to fight."[9] Honorable states and societies, therefore, are extremely conflict prone.[10]

Honor always counsels belligerence. In societies where resolute retaliation is a virtue there will be persistent challenges, responses, and conflict, no matter how irrational or futile fighting may appear.[11] Historically, international society has often dictated that violence was an acceptable and indeed necessary method with which to address challenges to personal or national honor. For most of human history, leaders routinely demonstrated a willingness to bring their nations to war rather than lose face or be dishonored. To be a man, and to be a country, was to be eternally ready and willing to go to battle.

Honor has been at the heart of conceptions of masculinity for nearly every culture across eras.[12] Although the social construction of its meaning has widely varied, the same basic motivation shaped behavior from antiquity through the industrial revolution. Explicit references to honor became rare where liberal notions of human rights and obligations came to dominate, but it survives, if most obviously

adherence to social norms." Christopher Ball, ed., "Review of Richard Ned Lebow, A Cultural Theory of International Relations," H-Diplo/ISSF Roundtable, Vol. 3, No. 7 (February 9, 2012), available at http://www.h-net.org/~diplo/ISSF/PDF/ISSF-Roundtable-3-7.pdf.

[9] Best, *Honour among Men and Nations*, p. 46.

[10] Lebow, *A Cultural Theory of International Relations*; and *Why Nations Fight*, esp. p. 75.

[11] Donald Kagan discusses the concept of honor and its relationship to the outbreak of war in *On the Origins of War and the Preservation of Peace* (New York: Doubleday, 1995).

[12] For a discussion of masculinity's relationship to war, see Joshua S. Goldstein, *War and Gender: How Gender Shapes the War System and Vice Versa* (New York: Cambridge University Press, 2001).

among traditional societies that liberalism has not (yet) reached.[13] Honor is also alive in the American South, for instance, where men are much quicker to fight one another than in any other region of the country.[14] It remains important in the inner cities, where challenges are common and the insulted (or "disrespected") feel compelled to respond with violence, largely because they cannot depend on the police for protection.[15] And it is certainly present in the international system, where long ago personal honor was very easily translated into national, without which no state would be respected by its peers. As Teddy Roosevelt once explained, "We despise a nation just as we despise a man who fails to resent an insult."[16]

Honor is a difficult subject for today's positivist scholar to grasp, since it is immeasurable, culturally specific, and mutable. Though clearly a correlate of war, it is difficult to capture in even the most sophisticated of equations, even if many international conflicts are mystifying without an understanding of the central role it plays.[17] It was honor at least as much as interest that propelled the great powers – especially the United States – into World War I, and that prevented them from finding a compromise solution long after it became clear the costs were far outpacing any potential benefit victory could bring.[18] It is only because that explanation seems so incredible to modern ears, according to Michael Donelan, "that the search for other explanations has been incessant."[19] Insults to its honor compelled the

[13] On the indirect relationship between honor and liberalism, see Kevin McAleer, *Dueling: The Cult of Honor in Fin-de-Siècle Germany* (Princeton, NJ: Princeton University Press, 1994); and Dick Steward, *Duels and the Roots of Violence in Missouri* (Columbia: University of Missouri Press, 2000).

[14] Nisbett and Cohen, *Culture of Honor*. See also Steven Pinker, *The Better Angels of Our Nature: Why Violence has Declined* (New York: Viking, 2011), pp. 84–99.

[15] Steven Pinker reviews the criminology literature on this subject, and why some consider the lower classes effectively "stateless," in *The Better Angels of Our Nature*, p. 84.

[16] Quoted by Norman Angell, *The Great Illusion: A Study of the Relation of Military Power to National Advantage*, 2nd ed. (London: William Heinemann, 1913), p. 203.

[17] Barry O'Neill does operationalize honor and glory in *Honor, Symbols, and War*.

[18] See Avner Offner, "Going to War in 1914: A Matter of Honor?" *Politics & Society*, Vol. 23, No. 2 (June 1995), pp. 213–41; Justus D. Doenecke, *Nothing Less than War: A New History of America's Entry into World War I* (Lexington, KY: University Press of Kentucky, 2011); and Galen Jackson, "The Offshore Balancing Thesis Reconsidered: Realism, the Balance of Power in Europe, and America's Decision for War in 1917," *Security Studies*, Vol. 21, No. 3 (August 2012), pp. 455–89.

[19] Donelan, *Honor in Foreign Policy*, p. 106. For that incessant search, see James Joll, *The Origins of the First World War*, 2nd ed. (New York: Longman, 1992); Jack L. Snyder,

United States to fight Great Britain in 1812, Spain in 1898, Germany in 1917, and Vietnam in the 1960s. Many generations of leaders would agree with Czar Alexander, who explained why it was necessary to go to war with Turkey in 1877 despite the fact that neither he nor his ministers could identify any tangible interests at stake: "In the life of states just as in that of private individuals there are moments when one must forget all but the defense of his honor."[20] Two hundred thousand Russians would die in that defense.

What seventeenth-century leaders unashamedly referred to as *honor* today's statesmen generally call *credibility*.[21] Like honor, the credibility of a state is a mixture of its competence, legitimacy, resolve, trust-worthiness, willingness to take casualties, and/or rigidity of purpose. It is, in Henry Kissinger's words, "the coin with which we conduct our foreign policy," an intangible asset without which a state cannot influence the actions of others.[22] In periods of high credibility, a state can deter and compel behavior and accomplish goals short of war, or so the argument goes. When credibility is low, skeptical adversaries and allies may be tempted to ignore a state's threats and promises. To policy makers, therefore, unimpeachable credibility is worth many divisions at the negotiating table.

The modern understanding of credibility shares the essential behavioral characteristic of honor: it is worth preserving primarily to send messages to others about likely future reactions to aggression in the hopes of affecting their decisions. Like honor, the credibility of a state forms the basis of its reputation, which is little more than an impression of fundamental national character that serves as a guide for others trying to anticipate future actions.[23] Threats made by a state

The Ideology of the Offensive: Military Decision Making and the Disasters of 1914 (Ithaca, NY: Cornell University Press, 1984); and the essays in Stephen E. Miller, ed., *Military Strategy and the Origins of the First World War* (Princeton, NJ: Princeton University Press, 1985).

[20] Quoted by William Wohlforth in "Honor as Interest in Russian Decisions for War, 1600–1995," in Elliot Abrams, ed., *Honor among Nations: Intangible Interests and Foreign Policy* (Washington, DC: Ethics and Public Policy Center, 1998), p. 35.

[21] Steven Pinker is the most recent one to make this point, in *The Better Angels of Our Nature*, p. 34.

[22] Dan Williams and Ann Devroy, "U.S. Policy Lacks Focus, Critics Say: Bosnia Cited as Prime Case," *Washington Post*, April 24, 1994, p. A1.

[23] Jonathan Mercer, *Reputation and International Politics* (Ithaca, NY: Cornell University Press, 1996), p. 6.

without credibility may not be believed, setting off a cascading domino effect of aggression from emboldened rivals, possibly until they challenge an interest that is truly vital, making major crises unavoidable. Thus the impulses of honor have not left our national marketplace of ideas, even if the word has come to seem old-fashioned, ridiculous, even quaint. The credibility imperative inspires the kinds of reactions Thucydides and Napoleon would recognize immediately as honor under a different guise.

Honor Cultures and their Effects

A shared belief in the importance of honor among actors exists in an "honor culture," where a set of specific behavioral norms and expectations are assimilated throughout society. Members of such a society can be expected to respond quickly to insults with violence, since failure to do so can be catastrophic to status, reputation, and security. Challenges will be common, even expected, as actors jockey for position and prestige (what the next chapter explains is the modern equivalent of glory). The status of he (and it is almost always a "he") who defeats an honorable foe, or forces one to back down from a challenge, rises. Although details and nuances of honor cultures vary, they are particularly likely to arise when two conditions are met: first, when the members of society are vulnerable to attack or theft from other members; and second, in an overriding condition of anarchy, or absence of a central authority able to create rules and enforce order.[24] Honor cultures, whether among European noblemen, Greek goat herders, U.S. inner city residents, or states, arise in self-help systems under anarchy. When actors perceive no government is capable of ensuring their security, they take steps to do it themselves.

The rational individual in an honor culture makes it clear to potential adversaries that he is willing to defend his interests at any cost, even if the risks involved seem grossly disproportionate to the insult. Those contemplating future challenges on serious matters would

---

[24] Nisbett and Cohen, *Culture of Honor,* p. 4. See also Todd K. Shackleford, "An Evolutionary Psychological Perspective on Cultures of Honor," *Evolutionary Psychology,* Vol. 3 (2005), pp. 381–91.

presumably learn important lessons about the disposition of the target from its violent reaction to relatively minor provocation. Thus seemingly bizarre behaviors – such as fatal encounters on the dueling field over, say, minor flirtation with a spouse – make some sense if they are aimed at deterring more serious overtures. The message sent to potential aggressors is clear: even the slightest challenge to the security of the target might well entail enormous costs. The chances for the success of deterrence are enhanced when targets demonstrate no hesitation to escalate violence to extreme ends. Sometimes it helps to be perceived as a bit of a madman.[25]

To act honorably is to send a signal, to make it clear costs are associated with future transgressions. The goat herder who failed to rise to an insult invited far more serious challenges to the security of his flock. Anthropologist Pierre Bourdieu notes that among the Kabyles of Algeria a man with honor can "sleep and leave the door open," and that his women "can walk alone, with a golden crown on their head, without anyone dreaming of attacking them."[26] In such societies honor is equivalent to security: families that have one automatically have the other. "The man of honour," Bourdieu explained, "is immune from any attack, including the most ill-judged," for "even when he is absent, there is someone in his house."[27] Honor deterred challenge where no authority existed to punish it.

This same logic applied for centuries to the international system, the ultimate anarchic arena. The absence of a central world government essentially created a global honor culture, where failure to respond to insults invited more serious challenges in the future. Those states willing to defend their honor at any costs would be those least likely to be trifled with. "Once honor was gone, reputation was gone," explained Quincy Wright in his magisterial examination of war. "No one would fear to commit trespasses against the dishonored, who would rapidly sink in the world." For individuals and states alike, reputation, prestige,

---

[25] Scott Sagan and Jeremi Suri, "The Madman Nuclear Alert: Secrecy, Signaling and Safety in October 1969," *International Security*, Vol. 27, No. 4 (Spring 2003), pp. 150–83.

[26] Pierre Bourdieu, "The Sentiment of Honour in Kabyle Society," in J. G. Peristiany, ed., *Honour and Shame: The Values of Mediterranean Society* (London: Weidenfeld and Nicolson, 1965), p. 214.

[27] Bourdieu, "The Sentiment of Honour in Kabyle Society," p. 215.

and honor were "the practical road to security and advancement."[28]
Such concerns were perfectly rational in these specific international
societies. Political leaders in times past had to be concerned with their
reputations for at least three important reasons: if the general perception arose that they lacked honor – or, more specifically, the willingness to fight – leaders might well have faced internal challenges from
ever-present domestic enemies, external challenges from rivals, and/
or blows to their own self-esteem, which was itself constructed in a
society that valued honor above all other virtues. At many times in the
past, therefore, honor had a basis in interest.[29]

HONOR AND CREDIBILITY IN U.S. FOREIGN POLICY

Deterrence theorists used the same logic when discussing the importance of credibility during the Cold War.[30] Since state actions send
messages to others about likely future behavior, irresolution in crises
can teach rivals and allies alike that the state would be unwilling to
respond to any challenge.[31] Emboldened by such perceptions, adversaries might soon press their advantage. If instead the state is resolute in honoring its commitments, even in cases of seemingly little
importance, potential aggressors would take note, making more serious future crises less likely. "Essentially," explained Thomas Schelling
during the Cold War, "we tell the Soviets that we have to react here
because, if we did not, they would not believe us when we say that we
will react there."[32] The imperative to remain credible became part
of the training of nearly every American foreign policy professional
for decades, becoming the political science equivalent of settled law.
Since actions were interdependent, according to deterrence theorists,

---

[28] Quincy Wright, *A Study of War* (Chicago, IL: University of Chicago Press,
1965), p. 177.

[29] Donelan, *Honor in Foreign Policy*, p. 152.

[30] Thomas C. Schelling, *The Strategy of Conflict* (Cambridge, MA: Harvard University
Press, 1960) and *Arms and Influence* (New Haven, CT: Yale University Press, 1966);
Glenn H. Snyder, *Deterrence and Defense: Toward a New Theory of National Security*
(Princeton, NJ: Princeton University Press, 1961); and Glenn H. Snyder and Paul
Diesing, *Conflict among Nations: Bargaining, Decision-Making, and Systemic Structure in
International Crises* (Princeton, NJ: Princeton University Press, 1977).

[31] Schelling, *Arms and Influence*, pp. 35–91.

[32] Schelling, *Arms and Influence*, p. 55.

the surest way to prevent World War III was to display belligerence at every challenge.

The imperative was thus central to the development of Cold War grand strategy. U.S. leaders were reluctant to show any irresolution to the Soviet Union and worried obsessively about disheartening their allies or giving neutrals any reason to tilt toward Moscow. All of this led them to fight minor wars in otherwise irrelevant parts of the world; indeed many of the major actions during the Cold War make little sense absent an understanding of the importance U.S. policy makers placed on their credibility. South Korea had little bearing on the balance of power, for example, but it was perceived as vital to the United States' reputation. "We lost thirty thousand dead in Korea to save face for the United States and the United Nations," wrote Schelling, adding that "it was undoubtedly worth it."[33] Assistant Secretary of Defense John McNaughton summarized U.S. aims in Vietnam as motivated 10 percent to help the South Vietnamese, 20 percent to prevent falling dominoes in Eurasia, and 70 percent to avoid the reputational costs of a defeat.[34]

Jerome Slater has argued that "it does not occur to ordinary states to imagine that their 'vital interests' are integrally linked to outcomes of local wars in tiny countries thousands of miles away from their borders."[35] The United States, of course, has never been an "ordinary" state. Throughout the Cold War, it demonstrated a greater concern with its credibility than its rivals or allies. As mentioned earlier, there was never much evidence from Soviet actions or strategic literature to suggest that the Kremlin feared the potential catastrophic consequences of lost credibility to the same extent.[36] Its allies never seemed to doubt U.S. credibility as much as Washington feared they would, and certainly never considered separate accommodations with Moscow. The Cold War U.S. obsession with credibility puzzled, rather than reassured, outsider observers.

---

[33] Schelling, *Arms and Influence*, p. 124.
[34] Quoted in Bruce W. Jentleson, "American Commitments in the Third World: Theory vs. Practice," *International Organization*, Vol. 41, No. 4 (Autumn 1987), p. 676.
[35] Jerome Slater, "The Domino Theory and International Politics: The Case of Vietnam," *Security Studies*, Vol. 3, No. 2 (Winter 1993/94), p. 218.
[36] See Patrick M. Morgan, "Saving Face for the Sake of Deterrence," in Robert Jervis, Richard Ned Lebow, and Janice Stein, *Psychology and Deterrence* (Baltimore, MD: Johns Hopkins University Press, 1985), esp. p. 142.

The collapse of the Soviet Union did not significantly weaken the U.S. imperative to remain credible. Though the state most likely to make challenges and be encouraged by irresolution was gone, new enemies emerged in the form of rogue states and terrorists who posed threats to the new world order Washington was trying to create. The real, unspoken danger has been chaos itself; during the Cold War, the credibility imperative drew strength from the belief that communism could spread in a domino-like fashion, and after its end similar fears were common, with disorder as the new focus. Credibility was a key concern of the Bush and the Clinton administrations as all the crises of the 1990s unfolded, from Bosnia and Kosovo to Somalia and Haiti. If the United States failed to react to these chaotic situations, the argument always went, malevolent opportunists would arise to spread chaos to other regions. "Our credibility must be preserved or all the would-be Milosevics around the world will believe that they, too, can kill and maim with impunity," explained former Secretary of State Lawrence Eagleburger.[37] "In Pyongyang and Baghdad and Tripoli, they are paying close attention," argued Senator John McCain during the crisis in Kosovo. "If a military establishment that was defeated by the Croatian Army prevails, one led by a Balkan thug prevails, then we will be vulnerable to many challenges in many places."[38] Indeed all manner of undesirable international events, from Russian intransigence to rioting across the Arab world in response to YouTube videos, have been blamed at various times on insufficient U.S. resolve.[39]

Many have feared that not just rogue states but dangerous nonstate actors would be encouraged by low U.S. credibility, especially since the leadership of Al Qaeda repeatedly cited a lack of resolution in Washington as inspiration for its actions. Bin Laden accused America of being a "paper tiger," a state that will back away at the slightest use of force. "We have seen in the last decade," he declared in one of his periodic rants, "the decline of the American government and the weakness of the American soldier who is ready to wage Cold Wars

[37] Lawrence S. Eagleburger, "NATO, in a Corner," *New York Times*, April 4, 1999, p. D11.
[38] Alison Mitchell, "McCain Keeps Pressing Case for Troops," *New York Times*, April 4, 1999, p. 7.
[39] See Liz Cheney, "Cairo, Benghazi and Obama Foreign Policy," *Wall Street Journal*, September 13, 2012, p. A15.

and unprepared to fight long wars. This was proven in Beirut when the Marines fled after two explosions. It also proves they can run in less than twenty-four hours, and this was also repeated in Somalia."[40] Some analysts take bin Laden at his word and argue that Al Qaeda has drawn inspiration from perceptions of American irresolution. Had the United States taken steps to bolster its credibility, the argument goes, the attacks of September 11 might never have occurred.[41]

If decreased U.S. credibility has altered the calculations of militant fundamentalist groups, then states combating terrorism would be justified in worrying about the messages their actions send, and should consider the likely impact current decisions will have on future crises. The credibility imperative would be a rational response to international anarchy, rather than the foundation for pathological beliefs. The following sections explore the costs and benefits of our national obsession with credibility, beginning with a deeper examination of the behavior it inspires.

HONOR'S EFFECTS

The credibility imperative has three observable effects on foreign policy discourse: like honor, it counsels stubborn belligerence; second, it leads to worst-case-scenario thinking, producing at times astonishing hyperbole and illogic; and third, its employment in a debate strongly indicates that no tangible, measurable national interests are otherwise at stake. All of these drive the "battlefield of beliefs" in pathological directions, making unnecessary, counterproductive actions more likely.

Belligerence

First and most obviously, the credibility imperative is almost always employed to bolster the most hawkish position in any discussion, counseling belligerent responses to all perceived challenges. Failure

---

[40] Osama bin Laden, in an interview with John Miller, in Laura Egendorf, ed., *Terrorism: Opposing Viewpoints* (San Diego, CA: Greenhaven Press, 1999), p. 125.

[41] See Norman Podhoretz, *World War IV: The Long Struggle against Islamofascism* (New York: Doubleday, 2007); and David Frum and Richard Perle, *An End to Evil: How to Win the War on Terror* (New York: Random House, 2003).

to react with appropriate strength, its adherents warn, would risk appeasement, disgrace, and far worse crises in the future. The examples are almost too numerous to review: hawks argued U.S. credibility would be irreparably harmed if Washington failed to get involved in Vietnam, and then if it did not stay until the war was won; if it did not use air strikes against the Soviet missiles in Cuba; if it did not respond to Bosnian Serb provocations with sufficient force; if it failed to attack the leaders of the military coup in Haiti in 1994; and if it did not "stay the course" in Iraq. At other times, the credibility imperative was employed to urge two presidents to use military force to prevent nuclear proliferation in North Korea and to punish the recalcitrant Saddam Hussein.[42] Cheney reveals in his memoirs that he bolstered his case for a strike on Syrian nuclear facilities in 2007 by arguing at a National Security Council meeting that doing so "would enhance our credibility in that part of the world."[43] The credibility of the United States is always endangered by inaction and affirmed by action, irrespective of the importance of the issue at hand. The reputation for sound policy judgment never seems to be as important as the reputation for belligerence.

The credibility imperative encourages hawkish behavior during negotiations as well, supporting rigidity and decrying concessions as demonstrations of weakness. Only victory can legitimate diplomacy; compromised settlements encourage further challenges and are synonymous with appeasement. Madeleine Albright reported a typical example in her memoirs, explaining that during Bosnia negotiations "the ordinarily hawkish Jamie Rubin urged me to compromise on a particular measure. I glared and said, 'Jamie, do you think we're in Munich?'"[44] *Washington Post* columnist Charles Krauthammer complained that the negotiations that headed off war on the Korean peninsula in 2003 would prove a "threat to

---

[42] On the former, see the floor speeches of Senator John McCain, such as "The Nuclear Ambitions of North Korea," October 7, 1994, available at http://www.fas.org/spp/starwars/congress/1994/s941007-dprk.htm, accessed December 17, 2012; on the latter, see Eliot A. Cohen, "Sound and Fury," *Washington Post*, December 19, 1998, p. A25 and Charles Krauthammer, "Saddam: Round 3," *Washington Post*, November 13, 1998, p. A23.

[43] Dick Cheney, *In My Time: A Personal and Political Memoir* (New York: Simon and Schuster, 2011), p. 471.

[44] Madeleine Albright, *Madame Secretary* (New York: Miramax, 2003), p. 382.

American credibility everywhere."[45] Diplomacy with aggressors is always suspect.

Once engaged, credibility can only be maintained by victory, whatever the cost. As the situation began to deteriorate in Somalia, for example, President Clinton was quite hesitant to pull U.S. troops out. "Our own credibility with friends and allies would be severely damaged," he said. "Our leadership in world affairs would be undermined at the very time when people are looking to America to help promote peace and freedom in the post–Cold War world. And all around the world, aggressors, thugs and terrorists will conclude that the best way to get us to change our policies is to kill our people. It would be open season on Americans."[46] A decade later, Secretary of Defense Donald Rumsfeld warned that if the United States withdrew "prematurely" from Iraq "the enemy would tell us to leave Afghanistan and then withdraw from the Middle East. And if we left the Middle East, they'd order us and all those who don't share their militant ideology to leave what they call the occupied Muslim lands from Spain to the Philippines." Ultimately, America would be forced "to make a stand nearer home."[47] Kissinger agreed, predicting that "our leadership and the respect accorded to our views on other regional issues from Palestine to Iran would be weakened; the confidence of other major countries – China, Russia, Europe, Japan – in America's potential contribution would be diminished. The respite from military efforts would be brief before even greater crises descended upon us."[48] President Bush wrote in his memoirs that withdrawal would "embolden a hostile Iran in its pursuit of nuclear weapons," and that "ultimately, our enemies could use their sanctuary to attack our homeland."[49] The United States always needs to stay engaged, lest others lose faith in its tenacity and determination, after which greater disasters would follow.

The actors employing the imperative are not always the same – many of the doves of the 1980s became hawks by the 1990s – but their prescription never waivers: those citing credibility always do so

45 Charles Krauthammer, "Korea Follies," *Washington Post,* January 17, 2003, p. A23.
46 John M. Broder, "Clinton Orders 5,300 Troops to Somalia," *Los Angeles Times,* October 8, 1993, p. A1.
47 *New York Times,* "The Sound of One Domino Falling," August 4, 2006, p. 16.
48 Henry Kissinger, "How to Exit Iraq," *Washington Post,* December 19, 2005.
49 George W. Bush, *Decision Points* (New York: Crown Publishers, 2010), p. 367.

on the side of belligerence. The credibility imperative is the rhetorical instrument of the hawk.

Hyperbole

The credibility imperative tends to produce rather gaudy hyperbole, or at best seriously underexplained projections of danger, even in otherwise sober analysts. If the United States were to lose credibility, hawks warn, the floodgates would open to a variety of catastrophes, setting off chains of dominoes that would eventually not only threaten vital interests and make major war necessary but that might somehow lead to the end of the republic itself (or to the death of freedom, or to the destruction of civilization, or other such horrific disaster). Momentum toward the abyss can begin with the smallest demonstration of irresolution, since in the interdependent system there are no inconsequential events. Even tiny slips can begin the United States down the slope toward unmitigated disaster.

Quemoy and Matsu might not have seemed terribly important to U.S national security in 1955, for example, but if they fell to the Chinese without response the resulting loss of credibility would enable the communists "to begin their objective of driving us out of the western Pacific, right back to Hawaii and even to the United States," according to John Foster Dulles.[50] In 1983, President Reagan told Congress that if U.S. efforts failed in Central America, "our credibility would collapse, our alliances would crumble, and the safety of our homeland would be put at jeopardy."[51] Five years earlier, he had warned the nation that giving up direct rule of the Panama Canal would embolden America's enemies to the point that it could well lead to a loss "of our own freedom."[52] Michael Ledeen of the American Enterprise Institute argued that the negotiations with China over the return of the crew during the EP-3A mini-crisis with China in 2001 were "part of an enormously

[50] Quoted in John Lewis Gaddis, *Strategies of Containment: A Critical Appraisal of Postwar American Security Policy* (New York: Oxford University Press, 1982), p. 144.

[51] Steven R. Wiesman, "President Appeals before Congress for Aid to Latins," *New York Times*, April 28, 1983, p. A1.

[52] Reagan spent the seventies warning about the perils of letting the Panamanians operate the canal. See Adam Clymer, *Drawing the Line at the Big Ditch: The Panama Canal Treaties and the Rise of the Right* (Lawrence: University Press of Kansas, 2008); the quotation comes from p. 72.

important process, in which the survival of the United States may very well be at stake."⁵³ Four years later former Secretary of Defense Melvin Laird warned that the stakes in Iraq "could not be higher for the continued existence of our own democracy."⁵⁴

The hyperbole produced by Vietnam was in a class by itself. Vice President Johnson worried in 1961 that if Saigon were to fall to the communists, "the United States must inevitably surrender the Pacific ... and pull back our defenses to San Francisco."⁵⁵ Secretary of State Dean Rusk wrote that if U.S. commitments became discredited through defeat, "the communist world would draw conclusions that would lead to our ruin and almost certainly to a catastrophic war."⁵⁶ As president, Johnson warned his cabinet that "if we run out on Southeast Asia, there will be trouble ahead in every part of the globe – not just in Asia, but in the Middle East and in Europe, in Africa and Latin America. I am convinced that our retreat from this challenge will open the path to World War III."⁵⁷ His successor warned in 1965 that defeat would lead to the end of free speech throughout the world.⁵⁸ While in office, Nixon argued that defeat "would spark violence wherever our commitments help maintain the peace – in the Middle East, in Berlin, eventually even in the Western Hemisphere."⁵⁹ And Kissinger felt that if South Vietnam were allowed to fall, it would represent a "fundamental threat, over a period of time, to the security of the United States."⁶⁰ Somehow "untold millions would be in jeopardy."⁶¹

Audiences often prove distressingly willing to accept projections of catastrophe at face value. Rarely are policy makers or analysts asked

53 Michael Ledeen, "Handling China," *National Review Online*, April 19, 2001, available at http://www.aei.org/news/newsID.12741,filter.all/news_detail.asp.
54 Melvin Laird, "Iraq: Learning the Lessons of Vietnam," *Foreign Affairs*, Vol. 84, No. 6 (November/December 2005), p. 36.
55 Quoted in Barbara W. Tuchman, *The March of Folly: From Troy to Vietnam* (New York: Ballantine Books, 1984), p. 293.
56 Quoted in Gaddis, *Strategies of Containment*, p. 240.
57 Lyndon Baines Johnson, *The Vantage Point* (New York: Holt, Rinehart and Winston, 1971), pp. 147–48.
58 Quoted in Theodore H. White, *The Making of the President 1968* (New York: Harper Collins, 2010), p. 57.
59 McMahon, "Credibility and World Power," p. 467.
60 Quoted in Tuchman, *The March of Folly*, p. 375.
61 Henry Kissinger, *White House Years* (Boston: Little, Brown & Co., 1979), p. 196.

to justify these visions or pressed to examine the logic connecting the present decisions to horrifying future disasters. No one thinks to ask why anyone should accept the notion that the loss of credibility would result in such unprecedented, unimaginable consequences. When the United States did not respond with instant belligerence to the seizure of the *Pueblo* in 1968, Kissinger believed that it "paid for" that seemingly long-forgotten event "in many intangible ways, in demoralized friends and emboldened adversaries."[62] No one asked in *what* ways, or *which* friends, or *which* adversaries, or if in general one should allow such imprecise, borderline delusional beliefs to drive policy. In this case and others, the shadow of the future blinded the policy makers to the present.

During debates, establishing logical connections is never as important as establishing the potential, however slim, for catastrophe. The public is meant to accept these warnings on faith alone, with the understanding that the elite have more experience and expertise in these matters. Few would oppose the defense of Quemoy and Matsu once it was explained that belligerence would prevent a "catastrophic war." Similarly, it was difficult to argue that aid to the Contras was not in the national interest once it became linked to the survival of NATO and the safety of "our homeland." When policy makers internalize the imperative to remain credible, logic and reason can become casualties of fear.

The desire to prevent negative outcomes is prudent; the fear of triggering impossible outcomes is pathological. The credibility imperative inspires decision makers to cross the line between the two time and time again. It never seems necessary to explain precisely how the predicted string of catastrophes could occur, since the mere suggestion that inaction could lead to ruin is often sufficient to shout down those who object to demonstrations of belligerence in minor crises. Once leaders internalize the belief that threats are interdependent, it seems to follow that the loss of credibility anywhere would be disastrous for U.S. interests everywhere. Foreign policy is by necessity a worst-case-scenario business, after all, and decision makers are always wise to hedge against negative outcomes.[63] Since a loss of credibility

---

[62] Kissinger, *White House Years.*, p. 321.
[63] Jack Snyder, "Introduction," in Robert Jervis and Jack Snyder, eds., *Dominoes and Bandwagons: Strategic Beliefs and Great Power Competition in the Eurasian Rimland* (New York: Oxford University Press, 1991), pp. 9–12.

offers an imaginable (if implausible) route to national ruin, it seems logical for policy makers to pay limited costs in the present if by doing so they can avoid unlimited disasters in the future. The costs of tomorrow's catastrophe can always be portrayed as outweighing those of today's resolution. George Ball stood little chance against Robert McNamara.

It is tempting to doubt the sincerity of those employing hyperbole. Perhaps at times these decision makers did not really believe what they said, and were instead attempting to instill fear in the public for political purposes. While divining the ulterior motives of political leaders is a popular cottage industry, it is also necessarily speculative and tendentious. There is little reason to doubt that those under the spell of the credibility imperative mean exactly what they say. After all, it is not only leaders who are guilty – analysts and scholars with little political pressure often reach much the same conclusions. Ultimately, whether statements like these are expressions of actual belief or merely attempts to sell unpopular policies to a skeptical public is not as important as the recognition of hyperbole in debates, understanding of its origins, and minimization of its effects.

Absence of Tangible Interests

"Few parts of the world are intrinsically worth the risk of serious war," noted the intellectual father of the credibility imperative, "but defending them may preserve one's commitment to action in other parts of the world and at later times."[64] In practice the imperative often encourages action in parts of the world that are manifestly not worthy of the risk involved. In other words, there is a loose inverse relationship between the rhetorical employment of the credibility imperative and the presence of vital, tangible national interests. Roosevelt did not make reference to the reputation of the United States when he asked Congress for a declaration of war against Japan in 1941. Similarly, Churchill's stirring speeches rallying his countrymen at their darkest hour did not mention the importance of maintaining

[64] Schelling, *Arms and Influence*, p. 124.

the credibility of the realm. When a clear national interest is at stake, policy makers have no need to defend (or sell) their actions with reference to the national reputation or credibility. The more tangible the national interest, the smaller the role intangible factors play in either decisions or justifications for policy. The credibility imperative helped the United States become willing to use force to keep Korea, Lebanon, Vietnam, Laos, Grenada, El Salvador, Nicaragua, and many other countries that had no measurable impact on the global balance of power in the camp of free nations. "El Salvador doesn't really matter," one of Ronald Reagan's foreign policy advisors admitted in 1981, but "we have to establish credibility because we are in very serious trouble."[65]

When credibility is the primary justification for action, it should be an indicator that the interest at stake is probably not vital to the United States. Since Washington had no strategic interests in the Balkans in the 1990s, for example, it was forced to invent some. Rather than sell policies based solely on what they were – humanitarian interventions – the Clinton administration repeatedly linked the fate of the Muslims of southeastern Europe to the credibility of the United States and NATO. By doing so, according to Owen Harries, Clinton "managed to create a serious national interest in Bosnia where none before existed: an interest, that is, in the preservation of this country's prestige and credibility."[66] The credibility imperative rose to prominence precisely because no tangible U.S. interest in Bosnia existed.

Earl Ravenal called this the "paradox of credibility": reputations are unlikely to be formed when states act to preserve vital national interests, since they are compelled to do so. "In order to buttress its credibility," he wrote, "a nation should intervene in the least significant, the least compelling, and the least rewarding cases, and its reaction should be disproportionate to the immediate provocation or the particular interest at stake." In other words, "the less the occasion, the greater the response."[67]

---

[65] Quoted in William M. LeoGrande, "A Splendid Little War: Drawing the Line in El Salvador," *International Security*, Vol. 6, No. 1 (Summer 1981), p. 27.

[66] Owen Harries, "An Anti-Interventionist No More: America's Credibility is Now at Stake," *Washington Post*, April 21, 1994, p. A31.

[67] Earl C. Ravenal, "Counterforce and Alliance: The Ultimate Connection," *International Security*, Vol. 6, No. 4 (Spring 1982), p. 28.

In fact, since the stakes involved are low, credibility is usually pursued at the *expense* of measurable state interests. The costs of the actions it supports often negatively affect the state's bottom line, doing more harm than good. Most of the time, when arguments for action are based on credibility, nothing of importance is likely at stake. Leaders would be wise to ignore the counsel of those who insist upon its importance.

Nothing of particular importance was at stake during the most dangerous moment of the Cold War, for example. Although the introduction of Soviet missiles into Cuba in 1962 posed a negligible security threat to the United States, the Kennedy administration was willing to push the world to the brink of nuclear war to have them removed. Contrary to widespread mythology, medium-range missiles deployed near the United States would hardly have given the Soviets an undeterrable first-strike capability: missiles launched from Cuba would not even be the first to hit U.S. targets in this scenario, which is an honor that would have gone to the scores of submarine-launched ballistic missiles the Soviets could have quite legally parked twelve miles off the U.S. coast. The Soviet action did not represent an alteration of the nuclear balance, as participants in Kennedy's "ExComm" meetings were well aware. The president stated on the first day of the crisis that "it doesn't make any difference if you get blown up by an ICBM flying from the Soviet Union or one that was ninety miles away. Geography doesn't mean that much."[68] On October 17 (the second day of the crisis and five days before a blockade was ordered), Theodore Sorensen summarized the views of the ExComm in a memorandum to the president by saying that "it is generally agreed that these missiles, even when fully operational, do not significantly alter the balance of power – i.e., they do not significantly increase the potential megatonnage capable of being unleashed on American soil, even after a surprise American nuclear strike."[69] Secretary of Defense Robert McNamara noted on that same day that "it's not a military problem that we're

---

[68] Sheldon M. Stern, *The Cuban Missile Crisis in American Memory: Myths versus Reality* (Palo Alto, CA: Stanford University Press, 2012), p. 21.

[69] Quoted by James A. Nathan, "The Missile Crisis: His Finest Hour Now," *World Politics*, Vol. 27, No. 2 (January 1975), p. 264.

facing; it's a political problem; it's a problem of holding the alliance together; it's a problem of properly conditioning Khrushchev for our future moves."[70] It was a problem, in other words, of credibility, and the United States was willing to run a very real risk of nuclear catastrophe to preserve it. It is hard to think of an act that was less rational in terms of potential costs and benefits than forcing a show-down over strategically irrelevant weapons.

Overall, when the credibility imperative drives policy, states are likely to follow hawkish recommendations regarding crises in which few tangible interests are at stake in order to head off terrifying, if vague and underexplained, future catastrophes. To justify such actions, the benefits would need to be clear, significant, and consistent. However, as the next section argues, this is not the case.

HONOR AS PATHOLOGY

If credibility kept a state safe in a dangerous world, then the occasional war to bolster it would be a small price to pay. However, there are good reasons to believe that this is not the case. For credibility to be a useful, rational motivation for action, two criteria must be met: at least some of the actors in society must have the desire and capability to take advantage of perceived low credibility; and second, there must be good reason to believe that these challenges can be deterred by a reputation for resolve. For the United States in the twenty-first century, neither of these criteria is met. The current international system is not the kind of dangerous, chaotic, unpredictable world where honor and credibility can deter aggression. No major enemies stand poised to take advantage of U.S. irresolution. Furthermore, decades of research cast doubt on the deterrent ability of honor among states, suggesting its benefits are illusory. Targets rarely learn the lessons we try to teach them. Credibility does not keep a country safe; fortunately, in today's world, the United States is safe with or without it.

[70] Stern, *The Cuban Missile Crisis in American Memory*, p. 58. See also Richard Ned Lebow, "The Traditional and Revisionist Interpretations Reevaluated: Why Was Cuba a Crisis?" in James A. Nathan, ed., *The Cuban Missile Crisis Revisited* (New York: St. Martin's Press, 1992), pp. 161–86.

Credibility Matters Little in a World at Peace

Honor can foster a sense of security in societies where challenges are common and no central authority exists to curtail them. In such circumstances, its pursuit is a rational response to a world of danger, an attempt to send understandable and logical messages in the search for safety. When no dire threats exist, however, it is irrational to be concerned with honor and can be pathological to act to maintain it. "If resources are abundant or are not subject to theft," noted psychologists Richard Nisbett and Dov Cohen, "then a reputation for toughness has little value."[71] In today's system, it is hard to identify either resources that are subject to theft or just who might be preparing to steal them.

The discussion in the previous chapter about the decline of war and the death of conquest should be sufficient to convince all but the most die-hard of skeptics that modern states no longer inhabit a world where their basic security is in constant danger. While anarchy is still a central feature of the international system in the literal sense that no central international authority exists to enforce order, this does not imply that those members face much risk. Twenty-first-century states simply do not live amid existential dangers, nor do they need to worry that neighbors will plunder their resources. In a world where conquest is dead and conventional attack rare, healthy credibility is not necessary to keep states safe.

Threats are particularly low – and assault unthinkable – for the unipole. Of all the members of the current system, the United States should be least concerned with maintaining its honor. However, as was the case with fear, the United States has been comparatively slow to realize that a concern for its credibility is no longer a rational motivation for behavior. No competing superpower stands ready to take advantage of perceived U.S. irresolution, no revisionist state probes the "new world order" for weaknesses. The credibility imperative should have waned in importance with the collapse of the Soviet Union, as neutrals were robbed of bandwagoning alternatives and allies relieved of the fear that a U.S. president would be unlikely to trade New York for Hamburg. Contagion or rapidly spreading disorder has not proven

---

[71] Nisbett and Cohen, *Culture of Honor*, p. xv.

much of a problem, despite the many times hawks have warned about the effects of lost U.S. credibility on one issue or another. The world has remained stubbornly stable.

The concern with credibility actually serves to decrease U.S. power by effectively yielding control over events to its junior partners. The assurance that the United States will act to bolster its reputation on a consistent basis allows smaller states to exert influence over the actions of their senior partner in ways they would otherwise be incapable of doing. The United States would be hard pressed, for example, to stay on the sidelines of an Israeli-Iranian war because of the perceived need to maintain the credibility of its commitments. "Even when allies are of considerable value to us, we still have the most leverage in nearly every case," notes Stephen Walt. "As soon as we start obsessing about our credibility, however, we hand that leverage back to our weaker partners and we constrain our ability to pursue meaningful diplomatic solutions to existing conflicts. Fetishizing credibility, in short, is one of the reasons American diplomacy has achieved relatively little since the end of the Cold War."[72] Defetishizing, or at least recognizing the pathological influence of, the credibility imperative would go a long way toward improving the performance of U.S. diplomacy in many areas.

The Illusion of Control: Credibility and Future Events

"Credibility is a nation's greatest asset in international affairs," John McCain believes. "It is the hardest to earn and the most difficult to maintain, but once possessed it makes it possible to compel changes in behavior."[73] Is this true? Can credibility compel changes in the behavior of others? Or, perhaps more important, does its possession make a country safe, or at least safer? Decades of research into these questions cast doubt on the assertion that honor serves the same purpose in international society that it does for domestic honor cultures. Greek goat herders with it might be safer than those without, but there is scant evidence that credibility keeps modern states any

---

[72] Walt, "Why are U.S. Leaders so Obsessed with Credibility?"
[73] John McCain, "No Time to Sleep," *Washington Post*, October 24, 2002, p. A35.

more secure. National credibility does not appear nearly as valuable as generations of policy makers have assumed it to be.

Research into the importance of credibility began in earnest as the war in Vietnam was coming to a close. Despite dire warnings from many of its leaders, the United States not only withdrew its forces from Southeast Asia but also cut back on its aid and watched North Vietnamese troops overrun Saigon in 1975. Since this "cut-and-run" and subsequent loss of an ally seemed to be unmitigated disasters for the credibility of the United States, presumably a string of foreign policy setbacks should have followed. If international actions are truly interdependent, as so many policy makers believe, then the 1970s would likely have seen evidence of allies beginning to question U.S. commitments, dominoes falling where the reputation of the United States maintained the status quo, and increased levels of Soviet activity in the third world. The conventional wisdom would suggest that the humiliating rooftop helicopter evacuation from the U.S. embassy in Saigon should have heralded a dark period for U.S. foreign policy.

However, no such string of catastrophes took place. Perhaps most obviously, there is no evidence that any allies of the United States were significantly demoralized or questioned the wisdom of their allegiance. If anything, many of Washington's closest allies seemed relieved when the war ended, since many of them doubted its importance in the first place and feared it distracted the United States from other, more pressing issues.[74] Newly opened archives in Western Europe and Canada, as well as those in the United States, make it clear that U.S. allies believed its credibility would suffer more from escalation than from retreat.[75] No state, not even in the nonaligned third world, changed its geopolitical orientation as a result of the defeat in Vietnam.

Neither did damage to U.S. credibility lead to the long-predicted spread of communism throughout the region, as even Kissinger today

---

[74] Robert H. Johnson, *Improbable Dangers: U.S. Conceptions of Threat in the Cold War and After* (New York: St. Martin's Press, 1994), pp. 160–61.

[75] Fredrik Logevall, "America Isolated: The Western Powers and the Escalation of the War," in Andreas W. Daum, Lloyd C. Gardner, and Wilfried Mausbach, eds., *America, the Vietnam War, and the World* (New York: Cambridge University Press, 2003), pp. 175–96.

acknowledges.[76] On the contrary, in the ten years that followed the fall of Saigon, the noncommunist nations of Southeast Asia enjoyed a period of unprecedented prosperity.[77] The only dominoes that fell were two of the very few countries even less relevant than Vietnam to the global balance of power: Cambodia and Laos, neither of which qualified as a major loss for the West, especially given the tragedies that were to follow. Nationalism proved to be an impervious bulwark against the spread of communism, irrespective of the U.S. reputation for resolve.

Most important, the Soviet Union apparently failed to become emboldened by the U.S. withdrawal, and did not appreciably increase its "adventurism" in the third world compared to the fifties and sixties, when U.S. credibility was high.[78] Although it is an article of faith among those under the spell of the credibility imperative that a string of foreign policy disasters followed Vietnam, such assertions are unconvincing, for at least two reasons. First, nothing that happened can be realistically considered disastrous. Michael Lind recites a list of countries that experienced Soviet-sponsored turmoil in the wake of Vietnam to support his claim that "by the mid-1970s, the U.S. position in the world had declined dramatically": Angola, Ethiopia, Mozambique, Southern Yemen, Benin, Congo-Brazzaville, Zaire, Guinea-Bissau, Cape Verde, and Madagascar.[79] Though the communists did not succeed in adding all of these places to their camp, the world would not have changed much if they had. If anything, such adventures helped bleed the USSR dry. The Cold War ended in victory within two decades of these supposed catastrophes.

Second, and more important, no one has made a convincing (or even weak) causal connection between Vietnam and these other "disasters." Lind asserts the events are connected, but offers no

[76] Henry Kissinger, *Ending the Vietnam War: A History of America's Involvement in and Extrication from the Vietnam War* (New York: Simon and Schuster, 2003), p. 561. See also Shiping Tang, "Reputation, the Cult of Reputation, and International Conflict," *Security Studies*, Vol. 14, No 1 (January–March 2005), pp. 34–62; and Slater, "The Domino Theory and International Politics," pp. 186–224.

[77] George C. Herring, *America's Longest War: The United States and Vietnam, 1950–1975*, 2nd ed. (New York: Knopf, 1979), p. 270.

[78] Ted Hopf, *Peripheral Visions: Deterrence Theory and American Foreign Policy in the Third World, 1965–1990* (Ann Arbor: University of Michigan Press, 1994).

[79] Michael Lind, *Vietnam: The Necessary War* (New York: Free Press, 1999), p. 25.

support. Some scholars have even attempted to make a connection between Vietnam and the Iranian revolution, asking the reader to accept the notion, without anything resembling evidence, that students in Tehran would not have overthrown the Shah if the United States had not abandoned the South Vietnamese government.[80] We are asked to accept such assertions on faith alone.

All the evidence that does exist actually points in the opposite direction, suggesting that international events are generally independent. Ted Hopf examined over 500 articles and 300 leadership speeches made by Soviet policy makers throughout the 1970s, and found that their public pronouncements did not demonstrate a belief that U.S. setbacks in the third world signaled a lack of resolution. "The most dominant inference Soviet leaders made after Vietnam," concluded Hopf, "was not about falling regional dominoes or bandwagoning American allies, but about the prospects of détente with the United States and Western Europe."[81] Soviet behavior did not change despite the perception of incompetence many Americans feared would inspire increased belligerence. In fact, Hopf found little evidence that perceptions of U.S. credibility affected Soviet decision makers in either direction. Their interventions in those geopolitically irrelevant states were independent events that would have probably occurred no matter what had happened in Southeast Asia. As it turns out, in other words, Vietnam was all but irrelevant to international politics, which is of course exactly what critics of the war had maintained all along.

The immediate post-Vietnam era actually contains a good deal of evidence to support a conclusion opposite to the presumptions of deterrence theorists. Robert Jervis has argued that states often act more aggressively in periods of low credibility following a reversal or in response to the perception of irresolution. "A statesman's willingness to resist," Jervis argued, "may be inversely related to how well he has

[80] Norman Podhoretz, *Why We Were in Vietnam* (New York: Simon and Schuster, 1982); Richard M. Nixon, *No More Vietnams* (New York: Arbor House, 1985); and Kissinger, *Ending the Vietnam War*, p. 561.

[81] Ted Hopf, "Soviet Inferences from their Victories in the Periphery: Visions of Resistance or Cumulating Gains?" in Robert Jervis and Jack Snyder, eds., *Dominoes and Bandwagons: Strategic Beliefs and Great Power Competition in the Eurasian Rimland* (New York: Oxford University Press, 1991), p. 167.

done in the recent past."[82] The Soviets might well have expected
the United States to act like a wounded animal after Vietnam, one
even more willing to defend its interests than before the withdrawal.
Indeed U.S. policy makers, believing that the national credibility had
been damaged, seemed eager to reverse such perceptions abroad.

The seizure of the merchant vessel *Mayaguez* by the Khmer Rouge
in May 1975, immediately after the fall of Saigon, provided the
opportunity to do so. The response of the Ford administration was
rapid, decisive, and belligerent; as the president said at the time, "I
have to show some strength in order to help us ... with our credibility
in the world." Kissinger had told reporters off the record that "the
United States must carry out some act somewhere in the world which
shows its determination to continue to be a world power." He wanted
to react rapidly, arguing that "indecision and weakness can lead to
demoralized friends and emboldened adversaries." Even though
a military response might have put the captured crew at risk, their
lives were a "secondary consideration," argued Kissinger, since the
"real issue was international credibility and not the safe return of the
crew."[83] At National Security Council meetings discussing the matter he had argued that "negotiation, even if we get the ship back ...
is not to our advantage" and advocated seizing the island to which
the *Mayaguez* had been towed and attacking the Cambodian mainland. "I think a violent response is in order," Vice President Nelson
Rockefeller agreed. "The world should know that we will act and that
we will act quickly."[84]

As a result of this reasoning, a rescue mission was rapidly put
together and an attack on the island followed, during which forty-
one servicemen lost their lives.[85] The mission recaptured the ship but

[82] Robert Jervis, "Domino Beliefs and Strategic Behavior," in Robert Jervis and Jack
Snyder, eds., *Dominoes and Bandwagons: Strategic Beliefs and Great Power Competition in
the Eurasian Rimland* (New York: Oxford University Press, 1991), p. 37.

[83] Christopher Jon Lamb, *Belief Systems and Decision Making in the Mayaguez Crisis*
(Gainesville: University of Florida Press, 1989), pp. 68, 72, 73, 81, and 149.

[84] Trevor B. McCrisken, *American Exceptionalism and the Legacy of Vietnam: US Foreign
Policy Since 1974* (New York: Palgrave MacMillan, 2003), pp. 49–51.

[85] This number includes twenty-three killed in a helicopter crash off the island's coast
and eighteen servicemen killed by hostile fire. Lamb, *Belief Systems and Decision
Making in the Mayaguez Crisis*, p. 29.

none of the crew, who were elsewhere, already in the process of being released unharmed. That the whole incident was a pointless tragedy seems to have been lost on many hawks: in 1978, National Security Advisor Zbigniew Brzezinski commented privately to Senate staff members that the Carter administration needed a *Mayaguez* incident so the president could "get tough with the communists."[86]

Perhaps needless to say, predictions of doom that usually accompany apparent losses of U.S. credibility are rarely borne out by events. When the Reagan administration pulled U.S. troops out of Lebanon following the 1983 barracks bombing, for example, hawks were predictably apoplectic. "If we are driven out of Lebanon, radical and rejectionist elements will have scored a major victory," Secretary of State George Shultz said in briefings on Capitol Hill. "The message will be sent that relying on the Soviet Union pays off and that relying on the United States is a fatal mistake."[87] Michael Ledeen was more explicit: "Our defeat in Lebanon will encourage our enemies, in the Middle East and elsewhere," he wrote. "In all probability, we shall pay a disproportionate price for our Lebanese failure," from the Middle East to Central America, where Soviet-sponsored guerrillas would be disastrously encouraged. As always, U.S. allies and potential friends would be powerfully disillusioned, including the Egyptians, whom Ledeen felt would "increasingly distance themselves from the Camp David agreement."[88] Fortunately for the United States, Soviet influence in the Middle East did not increase, their guerrilla allies did not change their behavior, and the Egyptians did not abandon their treaty commitments. The fears generated by lost honor proved, as usual, baseless.

Just as low credibility is rarely harmful, high credibility rarely helps. Scholars have struggled to identify cases where apparently healthy credibility aided the United States in achieving its goals during the Cold War. The short-term aftermath of the Cuban Missile Crisis, for example,

[86] Quoted in Walter LaFeber, "The Last War, the Next War, and the New Revisionists," *Democracy*, Vol. 1, No. 1 (January 1981), p. 96.

[87] Lou Cannon and Don Oberdorfer, "Standing Fast: 'Vital Interests' of U.S. at Stake," *Washington Post*, October 25, 1983, p. A1.

[88] Michael Ledeen, "The Lessons of Lebanon," *Commentary*, Vol. 77, No. 5 (May 1984), pp. 21–22.

included neither a string of Soviet reversals nor a display of bandwagoning with the West throughout the third world.[89] In fact, the perceived reversal seemed to harden Soviet resolve. As the crisis drew to a close, Soviet diplomat Vasily Kuznetsov angrily told his counterpart, "you Americans will never be able to do this to us again."[90] Kissinger commented in his memoirs that "the Soviet Union thereupon launched itself on a determined, systematic, and long-term program of expanding *all* categories of its military power.... The 1962 Cuban crises was thus an historic turning point – but not for the reason some Americans complacently supposed."[91] The reassertion of the credibility of the United States, done at the brink of nuclear war, had few long-lasting benefits. The Soviets seemed to have learned the wrong lesson.

There is actually scant evidence that target states ever learn the *right* lessons. Cold War history contains little reason to believe the superpowers' credibility had very much effect on their ability to influence others. Since Vietnam, a series of major scholarly studies have cast serious doubt on the fundamental assumption of interdependence across foreign policy actions. Jonathan Mercer argued that while policy makers may feel their decisions send messages about their basic *dispositions* to others, most of the evidence from social psychology suggests otherwise. Groups tend to interpret the actions of their rivals as *situational*, dependent on the constraints of place and time, and are therefore unlikely to form lasting impressions of irresolution from single events. Mercer pointed out that the interdependence assumption needed to be accepted on faith, since on those rare occasions when it was put to a coherent test, it almost invariably failed.[92]

Other studies on the utility of credibility have tended to yield similar results. A reputation for belligerence has not been shown to be of much value in deterring challenges in large N analyses, or in-depth case studies, whether in modern or ancient times.[93] Even seemingly

---

[89] Gaddis, *Strategies of Containment*, pp. 267–68.

[90] Michael R. Beschloss, *The Crisis Years: Kennedy and Khrushchev, 1960–1963* (New York: Edward Burlingame Books, 1991), p. 563; and Charles E. Bohlen, *Witness to History 1929–1969* (New York: W. W. Norton and Co., 1973), pp. 495–96.

[91] Henry Kissinger, *White House Years* (Boston: Little, Brown & Co., 1979), p. 197 (emphasis in original).

[92] Mercer, *Reputation and International Politics*, pp. 28–42.

[93] Alexander L. George and Richard Smoke, *Deterrence in American Foreign Policy: Theory and Practice* (New York: Columbia University Press, 1974); Snyder and Diesing,

easy cases for the credibility imperative have failed: for instance, Daryl Press found no evidence from the interwar years that either German or American leaders made predictions about the likely actions of the other based on behavior in previous crises.[94] Soviet archives have not revealed instances when the Kremlin acted primarily because it doubted U.S. resolve, Vietnam, Lebanon, and the Shah notwithstanding.[95] Although at times credibility perhaps seemed helpful in limited ways – such as in multiple interactions with the same leader, or in alliance formation – there is no reason to believe that third parties learn much from the actions of a state in other matters.[96]

Overall, the overwhelming majority of the evidence suggests international actions are much more independent than early deterrence theorists believed. This is about as close as security studies scholarship ever gets to a settled question: *credibility gained in one instance does not help states in future endeavors,* and neither does damaged credibility cause much harm. There is little reason for leaders to be concerned

Conflict among Nations; Richard Ned Lebow, *Between Peace and War* (Baltimore, MD: Johns Hopkins University Press, 1981); Paul Huth and Bruce Russett, "What Makes Deterrence Work? Cases from 1900 to 1980," *World Politics*, Vol. 36, No. 4 (July 1984), pp. 496–526; Janice Stein, "Deterrence and Learning in an Enduring Rivalry," *Security Studies*, Vol. 6, No. 1 (Autumn 1996), pp. 104–52; Vesna Danilovic, "The Sources of Threat Credibility in Extended Deterrence," *Journal of Conflict Resolution*, Vol. 45, No. 3 (June 2001), pp. 341–69; and Richard Ned Lebow, "Thucydides and Deterrence," *Security Studies*, Vol. 16, No. 2 (April–June 2007), pp. 163–88.

[94] Daryl G. Press, *Calculating Credibility: How Leaders Assess Military Threats* (Ithaca, NY: Cornell University Press, 2006).

[95] Hopf, *Peripheral Visions*; and Richard Ned Lebow and Janice Stein, *We All Lost the Cold War* (Princeton, NJ: Princeton University Press, 1994).

[96] Paul Huth, "Extended Deterrence and the Outbreak of War," *American Political Science Review*, Vol. 82, No. 2 (June 1988), pp. 423–43; Paul Huth, Christopher Gelpi, and D. Scott Bennett, "The Escalation of Great Power Militarized Disputes: Testing Rational Deterrence Theory and Structural Realism," *American Political Science Review*, Vol. 87, No. 3 (September 1993), pp. 609–23; and James D. Fearon, "Signaling versus the Balance of Power and Interests: An Empirical Test of a Crisis Bargaining Model," *Journal of Conflict Resolution*, Vol. 38, No. 2 (June 1994), pp. 236–69. Mark J. C. Crescenzi and others have found some effect of reputation on dyadic interaction; see his "Reputation and Interstate Conflict," *American Journal of Political Science*, Vol. 51, No. 2 (April 2007), pp. 382–96; and Mark J. C. Crescenzi, Jacob D. Kathman, Katja B. Kleinberg, and Reed M. Wood, "Reliability, Reputation, and Alliance Formation," *International Studies Quarterly*, Vol. 56, No. 2 (June 2012), pp. 259–74. For evidence that reputation may affect alliance formation, see Gregory D. Miller, *The Shadow of the Past: Reputation and Military Alliances before the First World War* (Ithaca, NY: Cornell University Press, 2012).

about their reputations, and it is certainly never wise, especially in today's world, to fight for honor.

A belief that it is worthwhile to bear enormous costs can only be considered rational when the benefits are clear and substantial. History does not contain anywhere near the kind of evidence necessary to make the credibility imperative seem reasonable. Throughout the Cold War era, it was a deeply pathological influence on policy making, and there is little to suggest that this judgment should be altered since its end.

Overall, since honor is a socially determined good, the community is the ultimate arbiter of whether any individual actor possesses it. The status of its credibility is therefore ultimately beyond the control of the United States. Neither people nor states own their reputation, which can be affected by actions to some extent but ultimately exist primarily in the minds of others. "Credibility exists," noted the recent U.S. politician most obsessed with its maintenance, "only in the eye of the beholder."[97] Target adversaries and allies will ultimately form their own perceptions, ones affected by their needs and goals as much as our actions. Even if states were to take what appeared to be the logical actions to protect their credibility, it is possible (and perhaps likely) that others will not receive the messages in the way they were intended.[98] Sending messages for their consideration in future crises, therefore, is all but futile.

Credibility and Nonstate Actors

At first glance, Islamic fundamentalists might appear to pose a difficult challenge to the credibility imperative's many academic skeptics. Osama bin Laden and his allies apparently considered the United States a feckless, cowardly "paper tiger," a perception that may have emboldened them to strike. When attacked, effete Americans sue; they send lawyers, not soldiers. September 11 may even have been

---

[97] McCain, "No Time to Sleep," p. A35. See also Lebow, *A Cultural Theory of International Relations*, p. 64.

[98] For a discussion of the many reasons this is the case, see Robert Jervis, *Perception and Misperception in International Politics* (Princeton, NJ: Princeton University Press, 1976). See also his "Deterrence and Perception," *International Security*, Vol. 7, No. 3 (Winter 1982–83), pp. 3–20.

prevented, so this logic goes, if Washington had responded to previous Al Qaeda attacks with a more determined show of force. Perhaps the "war on terror" will prove the conventional wisdom of the practitioner regarding the lessons of credibility. Did a lack of American "credibility" lead Al Qaeda to believe that it could strike the United States with impunity? Would a reputation for resolve keep a country safer during the war on terror?

There are actually several good reasons to believe that credibility is, if anything, even less helpful for states combating terrorists. First of all, it is not clear that the United States can control the perceptions of nonstate actors in the current era any more easily than it could those of states during the Cold War.[99] It is quite a stretch to believe that if U.S. troops had not been pulled out of Lebanon or Somalia, Al Qaeda would have acted any differently throughout the 1990s. For the policy maker's conventional wisdom about the importance of credibility to be correct, Al Qaeda's behavior would have to have been different had the United States remained engaged in Somalia until something resembling victory had been achieved. If the terrorists would have attacked either way – and it is certainly plausible to think they would have – then concerns for reputation are still irrelevant, and it remains unwise for policy makers to look beyond the current crisis when making decisions. There is little reason to believe that Al Qaeda learned anything of importance from the U.S. withdrawal from Somalia, or that it would have proven insufficiently emboldened without it.

Second, Al Qaeda's perceptions are unlikely to be affected by Washington's attempts to shape them. The strategy of a weak actor in extreme asymmetry must be based on the premise that since it may not be able to employ tangible assets to win the war, intangible, moral elements will prove decisive. No matter what the behavior of the strong actually is, the weak are likely to accuse it of being irresolute. Thus, Al Qaeda is pursuing a propaganda strategy nearly immune to rational influence. Since they lacked the power to force a retreat, the *mujahadeen* in Afghanistan needed to preach that the Soviet Union would prove morally inferior to convince its fighters that resistance was not utterly pointless. Likewise, bin Laden had to paint the United

---

[99] Vaughn P. Shannon and Michael Dennis, "Militant Islam and the Futile Fight for Reputation," *Security Studies*, Vol. 16, No. 2 (April–June 2007), pp. 287–317.

States as a paper tiger or no one would have rallied to his cause. Since *jihadi* groups have no hope of success without a certain degree of superpower irresolution, it is unlikely that any amount of credibility will cause these groups to abandon that belief (or hope). Once again, Washington will likely not be able to control its reputation in the eyes of others. The future actions of these groups will likely remain unaffected by their perceptions of U.S. credibility.

Finally, it is quite possible that bin Laden's pronouncements of American irresolution are less explanations for his behavior than tools for attracting new recruits. Might resolute, credible superpowers then be able to prevent *jihadi* groups from recruiting new generations of terrorists? Probably not, since Al Qaeda and its allies have shown no particular interest in the accuracy of their statements. Their preposterous exaggeration of both their involvement in and the scale of the battles in Somalia, for example, suggests the event was much more significant for their propaganda that it was for the formulation of their perceptions of U.S. resolve. Although there is little evidence that the battle in Mogadishu was fought by anyone other than Somalis, to listen to bin Laden one would think *mujahadeen* from all over the region had converged to oust the imperialists. He repeatedly claimed three hundred thousand Americans turned tail and fled, which is ten times more than were ever in the country and almost one hundred times the actual number that left after the battle.[100]

No matter what the United States did in Somalia, in other words, Al Qaeda would likely have continued its tangible and intangible assaults, which even in extreme exaggeration would have found eager ears among the disaffected, angry masses. Many regions of the world have populations quite sympathetic to the argument that despite its apparent strength, the United States is actually a weak, feminized, immoral, corrupt paper tiger. The Middle East, where conspiracy theories often find wide audiences, is seemingly fertile ground for twisted interpretations of U.S. irresolution. In other words, U.S. actions are not likely to have direct bearing on the interpretation of its credibility in the region, or on the outcome of the war on terror, for better or for worse.

[100] Usama bin Laden, "American Soldiers are Paper Tigers," *Middle East Quarterly*, Vol. 5, No. 4 (December 1998), pp. 73–79.

Israel's experience is instructive in this regard, since no one doubts the credibility of its response to provocation. If anything, the Israelis tend to err on the side of overreaction, of excessive use of retaliatory force, rather than run the risk that a display of irresolution might embolden their enemies. Yet despite the fact that the various nonstate groups must know Israel will not passively absorb their blows, attacks from nonstate actors continue. Israel is no safer because of its resolve to maintain a credible threat of retaliation against terror.

The United States is not likely able to affect the actions of today's nonstate actors through displays of resolution. Fortunately, it also has no reason to fear negative reactions of regional allies to diminished U.S. credibility. Even if some Middle Eastern states began to doubt U.S. credibility, it is hard to believe fundamentalism would sweep across the region somehow, or that our allies would become so disheartened that they would rethink their allegiance to the United States. During the Cold War, theoretically states had the option to flip sides and rely on the Soviets if they began to doubt the credibility of the United States (although none ever did so). Today it is impossible to imagine that any state would cast its lot with Al Qaeda. If anything, the perception that they could not rely on the United States would likely make other states intensify their effort to fight their local, anti-regime fundamentalists. Even if states of the Persian Gulf do begin to doubt the credibility of U.S. commitments, Islamic fundamentalist victories are not likely. And while it is obviously preposterous to suggest that the United States would soon have to fight them "nearer home," or that the continued existence of U.S. democracy is at stake, such statements will continue, as predictable products of the credibility imperative.

Although our national obsession with honor and credibility imperative lingered on to address the threats of the post–Cold War era, it is not any more useful as a guide for U.S. foreign policy. Today its academic defenders are small in number.[101] In the policy world, however, belief in the power of credibility lives on undiminished, and doubters are clearly in the minority. Shiping Tang has called the continued existence of the credibility imperative in spite of the overwhelming

---

[101] Defenders include Lind, *Vietnam: The Necessary War*; Dale C. Copeland, "Do Reputations Matter?" *Security Studies*, Vol. 7, No. 1 (Autumn 1997), pp. 33–71; and John Orme, "Deterrence Failures: A Second Look," *International Security*, Vol. 11, No. 4 (Spring 1987), pp. 97–124.

evidence to the contrary a sign of almost "cultish" behavior among policy makers.[102] The persistence of this cult should come as no surprise, since foreign policy beliefs are often impervious to change. Even pathological beliefs, those that lead to disaster and ruin, are passed down through the generations as received wisdom, as part of the initiation to top leadership positions. It would be helpful if at least occasionally those beliefs were subjected to periodic, rational reexamination.

That reexamination would certainly reveal that the almost overwhelming tendency to try to send messages through national actions increases the odds of policy mishaps and outright folly, for at least two reasons. First, and most basically, an eye toward the future prevents complete focus on the present. During a crisis, the national interest cannot be correctly ascertained unless policy makers de-link present concerns from future expectations. Second, as unsettling as it may be, the future is not subject to our control. There is much that can and will occur between the current crisis and the next, and the international environment will change in quite unpredictable ways. Target actors – whether superpowers or terrorist groups or vaguely defined "threats" – are not likely to believe that the actions a state takes today provide meaningful clues about its future choices. In other words, as Mercer makes clear, *they* believe that *our* actions are independent, and little can be done to change that.[103] Generally speaking, therefore, policy makers are wise to fight the natural temptation to look beyond the current crisis when making decisions.

PATHOGENESIS

Why does the credibility imperative – the remnants of honor – linger in the United States? There are reasons why this country has not modified this pathological foreign policy belief, ones that emanate from each of Waltz's levels of analysis. The following sections proceed from least important causes to most.

---

[102] Tang, "Reputation, the Cult of Reputation, and International Conflict," pp. 34–62.

[103] The argument is made most clearly by Jonathan Mercer in *Reputation and International Politics*.

Individual Level

The suggestion that credibility is in fact overvalued in international politics is somewhat counterintuitive, and contradictory to various events individuals experience on a daily basis. People certainly develop reputations in their daily lives that influence the way others treat them. Parents understand that they must carry through on their threats and promises if they want their children to take their future instructions seriously, and we all have friends whose repeated failures to deliver on past promises make us skeptical of their future assurances. However, international relations differ drastically from interpersonal. On this point Daryl Press is worth quoting at some length.

Children use past actions when they evaluate their parents' credibility to punish them, and perhaps we all use past actions to assess whether a friend will show up at the movies. But there is no logical basis to generalize from these mundane situations to the most critical decisions made by national leaders during crises. In fact it would be odd – even irrational – if people relied on the same mental shortcuts that they use to make unimportant split-second decisions of daily life when they confront the most important decisions of their lives – decisions on which their country's survival depends.[104]

The credibility imperative has a powerful intuitive logic behind it, therefore, one based on lifetimes of interpersonal experience that places significant impediments in front of those who would challenge the wisdom of the policy maker's obsession with reputation. It has a basis in everyday life, even if the extrapolation to the system cannot be done without introducing error.

Furthermore, surely it is comforting for actors to believe that they can control future events. The world is a complex and unpredictable place, especially for leaders burdened with the responsibility of charting a course for entire nations. Any actions that can make future crises easier to predict, avoid, and/or manage have tremendous appeal. The credibility imperative acts as a heuristic device, in other words, that helps bring the perception of order and even a measure of stability to world events. It aids in decision making and serves a significant cognitive purpose, since it is psychologically important for actors to believe

[104] Press goes on to argue that national capabilities and interests, not past behavior, provide the foundation for the formation of perceptions. Press, *Calculating Credibility*, p. 23.

that they can affect the future, to have some measure of control over their own lives. By the time that perception proves illusory, after all, one will likely have forgotten the pressures of the current crisis. So even if the imperative actually does not serve the needs of the future, it still can play the understandable role of relieving the anxiety of the present.

State Level

Waltz's second image might contain better explanations as to why the imperative persists. A number of factors unique to, or at least more influential in, the United States have contributed to its development. For example, geography surely plays a role. The great distance over which the United States must project its power has fostered a suspicion on the part of its policy makers that their threats and promises are inherently less believable than those of more proximate states.[105] They have at times carried the perception that they face a greater challenge in forging a reputation, and have as a consequence been quicker to act in the attempt to do so. The insecurity of the faraway power has led to occasional overcompensation by its leaders.

The actors within the U.S. marketplace of ideas also matter. Appeals to credibility – or even directly to honor, anachronistic or not – are much more common among some analysts and some world views than others. As is the case with the other beliefs under consideration in this volume, no group worries more about credibility, and therefore thinks more pathologically, than neoconservatives. Although many people across the foreign policy spectrum believe that honor is worth fighting for, neocons seem particularly passionate about its importance.

The association between neoconservatism and honor should come as no surprise, since the strength of the credibility imperative in any analyst is directly related to his or her beliefs about the existence of enemies. Low credibility is only dangerous if rivals exist who are prepared to press their perceived advantages. As discussed in the previous chapter, neoconservatives are among the most worried about the various dangers of the post–Cold War world, from Iraq to terrorists to chaos itself, and are therefore also among the most obsessed with

[105] George and Smoke, *Deterrence in American Foreign Policy.*

the national honor. The absence of a Soviet threat did not materially change the security environment, argued Frederick Kagan, "because there is another, perennial threat which has taken its place. That threat is global disorder."[106] His brother Robert warned that Russia's incursion into Georgia was evidence that "autocracy is making a comeback" and is on a collision course with the West (though it deserves mention that to this point there have been no follow-up events).[107] "Credibility matters deeply in a world of enemies," wrote Charles Krauthammer, whose world is always inhabited by many, both real and imaginary.[108] To neoconservatives, since danger always exists, even if it cannot always be clearly identified, honor and credibility are perpetually important. Three further characteristics of their world view contribute to its continuing obsession with reputation.

First of all, a central tenet of neoconservatism is that the establishment of a liberal world order ought to be a central goal of U.S. foreign policy.[109] Most foreign policy analysts would obviously welcome such a development, even if realists tend to doubt that it is a possibility. Neoconservatives and liberal internationalists differ primarily over the means that should be used to bring about that desirable end, with the latter giving a higher priority to international law and institutions than U.S. military power. But to the neoconservatives, great power gives the United States a unique opportunity – indeed a responsibility – to make the world a better place. "America has the capacity to contain or destroy many of the world's monsters," argued William Kristol and Robert Kagan. "A policy of sitting atop a hill and leading by example becomes in practice a policy of cowardice and dishonor."[110] U.S. credibility is therefore a central component in bringing about a stable,

---

[106] Frederick W. Kagan, "Back to the Future: NSC-68 and the Right Course for America Today," *SAIS Review*, Vol. 19, No. 1 (Winter–Spring 1999), p. 63.

[107] Robert Kagan, *The Return of History and the End of Dreams* (New York: Knopf, 2008), p. 68.

[108] Charles Krauthammer, "No Turning Back Now," *Washington Post*, January 24, 2003, p. A27.

[109] For some good explanations, see William Kristol and Robert Kagan, "Toward a Neo-Reaganite Foreign Policy," *Foreign Affairs*, Vol. 75, No. 4 (July/August 1996), pp. 18–33; Charles Krauthammer, "In Defense of Democratic Realism," *The National Interest*, No. 77 (Fall 2004), pp. 15–25; and Mackubin Thomas Owens, "The Bush Doctrine: The Foreign Policy of Republican Empire," *Orbis*, Vol. 53, No. 1 (Winter 2009), pp. 23–40.

[110] Kristol and Kagan, "Toward a Neo-Reaganite Foreign Policy," p. 31.

free, peaceful world, even if the United States must occasionally go to war against the world's monsters to make it so. Chaos offends our ideals and threatens our interests. "Were we to retreat from the position that history has bequeathed to us," warned Kaplan and Kristol, "the turmoil that would soon follow would surely reach our shores."[111]

Neoconservatives tend to see the mere existence of every autocratic ruler as a challenge to the U.S. reputation for resolve which imperils the national mission. Any failure to respond to injustice becomes a threat to the unified freedom edifice they are trying to construct. Even the most minor of setbacks calls for rapid, belligerent response, lest enemies be encouraged and allies disheartened. When the United States made a muddled apology to the Chinese to gain the release of its crew after the EP-3C incident in 2001, for example, Kagan and Kristol were apoplectic. "We can kid ourselves all we want, but we have suffered a blow to our prestige and reputation, a loss that will reverberate throughout the world if we do not begin immediately to repair the damage ... our reliability as defender of the peace and protector of friends and allies, especially in East Asia, has been thrown into doubt."[112] A liberal world order cannot be constructed by a dishonored or discredited United States.

Second, although many members of the U.S. foreign policy establishment have internalized the lessons of Munich, neoconservatives seem particularly focused on appeasement. Indeed it is hard to identify a lesson of history so dramatically mis-learned by any group; rare is the neoconservative work that fails to make mention of Munich in some form.[113] There is probably little need

[111] Lawrence F. Kaplan and William Kristol, *The War over Iraq: Saddam's Tyranny and America's Mission* (San Francisco, CA: Encounter Books, 2003), p. 120.

[112] Robert Kagan and William Kristol, "We Lost," *Washington Post*, April 13, 2001, p. A23.

[113] For exemplary explanations of its dangers, see Paul Wolfowitz, "Statesmanship in the New Century," in Robert Kagan and William Kristol, eds., *Present Dangers: Crisis and Opportunity in American Foreign and Defense Policy* (San Francisco, CA: Encounter Books, 2000), pp. 307–36; Norman Podhoretz, *The Present Danger* (New York: Simon and Schuster, 1980); Robert Kagan, *Of Paradise and Power: America and Europe in the New World Order* (New York: Knopf, 2003); William Kristol, "The Axis of Appeasement," *Weekly Standard*, Vol. 7, No. 47 (August 26, 2002) and "A World Without Nukes – Just Like 1939," *Washington Post*, April 7, 2009, p. A23; and Charles Krauthammer, "The Wages of Appeasement," *Washington Post*, December 15, 2011.

to repeat the well-known arguments about the effects of that conference on two generations of American policy makers.[114] If the overwhelming evidence that has already emerged has been insufficient to expunge the belief in the value of its "lessons," one more lengthy discussion would certainly be in vain. Few single events have had a more deleterious impact on international politics, or have created such incorrect impressions about how states behave. Munich has become the enemy of compromise, the emotional ammunition hawks trudge out every time the nation considers dishonorable accommodation rather than steadfast confrontation of various international evils. That it is incorrectly remembered matters little; today appeasement is a powerful, loaded term, one that warns against weakness and negotiation. The notion that the allies emboldened Hitler through concession and brought the Second World War on themselves is a great example of the most dangerous kind of belief that persists among the faithful, one immune to influence from the material world. It is so deeply held that it no longer is subject to examination, having long passed from historical event to myth. "The rest of the world," warned Kaplan and Kristol during the lead-up to Iraq, in proud defiance of logic and evidence, "plays by Munich rules."[115]

Finally, the current neoconservative patriarch, Norman Podhoretz, helped explain some of his movement's obsession with honor and credibility by offering his view of why appeasement occurred. British leaders waivered at Munich, he wrote, because they were the product of a culture weakened by, shall we say, insufficient machismo. "Homosexual feeling," he wrote, "accounted for a good deal of the pacifism that rose out of the trenches and into the upper reaches

---

[114] J. L. Richardson, "New Perspectives on Appeasement: Some Implications for International Relations," *World Politics*, Vol. 40, No. 3 (April 1988), pp. 289–316; Stephen R. Rock, *Appeasement in International Politics* (Lexington: University Press of Kentucky, 2000); Yuen Foong Khong, *Analogies at War: Korea, Munich, Dien Bien Phu and the Vietnam Decisions of 1965* (Princeton, NJ: Princeton University Press, 1992); Jeffrey Record, *Making War, Thinking History: Munich, Vietnam, and Presidential Uses of Force from Korea to Kosovo* (Annapolis, MD: Naval Institute Press, 2002) and *The Specter of Munich: Reconsidering the Lessons of Appeasing Hitler* (Washington, DC: Potomac Books, 2007); and Paul Kennedy, "A Time to Appease," *The National Interest*, No. 108 (July/August 2010), pp. 7–17.

[115] Kaplan and Kristol, *The War Over Iraq*, p. 117.

of the culture after the [first world] war was over."[116] A generation
affected by poets and pacifists could not be expected to demonstrate
honor at the negotiating table or on the battlefield. British credibility was therefore fatally undermined by "dandies and aesthetes," he
warned, and it can happen here too if Washington is not careful,
because "homosexual apologetics" are alive and well in the United
States. Appeasement is not just dishonorable, it is unmasculine, effete,
and gay, quite the opposite of everything the insecure neoconservative movement needs its country to be.

Honor, hypermasculinity, and Munich are linked in many ways.
Indeed the desire to respond to provocation is surely related to the
psychological need on the part of many males to assert their insecure
masculinity, to demonstrate that they are the kind of macho man
others can admire. Teddy Roosevelt, a hero for so many of today's
neocons, spoke constantly of manliness and virility and feared above
all that his nation was becoming effete.[117] "Psychologically I think it
is easier to get people emotionally involved in things that are expressive of macho," observed Paul Nitze during one of the periodic missile defense debates. "As far as macho is concerned, it is the offense
that is most attractive; the defense suggests somebody that is sly,
deceptive, dishonest."[118] In past ages, real men conquered and colo-
nized; today, at the very least, they must be prepared to fight, never
to appease.

The Munich analogy is trudged out with depressing regularity to
warn of the dangers of irresolution, compromise, and effeminacy. No
one employs it more than the neoconservative, who apparently labors
under the impression that Americans must be periodically reminded
of Munich's lessons to remain virile. As always, to the extent that
neoconservatism influences policy, it can be expected to tilt toward
the irrational, pathological, and counterproductive, at least in part
because of its insecure vision of American masculinity.

[116] Norman Podhoretz, "A Culture of Appeasement," *Harper's*, Vol. 255, No. 1529
(October 1977), pp. 25–32. The quotations are taken from pp. 30–31.

[117] Roosevelt had to overcome the stigma of being sickly in his youth and upper-
class, college-educated, and bespectacled as an adult. See Richard Hofstadter,
Anti-intellectualism in American Life (New York: Knopf, 1970), p. 192.

[118] Nicholas Thompson, *The Hawk and the Dove: Paul Nitze, George Kennan, and the History
of the Cold War* (New York: Henry Holt and Co., 2009), p. 225.

System Level

The credibility imperative survived the transition from bipolarity to unipolarity unscathed. It was originally a systemic phenomenon, a reaction to the anarchic honor culture that was international society. Though the attributes that helped make that society into such a culture are no longer present, the concern for credibility remains imbedded in policy making. The emphasis the United States places on reinforcing its reputation for resolve in the face of even the most minimal challenge lingers because of the legacy of bipolarity and the perceived demands of unipolarity. Today's leaders came of age when it seemed logical to worry about the credibility of the nation's myriad global commitments. Cold War policy makers, many of whom also mis-learned lessons about the importance of credibility from Munich, believed that their adversary was waiting for the slightest sign of U.S. irresolution for inspiration to press their advantage. The Cold War contributed to the construction of the credibility imperative for at least three reasons.

First, bipolarity leads naturally to zero-sum thinking. Though the Cold Warriors never fought each other directly, they waged a constant battle of ideas. Competing systems of socioeconomic organization struggled against each other in the minds of the masses as much as proxy armies did on the field. Intangible, psychological factors took on increased importance for security and stability, with success and failure often measured by perception as much as reality. U.S. credibility became essentially a measure of the viability of the system Washington espoused and promoted. When credibility was low, policy makers worried, others might get the impression that history was on the side of the Soviets and communism. Walt Rostow was hardly alone when he famously argued that because it was vitally important to convince the third world to follow a capitalist model of development reverses in the periphery could be strategic disasters.[119] On the Cold War scorecard, credibility points were won each time the United States kept its commitments and lost whenever it did not.

Second, the dominant weaponry of the Cold War also enhanced the imperative to remain credible. The nuclear revolution changed

[119] Gaddis, *Strategies of Containment*, pp. 208–209.

not only how states acted, but also how policy makers thought about international relations.[120] Since much about their use seemed irrational – after all, only madmen would contemplate nuclear war – security professionals were forced to deal with basic questions about sanity and insanity. The psychology of the opponent in particular became a much more important point of emphasis. As Robert McMahon has argued, "the very essence of security in the nuclear era has been based on conjectures about the cognitive process of others."[121] The wise policy maker took all possible steps to influence those cognitive processes in productive ways. Maintaining credible commitments was perhaps the most obvious way to do so.

Third, academic orthodoxy supported the belief in the importance of credibility. Unlike the case today, Cold War policy makers often had backgrounds in academic theories of international relations. Indeed no policy maker provides a better example of the interdependence belief in practice than Henry Kissinger, a former academic who often seemed to interpret all international events through zero-sum, interdependent lenses. Kissinger was but the most visible of a brand of foreign policy generalist who, along with such men as Acheson, Dulles, McNamara, Nitze, Nixon, and Brzezinski, tended to fit every event, no matter how local or peripheral it might have seemed, into a tightly knit framework of global competition. When India intervened in the Pakistani civil war in 1971, for example, Kissinger saw the hidden hand of the Soviets, which underlined the importance of maintaining the credibility of the U.S. threats. "Had we acquiesced in such a power play," he wrote, "we would have sent a wrong signal to Moscow and unnerved all our allies, China, and the forces for restraint in other volatile areas of the world. This was, indeed, why the Soviets had made the Indian assault on Pakistan possible in the first place."[122] When the Soviets threatened to construct a submarine base in Cienfuego in 1970, Kissinger thought that "the Kremlin had perhaps been emboldened when we reacted to the dispatch of combat

---

[120] See Michael Mandelbaum, *The Nuclear Revolution: International Politics before and after Hiroshima* (Cambridge: Cambridge University Press, 1981).

[121] McMahon, "Credibility and World Power," p. 469. See also Robert Jervis, Richard Ned Lebow, and Janice Stein, eds., *Psychology and Deterrence* (Baltimore, MD: Johns Hopkins University Press, 1985).

[122] Kissinger, *White House Years*, pp. 913–14.

troops to the Middle East by pressing Israel for a cease-fire."[123] The
Soviet invasion of Afghanistan was only possible, thought Zbigniew
Brzezinski, Kissinger's successor and a former academic himself,
because the United States had lost credibility by not responding more
forcefully to communist adventurism in the Horn of Africa, which in
turn was a result of the abandonment of Saigon.[124] Though the belief
in the importance of credibility began at least in part in the academy,
the current skepticism of scholars has not had similar real-world trac-
tion, perhaps as a result of the divide between the communities.[125]

Credibility and Great Power

Unipolarity has provided equally fertile ground for the credibility
imperative in the United States, in part because the strongest state
in any system tends to place a high value on maintenance of the status quo. It is perhaps natural for such states to be concerned with
challenges to international order that can be imagined as first steps
toward fundamental alteration of the system they have worked hard
to construct. As the power of the United States grew over the years,
perhaps it was quite natural for its leaders to become more concerned
with intangible assets. If credibility is only a concern for those participating in geopolitics on a global scale, today's United States ought to
be the state concerned the most.

Earlier hegemons showed similar concerns. Roman leaders certainly felt that the reputation of their legions was one of the key factors
maintaining order in the empire.[126] They were quite willing to spend
years and great amounts of resources on seemingly irrelevant tasks
primarily to send messages about their resolve. The siege of Masada,
for instance, does not make sense from a material perspective. The

[123] Kissinger, *White House Years*, p. 641.
[124] Zbigniew Brzezinski, *Power and Principle* (New York: Farrar, Strauss and Giroux,
1983), p. 429.
[125] On this oft-lamented state of affairs, see Alexander George, *Bridging the Gap: Theory
and Practice in Foreign Policy* (Washington, DC: U.S. Institute of Peace Press, 1993)
and Bruce W. Jentleson, "The Need for Praxis: Bringing Policy Relevance Back In,"
International Security, Vol. 26, No. 4 (Spring 2002), pp. 169–83.
[126] For a discussion of honor in the Roman Empire, see Vittorio Nicholas Galasso,
"Honor and the Performance of Roman State Identity," *Foreign Policy Analysis*, Vol.
8, No. 2 (April 2012), pp. 173–89.

Jewish War was all but over, and the fortress was of no strategic or economic importance. The Romans could have merely posted a few hundred men to starve the defenders out, but they chose instead to construct an enormous ramp up the mountain capable of supporting an invading army. The siege aimed to send a message to others about the determination of Rome to defeat all enemies, no matter the cost and time involved, in the hope that all other would-be rebels would take notice.[127] The few Jewish holdouts in Masada posed a threat to Rome's credibility, not its interests.

Although the credibility imperative did not drastically weaken Rome, subsequent powers that felt its pull were not so lucky. The kings of Hapsburg Spain believed in the domino theory long before the term was coined, worrying that any territory that managed to free itself from the empire would start a cascade of uncontrollable defections. The monarchy spent itself into penury fighting every revolt that arose, even when the treasury was already stretched well beyond the breaking point. The count-duke of Olivares, Philip IV's closest advisor, argued in 1635 that "the first and most fundamental dangers threaten Milan, Flanders and Germany. Any blow against these would be fatal to this monarchy; and if any one of them were to go, the rest of the monarchy would follow, for Germany would be followed by Italy and Flanders, Flanders by the Indies, and Milan by Naples and Sicily."[128] Philip chose to engage on new fronts (Portugal and Catalonia) at the height of the Thirty Years' War, since he felt that a threat to the integrity of his monarchy anywhere imperiled its existence everywhere. When those two rebellious provinces eventually won their freedom in 1640, however, no other defections from the empire followed. The expensive, bloody wars to maintain reputation were fought in vain.

Of all the wars the Spanish monarchy fought on behalf of its credibility, the eighty-year effort to smash rebellion in the Low Countries of modern-day Netherlands and Belgium was the most counterproductive. The cost of keeping those provinces in the empire far outweighed any possible material benefit. As the primary historian of the Dutch

---

[127] See Edward N. Luttwak, *The Grand Strategy of the Roman Empire: From the First Century A.D. to the Third* (Baltimore, MD: Johns Hopkins University Press, 1976), pp. 3–4.

[128] Quoted in J. H. Elliott, "Managing Decline: Olivares and the Grand Strategy of Imperial Spain," in Paul Kennedy, ed., *Grand Strategies in War and Peace* (New Haven, CT: Yale University Press, 1991), p. 97.

Revolt explained, "'Reputation,' or prestige, was recognized to have a tangible influence in politics and diplomacy, and Spain feared that acknowledgement of weakness in the Netherlands would decrease her stature as a world power."[129] The Netherlands didn't matter; Spanish credibility, however, did. The results were predictably disastrous. "The war in the Netherlands," observed one of Philip's advisors in 1623, "has been the total ruin of this Monarchy."[130] The effort to put down the rebellion in the northern provinces had at that point raged for fifty-six years, at enormous cost in blood and treasure. In the same speech, however, that advisor recommended a renewal of the effort to subdue the Dutch. Financial ruin and the loss of the empire were apparently small prices to pay to avoid a humiliating defeat. The Spanish were to go on bleeding and spending for another thirty-six years, suffering through bankruptcy after bankruptcy and eventual decline. While the credibility imperative may be a predictable accompaniment of great power, therefore, it is rarely a constructive one.

It will probably never be possible to determine the precise explanatory power of any of these proposed explanations for the existence of the credibility imperative, since they are hardly mutually exclusive. But in the final analysis, understanding the genesis of pathology, while important, is not as urgent as recognition, treatment, and cure. Indeed recognizing the existence of a problem is the first step toward dealing with, and perhaps eventually eliminating, its pernicious effects.

To summarize, when the credibility imperative drives policy, states fearful of catastrophic future consequences are likely to follow hawkish recommendations in otherwise unimportant situations, attempting to send messages that other states are unlikely to receive. Policy makers would be wise to beware of the credibility imperative while devising policy, question the beliefs it inspires, and remain skeptical of the fantastic disasters of which it warns. Most important, perhaps they should be given pause by the knowledge that scholars can supply virtually no evidence supporting the conventional wisdom about its importance.

---

[129] Geoffrey Parker, *Spain and the Netherlands, 1559–1659: Ten Studies* (Short Hills, NJ: Enslow Publishers, 1979), p. 53.
[130] Geoffrey Parker, *The Army of Flanders and the Spanish Road, 1567–1659*, 2nd ed. (New York: Cambridge University Press, 2004), p. 227.

Both logic and a preponderance of the evidence suggest that the current U.S. obsession with credibility is as insecure, misplaced, and mal-informed as all that have preceded it. There is no clear way to control the perceptions of others, whether they are superpowers, small states, or loosely connected nonstate groups. The belief that *their* thoughts can be controlled by *our* actions may be comforting, springing perhaps from basic human psychological needs, but it is pathologically misleading. In reality their perception of us is largely outside of our influence, and the messages we hope to send through our actions are unlikely to be successfully received. Washington would be well advised to avoid the understandable and natural temptation to look beyond the current crisis when making decisions. As unsettling as it may be, the future is largely outside our control. The tangible interests of the present, therefore, must outweigh the intangible ones of the future.

3

Glory

Hypercompetitiveness and U.S. Foreign Policy

"We need to out-innovate, out-educate, and out-build the rest of the world," said President Obama in his 2011 State of the Union Address. "That's how we'll win the future." In case anyone missed the theme, the president referred to "winning the future" eight more times during the speech, explaining after each how his administration planned to increase its efforts to lead the United States to victory. In many areas, the United States was losing to other countries: "Our infrastructure used to be the best, but our lead has slipped. South Korean homes now have greater Internet access than we do. Countries in Europe and Russia invest more in their roads and railways than we do. China is building faster trains and newer airports." All of this and more must be addressed if the future is to be won. "By the end of the decade," he predicted, if we pull together and enact wise policies, "America will once again have the highest proportion of college graduates in the world."

The president knew his audience. He could have hardly picked a slogan with a greater potential to resonate powerfully with the American people, who are among the most competitive on earth.[1] In fact, whenever its status as The Greatest is threatened – whether it be at the hands of Serbian basketball players, Indian science students,

---

[1] The president was hardly the first contemporary politician to use the phrase; see, for instance, Newt Gingrich, *Winning the Future: A 21st Century Contract with America* (Washington, DC: Regnery Publishing, 2005).

or Chinese high-speed rail – the public demands action. The United States cannot countenance being number two in any important category, at least not without a struggle. National glory, though rarely discussed, is an important motivator for action.

Thucydides, Hobbes, and Machiavelli would have immediately recognized this impulse, even if the details might have left them puzzled. Throughout most of human history, the desire – or obsession – to be number one, the need to improve one's status and prestige, has been ubiquitous. Though the pursuit of glory is one of the classic motivations for state behavior, it is not a major independent variable in modern models of international relations, perhaps because it is not only unmeasurable and subjective but also archaic and anachronistic. Indeed today it often seems as if only classicists are comfortable speaking openly of national glory and suggesting that it still matters for modern states.[2] Overt competition for national or personal greatness might have obsessed the Caesars and Napoleon, but it is simply not something information-age states are supposed to do. Ours is a postheroic age during which martial values like glory and honor have been replaced by ones more liberal, secular, and scientific.[3] Still, glory lingers. Direct reference might today be confined to dictatorial strongmen on the fringes of the international order, but its impulses are present in every country, especially in the United States.

Glory is the foundation for the next set of pathological beliefs in U.S. foreign policy. This chapter explores its continuing importance across three main sections: the first discusses the traditional meaning of glory in international and interpersonal politics, differentiating it from the related concepts of honor and credibility. While modern leaders rarely speak of national glory, this is once again a change in vocabulary rather than behavior; today *status* and *prestige* are more common terms, but the meaning is the same. Most important, the urge to compete in its pursuit remains unchanged. To the extent that

[2] Donald Kagan, *On the Origins of War and the Preservation of Peace* (New York: Doubleday, 1995); Victor Davis Hanson, *A War Like No Other: How the Athenians and Spartans Fought the Peloponnesian War* (New York: Random House, 2005).
[3] Edward Luttwak discusses this concept in "Toward Post-Heroic Warfare," *Foreign Affairs*, Vol. 74, No. 3 (May/June 1995), pp. 109–22.

the desire for prestige drives decision making, it does so in irrational or counterproductive ways. The second section describes the predictable, consistent effects competition for status and glory has on state behavior in general and on U.S. foreign policy in particular. The chapter then speculates about the genesis of what might be considered the prestige imperative, and why it continues to have such salience in the new century.

The belief that it is important to be the best, the number one state in the international hierarchy in whatever category is being discussed, often leads to counterproductive policies that waste assets in pursuit of unimportant goals. It is, therefore, deeply pathological. In an era when the United States may soon face challengers to its status that put its prestige in peril, it is a particularly important pathology to understand and control.

GLORY, STATUS, AND THE POLITICS OF PRESTIGE

In contemporary practice and scholarship, the terms *glory, prestige, honor, credibility, reputation,* and *status* are often used interchangeably, their meanings merged and rendered nearly indistinguishable. At the root of all of them are two ancient concepts, the desires for honor and for glory, which are distinct and arise from different foundations. Actors pursue honor (or its more common modern cousin, credibility) to influence future behavior of other actors; as discussed in the previous chapter, states often feel compelled to protect their credibility to deter challengers, reassure allies, and attract neutrals. A reputation for resolve and belligerence is thought – however erroneously – to have practical value in crises to come. By contrast, glory (or its modern equivalent, prestige) is not a means but an end in itself. It is pursued for its own sake, not because its possession is thought to make goals easier to achieve in the future.

Glory, like prestige, is simply *the perception of the esteem of the community*. It is manifest in the admiration of others and pursued in expectation of that admiration, based on criteria communicated by society. Though glory is bestowed from without, its importance comes from within; its presence brings benefits to our psyches, not to our interests. Actors are not motivated by the expectation that others will treat them differently because of their relative level of prestige, only that they will admire them more.[4] Daniel Markey has argued that "men suffer from an intense desire to perceive themselves better than their fellows," and it often seems as if states do as well.[5] At times the belief that it is important to be the best, or to compete for prestige, inspires states to take actions that produce tangible costs for that intangible, internal benefit. It is at those times when that belief can be profoundly pathological.

Glory has no functional value, nor any potential material importance. Those who pursue it do not harbor the expectation that having high prestige will help them achieve future goals. It is important, in other words, only because actors believe it to be important. Society rewards those who have it, but it does not make the attainment of goals or the deterrence of challenges any more likely in crises to come.

The prestige and credibility imperatives differ in at least two other ways. First, the desire for glory, unlike that for honor, cannot be sated. States either possess a reputation for resolve or they do not, at least according to its believers. Once that reputation is established, once honor has been affirmed or restored, there is no need to amass more. It may have to be defended at times, but honor is a dichotomous variable. Prestige, on the other hand, is continuous; it has no maximum, no point of satiation. Its pursuit is perpetual and human desire for it boundless.[6] No matter how much prestige any actor has, the perception will persist that more can be acquired, and that more would be better. Not even the most prestigious of actors stop their quest. Should one win greater glory than all living competitors, the competition against history sets in. States in pursuit of prestige compare themselves against all real and imaginable others from the present and the past, and never cease their efforts to improve since the future may contain ever more glorious challengers. Thus while honor is only

---

[4] For an economic explanation of this phenomenon, see Robert H. Frank's brilliant *Choosing the Right Pond: Human Behavior and the Quest for Status* (New York: Oxford University Press, 1985).

[5] Daniel Markey, "Prestige and the Origins of War: Returning to Realism's Roots," *Security Studies,* Vol. 8, No. 4 (Summer 1999), p. 150.

[6] Daniel Markey elaborates upon this point in "Prestige and the Origins of War," p. 157.

useful to the living, glory can be permanent, echoing down through the ages.[7] Winning it is the closest mortal man (or state) can come to achieving eternal life.[8]

Second, unlike honor, glory is zero-sum. When Hobbes observed that "glory is like honor, if all men have it, no man hath it," he was not completely accurate.[9] All actors in a society can theoretically be honorable or possess credibility. The honor of one nobleman did not necessarily degrade that of his peers. Not all actors can be glorious, however, without fundamentally weakening the importance of the concept. Glory implies a hierarchy, a competition for status, that honor does not necessarily demand. The future can only be won by one state.

Realists tend to assume that prestige is merely a function of military and economic power.[10] Although throughout much of history this may have been the case, today it can be won through victory in competitions outside the realm of traditional measures of state strength. In fact, the rules regarding the specific kinds of actions that generate the esteem of others depend on time and place. For the Spartans, sacrificial struggle against impossible odds was the quickest route, while Napoleon won glory through conquest. Modern states have won prestige through moral actions as well, such as that afforded to Great Britain for its part in bringing the slave trade to an end in the first half of the nineteenth century.[11]

While social conceptions of prestige evolve, one aspect remains constant: action is generally necessary to attain it. Though glory is essentially externally controlled, one can attempt to influence it through deeds, by appearing so superior to all potential challengers that no reasonable person could cast doubt on the obvious position of

[7] Barry O'Neill has argued that prestige is only possible for living actors, which makes his conception very different from glory, which surely can be eternal, or at least posthumous. *Honor, Symbols, and War* (Ann Arbor: University of Michigan Press, 1999), pp. 193–98.

[8] Richard Ned Lebow makes a similar point in *A Cultural Theory of International Relations* (New York: Cambridge University Press, 2008), p. 143.

[9] Quoted in Markey, "Prestige and the Origins of War," p. 157.

[10] Robert Gilpin, *War and Change in International Politics* (New York: Cambridge University Press, 1981), p. 31.

[11] Oded Löwenheim, "'Do Ourselves Credit and Render a Lasting Service to Mankind': British Moral Prestige, Humanitarian Intervention, and the Barbary Pirates," *International Studies Quarterly*, Vol. 47, No. 1 (March 2003), pp. 23–48.

greatness. In other words, glory is *won*, not bestowed; it is the product of victory, or at least valiant competition, not passivity, patience, or cooperation. The glory imperative is thus manifest in modern times by the obsessive desire to compete, to win, to be the best state there is, to achieve and maintain top status. Although it can have tangible benefits, such as among firms in a market economy, generally speaking in international politics *competiveness* is little more than *the desire for glory*, the change in vocabulary rather than substance that connects modern society to that of the ancients. What credibility is to honor, therefore, competitiveness is to glory: the current application of a long understood, primal concept, made more palatable for modern ears.

The United States seeks glory through competition, in ways large and small. It may well be the most competitive or glory seeking of modern states, and its eternal quest for victory, while useful in some ways, can also manifest itself in a number of deeply pathological beliefs.

Competition as Pathology

"Of all human powers operating on the affairs of mankind," Henry Clay told the Senate in 1832, "none is greater than that of competition."[12] Not only is it natural to compete, many people believe, but doing so brings out the best in people and societies. Of all the beliefs explored in this volume, this one may well be the most deeply ingrained in American culture: *competition is productive and positive.* Any suggestion that this might not be the case would certainly bear the burden of proof. This section takes up that burden.

Competitiveness is certainly not uniformly pathological. There are circumstances in which it can be quite useful and lead to positive outcomes. Consumers benefit from the competition between firms, for instance, which also stimulates overall economic growth and development. It was the competition of capitalism that brought about the industrial and then information ages, and that continues to be the best hope of those left behind. Under certain conditions, some people – and not just athletes – perform better when competing. What follows is not, therefore, an argument that competitiveness is always negative,

---

[12] Quoted in Wolfgang Kasper, "Competition," in David R. Henderson, ed., *The Concise Encyclopedia of Economics*, 2nd ed. (Indianapolis, IN: The Liberty Fund, 2007), p. 75.

merely that neither is it always positive. There is reason to believe that in many circumstances it does far more harm than good, especially in those instances when the competitors happen to be states.

Competition is one of the most thoroughly researched topics in the social sciences, examined by psychologists, anthropologists, sociologists, economists, political scientists, and many others.[13] Modern scholarship on the subject began with social psychologist Morton Deutsch, who laid the foundation for what today is known as social interdependence theory, which explores the relative merits of competition, cooperation, and individual efforts toward goals, seeking to determine the circumstances under which each is most productive and appropriate.[14] Prior to Deutsch's work, the conventional wisdom about competition was similar to that in popular circles today – that it is desirable and even necessary to create high levels of productivity and achievement.[15] Deutsch corrected a number of errors in that wisdom and found that the consequences of competition are actually largely negative in a variety of ways, especially when compared to those of cooperation or individual activities.[16] His work was immediately attacked by a variety of skeptics, many of whom were eventually converted as the results of their own experiments supported his basic conclusions. Over the last six decades, research carried out in many different settings, across cultures, age groups, disciplines, and generations has been remarkably uniform in its findings.

Alfie Kohn popularized the first fifty years of these findings from the academy in his award-winning 1986 best seller, *No Contest: The Case*

---

[13] For a multidisciplinary literature review, see Pauline Vaillancourt Rosenau, *The Competition Paradigm: America's Romance with Conflict, Contest, and Commerce* (Lanham, MD: Rowman and Littlefield, 2003).

[14] Morton Deutsch, "A Theory of Cooperation and Competition," *Human Relations*, Vol. 2, No. 2 (May 1949), pp. 129–52.

[15] The two most influential pre-Deutsch studies were Mark A. May and Leonard W. Doob, "Cooperation and Competition: An Experimental Study in Motivation," *Social Science Research Council Bulletin*, No. 25 (April 1937), pp. 1–191; and Gardner Murphy, Lois Barclay Murphy, and Theodore M. Newcomb, *Experimental Social Psychology: An Interpretation of Research upon the Socialization of the Individual* (New York: Harper & Brothers, 1937).

[16] Deutsch, "A Theory of Cooperation and Competition," pp. 129–52; *The Resolution of Conflict: Constructive and Destructive Processes* (New Haven, CT: Yale University Press, 1973); and *Distributive Justice: A Social Psychological Perspective* (New Haven, CT: Yale University Press, 1985).

against Competition, in which he sought to debunk what he called the four "central myths" about competition present in American culture: that it motivates people to achieve their best, to reach heights impossible without it; that people enjoy competing; that it is part of human nature; and that it builds character.[17] A great deal of experimental evidence casts doubt on every one of these beliefs.

First of all, competition does not appear to bring out the best in its participants. Although it may appear counterintuitive to many Americans, the productivity of people in competitive circumstances tends to be lower than that of those operating in cooperative or even individual environments. Hundreds of studies have examined how people best achieve goals and perform, and almost all conclude that cooperative interaction results in better results across a host of outcomes, including higher academic achievement, industrial productivity, motor skills, and cognitive development.[18] It is not necessary to compete to discover the heights to which people can rise; in fact, competition often proves counterproductive.

There is little evidence that people actually enjoy competing. They may well appreciate emerging victorious and extol the virtues of competition from their easy chairs afterward, but during the competition itself people generally report high levels of anxiety and discomfort.[19] Since our society places such a high premium on winning, for many people the fear of losing can overwhelm any enjoyment they might

[17] Alfie Kohn, *No Contest: The Case against Competition* (Boston, MA: Houghton-Mifflin, 1986).
[18] See two meta-analyses of this issue: David W. Johnson, Geoffrey Maruyama, Roger Johnson, Deborah Nelson, and Linda Skon, "Effects of Cooperative, Competitive and Individualistic Goal Structures on Achievement: A Meta-Analysis," *Psychological Bulletin,* Vol. 89, No. 1 (January 1981), pp. 47–62; and Mary Beth Stanne, David W. Johnson, and Roger T. Johnson, "Does Competition Enhance or Inhibit Motor Performance: A Meta-Analysis," *Psychological Bulletin,* Vol. 125, No. 1 (January 1999), pp. 133–54. More recent literature on the subject is reviewed in John Hattie, *Visible Learning: A Synthesis of over 800 Meta-Analyses Relating to Achievement* (New York: Routledge, 2009), esp. pp. 212–15; and David W. Johnson and Roger T. Johnson, "An Educational Psychology Success Story: Social Interdependence Theory and Cooperative Learning," *Educational Researcher,* Vol. 38, No. 5 (June/July 2009), pp. 365–79.
[19] Thomas Tutko and William Bruns, *Winning is Everything and other American Myths* (New York: MacMillan Publishing Co., 1976); and Graham Jones, "More than Just a Game: Research Developments and Issues in Competitive Anxiety in Sport," *British Journal of Psychology,* Vol. 86, No. 4 (November 1995), pp. 449–78.

otherwise gain through the activity. And most of the time, most people do lose: while 50–50 games allow as many winners as losers, many of society's contests are structured to determine one winner out of a field of participants. Only one person wins a 100-yard dash, for instance, or can become professor of the year, or valedictorian, or employee of the month. One team wins a tournament. And only one country, presumably, can win the future. The more a society values winning, the greater the anxiety about and shame following loss. We feel bad about ourselves when we lose, and sometimes even a bit subconsciously guilty when we win.[20]

People are also not born competing. Another broad, multidisciplinary consensus holds that competition is learned behavior rather than an intrinsic part of human nature. Seventy-five years ago, anthropologist Margaret Mead and her colleagues studied thirteen different cultures around the world to try to determine the extent to which competitiveness is a natural outgrowth of human existence. Their "most basic conclusion," wrote Mead, was that "competitive and cooperative behavior on the part of individual members of a society is fundamentally conditioned by the total social emphasis of that society, that the goals for which individuals will work are culturally determined."[21] That conclusion has stood the test of time among anthropologists, for whom it is common knowledge that our society, not our genetics, instructs people to compete.[22] The brain, according to recent research in neurobiology, is equipped with the potential for both behaviors.[23] The extent to which one is emphasized over the other is a result of nurture, not nature. Indeed competitiveness is directly related to age in American children to a far greater degree than in those of other countries.[24] Americans, like people everywhere, seem

[20] For support of the claims in this paragraph, see Kohn, *No Contest*, pp. 96–131.

[21] Margaret Mead, ed., *Cooperation and Competition among Primitive Peoples* (New York: McGraw Hill, 1937), p. 16.

[22] Bruce D. Bonta, "Cooperation and Competition in Peaceful Societies," *Psychological Bulletin*, Vol. 121, No. 2 (March 1997), pp. 299–320.

[23] Jean Decety, Philip L. Jackson, Jessica A. Sommerville, Thierry Chaminade, and Andrew N. Meltzoff, "The Neural Bases of Cooperation and Competition: An fMRI Investigation," *NeuroImage*, Vol. 23, No. 2 (October 2004), pp. 744–51.

[24] Sports psychologist Dorcas Susan Butt defends this claim and refers to it as a "constant one in the current literature" in *Psychology of Sport*, 2nd ed. (New York: Van Nostrand Reinhold Co., 1987), p. 58.

to be born cooperating and only learn to compete as they age and learn from those around them. "It would be unreasonable to assume," Deutsch concluded, "that there is an innately determined human tendency for everyone to want to be 'top dog.'"[25]

To the extent that competition builds character, it does so in a negative direction. Highly competitive people develop jaundiced views of others, ones marked by stereotype and prejudice, and have a far more difficult time maintaining healthy interpersonal relationships. Competition tends to enhance antisocial personality traits, making it more difficult for participants to form relationships even within groups. Once again hundreds of studies have been consistent in the conclusion that overall levels of stress, hostility, and aggression rise significantly in competing people, in ways that often spill over to other aspects of their lives.[26] Positive correlations exist between competition and a variety of personal and social ills, from insecurity to low levels of self-esteem to general unhappiness. Those like Vince Lombardi for whom winning is "not everything but the only thing" will often do whatever it takes to improve their chances, including undermining the other side and cheating whenever possible.[27] Whatever minimal benefit can be bestowed by helping children learn to lose with dignity is far outweighed by the harm that accompanies the inculcation of the competitive ethic.

Since we choose to teach our children that competitiveness is positive, we can presumably choose not to do so as well. As Kohn points out, "human nature" is almost always used to explain unsavory acts or impulses; generosity or kindness is rarely dismissed on the grounds that it is "just human nature."[28] Arguments that competitiveness is ubiquitous, natural, or welcome are ways people have developed to justify or rationalize what would otherwise seem to be antisocial, even selfish behavior.

---

[25] Deutsch, *The Resolution of Conflict*, p. 89.
[26] For a meta-analysis of 133 studies about this issue, see David W. Johnson and Roger T. Johnson, "Research Shows the Benefits of Adult Cooperation," *Educational Leadership*, Vol. 45, No. 3 (November 1987), pp. 27–30.
[27] David Callahan, *The Cheating Culture: Why More Americans Are Doing Wrong to Get Ahead* (New York: Harcourt, Inc., 2004).
[28] Kohn, *No Contest*, p. 12.

For three generations, psychologists have identified competitiveness as a key component in a variety of neuroses. Psychoanalyst Karen Horney argued in 1936 that competition "appears to be a never-failing center of neurotic conflicts," leading in some individuals to "hypercompetitiveness," or the obsessive psychological need to win all the time in every instance and to turn every aspect of life into a competition.[29] The hypercompetitive individual has an "incapacity to have fifty-fifty relationships. He either has to lead or he feels entirely lost, dependent and helpless."[30] Hypercompetitiveness is also highly correlated with narcissism, a subject to which we return in the next chapter.[31] For now it is merely important to note that there is little dissent among psychologists that cooperation, not competition, builds self-esteem, social support, and general well-being.[32]

One of the most famous experiments in the history of the social sciences may help make the overall point and illuminate the pathological effects of competitiveness. In the 1950s, in the halcyon days before universities created institutional review boards to oversee experiments on human subjects, two University of Oklahoma psychologists took a couple of dozen twelve-year-old boys to what appeared to be an ordinary summer camp.[33] At first the boys were assigned cooperative tasks they completed together. After about a week they were split into two teams that competed with one another constantly. Tension grew between the groups as the days went by, eventually descending into rabid prejudice and vandalism. On a number of occasions the boys had to be physically separated. After the competitive week, the researchers recombined the groups and reinstituted cooperative goals, and harmony was restored.

---

[29] Karen Horney, "Culture and Neurosis," *American Sociological Review*, Vol. 1, No. 2 (April 1936), p. 221.

[30] Karen Horney, *The Neurotic Personality of Our Time* (New York: W. W. Norton & Co., 1937), p. 175.

[31] Richard M. Ryckman, Bill Thornton, and J. Corey Butler, "Personality Correlates of the Hypercompetitive Attitude Scale: Validity Tests of Horney's Theory of Neurosis," *Journal of Personality Assessment*, Vol. 62, No. 1 (Winter 1994), pp. 84–94.

[32] See especially Johnson and Johnson, "An Educational Psychology Success Story," pp. 365–79.

[33] Muzafer Sherif, O. J. Harvey, Jack White, William R. Hood, and Carolyn W. Sherif, *The Robbers Cave Experiment* (Middletown, CT: Wesleyan University Press, 1988).

Throughout the experiment the boys gave feedback about their feelings and attitudes. They consistently reported being happier when working together, and had higher levels of anxiety while competing. Their attitudes toward themselves during the competitive round became inflated, while those toward the other group were uniformly – and increasingly – negative. Stress levels rose during the competitive periods, and enjoyment plummeted. There is a limited amount that can be learned from such experiments, of course, but many more have followed, all of which have reached the same conclusions: competition seems to lead to hostility, prejudice and, if not controlled, open aggression.[34] It poisons relationships and intensifies personal neuroses, while producing results inferior to those found through cooperation toward a common goal. And it generally brings out the worst in people, turning them into unhappy, self-absorbed, hostile cranks.

Does competition have any aspects that are beneficial for society? Freud believed so, arguing that sports and other nonviolent competition could provide people with useful, much needed outlets for their subconscious anxiety and rage.[35] This idea, known today as *catharsis theory*, was developed in greater depth by biologist Konrad Lorenz and subjected to a great number of tests over time.[36] It has not performed well. Over and over again, researchers have found that people grow more aggressive, not less, through exposure to competition, either directly or merely as spectators. Those who participate in sports, for instance, tend to carry lessons learned on the field to their homes or offices.[37] Cross-cultural studies suggest people simply do not possess a reservoir of aggression that can be released harmlessly on the

34 For some, see Robert R. Blake and Jane Srygley Mouton, "Reactions to Intergroup Competition under Win-Lose Conditions," *Management Science*, Vol. 7, No. 4 (July 1961), pp. 420–35; Jacob M. Rabbie and Murray Horwitz, "Arousal of Ingroup-Outgroup Bias by a Chance Win or Loss," *Journal of Personality and Social Psychology*, Vol. 13, No. 3 (November 1969), pp. 269–77; and Michael A. Zarate, Bernice Garcia, Azenett A. Garza, and Robert T. Hitlan, "Cultural Threat and Perceived Realistic Group Conflict as Dual Predictors of Prejudice," *Journal of Experimental Social Psychology*, Vol. 40, No. 1 (January 2004), pp. 99–105.
35 See Russell G. Geen and Michael B. Quanty, "The Catharsis of Aggression: An Evaluation of a Hypothesis," *Advances in Experimental Social Psychology*, Vol. 10 (1977), pp. 1–37.
36 Konrad Lorenz, *On Aggression* (New York: Harcourt, 1966).
37 Richard H. Cox, *Sport Psychology: Concepts and Applications*, 6th ed. (New York: McGraw Hill, 2007), esp. pp. 353–54.

field of play; instead it quickly becomes learned behavior carried over into all aspects of life.[38] Indeed sports are more likely to result in hooliganism among fans – or war, as was the case between El Salvador and Honduras following soccer riots in 1980 – than anything resembling healthy catharsis.[39] "There are few beliefs," argued Kohn in a review of catharsis theory, "so widely held by the general public that have been so decisively refuted by the evidence."[40] Even Lorenz was to tell a researcher less than a decade after writing his book that he had "developed strong doubts about whether watching aggressive behavior even in the guise of sport has any cathartic effect at all."[41]

In 2005, psychologists David and Roger Johnson conducted a massive meta-analysis of the over 750 studies on the effects of cooperation and competition in psychology, sociology, education, and business. The results across fields were quite consistent, confirming Deutsch's initial, counterintuitive findings. Not only do individuals perform far better in cooperative situations (about two-thirds of a standard deviation above the average person in a competitive situation, to be exact), but they also report higher levels of motivation and tend to complete assigned tasks much more quickly. Cooperation is far more conducive to psychological health across many indicators, such as morale and self-esteem, whereas competition generally proves harmful. Cooperators experience more satisfaction with their performance and far more positive attitudes toward others. Abstract reasoning and critical thinking also improve for those in cooperative situations compared to competitive. Overall, cooperation has outperformed competition across every imaginable indicator, nearly every time the two have been put to the test.[42]

[38] One early and influential study on this was Richard Sipes, "War, Sports and Aggression: An Empirical Test of Two Rival Theories," *American Anthropologist*, Vol. 75, No. 1 (February 1973), pp. 64–86.

[39] Ryszard Kapuscinski, *The Soccer War* (New York: Vintage Books, 1992).

[40] Kohn, *No Contest*, p. 144. For an update, see Brad J. Bushman, "Does Venting Anger Feed or Extinguish the Flame? Catharsis, Rumination, Distraction, Anger and Aggressive Responding," *Personality and Social Psychology Bulletin*, Vol. 28, No. 6 (October 2002), pp. 724–31.

[41] Richard Evans, "A Conversation with Konrad Lorenz about Aggression, Homosexuality, Pornography, and the Need for a New Ethic," *Psychology Today*, Vol. 8, No. 6 (November 1974), p. 83.

[42] David W. Johnson and Roger T. Johnson, "New Developments in Social Interdependence Theory," *Genetic, Social and General Psychology Monographs*, Vol. 131, No. 4 (November 2005), pp. 285–358.

To find unanimity of opinion in a field about any single subject is exceedingly rare; consensus across the social sciences is almost unheard of. The research on competition, however, is one of those impossibly rare cases. The findings are quite firm and by now nearly uncontested: Competition is pathological in a variety of ways, for both the individual and the society at large. "Healthy competition," as the phrase goes, is oxymoronic.[43]

National Competitiveness

To those unfamiliar with the scholarship on competition, the review of its findings, because of its relative brevity and abject novelty, may not be immediately convincing. It generally takes more than a few paragraphs to alter deep, long-held beliefs. One need not be convinced by the broad consensus among social scientists about the utility of competitiveness for individuals, however, to recognize that it can be a pathological influence on foreign policy. In fact, a good case can be made that competitiveness is even *more* destructive for a country than it is for a person, whether it be in security, economics, or social realms. Winning the future might not be such a great goal for the United States after all.

Security affairs appear to be a naturally competitive environment. Indeed there is no more obvious arena of competition than the battlefield, where the fate of states rests on the ability of militaries to outperform their opponents. The state overtaken by rivals is in danger of being permanently removed from the map. Leaders ought not to be concerned with strength and growth in relation to others, therefore, rather than in absolute terms.[44] Nearly a half century ago Kenneth Waltz summarized the conventional wisdom by stating that "relative

---

[43] Alfie Kohn makes this point in *No Contest*, p. 9.

[44] Good discussions of the relative versus absolute gains issue include Duncan Snidal, "Relative Gains and the Pattern of International Cooperation," *American Political Science Review*, Vol. 85, No. 3 (September 1991), pp. 701–26; Robert Powell, "Absolute and Relative Gains in International Relations Theory," *American Political Science Review*, Vol. 85, No. 4 (December 1991), pp. 1303–20; and Joseph Grieco, Robert Powell, and Duncan Snidal, "The Relative Gains Problem for International Cooperation," *American Political Science Review*, Vol. 87, No. 3 (September 1993), pp. 729–43.

gain is more important than absolute gain" in the anarchic, zero-sum, self-help system where war is a constant possibility.[45]

This Hobbesian, all-against-all vision of the international system hardly matches twenty-first-century reality. Competing to have the largest military is only rational if winning would assure security or increase the amount of influence a state wields. Today, it is not clear that either is true: the size of modern militaries has little relation to state security, and force is simply not as useful in achieving national goals as it once was.[46] The insights about the nature of the system reviewed in Chapter 1 deserve multiple repetitions until they become widely understood: the world has entered a golden age of peace and security during which both the incidence and intensity of warfare are declining. States no longer disappear, no matter how far behind their competitors they fall. Great Britain's relative power has shrunk markedly over the last century, but its people are no less safe today – in fact, they are much more so. The odds of Thailand surviving as a state through the next century are equivalent to the odds for Russia and Burkina Faso. The number of UN members that have disappeared against their will has held steady at zero for nearly seven decades. It is not only inveterate optimists who have concluded that conquest is dead.

Security competition is unrelated to overall state safety in the twenty-first century, and it has little relation to influence either. Militaries are useful only to the extent that they will be used; when that threat is absent, weaker states are free to call the bluff of the larger. Gone are the days when the presence of a superior fleet off the coast of another state was sufficient to compel changes in behavior. The overwhelming hard-power superiority of the United States, for example, does not necessarily help it achieve its goals. It cannot seem to coerce the Chinese into letting their currency float, for example, or get the Israelis to stop building settlements in the West Bank, or convince OPEC to produce more oil. The military balance does not

45 Kenneth N. Waltz, *Man, the State, and War: A Theoretical Analysis* (New York: Columbia University Press, 1959), p. 198.
46 For an explanation, see David Baldwin, *Paradoxes of Power* (New York: Blackwell, 1989); Evan Luard, *The Blunted Sword: The Erosion of Military Power in Modern World Politics* (New York: New Amsterdam Books, 1989); and Joseph Nye, *Soft Power: The Means to Success in World Politics* (New York: Public Affairs, 2004).

even enter into the discussions regarding most issues, since the idea that they would be decided by force is ludicrous. The practical utility of military superiority is limited if all parties in a dispute are confident force will not be employed. None of this is to imply that militaries have no utility, of course, only to make the point that, in a world where major war has become all but unthinkable, the maintenance of military status should not be of urgent, pressing concern. Its loss is not terribly dangerous.

Competition among state economies is even less useful. For people educated in a capitalist system this must seem especially counterintuitive, since competition is one of the main drivers of innovation and development among firms. But the forces that propel firms forward are not the same as those that affect states, which are much more complex and diverse in their interests. Once states make economic status a priority, they tend to enact policies that, while well meaning, can create inefficiencies and distort the function of the free market, in part by encouraging a variety of rent-seeking behaviors.[47] Macroeconomic competition, in other words, can interfere with the healthy, productive, microeconomic competition that spurs growth. When nations compete with one another over economic issues, both firms and consumers tend to suffer.

More important, those who urge the United States to compete with other countries in various indicators of economic performance misunderstand the nature of the current globalized system. Measuring one state against others in terms of productivity, growth, and/or overall size offers little practical utility, no matter what leaders may say, since the postmercantilist international economic system is not zero-sum. The United States benefits from growth in other countries, which opens markets and offers opportunities for investment. As Paul Krugman has argued on behalf of the majority of macroeconomists, "it is simply not the case that the world's leading nations are to any important degree in economic competition with each other, or that any of their major economic problems can be attributed to failures

---

[47] For a review, see Philippe Aghion and Rachel Griffith, *Competition and Growth: Reconciling Theory and Evidence* (Cambridge, MA: MIT Press, 2005). See also William J. Baumol, Robert E. Litan, and Carl J. Schramm, *Good Capitalism, Bad Capitalism and the Economics of Growth and Prosperity* (New Haven, CT: Yale University Press, 2007).

to compete on world markets."[48] Prosperity and standard of living – not to mention security – are not necessarily related to international rankings of the U.S. economy. Growth in one country helps that of others, as long as there are minimal restrictions on trade and investment. Krugman summed up a book-length explanation of this in his typically understated style: "Certainly anyone who wants to be considered an expert on economics has no excuse for not getting the arguments and facts just described here straight," he argued. "So, if you hear someone say something along the lines of 'America needs higher productivity so that it can compete in today's global economy,' never mind who he is, or how plausible he sounds. He might as well be wearing a flashing neon sign that reads: 'I DON'T KNOW WHAT I'M TALKING ABOUT.'"[49]

Samuel Huntington raised an important objection to this argument, if somewhat inadvertently. Although economists may insist that global trade and investment are positive-sum games, even to the point that they regard it as "self-evident truth," Huntington pointed out that such a conclusion is "self-evident to almost no one but economists. The American public as a whole, various groups in American society, and the leaders and publics in other societies do not buy it for a moment."[50] In other words, international economic competition is relevant precisely because people believe it to be so, irrespective of evidence and economic reality. To Huntington, this is enough to dismiss the argument that economic primacy is unimportant. For purposes of this project, however, it is evidence of a pathological belief, one based on an incorrect foundation in need of further examination and eventual elimination.

Finally, the social ramifications of national prestige are so minimal as to merit almost no discussion. While there are many reasons why it should be a top priority for every state to provide a good education for its children, for instance, competition with those of other countries

---

[48] Paul Krugman, "Competitiveness: A Dangerous Obsession," *Foreign Affairs*, Vol. 73, No. 2 (March–April 1994), p. 30.

[49] Paul Krugman, *Peddling Prosperity: Economic Sense and Nonsense in the Age of Diminished Expectations* (New York: W. W. Norton & Co., 1994), p. 280, capitalization in the original.

[50] Samuel Huntington, "Why International Primacy Matters," *International Security*, Vol. 17, No. 4 (Spring 1993), p. 72.

should not be one of them. The goal of an education system should be to equip students with the best chance for a fulfilling twenty-first-century life, not to win an imaginary competition over math scores with other states. To the extent that outrage over underperforming schools is motivated by concern for students, it is wise and proper; where it is motivated by fear of losing the future to other states, it is pathological. American students should learn math and science to improve their minds and prepare themselves for a more rewarding future, not to outscore their counterparts in Shanghai.

Social competition between states does not generally lead to improvements in national performance or maximization of efficiency. In fact, the opposite is often true: the pursuit of victory can distract from what ought to be more pressing concerns. Although there are times when actions taken in order to win are the same as those that would lead to optimal outcomes, this is not always the case. The remedy for lagging behind Chinese math students has been the monomaniacal imperative to improve American test scores, which has put additional pressure on a public education system already under considerable stress. Despite the fact that nearly every study of the factors correlated with student achievement conducted over the last five decades has reached the same conclusion – student outcomes are closely related to two factors, and two factors alone, the income and education level of parents – today's reformers believe that the way to improve schools is by injecting the competitive ethic.[51] As "virtually every scholar of teaching and schooling knows," according to one of the major members of that group, those factors under the control of educators, such as class size, spending per pupil, teacher pay or unionization, principal leadership, and the like – the "school factors," to use the parlance of Secretary of Education Arne Duncan – account for less than 20 percent of the variation in student performance.[52] The rest is a result of variables students bring into the classroom, ones beyond the reach of reformers. Input is decisive, in other words;

[51] Former George H. W. Bush administration Department of Education official Diane Ravitch reviews this research in *The Death and Life of the Great American School System: How Testing and Choice are Undermining Education* (New York: Basic Books, 2010).
[52] David C. Berliner, "Effects of Inequality and Poverty vs. Teachers and Schooling on America's Youth," *Teachers College Record*, Vol. 116, No. 1 (January 2014), forthcoming.

there is a limit to what schools can do to overcome the influence, both positive and negative, of the parents and community. In practice this means that troubled communities produce troubled schools. Rather than address broader social problems, however, the hypercompetitive society has focused instead on efforts to raise test scores so the United States can rise in the international rankings.

Furthermore, the oft-expressed belief that there is a "crisis" in education is incorrect, and pathologically so because it inspires poor public policy. By any reasonable measure public education is not deteriorating: student test scores are actually improving, while dropout rates are not increasing and a higher percentage of students go on to – and complete – college than ever before.[53] In other words, public schools are not failing, and when compared to any previous time they are actually performing better. To the extent the charter school/ school choice movement was implemented to address deteriorating schools, it aimed at a problem that did not exist. That is not to say that many school districts are without problems, of course, or that nothing can or should be done to improve the state of public education, just that there is little reason to believe that American schools will provide better educations at the end of the charterization/privatization process. But perhaps, by mandating that schools train students not to think but to test well, at least the rest of the world will no longer be able to lord it over Uncle Sam quite so much.

Fortunately, the fact that the United States lags behind other OECD countries in some measures of educational attainment is unrelated to economic performance. U.S. students have never performed well on the standardized tests that hope to measure the performance of our schools, at least in comparison to students abroad, and their rank has not changed since the 1960s when the tests were first administered. Those results have had no relation whatsoever to economic

[53] The classic explanation of this remains David C. Berliner and Bruce J. Biddle, *The Manufactured Crisis: Myths, Fraud, and the Attack on America's Public Schools* (Boston, MA: Addison-Wesley, 1995). Its points are even more relevant today. For a comprehensive overview of statistics related to U.S. public education, see U.S Department of Commerce, *Educational Attainment in the United States: 2009* (Washington, DC: U.S. Census Bureau, February 2012), available at http://www.census.gov/ prod/2012pubs/p20–566.pdf. A little historical perspective can be found in Thomas D. Snyder, ed., *120 Years of American Education: A Statistical Portrait* (Washington, DC: Department of Education, National Center for Education Statistics, 1993).

performance, innovation, or entrepreneurship – much less state power – and there is no reason to think they will in the future.

Overall, competition between states is certainly not a natural phenomenon. Since states are not people, they lack natural inner drives or subconscious impulses. The sex imperative that drives lions to compete for alpha status, for instance, is absent for states. Even if Freud, Lorenz, and other theorists of aggression were correct about the need for cathartic releases – and, to repeat, there is precious little reason to think they were – their insight would not apply to abstract, theoretical entities. Aggression is a human trait, not a national one. The suggestion that competition is natural for the international system cannot survive the requisite jump between levels of analysis. Anthropomorphizing states may be fashionable in some quarters, but it cannot change the fact that states have no independent existence.[54] They are not creatures whose behavior can be separated from their components and studied and understood as if they were so many crawfish.

Interstate competition is also not inevitable. The rules by which any anarchic system operates depend on the perceptions and expectations of its members. As those perceptions and expectations change, so too do the rules that govern the system. Perhaps the most basic, most central insight from constructivist theory in international politics is that the fundamental character of the system of states is neither set nor predetermined, but evolutionary and socially constructed. Competition is natural only if states believe that it is natural to compete; as those beliefs evolve, which they do over time, such underlying assumptions can change. That "anarchy is what states make of it" has become almost a cliché.[55] What is true today need not be tomorrow, because people learn, evolve, and change their minds, occasionally even regarding their most deeply held beliefs.

States that perceive themselves in military competition with others divert resources away from more productive, useful priorities. Those that believe they are locked in national economic competition will seek to protect their own industries, or bolster entire

[54] Alexander Wendt, "The State as Person in International Theory," *Review of International Studies*, Vol. 30, No. 2 (April 2004), pp. 289–316.

[55] Alexander Wendt, "Anarchy is What States Make of It: The Social Construction of Power Politics," *International Organization*, Vol. 46, No. 2 (Spring 1992), pp. 391–425.

sectors, or even weaken competitors and therefore hurt themselves. Education systems in competition will concentrate on student test scores rather than performance and learning as a whole. If the United States were to stop measuring its progress and standing against that of others, it would usually be better off. In other words, today *absolute national performance is more important than relative*, in almost all areas.

The Costs of State Competition

The competition for national glory would be rather harmless if there were no substantial costs associated with it. Unfortunately, however, its effects are rarely neutral. Like the credibility imperative, competition increases belligerent behavior and discourages cooperation. Research on the interpersonal effects of competition helps explain how the insistence on viewing the international system as a competitive environment can exacerbate at least three interrelated perceptions – of self, others, and the nature of the system – each of which can be poisonous to the pursuit of national interests.

First, competition affects the way actors view themselves, encouraging egocentrism and self-oriented action. The focus of competitors will naturally drift inward, toward what they feel is necessary for victory, which puts the needs of others a poor second. Sports psychologist Dorcas Butt noted that the "character of the competitive athlete becomes increasingly undesirable as he or she develops an intense egocentric orientation with rigid psychological defenses and insensitivity. Obsession with his or her own winning status dominates the athlete's being."[56] The people of the United States need little reason to become more self-obsessed than they already are.

Second, competition breeds unfavorable views of the character and intentions of the other, identifying all as potential rivals. Mitt Romney was guilty of this when he emphasized his experience in the business world and extrapolated lessons he learned in that competitive environment to international politics in his campaign memoir, as if microeconomics were the direct equivalent of geopolitics. He referred to China and Russia as political "competitors" throughout the book and

---

[56] Butt, *Psychology of Sport*, p. 72.

on the stump during his 2012 presidential campaign.[57] These were
rivals to be defeated, in his calculation, rather than relationships to
be managed. Like many American leaders, Romney was unable to dif-
ferentiate between those realms where competition could be useful
from those where it is not.

Not only do competitors assume that others harbor malign intentions and act accordingly, but they tend to envy winners and hold
contempt for losers. "In an extremely competitive society," argued
Richard Payne, "where victory is widely seen as the ultimate determi-
nant of what is right, just, and good, defeat is tantamount to evil."[58]
Winning is sometimes seen as just rewards for effort, preparation, and
talent, while losers are thought to have brought their condition on
themselves and deserve no sympathy. As a result, Americans feel that
the United States has achieved its position of dominance not by geographic gifts of isolation, resources, and weak neighbors, but through
hard work, smart choices, and God's grace. The other states of the
world have earned their lower status and our (perhaps subconscious)
contempt rather than empathy.

Finally, competition between states shapes the way they perceive the
system. Actors in competition naturally distrust one another, and relations between them are likely more hostile than necessary. Deutsch
argued that both sides in competitive relationships are predisposed to
regard the other negatively, "to have a suspicious, hostile, exploitative
attitude toward the other, to be psychologically closed to the other, to
be aggressive and defensive toward the other, to seek advantage and
superiority for self and disadvantage and inferiority for the other, to
see the other as opposed to oneself and basically different, and so
on. One is predisposed to expect the other to have the same orientation."[59] Leaders who believe that their states are operating in a competitive, dog-eat-dog world perceive the intentions and motivation of

---

[57] Mitt Romney, *No Apology: The Case for American Greatness* (New York: St. Martin's Press,
2010). For an analysis of how competition was a central theme of Romney's foreign
policy, at least as outlined on the campaign trail, see Paul Lettow, "A Romney-Ryan
Foreign Policy," *National Review Online*, November 5, 2012, available at http://www.
nationalreview.com/articles/332488/romney-ryan-foreign-policy-paul-lettow.

[58] Richard J. Payne, *The Clash with Distant Cultures: Values, Interests, and Force in American
Foreign Policy* (Albany: State University of New York Press, 1995), p. 62.

[59] Deutsch, *Distributive Justice*, p. 85.

others as ominous, threatening, and devious. They are also tempted to welcome such a perception, in the belief that it will bring out their best. Vince Lombardi once noted that to compete one needed a fire, and that "there is nothing that stokes fires like hate."[60]

Once members become convinced that the system is inherently competitive, they quickly learn to perceive threats and assume the worst in other members. In other words, competition exacerbates the already strong American tendency to think in Manichaean terms, to see the world as a battle between good and evil, black versus white. "Dichotomous thinking is both conducive to and a consequence of competing," argued Kohn. "Those inclined to see the world in an either/or fashion will be attracted to the competition, but, by the same token, competition will help to shape such an orientation."[61] Rarely are international affairs that simple. Dichotomous perceptions, while sometimes not completely mistaken, often lead to national folly.

It is also worth noting that the prestige imperative tends to inspire unnecessarily high intensity levels in actions it helps to motivate. Since glory is won only through the perceptions of others, actors will tend to be insecure about the effectiveness of their attempts to win it. Insecure actors overcompensate. They do more to achieve their goals than may be necessary to make the outcome, which is uncomfortably outside of their control, more likely to occur. Thus the passion (and violence) inspired by the prestige imperative is apt to be disproportionate to the goal at hand.[62]

Centuries ago, Hobbes recognized that the pursuit of prestige is an enemy of political stability.[63] That insight remains true today, whether or not modern states recognize it to be so. To the extent that it can be minimized, especially in the unipolar power, the world will be a more stable, more rational place. The most powerful members of any system have a disproportionate effect upon its rules, norms, and overall character. Unfortunately, today the United States is the most glory-obsessed, most competitive country of them all.

[60] Quoted in James A. Michener, *Sports in America* (New York: Random House, 1976), p. 420.
[61] Kohn, *No Contest*, p. 127.
[62] Markey, "Prestige and the Origins of War,"," p. 157.
[63] Quoted in Markey, "Prestige and the Origins of War," p. 148.

THE UNITED STATES, COMPETITIVENESS, AND GLORY

Although most twenty-first-century Americans may consider themselves immune from atavistic motivations like the prestige imperative, no state harbors a greater concern with competition, status, and victory. If any country exhibits the hypercompetitive spirit, according to social psychologist Elliot Aronson, it is the United States, which manifests a "staggering cultural obsession with victory."[64] Although many societies are organized into fundamentally hierarchical, status-oriented systems, those who make cross-cultural comparisons report that few take it as seriously, or encourage competition to be as pervasive, as does the United States. It is, according to economist Paul Wachtel, "almost our state religion."[65] The competitive ethic is inculcated into Americans in childhood and reinforced in virtually every aspect of their lives as they grow up. Actually, for many American children, the prestige imperative predates birth, as hypercompetitive parents pump Mozart into wombs in the hope of aiding brain development and increasing the odds of qualifying for those precious few slots in the best, most exclusive nursery schools and the fast track to the Ivy League.

An early, widely cited and oft-repeated study compared the way Mexican and American children approach play, concluding that the Americans were far less cooperative, less likely to share, and generally more competitive when playing similar games.[66] (It deserves mention that researchers have not been able to connect the lack of competitiveness among Mexican children with lower achievement in school. Competitiveness does not serve American children well, since it makes them less satisfied with their performance and with

[64] Eliot Aronson, *The Social Animal*, 3rd ed. (San Francisco, CA: W. H. Freeman, 1980), p. 154.
[65] Paul L. Wachtel, *The Poverty of Affluence: A Psychological Portrait of the American Way of Life* (New York: Free Press, 1983), p. 284.
[66] Spencer Kagan and Millard C. Madsen, "Cooperation and Competition of Mexican, Mexican-American, and Anglo-American Children of Two Ages under Four Instructional Sets," *Developmental Psychology*, Vol. 5, No. 1 (July 1971), pp. 32–39. See also J. Avellar and Spencer Kagan, "Development of Competitive Behaviors in Anglo-American and Mexican-American Children," *Psychological Reports*, Vol. 39, No. 1 (August 1976), pp. 191–98; and Charles McClintock, "Development of Social Motives in Anglo-American and Mexican Children," *Journal of Personality and Social Psychology*, Vol. 29, No. 3 (March 1974), pp. 348–54.

themselves.[67] Competitiveness in education simply does not lead to better outcomes.) The cultural differences only seem to strengthen with age.[68]

Our national pastimes are almost all competitive in nature. No nation is more obsessed with participating in and watching others play sports as is America.[69] Four major professional sports leagues make millionaires of their members, while spectators spend billions of dollars annually at a variety of other individual, amateur, and other kinds of events. As President Clinton said in 1998, "America, rightly or wrongly, is a sports-crazy country."[70] American sporting events are of course deeply intertwined with patriotic imagery, often in ways that cannot help but make outsiders uncomfortable. Not only is the national anthem a requirement before any game can begin, for example, but the post-9/11 innovation of playing "God Bless America" during the seventh-inning stretch seems to have become a permanent feature for many teams. Country and sport go hand in hand.

Inherently antagonistic activities like sports only tell part of the story of American hypercompetitiveness, however. "Not only do we get carried away with competitive activities," argued Kohn, "but we turn almost everything else *into* a contest," as if events have no meaning absent a win/lose, hierarchical framework.[71] We obsessively rank the unrankable, from the quality of universities and cars to the beauty of women to "most livable" cities. It is no coincidence that the United States was the first to create awards for its best movies, finest restaurants, top canines, and fattest twins. We make contests out of singing,

[67] Spencer Kagan, G. Lawrence Zahm, and Jennifer Gealy, "Competition and School Achievement among Anglo-American and Mexican-American Children," *Journal of Educational Psychology*, Vol. 69, No. 4 (August 1977), pp. 432–41.

[68] Butt, *Psychology of Sport*, p. 60.

[69] The others that may be close – Australia, England, and South Africa – are all part of the so-called Anglosphere, where virtually all major international sports were born. See William J. Baker, *Sports in the Western World* (Chicago: University of Illinois Press, 1988); Richard O. Davies, *America's Obsession: Sports and Society Since 1945* (New York: Harcourt Brace & Co., 1994); Allen Guttman, *Games and Empires: Modern Sports and Cultural Imperialism* (New York: Columbia University Press, 1994); and David Kenneth Wiggins, ed., *Sport in America: From Wicked Amusement to National Obsession* (Champaign, IL: Human Kinetics, 1995).

[70] Quoted in Kathryn Jay, *More than Just a Game: Sports in American Life since 1945* (New York: Columbia University Press, 2004), p. 2.

[71] Kohn, *No Contest*, p. 2, emphasis in original.

architecture, and hot dog consumption. When Michael Mandelbaum argued that "contemporary Americans are perhaps the most competitive people since the Ancient Greeks," one wonders what led him to apply that limitation.[72] The United States certainly seems a strong contender for "most competitive society in history" – a title that, no doubt, would please many Americans to win.

Foreign policy cannot remain untouched by the hypercompetitive characteristics of American society. Behaviors learned and reinforced in one arena are commonly, perhaps inevitably, transferred into others. International society can shape the behavior of its members, but it cannot completely overcome national culture. Few scholars of international politics would argue that cultural characteristics have no impact on decision making. There is some disagreement over exactly how much they can explain – many realists contend that power and/or structural constraints are more decisive – but there is a broad and growing consensus that when it comes to foreign policy, to some degree at least, culture matters.[73] In theory, states can be considered unitary actors that respond primarily to systemic incentives; in practice, the people who run states are the products of national cultures, and cannot be fully immune from the lessons learned from their society. The most competitive, status-oriented societies ought to produce the most competitive, status-oriented foreign policies. In the case of the United States, that is precisely the case.

One of the main lessons culture teaches Americans is that victory is vitally important. During the Cold War, for example, competition with the Soviet Union colored every aspect of U.S. foreign policy. When any part of the globe switched from blue to red it was seen by some

---

[72] Michael Mandelbaum, *The Meaning of Sports: Why Americans Watch Baseball, Football, and Basketball and What They See When They Do* (New York: Public Affairs, 2004), p. 30.

[73] Lucian W. Pye, "Political Culture Revisited," *Political Psychology*, Vol. 12, No. 3 (September 1991), pp. 487–508; Judith Goldstein and Robert O. Keohane, eds., *Ideas and Foreign Policy: Beliefs, Institutions, and Political Change* (Ithaca, NY: Cornell University Press, 1993); Alastair Iain Johnston, "Thinking about Strategic Culture," *International Security*, Vol. 19, No. 4 (Spring 1995), pp. 32–64; Peter J. Katzenstein, *Cultural Norms and National Security* (Ithaca, NY: Cornell University Press, 1996); Richard J. Ellis and Michael Thompson, eds., *Culture Matters: Essays in Honor of Aaron Wildavsky* (Boulder, CO: Westview Press, 1997); Theo Farrell, "Culture and Military Power," *Review of International Studies*, Vol. 24, No. 3 (July 1998), pp. 407–16; and Michael C. Desch, "Culture Clash: Assessing the Importance of Ideas in Security Studies," *International Security*, Vol. 23, No. 1 (Summer 1998), pp. 141–70.

as a loss for the United States, whether or not it affected the balance of power. Both sides turned local conflicts in places like Angola, Laos, and Guatemala into proxy competitions, even though it was hard even for supporters to describe precisely what tangible benefits would accompany victory. Complex rationales were devised to explain why it was important for the United States to remain ahead of the Soviets in the size of the nuclear stockpile. Were the Soviets ever to catch up or (heaven forbid) pull ahead, the Nitze-Wohlstetter wing of the debate maintained, Moscow would be tempted to use that superiority during a "window of opportunity" to blackmail, or perhaps even attack, the United States.[74] Concerns about hypothetical "missile gaps" or "bomber gaps" kept strategists awake at night, as if tens of thousands of nuclear weapons on three different platforms would be rendered insufficient to maintain strategic stability if the U.S. numerical advantage ever wavered. "What in the name of God is strategic superiority?" asked Henry Kissinger in exasperation as hawks attempted to derail détente. "What is the significance of it, politically, militarily, operationally, at these levels of numbers? What do you do with it?"[75] There were theories behind these notions, of course: the spread of red on the map may have created the impression that momentum was on the side of the Soviets; losses in irrelevant areas might spread to those that were more important; the United States had to show resolve in the periphery to avert challenges in the core; Moscow knew it could not compete economically in the long run, so if it achieved nuclear superiority at any point the window of opportunity for action might be small; and so forth. But the primary reaction to Soviet victories was visceral, not intellectual. We could not abide the notion of losing anything, no matter how big or small, to Moscow. Getting to the moon was a wonderful achievement, but beating the Russians there made it glorious.

---

[74] For good examples of this argument, see Paul H. Nitze, "The Strategic Balance between Hope and Skepticism," *Foreign Policy*, No. 17 (Winter 1974/75), pp. 136–56; and Albert Wohlstetter, "The Delicate Balance of Terror," *Foreign Affairs*, Vol. 27, No. 2 (January 1959), pp. 211–35.

[75] The episode is recounted by Nicholas Thompson in *The Hawk and the Dove: Paul Nitze, George Kennan, and the History of the Cold War* (New York: Henry Holt and Co., 2009), p. 245, and analyzed by Barry M. Blechman and Robert Powell, "What in the Name of God is Strategic Superiority?" *Political Science Quarterly*, Vol. 97, No. 4 (Winter 1992–93), pp. 589–602.

To the hypercompetitive element in the U.S. battlefield of beliefs, every action is recorded on an ongoing scorecard, with losses deemed intolerable national humiliations. Today's opponents, whether they be Iran, China, or Al Qaeda, are also keeping score. When the United States closed an embassy in Yemen for a couple of days in January 2010 following a security threat, for example, William Kristol lamented that it was a "victory for Al Qaeda."[76] It remains to be seen whether the Arab Spring will constitute a victory or defeat for Al Qaeda, Iran, or the United States. Although it is not always clear just how any of this scoring helps or harms, what is certain is that the United States has to win at all times.

"Americans love a winner and will not tolerate a loser," Patton told his troops on the eve of D-Day, "That's why Americans have never and will never lose a war. Americans play to win, all the time. I wouldn't give a hoot in hell for a man who lost and laughed.... The very thought of losing is hateful to an American."[77] No state competes like the United States, and no people like to bask in the reflected glow of national glory as do Americans. Perhaps little harm is done when astronauts rather than cosmonauts plant a flag on the moon, and we all feel proud to be associated with victory. The consequences for foreign policy of the continuing importance of glory are, however, uniformly pathological.

Competitiveness and War: Victory for Victory's Sake

For hypercompetitive societies, victory itself is a national interest. Determining victory or defeat in war – especially guerrilla war – is hardly a straightforward process, however. Prolonged ambiguity is a much more common outcome, one that allows room for debate about which side is the victor and which the vanquished.[78] The people of the United States have little tolerance for gray areas when it comes

[76] Remarks made on *Fox News Sunday,* January 31, 2010, transcript available at http://www.foxnews.com/on-air/fox-news-sunday/2010/02/01/transcript-bipartisan-blue-ribbon-panel.

[77] Quoted in Dominic D. P. Johnson and Dominic Tierney, *Failing to Win: Perceptions of Victory and Defeat in International Politics* (Cambridge, MA: Harvard University Press, 2006), pp. 14–15.

[78] Johnson and Tierney, *Failing to Win*; and Robert Mandel, *The Meaning of Military Victory* (Boulder, CO: Lynne Rienner, 2006).

to foreign policy. Even when it comes to war they place a great deal of value on winning for its own sake, irrespective of tangible costs and benefits, which has a number of pathological effects on national security policy.

At times victory can become the primary metric for judging the wisdom of foreign policy ventures. Wars won were worth fighting, by definition, and those lost were not. Since victory tends to forgive error, the public excuses nearly any mission, no matter how bloody or counterproductive, as long as the United States is successful in carrying it out. As a result, presidents do not have to worry as much about wisdom as they do about winning, since the glory that accompanies success will sanctify even the most pointless cause. Victory would make Iraq worthwhile, this thinking goes, and victory alone.

Recent research makes it quite clear that U.S. public opinion about war is highly correlated with the perception of success.[79] Support for Iraq began to wane as the public lost faith in the potential for ultimate victory, for example. The national interest and humanitarian concerns often seem of secondary consideration, as if wars are games that need only to be won to be just. Vietnam is remembered as a disaster not only because of its high costs for virtually no benefit but because it was a defeat, the first for the United States since at least 1812. Nixon maintained until the end of his life that the war was not in fact lost; one of the chapters of his 1985 Vietnam retrospective is titled "How We Won the War," which explains how his successful policies were ultimately undercut by a variety of rapscallions.[80] In his mind the perception of victory would have justified the cost.

A similar dynamic occurred as the United States prepared to pull out of Iraq. Hawks objected strenuously when the Obama administration chose to remove almost all U.S. troops in the fall of 2011, not because of the risk of humanitarian crises or implications for U.S. security (since they were minimal), but because it threatened to "lose" the war or – God forbid – hand Iran a victory. Charles Krauthammer

[79] Christopher Gelpi, Peter D. Feaver, and Jason Reifler, *Paying the Human Costs of War: American Public Opinion and Casualties in Military Conflicts* (Princeton, NJ: Princeton University Press, 2009).
[80] Richard M. Nixon, *No More Vietnams* (New York: Arbor House, 1985). See also Lewis Sorley, *A Better War: The Unexamined Victories and Final Tragedy of America's Last Years in Vietnam* (New York: Harcourt Brace, 1999).

argued that although Obama was "handed a war that was won," through mendacity, incompetence, and crass political calculations he had squandered the victory.[81] "Iran has just defeated the United States in Iraq," lamented Frederick and Kimberly Kagan, which added points to Tehran's side of the geopolitical scorecard in the neoconservative imagination.[82]

Wars are acts of politics, not self-contained contests like chess where the only object is to win. Victory can even be counterproductive, as King Pyrrhus of Epirus could attest, if the costs outweigh the benefits. Indeed successful ventures, if they do not lead to any appreciable positive outcomes for the winner, are often not worth the price. On the most basic level, to be considered worthwhile wars must lead to *a better peace*, not just to a positive addition to the national statistics. Success or failure is only one of the criteria that must be applied to render judgment on wars, especially those not fought out of necessity. For U.S. policy makers and historians alike, too many times winning is "the only thing" considered in the evaluation of the decision to fight wars of choice.

Hypercompetitiveness also hampers decision making *in bello*, lengthening wars by encouraging belligerence long past the point that any realistic benefits can be expected. Once victory becomes the goal, it can eclipse those that originally motivated the war. Expensive, counterproductive victory can seem preferable to lower-cost, but inglorious, defeat. Military professionals, for whom nothing is as anathema as losing, are particularly susceptible to this belief. Since their entire training focuses on delivering victory, officers in the field are rarely in the best position to judge the political ramifications of continuing the fight. Clausewitz should remind them, however, that politics must always be the reason for war, the element that distinguishes it from mere violence. Those who seek the advice of generals should be aware that their recommendations will rarely include cutting losses and withdrawing before the war is won. Presidents are hardly immune. Johnson, for example, famously kept American troops in Vietnam

---

[81] Charles Krauthammer, "Who Lost Iraq?" *Washington Post*, November 4, 2011, p. A19. See also Frederick W. Kagan, Kimberly Kagan, and Marisa Cochrane Sullivan, "Defeat in Iraq," *The Weekly Standard*, Vol. 17, No. 8 (November 7, 2011).

[82] Frederick W. Kagan and Kimberly Kagan, "Out of Iraq," *Los Angeles Times*, October 27, 2011, p. 29.

in large part because he worried about being the first president to lose a war, which historian Frederik Logevall puts "at the top of the causal hierarchy for the Americanization of the war in 1964–65."[83] His country would have been better off if he had focused less on winning and losing and more on the national interest, a rational evaluation of which would have brought about a much earlier exit from the Southeast Asian quagmire.

The victory compulsion resists ambiguous outcomes, even when missions are presumably accomplished. The war in Korea could have ended in October 1950, for instance, when North Korean forces were expelled from the south. Indeed many of President Truman's advisors and other prominent observers of U.S. foreign policy – including George Kennan and Paul Nitze, who found themselves on opposite sides of many other issues – urged the president to stop the war at the 38th parallel, even if complete victory had not been accomplished.[84] But a war half won was inadequate for both the administration and its military, and U.S. troops pressed on toward the Yalu River and an entirely predictable Chinese counterassault. The war would drag on for three more years before ending at that starting point, wasting tens of thousands of U.S. lives (as well as the lives of hundreds of thousands of civilians) and destroying the Truman presidency in the process. When George H. W. Bush faced a similar choice regarding Saddam Hussein forty years later, he chose the opposite and refused to drive on to Baghdad. While failing to achieve "complete victory" might have enraged neoconservatives and other hawks, it led to a clean end to a quick – and relatively cheap – war.

Rational decisions regarding war are difficult to make in societies where victory is a virtue. There are times when admission of failure, as distasteful as it may be, is the wisest choice. Former Defense Department official Fred Iklé once observed with resignation that it is "commonplace in human affairs that men continue to labor on major undertakings a long time after the ideas upon which these efforts

---

[83] Fredrik Logevall, *Choosing War: The Lost Chance for Peace and the Escalation of the War in Vietnam* (Berkeley: University of California Press, 1999), p. 400.

[84] James I. Matray, "Truman's Plan for Victory: National Self-Determination and the Thirty-Eighth Parallel Decision in Korea," *Journal of American History*, Vol. 66, No. 2 (September 1979), pp. 314–33.

were based have become obsolete."[85] The desire to win can inspire such irrational labor, long past the point where the value of victory can be said to be worth the cost.

Competitiveness and Grand Strategy: Primacy

It should not be surprising that the world's most competitive state has made it a national priority to achieve and maintain the top position in the global hierarchy. "Primacy," which can be considered either a status atop that hierarchy or a grand strategy to maintain it, is the current scholarly buzzword. As a grand strategy, primacy seeks to achieve and maintain unquestioned leadership in the international order, the number one position in every category related to national power.[86]

It did not take long after the fall of the Soviet Union for American policy makers to decide that primacy ought to be a central goal of the United States. In 1992, a memo was drafted in the Pentagon under the direction of Paul Wolfowitz and I. Lewis "Scooter" Libby that laid out a conception of U.S. grand strategy that aimed at preventing the rise of any challengers to U.S. dominance.[87] The "Defense Planning Guidance," as the document was known, was circulated outside the Pentagon for comments, including to at least one person who apparently found the document objectionable enough to leak it to the *New York Times*.[88] Excerpts of the report were enough to cause a good deal

[85] Fred Charles Iklé, *Every War Must End*, 2nd ed. (New York: Columbia University Press, 2005), p. 129.

[86] Charles Krauthammer, "The Unipolar Moment," *Foreign Affairs*, Vol. 70, No. 1 (1991/92), pp. 23–33; Huntington, "Why International Primacy Matters," pp. 68–83; William Kristol and Robert Kagan, "Toward a Neo-Reaganite Foreign Policy," *Foreign Affairs*, Vol. 75, No. 4 (July/August 1996), pp. 18–33; Robert Kagan, "The Benevolent Empire," *Foreign Policy*, No. 111 (Summer 1998), pp. 24–35; Niall Ferguson, *Colossus: The Price of America's Empire* (New York: Penguin Press, 2004); Robert J. Lieber, *The American Era: Power and Strategy for the 21st Century* (New York: Cambridge University Press, 2005); and Mackubin Thomas Owens, "The Bush Doctrine: The Foreign Policy of Republican Empire," *Orbis*, Vol. 53, No. 1 (Winter 2009), pp. 23–40.

[87] A heavily redacted version of the document declassified in 2007 is available at the National Security Archive at George Washington University, http://www.gwu.edu/~nsarchiv/nukevault/ebb245/doc04.pdf. As is often the case, it is hard to imagine what possible damage could be done at this point by declassifying the whole document.

[88] Patrick E. Tyler, "U.S. Strategy Plan Calls for Insuring No Rivals Develop," *New York Times*, March 8, 1992. The bureaucracy learned an unfortunate lesson during the

of controversy, and the document was scuttled and not declassified for fifteen years. The sentiment, though, certainly had its share of sympathizers.

Robert Jervis has pointed out that in prior eras there would have been no need to ask whether primacy was worth the cost.[89] The desire to be the best and the strongest has usually not been irrational, since with great power has come great security. In a world without existential threats, however, the United States is already safe. National security is only tangentially relevant to the desire for primacy, therefore; the interest that hypercompetitive societies have for status goes beyond the practical. Even if there were no measurable advantages in being the best, U.S. policy makers and citizens alike would still desire the prestige and the glory that goes along with being number one. The threats that would accompany the end of the unipolar moment are more psychological than physical.

Competitive impulses drive the size and composition of the armed services at least as much as any rational evaluation of danger. Maintenance of status for the U.S. military now implies not just advantage but dominance in every imaginable category, or "full spectrum dominance," the ability to "defeat any adversary and control any situation across the full range of military operations," in the air, on land, and at sea, as well as in space and regarding information, according to Pentagon planning documents.[90] A commitment to full spectrum dominance would demand that the United States not accept second place in any category of military competition, no matter how relevant to its actual security, which is in any event all but assured a priori.

---

affair: national security planning documents can cause a good deal of political harm. Those documents that followed the 1992 DPG debacle – an endless string of Quadrennial Defense Reviews, National Security Strategies, National Military Strategies, National Defense Strategies, Quadrennial Diplomacy and Development Reviews, and dozens of others – are written with the overriding objective of being politically uncontroversial. As a result, they are horribly unreadable and bland.

[89] Robert Jervis, "International Primacy: Is the Game Worth the Candle?" *International Security*, Vol. 17, No. 4 (Spring 1993), pp. 52–67.

[90] The first Department of Defense document to discuss full spectrum dominance was *Joint Vision 2020* (Washington DC: U.S. Government Printing Office, June 2000), available at http://www.fs.fed.us/fire/doctrine/genesis_and_evolution/source_materials/joint_vision_2020.pdf. The quotation is on p. 6.

For a grand strategy to be rational, it must separate actual threats and opportunities extant in the system from those conjured up by hypercompetitive national imagination. The desire to be the best for its own sake should never be allowed to drive policy making. Surely it is worth periodically asking ourselves just how valuable being the world political and military champion is, since defending that title entails substantial costs.

Declinism

Generally speaking, people tend to be insecure regarding the most important things in their lives. If it is true that the United States is quite concerned about its international status, then one would expect assessments of that status to be commonplace, along with insecurity about the future. Indeed this is what we see. For at least a generation, a wide variety of analysts, observers, and scholars in the United States have warned about the impending (or even present) drop in various international rankings. The current round of declinism began in earnest about 2005, suggesting that many Americans continue to place a high value on being the best country in the world.

Warnings about inexorable processes of decline seem to accompany great power.[91] As soon as the United States attained great power status, observers emerged to declare that its power was waning. "The United States cannot afford another decline like that which has characterized the last decade and a half," wrote Kissinger in 1962. "Fifteen years more of a deterioration on our position in the world such as we have experienced since World War II would find us reduced to Fortress America in a world in which we had become largely irrelevant."[92] The United States experienced at least five waves of declinism during the Cold War, the most significant of which was probably that of the late 1970s through the mid- to late 1980s.[93] Paul Kennedy, whose was perhaps the most prominent voice of this generation, shrouded his pessimism in historical patterns he claimed to find in empires,

---

[91] Arthur Herman, *The Idea of Decline in Western History* (New York: Free Press, 1997).

[92] Henry A. Kissinger, *The Necessity for Choice: Prospects of American Foreign Policy* (Garden City, NY: Anchor Books, 1962), p. 1.

[93] Samuel Huntington discusses the previous waves of Cold War declinism in "The U.S.: Decline or Renewal?" *Foreign Affairs*, Vol. 67, No. 2 (Winter 1988), pp. 94–95.

implying a natural life cycle of great power of which the United States was nearing the end.[94]

One might have expected a bit of modesty from the declinists when the Cold War ended, since the relative power of the United States dramatically increased to the point that it became greater than that of any country, ever. Rather than admit that perhaps their announcements of waning power were a bit hasty, however, declinists tended to dig in their heels. In 1993, Edward Luttwak predicted that the United States was on its way toward becoming a "third world country" by 2020.[95] As late as 1996, Robert Gilpin was proclaiming himself an "unreconstructed declinist," demonstrating that few scholars ever admit error, no matter how overwhelming the evidence to the contrary.[96] Declinism reappeared in earnest in the first decade of the new century, fueled this time by confidence-shaking events and trends such as the war in Iraq, Chinese economic growth, and the 2008 financial crisis. "America is in unprecedented decline," wrote Robert Pape. Because the relative size of its economy is shrinking, "the unipolar world is indeed coming to an end," which means the world is entering a "highly dangerous" period.[97] We stand once again, as ever, at the end of the American era.

[94] Among the most prominent "declinists" were Paul Kennedy, *The Rise and Fall of the Great Powers: Economic Change and Military Conflict from 1500 to 2000* (New York: Random House, 1987); Walter Russell Mead, *Mortal Splendor: The American Empire in Transition* (Boston, MA: Houghton-Mifflin, 1988); David Calleo, *Beyond American Hegemony: The Future of the Western Alliance* (New York: Basic Books, 1987); Robert W. Tucker, "America in Decline: The Foreign Policy of 'Maturity,'" *Foreign Affairs*, Vol. 58, No. 3 (1979), pp. 449–84; and Robert Keohane, *After Hegemony: Cooperation and Discord in the World Political Economy* (Princeton, NJ: Princeton University Press, 1984).

[95] Edward Luttwak, *The Endangered American Dream: How to Stop the United States from Becoming a Third World Country and How to Win the Geo-Economic Struggle for Industrial Supremacy* (New York: Simon and Schuster, 1993), p. 118. Apparently Luttwak did not notice that the "second world" had disappeared.

[96] Robert Gilpin, "No One Loves a Political Realist," *Security Studies*, Vol. 5, No. 3 (Spring 1996), p. 5. There were some exceptions: Kennedy, for instance, wrote in 1999 that "in virtually all dimensions of power … the United States seems at present in a relatively more favorable position in the world than at any time since the 1940s." Paul Kennedy, "The Next American Century?" *World Policy Journal*, Vol. 16, No. 1 (Spring 1999), p. 56.

[97] Robert A. Pape, "Empire Falls," *The National Interest*, No. 99 (January–February 2009), pp. 21–34. See also Fareed Zakaria, *The Post-American World* (New York: W. W. Norton, 2008); Charles Kupchan, *The End of the American Era: U.S. Foreign Policy and the Geopolitics of the Twenty-First Century* (New York: Knopf, 2002); T. R. Reid, *The*

The mere fact that none of these arguments are new – and that they have always proven wrong before – does not mean they are incorrect now. Perhaps in the near future America will not be as dominant, at least in relative terms, compared to various moments in the past. It is important to note, however, that the evidence of relative decline remains thin. A decade into the new millennium, the United States remains far more powerful in a comparative sense than any country has ever been, economic crises notwithstanding. The world is still in most measurable and unmeasurable senses unipolar; the United States towers over all other states militarily, economically, politically, scientifically, technologically, and even culturally, despite the recession and overall meager growth that marked the end of the Bush years. China may be gaining in overall size of its economy, but it remains a far second. "To say that the world is now unipolar," explained Jervis in a recent *World Politics* issue devoted to the topic, "is to state a fact."[98]

Yet declinism remains and thrives. The newest wave is reminiscent of many that have followed disastrous wars of the past. The mixed bag of emotions that tends to follow foreign policy catastrophe – anger, guilt, shame, doubt – seems to contribute to an overall sense of pessimism about the future, and of foreign policy in general. It is no coincidence that Kennedy wrote *Rise and Fall of the Great Powers* in the United States in the 1970s, or that Otto Spengler wrote of the decline of the West in Germany in the early 1920s.[99] Disasters seem to portend even greater ones to come.

Why exactly relative decline would bring about disaster in a world free of major war is something not usually addressed in the declinist literature. Great Britain is hardly less safe – and is certainly not less prosperous – despite the fact that it suffered a drastic

United States of Europe: The New Superpower and the End of American Supremacy (New York: Penguin, 2004); Gideon Rachman, "Think Again: American Decline," *Foreign Policy*, No. 184 (January/February 2011), pp. 59–63; Christopher Layne, "This Time It's Real: The End of Unipolarity and the *Pax Americana*," *International Studies Quarterly*, Vol. 56, No. 1 (March 2012), pp. 202–13; and Zbigniew Brzezinski, *Strategic Vision: America and the Crisis of Global Power* (New York: Basic Books, 2012).

[98] Robert Jervis, "Unipolarity: A Structural Perspective," *World Politics*, Vol. 61, No. 1 (January 2009), p. 188. See also Stephen G. Brooks and William C. Wohlforth, *World out of Balance: International Relations and the Challenge of American Primacy* (Princeton, NJ: Princeton University Press, 2008).

[99] Oswald Spengler, *The Decline of the West* (New York: Knopf, 1926–1928).

diminution of relative power throughout the twentieth century.[100] Similarly, once imperial Spain ceased fighting in order to maintain its position at the top of the European hierarchy, it found itself in a much more sustainable economic position.[101] Indeed the only studies we have of the subject suggest that, despite fears to the contrary, decline is usually not followed by catastrophe. Peaceful, successful retrenchment is far more common, even during times when neighbors could reasonably have been expected to try to take advantage of weaknesses.[102] In the relatively safe, stable post–Cold War era, the tangible dangers posed by decline, even if real, would be rather minimal. The national ego might take longer to recover, but recover it would.

Hypercompetitive societies are insecure about their status; the United States is simultaneously the world's most powerful country and its most insecure. The perception of decline, if not kept under control, may lead to foolish foreign policy decisions in the future. If Washington remains under the impression that it is important to be the best, and that its status is slipping, then it might be willing to take steps to address that decline. "States may no longer fight to win status," Christopher Coker has written, "but they do so to retain it."[103] So too might the United States as the new century unfolds, if it does not come to the realization that it is pathological to focus so heavily on being the best.

PATHOGENESIS

As with the other pathological foreign policy beliefs, the prestige imperative has multiple, complex roots. A number of factors unique to U.S. society and historical experience amplify its competitiveness. An enhanced concern for prestige may also be a common reaction

---

[100] George L. Bernstein, *The Myth of Decline: The Rise of Britain since 1945* (London: Pimlico, 2004).

[101] Henry Kamen, "The Decline of Spain: A Historical Myth?" *Past and Present*, No. 81 (November 1978), pp. 24–50.

[102] Paul K. MacDonald and Joseph M. Parent, "Graceful Decline? The Surprising Success of Great Power Retrenchment," *International Security*, Vol. 35, No. 4 (Spring 2011), pp. 7–44.

[103] Christopher Coker, "War, Memes and Memeplexes," *International Affairs*, Vol. 84, No. 5 (September 2008), p. 908.

of unipolarity, or at least of great power. In other words, once again insight can be gained from each level of analysis.

Individual Level

"Competition," argued Huntington, "we all recognize as natural among individuals, corporations, political parties, athletes and universities; it is no less natural among countries."[104] The most basic explanation for the competitiveness of the United States would be that human beings, no less than other animals, are biologically hardwired to compete. Evolutionary common sense appears to imply that only the fittest survive to pass on their genes, which makes competition inevitable. Perhaps it is only natural to crave what Markey called the "irrational desire for applause."[105] However, the mountain of research discussed in this chapter casts doubt on that wisdom, no matter how conventional it may be, since a number of societies have proven essentially resistant to competition's charms. There is little reason to believe that competitiveness comes naturally to human beings. Its origins in U.S. foreign policy probably lie elsewhere.

State Level

At least three factors seem to have helped the glory pathology take root and grow in the United States. First, as the next chapter explains in more detail, no country exhibits a greater sense of exceptionalism than the United States, which has meaning only in comparison. The people of the United States cannot know that their country is different and special unless they examine it next to all the rest. There is a mutually reinforcing relationship, in other words, between exceptionalism and competitiveness. Horney wrote that one of the hallmarks of the hypercompetitive, neurotic personality is the need to "be unique and exceptional. While he may think in the comparative his aim is always in the superlative."[106] Exceptionalism is both the goal of and force behind competitive actors such as the United States.

---

[104] Huntington, "Why International Primacy Matters," p. 71.
[105] Markey, "Prestige and the Origins of War," p. 152.
[106] Horney, *The Neurotic Personality of Our Time*, p. 189.

Second, there is clearly a cultural aspect to competitiveness. Part of America's exceptionalism, and of its identity, is the image of the rugged individualist waging a battle against various destructive elements. The United States has an individualistic national culture, as opposed to collectivist or communitarian, regarding basic rights and freedoms, interpersonal relations, and overall sense of identity. Indeed, according to historical and empirical measures, the American people are the most individualistic on earth.[107] Since the same methods rank England as Europe's most individualistic society, perhaps it should be no surprise that a country with English roots would reflect that sense. In addition, scholars have pointed to the relative affluence of the United States, its open frontier, and its social and geographic mobility as possible factors to explain its high individualism scores.[108] Most important for these purposes, there is a direct correlation between individualism and competitiveness, as anthropologist Francis Hsu has persuasively argued.[109] Members of individualistic (as opposed to collectivist) societies are not programmed to place the needs of the community – whether comprised of people or states – above their own, and as a result are much more likely to consider themselves as operating in hostile, self-help environments.[110] The American culture teaches its people that they have to compete to survive in a dangerous world.

The political, economic, and legal systems chosen for the United States at its founding have surely helped foster a sense of competition in all aspects of its national life. Capitalism depends on the struggle between firms, where competitive pressures and creative destruction drive innovation, benefit for consumers, growth for the economy, and

---

[107] See especially the work of Dutch social psychologist Geert Hofstede, *Culture's Consequences: Comparing Values, Behaviors, Institutions, and Organizations across Nations* (Thousand Oaks, CA: Sage Publications, 2001); and Robert N. Bellah, Richard Madsen, William M. Sullivan, Ann Swidler, and Steven M. Tipton, *Habits of the Heart: Individualism and Commitment in American Life* (Berkeley: University of California Press, 1985).

[108] Harry C. Triandis, *Individualism and Collectivism* (Boulder, CO: Westview Press, 1995).

[109] Francis L. K. Hsu, *Rugged Individualism Reconsidered: Essays in Psychological Anthropology* (Knoxville: University of Tennessee Press, 1983).

[110] Harry C. Triandis, Robert Bontempo, Marcelo J. Villareal, Masaaki Asai, and Nydia Lucca, "Individualism and Collectivism: Cross-Cultural Perspectives on Self-Ingroup Relationships," *Journal of Personality and Social Psychology*, Vol. 54, No. 2 (February 1988), pp. 323–38.

overall development. Coke and Pepsi are locked in a competition because customers choose one at the expense of the other. Similarly, parties help make the American political system a zero-sum game. Offices are won and lost by groups in perpetual competition, staffed by consultants whose job it is to give their clients the best chance at victory. In a two-party system, not only the candidates but voters come to see governance more as a competition for office rather than as the method to distribute public goods. Even its legal system is more competitive than most others. The United States operates what legal scholars refer to as an "adversarial" system, in which judges act like referees between contesting sides. The "inquisitorial" systems practiced in much of the rest of the world allow judges much more freedom to ask questions and probe the arguments of the lawyers. As a result, the former system emphasizes winning and losing cases, whereas the pursuit of truth remains the highest calling of the latter.[111] The American people have become conditioned to compete, therefore, by the most basic social systems into which they have been born.

Its national competitiveness cannot help but have an impact on U.S. foreign policy. Basic learning theory suggests that people commonly transfer behavior developed in one environment to others. Once the competitive ethic has been inculcated into people in the classroom or the boardroom, it quickly spills over to shape behavior in other aspects of their lives. Sports psychologists have long understood that athletes often have trouble removing the competitive urges from their private lives, for instance.[112] "It is simply unrealistic," writes Kohn, "to think that the hostility engendered by and experienced during a contest will evaporate into thin air, leaving the relationship between two individuals unaffected."[113] Over time, it seems, competition conditions people to adopt adversarial postures in all areas of life. It should be no surprise that a country established with a competitive ethic at the core of its economic, political, and legal systems should have driven innovation in sports and other competitive ventures, or that it developed a

[111] Robert A. Kagan, *Adversarial Legalism: The American Way of Law* (Cambridge, MA: Harvard University Press, 2001); and Francesco Parisi, "Rent-Seeking through Litigation: Adversarial and Inquisitorial Systems Compared," *International Review of Law and Economics*, Vol. 22, No. 2 (August 2002), pp. 193–216.
[112] See Tutko and Bruns, *Winning is Everything*.
[113] Kohn, *No Contest*, p. 135.

very status-oriented view of its role in the international system. Once the competitiveness pathogen emerges, it is very difficult to contain.

System

Though unipolarity is not a sufficient condition to explain the enhanced importance Americans seem to place on status and victory, it may be a necessary one. A certain amount of prestige and glory accompanies unipolarity, even if that status was somewhat accidental, so the people of the United States take understandable pride in being the best. As a result, the suggestion that the United States may at some point no longer be the world's top power generates anxiety in the American public out of proportion to any actual threat such an outcome would pose to its security or prosperity.

Scholars have only recently begun to reexamine competition for status as an underlying motive for state behavior.[114] It is difficult for any person or group to decline, to relinquish the top position in a seemingly competitive system without a struggle. People often resist losses to a degree that is often not strictly rational. Psychologists Daniel Kahneman and Amos Tversky were awarded the Nobel Prize in economics for explaining how and why people react so disproportionately to losing.[115] Their insight, which has become known as *prospect theory*, is the academic expression of a phenomenon long understood by athletes: losing hurts far more than winning feels good.[116] Over and over again in hundreds of laboratory experiments subjects have reported depths of misery following losses that are lower than the

[114] Randall L. Schweller, "Realism and the Present Great Power System: Growth and Positional Conflict over Scarce Resources," in Ethan B. Kapstein and Michael Mastanduno, eds., *Unipolar Politics: Realism and State Strategies after the Cold War* (New York: Columbia University Press, 1999), pp. 28–68; William Wohlforth, "Unipolarity, Status Competition, and Great Power War," *World Politics*, Vol. 61, No. 1 (January 2009), pp. 28–57; Deborah Welch Larson and Alexei Shevchenko, "Status Seekers: Chinese and Russian Responses to U.S. Primacy," *International Security*, Vol. 34, No. 4 (Spring 2010), pp. 63–95.

[115] Only Kahneman was alive to accept the award. See especially Daniel Kahneman and Amos Tversky, "Prospect Theory: An Analysis of Decision under Risk," *Econometrica*, Vol. 47, No. 2 (March 1979), pp. 263–91.

[116] This quotation has been attributed to Hall of Fame baseball manager Sparky Anderson; see Christopher J. Fettweis, *Losing Hurts Twice as Bad* (New York: W. W. Norton, 2008).

height of satisfaction for equivalent gains.[117] As a consequence, we are much more liable to choose more risky options when facing a potential loss, and less risky ones when facing a gain.

Kahneman and Tversky found that people adjust quickly to a new status quo and judge all consequent events according to that standard. For example, they discovered that people who won one hundred dollars and then lost fifty reported being less happy than those who merely won fifty, even though the net gain was the same. Human beings just do not appear capable of remaining too happy or sad for long. The same process that allows us to recover after negative events (adaptation or "renormalization") also limits the time that we experience pleasure when positive things occur.[118] Good fortune and improvements to our lives quickly become part of our status quo, our reference point through which we judge new information.[119] Losses, however, are far more difficult to accommodate. Rarely are people or nations content to accept less than they currently have, whether that is measured in money, lower living standards, or status. Grievances can last generations, as the sons of the Confederacy can attest. It is irrational, perhaps, but universal: forward steps are soon forgotten, while those that go backward are remembered forever.

Prospect theory helps explain why the unipole might be expected to be more reluctant to accept a lower status than a rational evaluation of costs would suggest it should be. The nation's prestige is also our personal prestige; its honor is our honor. When our country wins, we file into the streets and celebrate our glorious victory. When it loses, we share the agony of defeat, whether or not we actually suffered in any serious way while war raged. No one wants to be associated with

---

[117] For more recent views from different fields, see Colin Camerer, "Prospect Theory in the Wild: Evidence from the Field," in Colin Camerer, ed., *Advances in Behavioral Economics* (Princeton, NJ: Princeton University Press, 2004), pp. 148–61; William A. Boettcher, "The Prospects for Prospect Theory: An Empirical Evaluation of International Relations Applications of Framing and Loss Aversion," *Political Psychology*, Vol. 25, No. 3 (June 2004), pp. 331–62; and Rose McDermott, James H. Fowler, and Oleg Smirnoff, "On the Evolutionary Origin of Prospect Theory Preferences," *Journal of Politics*, Vol. 70, No. 2 (April 2008), pp. 335–50.

[118] This process is described by psychologist Barry Schwartz in *The Paradox of Choice: Why More is Less* (New York: Harper Collins 2004), chapter 8.

[119] Robert Jervis, "Political Implications of Loss Aversion," in Barbara Farnham, ed., *Avoiding Losses/Taking Risks: Prospect Theory and International Conflict* (Ann Arbor: University of Michigan Press, 1994), p. 36.

a loser, whether it be a team, a presidential candidate, or a nation. It may be natural for the possibility of lost prestige to cause angst, but that does not make it rational, much less productive.

"For a prince," observed Machiavelli, "the first order of business is to escape mediocrity."[120] That seems to be the first order for the United States as well. Though it is no longer fashionable to discuss glory as a motivation for action, it persists as prestige, inspiring combative, competitive behavior and aggression in the hope of producing results that will outlive those who choose them. No matter what term is used, the belief in the importance of glory marches states toward folly. When the prestige imperative drives policy making in competitive directions, the United States is likely to behave in manifestly pathological ways.

Criticizing the obsession with competition is not merely an academic exercise, since its dangers may well increase over time. Although national decline may be more perception than reality, perceptions often drive behavior. If the people of the United States believe that it is important to stay ahead of the Chinese, they may support steps to maintain their status, to "win the future" by any means necessary. Unless this pathological belief is identified and its effects minimized, it has the potential to inspire unnecessary or counterproductive actions in the future, as it has throughout history.

"Peace is a word devoid of meaning," Napoleon wrote to his brother Joseph after Austerlitz. "What we need is a glorious peace."[121] Hopefully the leaders of the twenty-first century will come to appreciate peace and prosperity at face value, no matter what the status of their country happens to be.

[120] Markey, "Prestige and the Origins of War," p. 146.
[121] Michael Donelan, *Honor in Foreign Policy* (New York: Palgrave Macmillan, 2007), p. 65.

4

Hubris

The Superpower as Superhero

The aide said that guys like me were "in what we call the reality-based community," which he defined as people who "believe that solutions emerge from your judicious study of discernible reality." I nodded and murmured something about enlightenment principles and empiricism. He cut me off. "That's not the way the world really works anymore," he continued. "We're an empire now, and when we act, we create our own reality. And while you're studying that reality – judiciously, as you will – we'll act again, creating other new realities, which you can study too, and that's how things will sort out. We're history's actors ... and you, all of you, will be left to just study what we do."

A "senior advisor" to President Bush, speaking with reporter Ron Suskind, 2002[1]

The civil war that slowly filled the vacuum left by Saddam's regime horrified the Bush administration and other supporters of the war, and left them somewhat flabbergasted as well. The conquest had been as swift as expected, but the aftermath was not going as planned. By the time the 2007 surge of troops and change in strategy helped to reduce the sectarian violence to perhaps more tolerable levels, untold tens – perhaps hundreds – of thousands were dead, including more than four thousand Americans, and millions more had fled. The Iraqi economy was a wreck and de facto ethnic cleansing had divided the country.[2]

---

[1] Ron Suskind, "Without a Doubt," *New York Times Magazine*, October 17, 2004.
[2] Rajiv Chandrasekaran paints a clear picture of the Iraqi economy meltdown in *Imperial Life in the Emerald City: Inside Iraq's Green Zone* (New York: Knopf, 2007).

The United States had managed to do the impossible: it had actually made life in Iraq worse than it had been under Saddam Hussein.

It was not supposed to have gone this way. In the lead-up to the war, the administration had assured a wary public that toppling Saddam would be quick, easy, cheap, and glorious. Former Pentagon official Kenneth Adelman famously predicted that liberating Iraq would be a "cakewalk," which was the dominant message promoted by the war's proponents, even if some bristled a bit at the use of that word.[3] The Hussein regime was a house of cards, the American people were told, one that would collapse with the slightest nudge (or the "first whiff of gunpowder," according to Richard Perle).[4] American troops would be greeted as liberators, not conquerors; the streets of Baghdad and Basra, according to the vice president, were "sure to erupt with joy."[5] And while "ethnic differences" existed in Iraq, Deputy Secretary of Defense Paul Wolfowitz assured the American public they were exaggerated.[6] A healthy Iraqi democracy was waiting to replace Saddam's tyranny, needing only a little push to help bring it about. Furthermore, Iraqi oil would pay for it all. Extensive postconflict planning done by the State Department prior to the war was pushed aside, since there would be no need for its insights.[7] "Today," William Kristol and Lawrence Kaplan wrote in 2002, "we may attack Iraq with minimal risk."[8] The fact that many – if not most – military professionals did not share this optimism was apparently of no consequence.[9]

[3] Kenneth Adelman, "Cakewalk in Iraq," *Washington Post*, February 13, 2002, p. A27. Discerning optimists can perhaps detect a subtle distinction between "cakewalk" and "walk in the park," which he had predicted six months earlier. Kenneth Adelman, "Desert Storm II Would Be a Walk in the Park," *London Times*, August 29, 2002.

[4] Remarks made on the PBS series *Wide Angle*, July 11, 2002.

[5] Dick Cheney, Speech to Veterans of Foreign Wars, Nashville, TN, August 26, 2002.

[6] Quoted by Thomas Ricks in *Fiasco: The American Military Adventure in Iraq* (New York: Penguin, 2006), p. 96.

[7] See Chandrasekaran, *Imperial Life in the Emerald City*, pp. 29–37.

[8] Lawrence F. Kaplan and William Kristol, *The War over Iraq: Saddam's Tyranny and America's Mission* (San Francisco, CA: Encounter Books, 2003), p. 83.

[9] Army Chief of Staff Eric Shinseki was the most prominent officer to suggest toppling Saddam might be a bit more difficult than the rosy analyses suggested. Though he was forced into retirement as a result, events vindicated his views and his reputation has risen accordingly.

Iraq was not the first case of U.S. leaders misled by cakewalk expectations, and it probably will not be the last. Over and over again, the United States has overestimated its capabilities and as a result made decisions that, in retrospect, appear bafflingly ill advised. From the Bay of Pigs invasion through the wars in Vietnam and Iraq, Washington has repeatedly exhibited the kind of overconfidence the Greeks would immediately recognize as hubris, or inflated self-esteem that leads inevitably to folly.

In fact, no country displays the symptoms of hubris more clearly than does the United States. Only in the United States could a secretary of state not be mocked for claiming that "if we have to use force, it is because we are America; we are the indespensible [*sic*]nation. We stand tall and we see further than other countries into the future."[10] Only a U.S. leader could proclaim that it was "our responsibility to history" to "rid the world of evil," as did George W. Bush, and have his people rally behind him as if such a thing were actually possible.[11] Only the United States feels its ideals and system are not only universally applicable but gifts from God, deserving of aggressive promotion in all corners of the world. The United States is more evangelical in its foreign policy than any other state, and committed evangelicals cannot help but display the haughtiness and intellectual arrogance we normally see as hallmarks of hubris.

Derek Reveron has written that the disaster in Iraq taught the United States "that being a superpower does not make it a superhero that can accomplish anything it desires."[12] This is probably true in the short term; temporary periods of humility have followed previous overextensions in Vietnam, Somalia, and elsewhere. Rather than seek enduring lessons, however, Americans have dismissed these periods as aberrations or even "syndromes" from which the nation needs to recover, to regain its normal level of confidence. Recent history gives

[10] Madeleine K. Albright, Interview on NBC's *The Today Show*, February 19, 1998, available at http://secretary.state.gov/www/statements/1998/980219a.html, accessed September 14, 2010.
[11] President George W. Bush, Remarks at the National Cathedral, September 14, 2001.
[12] Derek S. Reveron, "Military Diplomacy and the Engagement Activities of Combatant Commanders," in Derek S. Reveron and Judith Stiehm, eds., *Inside Defense: Understanding the U.S. Military in the 21st Century* (New York: Macmillan, 2008), p. 51.

little reason to believe that Iraq's lessons will endure, either. It will not be long before the limits to their power are again obscured to the point that they will be impossible for U.S. leaders to recognize. A certain degree of self-analysis might be needed before the United States realizes that it is not a superhero, and that the national interest occasionally compels presidents to say "no, we can't." A dash of modesty now and again would probably help as well.

HUBRIS AS A CATEGORY OF PATHOLOGICAL BELIEFS

Barry Buzan has argued that the United States is particularly susceptible to what he called "middle kingdom syndrome," in which it sees itself as the center of the universe, the "exclusive holder of the only civilized values and standards that matter," a state that has nothing of importance to learn from the rest of the world.[13] What he meant, without saying it explicitly, was that the United States suffers from hubris, a malady as old as humanity itself. The common understanding of hubris has changed little since it was first described by the ancient Greeks. Arrogance, extreme haughtiness, or excessive pride before the gods led to the downfall of many characters in their histories and tragedies, usually at the hands of Nemesis, the avenging goddess.[14] Among moderns, Nemesis takes the form of overconfidence, overestimations of self-worth and excess self-esteem, or an "arrogance of power," to use the words of former Senator William Fulbright. The Greeks felt hubris was the chief sin common among leaders, and the principal fountain, not only of bad judgment and disaster, but of most political instability.[15] From that fountain springs a variety of pathological beliefs, all related to an inflated sense of the possible,

---

[13] Barry Buzan, *The United States and the Great Powers: World Politics in the Twenty-First Century* (Malden, MA: Polity, 2004), p. 164.

[14] Unfortunately, the Greek form of the word made its way into English rather than the Latin equivalent, *superbia*, which strikes this author as having a bit more panache.

[15] Joseph J. Spengler, "Social Science and the Collectivization of Hubris," *Political Science Quarterly*, Vol. 87, No. 1 (March 1972), p. 3. See also Douglas L. Cairns, "Hybris, Dishonour, and Thinking Big," *Journal of Hellenistic Studies*, Vol. 116 (1996), pp. 1–32. Warren Hedges argues the Greeks actually defined hubris somewhat differently; for simplicity's sake, this chapter relies on the common understanding. See his entry in Simon Hornblower and Antony Spawforth, eds., *Oxford Classical Dictionary*, 3rd ed. (New York: Oxford University Press, 1996), p. 732.

overestimation of capabilities, and underestimation of cost. The United States is different from other countries, its public and leaders believe, and better. It is the indispensible nation, chosen by God to do His work on earth. Most important, hubris leads many in the United States to believe that there is virtually no limit to what their nation can accomplish, once its mind is made up. Icarus felt no danger in flying near the sun; likewise, Oedipus acted in willful disobedience of the gods, Alcibiades convinced the Athenians of the wisdom of invading Sicily, and George W. Bush led his country into Iraq.

Hubris can also be considered a behavioral manifestation of narcissism, or excessive love of self, which causes a grandiose sense of importance and confidence in those afflicted with it. According to the current *Diagnostic and Statistical Manual of Mental Disorders* of the American Psychiatric Association, those with "narcissistic personality disorder" entertain fantasies of unlimited power and success, as well as a sense of being special and unique.[16] Narcissists require "excessive admiration," and have a need for constant attention and praise.[17] It is possible to be narcissistic toward one's personal or national identity; in other words, the disorder can afflict both individuals and states. The influence of narcissism and hubris on foreign policy is predictable, understandable, and, in the end, one hopes, treatable.

HUBRIS AND FOREIGN POLICY

The beliefs associated with hubris shape foreign policy in a few general, pathological ways. First and most obviously, its overestimation of capabilities makes international action more likely by decreasing expectations of costs while increasing those of success, effectively lowering the bar for invasions and interventions. Hubris also causes states to misjudge the likely reactions of others to their initiatives. Finally, it causes actors to ignore outside counsel, trusting in their own judgment even when their closest allies are united in opposition.

[16] Michael B. First and Allan Tasman, eds., *DSM-IV-TR Mental Disorders: Diagnosis, Etiology, and Treatment* (Hoboken, NJ: John Wiley & Sons, 2004).

[17] Jerrold M. Post, "Current Concepts of the Narcissistic Personality: Implications for Political Psychology," *Political Psychology*, Vol. 14, No. 1 (March 1993), p. 100. See also Heinz Kohut, *The Analysis of the Self: A Systemic Approach to the Psychoanalytic Treatment of Narcissistic Personality Disorders* (Chicago, IL: University of Chicago Press, 2009).

All of these become perhaps a bit more understandable and even predictable when explained in the context of the underlying narcissistic personality disorder.

Overestimation of Capability

"The consequences of positive illusions in conflict and international politics are overwhelmingly harmful," Daniel Kahneman and Jonathan Renshon recently argued, because such illusions "generally favor hawkish, aggressive behavior."[18] Indeed hubris has its most pernicious influence on the cost-benefit analyses that precede any war of choice. This is particularly dangerous for the United States, for whom the majority of wars and all interventions are choices, as opposed to necessities, to use the current terms of art.[19] Very rarely do truly existential threats arise that demand action on part of the world's safest country. Today the United States always chooses whether or not to fight, since inaction is always a viable option. There have of course been times when the benefits of intervention have proven to outweigh the costs, making the choice of war the correct one – World War II, Somalia, and Afghanistan are examples – so "war of choice" need not be a pejorative label, only an accurate one. Choices they were, and choosing necessarily involves some prior analysis.

Such analyses suffer when made by policy makers in the throes of national hubris. Inflated senses of self-worth tend to be accompanied by unrealistic expectations for success. Hubris causes policy makers to underestimate risks, making the difficult appear easy and the impossible merely difficult.[20] In the words of Richard Ned Lebow, it leads actors to "embrace complex, risky and unrealistic schemes and to deny, distort, explain away or ignore information indicating

---

[18] Daniel Kahneman and Jonathan Renshon, "Hawkish Biases," in A. Trevor Thrall and Jane K. Cramer, *American Foreign Policy and the Politics of Fear: Threat Inflation Since 9/11* (New York: Routledge, 2009), p. 82.

[19] Lawrence Freedman appears to have first discussed the war of choice/war of necessity dichotomy in "Revolution in Strategic Affairs," *Adelphi Series*, No. 318 (International Institute for Strategic Studies, 1998).

[20] See Baruch Fischhoff, Paul Slovic, and Sarah Lichtenstein, "Knowing with Certainty: The Appropriateness of Extreme Confidence," *Journal of Experimental Psychology*, Vol. 3, No. 4 (November 1977), pp. 552–64.

that they were unlikely to succeed."[21] When the risks of action are underestimated, policy makers can be in for nasty, expensive surprises. The relationship of hubris to the invasion of Iraq – and to the decisions made post invasion, such as de-Ba'athification and the dismissal of the Iraqi army – needs little further discussion, since it has been discussed at length elsewhere and its consequences are well known.[22] Indeed the connections between unwarranted overconfidence and a variety of disasters should be quite clear. Doubt rarely enters into the mind of the narcissist for whom, according to psychiatrist Jerrold Post, "dogmatic certainty with no foundation of knowledge is a posture frequently struck."[23]

Hubris can overcome what seem to be the most obvious warning signs. Though it is often unfair for historians to pass harsh judgment on foreign policy decisions once retrospect has made their consequences clear, the April 1961 invasion of Cuba is not one of those cases. Many red flags should have at the very least given the Kennedy administration serious pause prior to the landings at the Bay of Pigs. There was no hope of surprise, for one thing, since the build-up, training, and impending invasion were closely covered by the U.S. media. "Anti-Castro Units Trained to Fight at Florida Bases," proclaimed a headline on the front page of the *New York Times* eight days before the invasion, with a subheadline that read "Invasion Reported Near." The Department of State expressed concern that "the operation was no longer secret but is known all over Latin America."[24] Castro, whose agents apparently paid attention to U.S. news reports, rounded up thousands of potential troublemakers in the days prior to the landings. Furthermore, though professional soldiers were among the invasion force, the majority were volunteers with no military experience at all. And though the planners felt

[21] Richard Ned Lebow, *A Cultural Theory of International Relations* (New York: Cambridge University Press, 2008), p. 100.

[22] Peter Beinart, *The Icarus Syndrome: A History of American Hubris* (New York: Harper Collins, 2010); David Owen, *The Hubris Syndrome: Bush, Blair and the Intoxication of Power* (London: Politico's, 2007); and Michael Isikoff and David Corn, *Hubris: The Inside Story of Spin, Scandal, and the Selling of the Iraq War* (New York: Three Rivers Press, 2006).

[23] Post, "Current Concepts of the Narcissistic Personality," p. 104.

[24] Piero Gleijeses, "Ships in the Night: The CIA, the White House and the Bay of Pigs," *Journal of Latin America Studies*, Vol. 27, No. 1 (February 1995), p. 12.

there was no way the operation could succeed without support from the Cuban people, the CIA was receiving (and apparently ignoring) reports that anti-Castro rebels were starving in their mountain outposts, shunned by the broader society.[25] Their internal estimates indicated Castro could count on the support of about 75 percent of the Cuban population.[26]

In other words, though a rational analysis should have concluded that the chances of success were quite slim, an overconfident United States pressed onward toward utterly predictable disaster (although it was probably a better outcome for the United States in the long run, since "success" would have resulted in a prolonged guerrilla war with inevitable U.S. involvement).[27] Afterward, President Kennedy asked Theodore Sorensen, his special counsel, a question many echoed at the time and since: "How could I have been so stupid to let them go ahead?"[28]

For the narcissist, writes Post, "there is a preoccupation with fantasies involving unrealistic goals."[29] The attractiveness of the foreign policy fantasies of the United States – whether they were of a Cuba without Castro or a democratic Middle East – have too often blinded policy makers to the difficulties of actually bringing them about. Dictators are fragile, therefore, not daunting, and their people will welcome our help rather than resent the interference. Fred Kagan predicted in early 2008 that we could turn Iraq into a "normal democratic country" replete with a thriving tourist industry "in a year or so."[30] So far, at least, few tourists have flocked to Baghdad, despite our best efforts. Douglas Feith, the number three person in the Pentagon

---

[25] For reviews of this rather exquisite folly that cover all of the events described in this paragraph, see Peter Wyden, *Bay of Pigs: The Untold Story* (New York: Simon and Schuster, 1979) and Howard Jones, *The Bay of Pigs* (New York: Oxford University Press, 2008).

[26] Gleijeses, "Ships in the Night," p. 30.

[27] Indeed Robert Kennedy assured the president that the operation "really can't be a failure," since the rebels could always take to the woods and become guerrillas. The CIA's head of the operation, Deputy Director for Plans Richard Bissell, admitted three decades later: "We had no plan on how to end the war." Gleijeses, "Ships in the Night," pp. 36, 28.

[28] Wyden, *Bay of Pigs: The Untold Story*, p. 8.

[29] Post, "Current Concepts of the Narcissistic Personality," p. 103.

[30] Derek Leebaert, *Magic and Mayhem: The Delusions of American Foreign Policy from Korea to Afghanistan* (New York: Simon & Schuster, 2010), p. 237.

during the first Bush administration, believed the war would allow the United States to "transform the Middle East and the broader world of Islam generally."[31]

For too many, these beliefs did not die in Iraq. In fact Iraq's descent into civil war did little to shake the neoconservative belief in the inherent fragility of authoritarian political order. Michael Ledeen has argued for two decades that overthrowing the regime in Iran would be a simple affair, or a "piece of cake."[32] Jonah Goldberg, editor-at-large of the *National Review Online* and a leading conservative public intellectual, recommended in a series of columns in 2000 that the United States invade Africa – the whole continent – to build stable societies and bring order, civilization, and enlightenment.[33] While neoconservatives may be the most blatantly confident in the capabilities of the United States to destroy and rebuild nations, they are hardly alone. Unchecked power has turned many people who were doves during the Cold War into hawks eager to demonstrate U.S. omnipotence by curing a variety of the world's ills. Liberals as well as conservatives have proven receptive to the image of the United States wearing the superhero's cape, willing and able to resist the forces of injustice wherever they rear their heads.

It is hubris that causes leaders to believe anything is possible if they just work hard enough, or that the United States can accomplish anything it wants. The "can-do optimism" of the United States may be an asset when it comes to innovation, education, and economics, but it can warp the appreciation for the dangers involved with foreign policy adventures. Superman is not only morally compelled to act but he risks nothing by doing so, and will always succeed in the end. Once the limits are taken off, once anything seems possible, only imagination

---

[31] Quoted in Andrew Bacevich, "He Told Us to Go Shopping: Now the Bill is Due," *Washington Post,* October 5, 2008, p. B3.

[32] Michael Ledeen, "The War on America," remarks made at Tulane University, March 30, 2011. His optimism extended beyond Iraq: he also suggested twenty U.S. Marines properly equipped and deployed to the Shi'ite areas of Saudi Arabia would be sufficient to bring down the monarchy.

[33] Jonah Goldberg, "A Continent Bleeds," *National Review Online,* May 3, 2000, available at http://www.nationalreview.com/articles/204646/continent-bleeds/jonah-goldberg, and "Goldberg's Africa Invasion," *National Review Online,* May 10, 2000, available at http://www.nationalreview.com/articles/204649/goldbergs-african-invasion/jonah-goldberg.

limits the set of options for the United States. Inaction, rather than intervention, begins to bear the burden of justification.

Exacerbated Misperception

Policy makers under the spell of hubris, especially those who tend toward narcissism, are likely to misperceive more than their own capabilities. Because they are so deeply ensconced in themselves, narcissists have an especially difficult time understanding others, whether adversary or ally.[34] The second effect hubris has on foreign policy is the repeated misjudgment of the likely reactions to our initiatives.

People tend to overestimate their influence on the decision making of others. "Because an actor's actions loom large to him," Robert Jervis argued in his classic work on misperception, "overgeneralizing often involves the belief that his behavior was a major influence on the outcome."[35] Since we are the most important actors in our world, it follows that we must be an important factor in theirs as well. None of this is meant to imply that the actions of others are not affected by our actions, of course, only that we are likely to place a greater explanatory role on us than is warranted. This phenomenon, which psychologists refer to as the "egocentric bias," blocks empathy and understanding, and has a great deal of experimental evidence to support it.[36]

President Carter and his administration, and indeed a large portion of the U.S. foreign policy community, interpreted the 1979 Soviet invasion of Afghanistan as a major new initiative in Cold War superpower relations.[37] They assumed that it was meant to test U.S.

---

[34] Post, "Current Concepts of the Narcissistic Personality," p. 112.

[35] Robert Jervis, *Perception and Misperception in International Politics* (Princeton, NJ: Princeton University Press, 1976), p. 234.

[36] Michael Ross and Fiore Sicoly, "Egocentric Bias in Availability and Attribution," *Journal of Personality and Social Psychology*, Vol. 37, No. 3 (March 1979), pp. 322–26.

[37] Richard Ned Lebow and Janice Gross Stein, "Afghanistan, Carter and Foreign Policy Change: The Limits of Cognitive Models," in Dan Caldwell and Timothy J. McKeown, eds., *Diplomacy, Force, and Leadership: Essays in Honor of Alexander L. George* (Boulder, CO: Westview Press, 1993), pp. 95–128. For other pessimistic conclusions about Soviet intentions, see Zbigniew Brzezinski, *Power and Principle: Memoirs of the National Security Advisor, 1977–1981* (New York: Farrar, Straus, and Giroux, 1983); Dennis Ross, "Considering Soviet Threats to the Persian Gulf," *International Security*, Vol. 6, No. 2 (Fall 1981), pp. 159–80; and Francis Fukuyama, *The Soviet Threat to the Persian Gulf* (Santa Monica, CA: RAND Corporation, No. 6596, March 1981).

mettle as the opening salvo of a drive to the Persian Gulf, rather than the final step in a prolonged effort to remove a puppet regime in the near abroad that had grown uncooperative, which was an alternate hypothesis readily available at the time (and that has since been fully confirmed).[38] Carter's reaction – he called the invasion the "greatest threat to peace since World War II" – turned a local crisis into a global one, and scuttled détente.[39]

Hubristic policy makers also tend to overestimate the extent to which others will cooperate with, or at least not overtly resist, their overtures. They assume their capabilities are as obvious to others as they are to themselves, which makes them assume others will choose to cast their lot with the side that will certainly succeed. Specifically, then, *hubris leads states to anticipate bandwagoning behavior,* even in cases where balancing would otherwise seem quite predictable. Hitler's hubris caused him to believe the British would seek an accommodation once France was crushed under Nazi armor, for example. Similarly, the Japanese were under the impression that the United States would sue for peace following a *fait accompli* at Pearl Harbor rather than resist. Both misjudgments, as is typical of those generated by hubris, proved quite costly. It comes as something of a shock to U.S. policy makers when other states choose to balance against the United States, if softly, rather than bandwagon with its benevolent hegemony.[40]

---

[38] Current scholarship makes it quite clear that the invasion was the result of mission creep, with quite local ends. See a new translation of the Russian original book by Vladimir Snegirev and Valery Samunin, published in English as *The Dead End: The Road to Afghanistan,* available as a free e-book on the webpage of the National Security Archive at George Washington University, National Security Archive Electronic Briefing Book No. 396, October 13, 2012, http://www.gwu.edu/~nsarchiv/ NSAEBB/NSAEBB396/Full%20Text%20Virus%20A.pdf, accessed December 18, 2012. The archive also has a collection of original documents from the era, available online and analyzed by Aleksandr Antonovich Lyakhovskiy, *Inside the Soviet Invasion of Afghanistan and the Seizure of Kabul, December 1979* (Washington, DC: Woodrow Wilson Center), Cold War International History Project, Working Paper #51, January 2007. See also Anatoly Dobrynin, *In Confidence* (New York: Random House, 1995), esp. p. 441.

[39] Carter quoted in Dobrynin, *In Confidence*, p. 443.

[40] For discussions of "soft balancing," which is currently itself a rather soft concept, see Robert Pape, "Soft Balancing against the United States," *International Security*, Vol. 30, No. 1 (Summer 2005), pp. 7–45; and Stephen G. Brooks and William C. Wohlforth, "Hard Times for Soft Balancing," *International Security*, Vol. 30, No. 1 (Summer 2005), pp. 72–108.

The Clinton administration's decision to expand rather than contract NATO was based on the belief that over time the Russians would come to see its presence as a stabilizing force and therefore positive, rather than ominous or threatening. President Clinton and his advisors were reportedly surprised by the angry Russian reaction to the news that the decision to expand the alliance had been made. Both the president and Secretary of State Warren Christopher were caught completely off guard by the hostility of their counterparts at a summit in Budapest in December 1994.[41] How they could have anticipated otherwise is a bit of a puzzle. Despite warnings from the vast majority of academic and policy experts about the likely Russian reaction and overall wisdom of expansion itself – historians and political scientists had been nearly united in opposition, a phenomenon John Lewis Gaddis called "uncharacteristic," which was an understatement – the administration failed to understand Moscow's position.[42] Expansion's proponents did not seem to give much consideration to what their reaction would have been had the situation been reversed, if the Warsaw Pact were expanding following a U.S. Cold War defeat. Would they have interpreted such a move as benevolent, as the extension of the sphere of stability and prosperity? Would they have accepted Russian assurances of benign intentions? Only a state blinded by hubris could convince itself that a former rival would accept and indeed welcome an expansion of potentially hostile security guarantees over territory that until very recently was under its control.

American leaders have also commonly misjudged popular reactions to their policies. The decision to invade Cuba was bolstered by a particular belief that has recurred with regularity throughout recent American history, one that holds that our interventions will be met by throngs of delighted locals. Time and again policy makers in Washington have been puzzled by the underappreciation of foreigners, who not only have failed to recognize the benevolence of our intentions but reacted with active hostility. Vice President Cheney was no doubt a bit surprised when eruptions of Iraqi joy and gratitude failed to materialize, or at least did not last long. From the

[41] James M. Goldgeier, *Not Whether But When: The U.S. Decision to Enlarge NATO* (Washington, DC: Brookings Institution Press, 1999), pp. 86–87.

[42] John Lewis Gaddis, "History, Grand Strategy and NATO Enlargement," *Survival*, Vol. 40, No. 1 (Spring 1998), pp. 145–51.

Philippines to Laos to Afghanistan, other peoples have repeatedly proven unenthusiastic about being conquered or have rapidly soured on the occupations that have followed.

Imbalances of power grossly complicate the already perilous process of perception among states. A number of factors make it even more difficult than usual for strong and weak states to truly understand one another. The strong state cannot really appreciate the paranoia asymmetric power generates; the weaker feels fundamentally threatened, and must always assume the worst to hedge against strategic disaster since its margin for error is small. The strong power tends to treat the weak as if it had the same freedom of maneuver it enjoys, and the weak assumes the strong must understand its small capabilities pose no significant threat. This natural elevated level of misunderstanding is exacerbated when the larger power is also the victim of hubris. Such states are even worse than usual at empathizing with others, which leads to intensified misperceptions. The gulf in understanding between the United States and Iran is perhaps the most obvious and important current example of this pathological phenomenon, but it is not alone. Indeed today power imbalances inevitably mark every bilateral relationship involving the United States. Unless its leaders are conscious of these predictable effects and take action to minimize them, misperceptions are likely to arise in each case.

Going It Alone: Hubris and Unilateralism

Finally, hubris makes actors less receptive to the counsel of others. Warnings of danger are readily dismissed as politically motivated, cowardly, or overly pessimistic. "It is difficult for the narcissist," according to Post, "to acknowledge ignorance and accordingly to seek or accept information or constructive criticism of his ideas."[43] To do so would be to admit flawed knowledge or insufficient wisdom, both of which are anathema to the fragile narcissistic ego. Hubris not only makes actors unreceptive to criticism or external advice, but it can make them downright hostile to it. This manifests itself in the willingness – and indeed sometimes the preference – to act alone.

[43] Post, "Current Concepts of the Narcissistic Personality," p. 110.

Often these solo preferences have to be somewhat hidden, for domestic political purposes. Multilateralism has become enough of a buzzword that even those who most oppose working in concert with others must pay lip service to it. Supporters of the Iraq war are quick to point out that the United States was supported by a "coalition of the willing" and that a group of over thirty states contributed to the effort. This is an effort at obfuscation, not analysis. Today multilateralism has become all but synonymous with actions taken under UN auspices, which the war in Iraq most certainly was not. Vice President Cheney argued vociferously against involving the United Nations in any stage of the deliberative process, in the belief that the institution would only weaken the entire effort.[44] Most of the Iraq coalition was willing only to curry favor with Washington in the expectation of payback in the future, an expectation that was often fulfilled.[45] The war in Iraq was essentially an American, or at best an Anglo-American, expedition.

Post–Cold War America, the state that sees farther and more clearly into the future, has rarely felt constrained by myopic poltroons in Old Europe and elsewhere. That the United States found no meaningful support for the war in Iraq outside of Great Britain and Australia was not a concern of the hawks, who dismissed warnings of others as the whining of effeminized, irresponsible weaklings.[46] The United States was quite prepared to act alone, and indeed often preferred it. The warning of allies, of course, proved prescient. As journalist Peter Beinart has suggested, the people of the United States needed not its allies' tanks, but their judgment.[47]

Recent history contains no shortage of similar instances when the United States would have been better off had it listened to voices of caution from its friends. Washington's allies were puzzled by its preoccupation with Cuba in the early 1960s, and consistently warned against

[44] The vice president's views on this and other preinvasion cooperation issues are discussed at length by Bob Woodward in *Bush at War* (New York: Simon and Schuster, 2002) and *Plan of Attack* (New York: Simon and Schuster, 2004).

[45] It is surely no coincidence that Georgia and Vanuatu, two willing coalition members, were among the first recipients of Millennium Challenge aid while many other theoretically more deserving states were left off the list.

[46] Robert Kagan, *Of Paradise and Power: America and Europe in the New World Order* (New York: Knopf, 2003).

[47] Beinart, *The Icarus Syndrome*, p. 7.

invasion. Historian Arthur Schlesinger, a senior advisor to President Kennedy, caught an earful of criticism when he visited Western European capitals shortly after the disaster. He noted deep "shock and disillusion" over the debacle among diplomats, political leaders, and private citizens alike.[48] Cautionary warnings from abroad continued as the United States increased its commitment to Southeast Asia as the decade wore on, even from Washington's closest friends, who never seemed to understand the importance the United States placed on irrelevant, postimperial backwaters like Vietnam and Laos.[49] "If the Americans are not too stupid," French president Charles de Gaulle told his cabinet in January 1964, "they will put an end to this absurd Vietnam War."[50] In both cases, the allies were correct.

The basic logic that the opinion of the many is often wiser than that of the one is lost on the hubristic, who trust their own views above all others whenever necessary. Overconfident actors welcome neither the assistance nor the opinions of others.

HUBRIS BEYOND WAR

Unnecessary military interventions are only the most obvious consequence of cakewalk thinking. Hubris makes a wide variety of unrealistic goals appear possible, if challenging, which has over the years led the United States to pursue a number of ill-considered policies in the belief that there are no limits to what it can do once its mind is set.

Nation Building

Many times since the end of World War II, the United States has attempted to reshape other countries to fit an image of its choosing. Washington made it a top Cold War priority to address the economic,

[48] Jones, *The Bay of Pigs*, p. 132.
[49] See Fredrik Logevall, *Choosing War: The Lost Chance for Peace and the Escalation of the War in Vietnam* (Berkeley: University of California Press, 1999), esp. pp. 123–25; and Eugenie M. Blang, *Allies at Odds: America, Europe, and Vietnam, 1961–1968* (New York: Rowman and Littlefield, 2011).
[50] Fredrik Logevall, "America Isolated: The Western Powers and the Escalation of the War," in Andreas W. Daum, Lloyd C. Gardner, and Wilfried Mausbach, eds., *America, the Vietnam War, and the World* (New York: Cambridge University Press, 2003), p. 180.

political, and even cultural strength of states that appeared vulnerable to communist infiltration. That impulse persists, providing the foundation for what has become known as *nation building* the modern version of which has replaced the anticommunist element with a paternalistic concern for the development of political and legal institutions, as well as economic growth and even religious evolution, for strategic purposes. A 2007 RAND study pointed out that since the end of the Cold War the United States has embarked on a nation-building exercise on average once every two years.[51] Such interventions are invariably based on the belief that target states will prove willing and even eager to receive U.S. aid and advice, and will come to accept the notion that outsiders know better than they do about what is best for their societies.[52]

As it happens, however, many nations prove stubbornly resistant to building. The experiences in Haiti, Bosnia, Kosovo, Afghanistan, Iraq, and elsewhere ought to suggest at the very least that nation building is a daunting and difficult task, one that takes years of effort and hundreds of billions of dollars to be successful. While sometimes worthwhile, these tasks should not be entered into lightly. "What is remarkable about this entire experience," observed Francis Fukuyama, "is how little institutional learning there has been over time; the same lessons about the pitfalls and limitations of nation-building have to be relearned with each new involvement."[53] One of those central lessons should be that other people, even those from less developed societies, are not likely to be passive consumers of received wisdom from the United States.

The experience in Somalia is instructive, if misunderstood. The United States led the efforts of the international community to relieve a man-made famine in late 1992, and saved somewhere between one hundred thousand and two hundred fifty thousand lives.[54] The

[51] James Dobbins, Seth G. Jones, Keith Crane, and Beth Cole DeGrasse, *The Beginner's Guide to Nation-Building* (Santa Monica, CA: RAND, 2007).
[52] Jeremi Suri, *Liberty's Surest Guardian: American Nation-Building from the Founders to Obama* (New York: Free Press, 2011).
[53] Francis Fukuyama, "Nation-Building and the Failure of Institutional Memory," in Francis Fukuyama, ed., *Nation-Building beyond Afghanistan and Iraq* (Baltimore, MD: Johns Hopkins University Press, 2006), p. 8.
[54] In the modern era, famines are man-made. See Amartya Sen, *Development as Freedom* (New York: Knopf, 1999). On the Somalia experience, see Walter Clarke and Jeffrey

mission was a resounding success, at least until the mission began to
evolve beyond famine relief. "Combatants must be disarmed, retrained
and re-employed," explained U.S. Ambassador to the United Nations
Madeleine Albright. "Development aid must be delivered and effi-
ciently used. Democratic institutions must be established. Those
who disrupt the peace must be stopped."[55] Once the United States
accepted the idea that its forces had to stay until a stable Somali state
emerged, it began to engage in a wholly different task. Nation building, not humanitarian intervention, failed in Somalia. The latter does
not necessitate the former. Presumably the international community
could have left Somalia with the promise to return if the warlords
allowed famine to break out again. The Somalis needed to work out
their own governance for it to succeed (and still do). They can benefit
from economic aid, training, and ideas, no doubt, but not direction
and micromanagement from outsiders.

The conventional wisdom that nation building inevitably follows
intervention is an underexamined intellectual relic of the Marshall
Plan. In 1994, for example, the Clinton administration could presumably have sent troops to Rwanda and brought an end to the genocide
without involving itself much in the details of postconflict reconstruc-
tion, which would have saved at least some innocent Tutsis. If genocide
had erupted again, the Marines could have returned. Kinetic military
operations are, after all, what this nation does best. The United States
does not have the responsibility to rebuild every time it intervenes.
The "Pottery Barn rule" Secretary of State Colin Powell supposedly
discussed with President Bush prior to Iraq – "if you break it, you
own it" – might be enforceable in malls, but it only has relevance to
international politics if the United States believes it does.[56] There are
times when things need to be broken, to extend the metaphor, even
if the United States is not capable of (or interested in) putting them
back together again.

The belief in the national security importance of nation building
has only strengthened since the attacks of September 11, after which

Herbst, "Somalia and the Future of Humanitarian Intervention," *Foreign Affairs*, Vol.
75, No. 2 (March–April 1996), pp. 70–85.

[55] Madeleine K. Albright, "Yes, There Is a Reason to Be in Somalia," *New York Times*,
August 10, 1993, p. A19.

[56] Woodward, *Plan of Attack*, p. 150.

many strategists and pundits arrived at the conclusion that the only long-term solution to terrorism is to aid in the development – economic, political, even religious – of the states from which it springs, or to address its "root causes." As a result, hundreds of billions of counter-terror dollars have been spent trying to drag Afghanistan out of the Middle Ages, to bolster moderates in Pakistan, and to spark development in Yemen. "We fight against poverty because hope is an answer to terror," President Bush told an audience in Mexico in March 2002.[57] The connection between poverty and terrorism is one of the few issues regarding which the former president found himself in agreement with the editors of the *New York Times*, who argued in 2004 that "economics cannot be separated from national security. Young Pakistanis who can't get jobs in factories that export to America sometimes go to training camps to learn how to kill Americans."[58]

The idea that the poor turn to terrorism as an outlet for their anger, and that therefore the solution for their violence is development, is a widespread, plausible fiction. If poverty led to terrorism, then presumably the poorest countries would produce the greatest numbers of terrorists, which clearly is not the case. Not only do terrorists rarely emerge from the least developed countries – precious few come from sub-Saharan Africa, for instance – but they do not even represent the poorest parts of the areas from which they do come, such as the Arab world. Complicated statistical analyses should not be necessary to demonstrate that there is no correlation between national poverty and terrorism, much less a causal relationship. Such analyses do exist, but common sense ought to suffice.[59] There does not appear to be any connection at the micro level either: a widely discussed, sophisticated study of Pakistanis released in May 2011 found no correlation

[57] Remarks by President George W. Bush at the International Conference on Financing for Development, Monterrey, Mexico, March 22, 2002, available at http://www.un.org/ffd/statements/usaE.htm.

[58] *New York Times*, "Nourishing the Muslim World," October 25, 2004.

[59] Alan B. Krueger and Jitka Malečková, "Education, Poverty and Terrorism: Is there a Causal Connection?" *Journal of Economic Perspectives*, Vol. 17, No. 4 (Fall 2003), pp. 119–44; Alberto Abadie, "Poverty, Political Freedom, and the Roots of Terrorism," *American Economic Review*, Vol. 96, No. 2 (May 2006), pp. 50–56; and James A. Piazza, "Rooted in Poverty? Terrorism, Poor Economic Development, and Social Cleavages," *Terrorism and Political Violence*, Vol. 18, No. 1 (March 2006), pp. 159–77.

between local poverty and support for extremist groups. In fact, poor
Pakistanis reported far more antipathy toward militant groups than
members of the middle class.[60] Alleviating poverty in developing
nations remains a great moral imperative, to be sure, but one that
should not be conflated with national security.

 . If the eradication of poverty cannot provide a magic bullet to eliminate terrorism, then perhaps religious evolution can. Al Qaeda and
its allies claim to practice a particularly conservative form of Islam,
one promoted by Saudi money in hundreds of schools, or *madrassas*, across the Muslim world. Some terrorism analysts have suggested
that Washington ought to engage in an ideological battle to shape the
course of that religion by providing funding to antiextremist elements
as a counterweight to the conservative, poisonous Saudi financing.[61]
The United States needs to change the Muslim faith, in other words,
nudging it toward moderation and modernity. "A forward strategy
of freedom cannot but give priority to religion-shaping," explained
former State Department official Tony Corn, which would involve
establishing American-funded madrassas and "putting an end to rote
learning" in the Arab world.[62]

The idea that an outsider could shape the development of one of
the world's great religions could only be promoted by those especially
blinded by hubris. If one were to believe the United States can do
anything it sets out to do, then it follows that changing the way hundreds of millions of people practice their ancient faith is within its
grasp. However, proponents of religion shaping might consider the
likely reaction in the United States or any predominantly Christian
country if outside powers attempted to shape the development of its
belief system. One might reach the conclusion that any attempt to do

[60] Graeme Blair, C. Christine Fair, Neil Malhotra, and Jacob N. Shapiro, "Poverty and Support for Militant Politics: Evidence from Pakistan," *American Journal of Political Science*, Vol. 57, No. 1 (January 2013), pp. 30–48.
[61] Angel Rabasa, Cheryl Benard, Lowell H. Schwartz, and Peter Sickle, *Building Moderate Muslim Networks* (Santa Monica, CA: RAND, 2007); and Ronald R. Krebs, "Rethinking the Battle of Ideas: How the United States Can Help Muslim Moderates," *Orbis*, Vol. 52, No. 2 (Spring 2008), pp. 332–46.
[62] Tony Corn, "World War IV as Fourth-Generation Warfare," *Hoover Institution Policy Review* (January 2006), available at http://www.hoover.org/publications/policy-review/article/6526. See also Norman Podhoretz, *World War IV: The Long Struggle against Islamofascism* (New York: Doubleday, 2007), pp. 214–15.

so would not only be a tremendous waste of time but might produce the opposite of what it intends.

The United States has supported what it sees as a more palatable form of Islam in Pakistan since 9/11, with predictably poor, counterproductive results. The version preferred by Washington, Sufism, has suffered under the perception of Western taint. Attempts to hide the source of financial support for initiatives like a Sufi council, concerts, and a university have failed, and as a result many Pakistanis have begun to consider all Sufis pawns of American intelligence. Their shrines have been attacked all over Pakistan.[63] The religion-shaping effort has backfired and has provided a boost to extremism.

Finally, it is worth noting that the belief that nation building is a viable possibility has turned those times when the United States failed to do so into points of contention that have occasionally shaped future policy in pathological ways. That the United States "abandoned" its allies in Afghanistan after the Soviets left, for example, allowing fundamentalism to grow amid the chaos, is a widely accepted charge, one that compelled policy makers to persevere in the effort to remake the country after the overthrow of the Taliban. As Senators McCain, Lieberman, and Graham wrote recently, "We abandoned Afghanistan in the 1990s, and the result was a fanatical regime that allowed its territory to become a base for global terror attacks, while inflicting medieval tyranny on the Afghan people, especially women. If we quit Afghanistan again," they warned, "the consequences will be disastrous for both our peoples."[64]

How exactly the United States could or should have engaged in the late 1980s is usually left to the imagination. As the events of the past decade should have made clear, Afghanistan is about as immune to foreign influence as it is possible to be. It is hard to imagine how U.S. intervention could have stopped the civil war that followed the Soviet withdrawal, or meaningfully effected economic growth, or prevented the rise of the Taliban. Had the United States continued or increased its aid to post-Soviet Afghanistan, it is quite likely events would have

[63] See Mohammed Hanif, "Survival State," *New York Times*, June 26, 2011, p. BR29; and Anatol Lieven, *Pakistan: A Hard Country* (New York: Public Affairs, 2011), esp. p. 141.

[64] John McCain, Joseph I. Lieberman, and Lindsey Graham, "Sustaining Success in Afghanistan," *Washington Post*, March 21, 2012.

unfolded in much the same way. This is of course hardly convincing to those who believe that the United States is capable of doing virtually anything to which it sets its mind. Washington failed to build a strong Afghan nation in the aftermath of the Soviet occupation, the belief goes, and it has been paying the price ever since.

During most attempts at nation building, local communities have shown little interest in having their societies reshaped by paternalistic outsiders, no matter how well meaning they might have been. They are happy to take money from Westerners, and have learned to say the things that will keep it flowing, but ignore their counsel whenever necessary. If the hubris pathology could be recognized and minimized, the impulse to build nations for strategic reasons would surely wane, development and humanitarian assistance would be kept separate from national security imperatives, and all parties would be better off.

In her analysis of the folly of Vietnam, historian Barbara Tuchman called nation building "the most presumptuous of all the illusions," and expressed amazement that the descendents of settlers to a virgin land "failed to learn from their success that elsewhere, too, only the inhabitants can make the process work."[65] It is comforting, but illusory, to think otherwise.

Public Diplomacy

All states make efforts to sell their policies to the world at large. When others do it, it is "propaganda"; when we do it, it is "public diplomacy" or diplomacy designed to reach the people of other countries. The Defense Department prefers a different term, one that perhaps better captures the intent of the effort: "strategic communications." But by any name the attempt to spread positive images of the United States has been pursued with renewed energy since 9/11.[66] The modern generation of public diplomats has been inspired by the victory

---

[65] Barbara Tuchman, *The March of Folly: From Troy to Vietnam* (New York: Ballantine Books, 1984), p. 375.

[66] On public diplomacy, see Peter G. Peterson, "Public Diplomacy and the War on Terrorism," *Foreign Affairs*, Vol. 81, No. 5 (September–October 2002), pp. 74–94; and Martha Bayles, "Goodwill Hunting," *The Wilson Quarterly*, Vol. 29, No. 3 (Summer 2005), pp. 46–56.

of ideas during the Cold War, when freedom and democracy proved more attractive to those who sat on ideological fences than communist tyranny. That the former was inherently more appealing than the latter is a point that often seems missed, however. No major sales job was necessary to convince the people of Eastern Europe that they would prefer to live like their counterparts on the other side of the wall. The West sold itself. The instances of concerted, targeted public diplomacy during the Cold War, such as the efforts to "win hearts and minds" in Vietnam, were often unsuccessful. Our post–Cold War efforts have been meeting a similar fate.

"Be it ethnic or religious," according to Corn, "identity-shaping is not rocket science. Since U.S. marketers do that routinely every day, it can be outsourced to a large extent by the public diplomacy bureaucracy."[67] While nation building addresses the political, economic, and legal systems of target states, public diplomacy hopes to shape their ideas and desires, in effect making them want to do what we want them to do. It is essentially an attempt to generate what Joseph Nye has called "soft power," or the "ability to get what you want through attraction rather than coercion or payments."[68] Unfortunately, soft power is quite difficult to produce – it is by-product, not product – and effectively impossible to yield in any constructive sense. The soft power of any state is largely outside of its control, since it is transmitted through the messages from society more than by official government actions. The admiration and adulation of other people simply cannot be manipulated as easily as optimists seem to think.

Their optimism led to the creation of the position of undersecretary of state for public diplomacy and public affairs in 1999. The first post-9/11 undersecretary was Charlotte Beers, a prominent Texas advertising executive, under whose guidance the Bush administration financed, among other things, a series of commercials portraying smiling, satisfied American Muslims and a couple of Arabic-language radio stations. Beers resigned in March 2003, and her immediate successor lasted less than seven months. Karen Hughes, one of President Bush's closest advisors, was next, and despite the high-profile appointment

---

[67] Corn, "World War IV as Fourth-Generation Warfare."
[68] Joseph S. Nye, *Soft Power: The Means to Success in World Politics* (New York: Public Affairs, 2004), p. x.

the image of the United States among Muslims failed to improve. Each undersecretary soon realized that the Middle East is particularly immune to manipulation by official sources, since its residents have a long and understandable tradition of greeting what governments tell them with skepticism.

If the relevant metric is favorable opinions of the United States and its policies, the billions spent on outreach to the Muslim world have been wasted. Over the course of the past decade, Arab views of U.S. foreign policy, already deeply skeptical, grew worse. Shibley Telhami has conducted extensive polling in six countries whose governments are (or were) considered friendly to Washington – Egypt, Jordan, Lebanon, Morocco, Saudi Arabia, and the United Arab Emirates – and has found that the percentage of people reporting favorable or somewhat favorable views of the United States has consistently been in or near the single digits, results more or less consistent with what has been found in other surveys from across the region.[69] Public diplomacy has failed to overcome the negative impressions the United States has generated through its actions, especially the invasion of Iraq and continued, unconditional support for Israel. As it turns out, selling the United States is not as easy as selling Coke. The only measurable changes in foreign public opinion of the United States have followed concrete actions, such as disaster relief or the election of Barack Obama, and even those have proven temporary.

Fortunately, this failure to sell a positive image has had little impact on U.S. national security: persistent high levels of anti-American sentiment have not translated into sympathy for its enemies. The fundamental assumption of post-9/11 public diplomacy – that anti-Americanism leads to terrorism – has not proven true. Despite the fact that Muslim antipathy toward U.S. policies has been at record highs throughout the period, Al Qaeda has not appeared to benefit.

[69] The latest of Shibley Telhami's annual reports is "2011 Arab Public Opinion Poll," University of Maryland in conjunction with Zogby International, November 21, 2011, available at http://www.brookings.edu/research/reports/2011/11/21-arab-public-opinion-telhami, accessed December 18, 2012. See also Gallup, "U.S. Approval Gains Nearly Erased in Middle East/North Africa," September 30, 2010, available at http://www.gallup.com/poll/143294/Approval-Gains-Nearly-Erased-Middle-East-North-Africa.aspx. For some analysis, see Peter J. Katzenstein and Robert O. Keohane, eds., *Anti-Americanism and World Politics* (Ithaca, NY: Cornell University Press, 2006).

Only 6 percent of Telhami's respondents report being sympathetic to Al Qaeda's Islamist goals, and 7 percent approved of its methods, which is another finding echoed from poll to poll.[70] Sympathy for a group does not necessarily translate into support, of course, much less active participation. The "war on terror" has never been zero-sum, in that ideological losses for Washington have translated into gains for fundamentalists. The people of the Arab world appear capable of disdaining both at once.

In fact there is some evidence that public diplomacy can actually be counterproductive, especially in places where it is most needed, where views of the United States are already negative. Two University of Toronto political scientists conducted fascinating experiments in Kyrgyzstan and Tajikistan during which they exposed locals to a variety of public diplomacy efforts; the locals' view of the United States actually grew worse.[71] "People do not merely *discount* a statement attributed to someone who lacks credibility," they conclude. "Their suspicions instead cause the expected framing effect to be *resisted* and *reversed*."[72]

A certain degree of anti-Americanism is inevitable in some corners of the world. Fortunately, the inability to control the opinions of others is hardly a catastrophic weakness. High levels of public antipathy do not necessarily lead other countries to oppose U.S. policies any more than pro-American sentiment delivers their support. Though the Bush administration was more reviled than any administration in memory, national interest often inspired other states to put aside popular ire and cooperate when appropriate. The United States did not become a pariah or boycotted outcast. Conversely, though the Obama

[70] Shibley Telhami, "What Arab Public Opinion Thinks of U.S. Policy," Brookings Institution Forum, December 2005, transcript available at http://www.brook.edu/fp/saban/events/20051212.pdf; see also Program on International Policy Attitudes (PIPA), "Large and Growing Numbers of Muslims Reject Terrorism, Bin Laden" (College Park: Center for International and Security Studies, University of Maryland), June 30, 2006, available at http://www.worldpublicopinion.org/pipa/articles/international_security_bt/221.php?nid=&id=&pnt=221&lb=btis, both accessed December 18, 2012.
[71] Edward Schatz and Renan Levine, "Framing, Public Diplomacy, and Anti-Americanism in Central Asia," *International Studies Quarterly*, Vol. 54, No. 3 (September 2010), pp. 855–69.
[72] Schatz and Levine, "Framing, Public Diplomacy, and Anti-Americanism in Central Asia," p. 866, emphasis in original.

administration was at first undoubtedly more popular in nearly every corner of the world than its predecessor, it has run into trouble attracting cooperation from other states when national interests are in conflict. So while it would be nice if the United States was liked by people abroad, in the final analysis international public opinion does not decisively determine the behavior of states. Relative levels of anti-Americanism are overrated, or at least not nearly as important as many people think they are. Public diplomacy is not harmful; it is merely pointless. Its failure does not imperil the interests of the United States, which will survive throughout the coming century just fine, no matter how many people across the Islamic world disapprove of what it does.

Public diplomacy assumes that other people are simple, malleable, facile, passive consumers of information. Only the most hubristic, least self-aware nation would believe that lipstick can change the perception of a pig, to paraphrase an old saying. The sooner U.S. leaders recognize that hearts and minds are won with action, not words (much less radio stations or thirty-second commercials), the better off all sides will be.

Aversion to Apology

Apologies are by their nature, at a minimum, somewhat humbling and potentially humiliating. In moments of crisis among individuals or states, however, few acts defuse tensions more rapidly than the simple act of contrition.[73] Not all states treat the admission of error the same way, though; to some, and in some cultures, apologies are expected in cases of clear blunder, while to others they are a debasing, unnecessary act of national humiliation.[74] The United States clearly falls into the latter category. Harry Truman's personal credo – "don't ever apologize for anything" – could easily be said to apply to the country he led.[75]

[73] Aaron Lazare, "Go Ahead: Say You're Sorry," *Psychology Today*, Vol. 28, No. 1 (January 1995), pp. 40–45; and Nicholas Tavuchis, *Mea Culpa: A Sociology of Apology and Reconciliation* (Stanford, CA: Stanford University Press, 1991).

[74] On the international politics of apologies, see Jennifer Lind, *Sorry States: Apologies in International Relations* (Ithaca, NY: Cornell University Press, 2008); and Alex Dudden, *Troubled Apologies among Japan, Korea and the United States* (New York: Columbia University Press, 2008).

[75] Quoted in Lind, *Sorry States*, p. 1.

Some of the staunch opposition to apologies has roots in the credibility imperative, which counsels that they may signal weakness and inadvertently embolden enemies. William Kristol and Robert Kagan warned, for example, that even considering an apology following the EP-3 incident in April 2001 had put the United States "on the path to humiliation," which would lead the Chinese to "try to exploit it again and again, most likely in a future confrontation over Taiwan."[76] There is also a cultural element to the U.S. aversion to contrition: in the hyper-litigious culture of the United States, legal counsel routinely cautions that apologies are de facto admissions of liability that open the door to legal action down the road. To avoid legal responsibility, in effect, people often abandon their social responsibility. It would be unheard of in the United States for a CEO of a U.S. airline to apologize in person to relatives after a crash before the investigation was complete, as did Yasumoto Takagi, the president of Japanese Air Lines, in August 1985. Though apologies may well make lawsuits less likely – indeed a good deal of evidence from the medical profession suggests that doctors who apologize are much less likely to be sued for malpractice – fear of liability prevents their more widespread use.[77] The American aversion to apology may therefore have more than simply hubristic roots.

But while concerns over credibility and liability can take some credit for the U.S. aversion to apology, surely there remains an element in society that instinctively recoils from any suggestion of U.S. imperfection. The United States always tries to do the right thing, they claim, so other states should realize that its errors are made in good faith. Furthermore, Americans really have little to apologize for, since the good they provide to the world far outweighs whatever bad might come from minor peccadilloes. As long as other countries refuse to apologize for whatever far more egregious sins they have committed,

---

[76] Fortunately, but not surprisingly, no such exploitation occurred. William Kristol and Robert Kagan, "A National Humiliation," *The Weekly Standard*, April 16–23, 2001, pp. 11–16.

[77] A meta-analysis of the effects of apologies on malpractice litigation can be found in Allen Kachalia, Samuel R. Kaufman, Richard Boothman, Susan Anderson, Kathleen Welch, Sanjay Saint, and Mary A. M. Rogers, "Liability Claims and Costs before and after Implementation of a Medical Error Disclosure Program," *Annals of Internal Medicine*, Vol. 153, No. 4 (August 17, 2010), pp. 213–21.

there is no imperative for the United States to do so. Narcissists, after all, cannot abide imperfection.

This element has been on particularly stark display since 2009, when President Obama's critics began complaining that he has appeared a bit too willing to apologize for past transgressions, even going on "apology tours" soon after taking office.[78] Former Secretary of Defense Donald Rumsfeld has repeatedly accused the president of "making a practice of trying to apologizing for America," which Rumsfeld himself would never have done, he explained, since he was proud of his country.[79] To emphasize the distinction between himself and the president, Mitt Romney titled his campaign memoir *No Apology: The Case for American Greatness.*[80] That the president actually offered no apologies on these "tours" was beside the point.[81]

For too many Americans, patriotism and contrition cannot coexist. Willingness to apologize is prima facie evidence of insufficient love of country. The United States, it seems, has no need to apologize for anything, ever; to do so is to admit imperfection, which cannot help but shake the foundations of fragile, hubris-ridden national egos. As a result, minor crises that could be quickly resolved through a little honest repentance, like those that follow mid-air collisions between spy planes and fighters, risk becoming elevated to national showdowns. Rarely is damage to egos worth the material cost often paid to avoid it.

Illusions of Hegemony

The final and in some ways most important pathological belief generated by hubris places the United States at the center of the current era of relative peace. "All that stands between civility and genocide, order

---

[78] Karl Rove, "The President's Apology Tour," *Wall Street Journal,* April 23, 2009.

[79] Quoted in Glenn Kessler, "Obama's 'Apology Tour,'" *Washington Post,* posted February 22, 2011, available at http://voices.washingtonpost.com/fact-checker/2011/02/obamas_apology_tour.html, accessed December 18, 2012.

[80] Mitt Romney, *No Apology: The Case for American Greatness* (New York: St. Martin's Press, 2010).

[81] The *Washington Post*'s fact checker gave the notion of an "apology tour" his highest rating for dishonesty, concluding it "never happened." Kessler, "Obama's 'Apology Tour.'"

and mayhem," explain Kaplan and Kristol, "is American power."[82] This belief is a variant of what is known as the "hegemonic stability theory," which proposes that international peace is only possible when one country is strong enough to make and enforce a set of rules.[83] Although it was first developed to describe economic behavior, the theory has been applied more broadly to explain eras of relative stability in the international system. At the height of Pax Romana between roughly 27 BC and 180 AD, for example, Rome brought an unprecedented level of peace and security to the Mediterranean. The Pax Britannica of the nineteenth century was an era of relative stability on the high seas. Perhaps the current era is peaceful because the United States has established a de facto Pax Americana with a set of clear rules that are generally in the interests of all countries to follow.

Opinion is split about how necessary the United States continues to be in the maintenance of that beneficial world order. Some scholars have suggested that stability could outlast direct U.S. hegemony, that the institutions, law, and norms promoted by the United States have become internalized by members of the system to the extent that their existence is not dependent upon active promotion.[84] The majority of those writing on this topic, however, think differently. A hegemon-free hegemonic stability strikes many as unlikely to last. For this larger group of strategists, a rather logical policy implication follows: since instability may break out around the globe in the absence of a rule enforcer, the United States must continue to play that role.[85] Were the United States to abdicate its responsibilities, unchecked conflicts

---

[82] Kaplan and Kristol, *The War over Iraq*, p. 118.

[83] On hegemonic stability theory, see Charles Kindleberger, *The World in Depression, 1929–1939* (Berkeley: University of California Press, 1974); Robert O. Keohane, *After Hegemony: Cooperation and Discord in the World Political Economy* (Princeton, NJ: Princeton University Press, 1984); and David A. Lake, "Leadership, Hegemony, and the International Economy: Naked Emperor or Tattered Monarch with Potential?" *International Studies Quarterly*, Vol. 37, No. 4 (December 1993), pp. 459–89.

[84] G. John Ikenberry, *Liberal Leviathan: The Origins, Crisis, and Transformation of the American World Order* (Princeton, NJ: Princeton University Press, 2011).

[85] William Kristol and Robert Kagan, "Toward a Neo-Reaganite Foreign Policy," *Foreign Affairs*, Vol. 75, No. 4 (July/August 1996), pp. 18–33; Niall Ferguson, *Colossus: The Price of America's Empire* (New York: Penguin, 2004); Michael Mandelbaum, *The Case for Goliath: How America Acts as the World's Government in the 21st Century* (New York: Public Affairs, 2005); and Robert Kagan, *The World America Made* (New York: Knopf, 2012).

would at the very least bring humanitarian disaster and, in today's interconnected world, send economic turmoil rippling throughout global financial markets. Former National Security Advisor Zbigniew Brzezinski warned of "outright chaos" and a string of specific horrors that could be expected to follow a loss of hegemony, including new or renewed attempts to build regional empires (by China, Turkey, Russia, and Brazil) and the collapse of the U.S. relationship with Mexico as emboldened nationalists south of the border reassert 150-year-old territorial claims. Overall, without U.S. dominance, today's relatively peaceful world would turn "violent and bloodthirsty."[86] The liberal world order that is so beneficial to all would come crumbling down.

There are good theoretical and empirical reasons, however, to doubt that U.S hegemony is the primary cause of the current stability. First of all, the hegemonic-stability argument displays the classic symptom of hubris: it overestimates the capability of the United States, in this case to maintain global peace. No state, no matter how strong, can impose peace on determined belligerents. The U.S. military may be the most imposing in history, but it can only police the system if the other members generally cooperate. Self-policing must occur, in other words; if other states had not decided on their own that their interests are best served by peace, then no amount of international constabulary work by the United States could keep them from fighting. The 5 percent of the world's population that lives in the United States simply cannot force peace upon an unwilling 95 percent. Stability and unipolarity may be simply coincidental.

For U.S. hegemony to be the explanation for global stability, the rest of the world would have to expect reward for good behavior and fear punishment for bad. Since the end of the Cold War, the United States has not proven eager to enforce rules on a consistent basis. Even rather incontrovertible evidence of genocide has at times not been enough to inspire action. Hegemonic stability can only take credit for influencing decisions that would have ended in war without the presence, whether physical or psychological, of the United States. Ethiopia and Eritrea are hardly the only states that could go to war without the slightest threat of U.S. intervention, yet few choose

---

[86] Zbigniew Brzezinski, "After America," *Foreign Policy*, No. 191 (January/February 2012), pp. 1–4. See also Kagan, *The World America Made*.

to do so. Since most of the world today is free to fight without U.S. involvement, something else must be affecting their calculations.[87] Stability exists today in many places to which U.S. hegemony does not extend.

It is worthwhile to repeat one of the most basic observations about misperception in international politics, one magnified by hubris: rarely are *our* actions as consequential upon *their* behavior as we believe them to be. Ego-centric biases suggest that while it may be natural for U.S. policy makers to interpret their role as crucial in the maintenance of world peace, they are almost certainly overestimating their own importance. At the very least, Washington is probably not as central to the myriad decisions in foreign capitals that help maintain international stability as it thinks it is.

If U.S. security guarantees were the primary cause of the restraint shown by the other great and potentially great powers, then those countries would be demonstrating an amount of trust in the intentions, judgment, and wisdom of another that would be without precedent in international history. If the states of Europe and the Pacific Rim detected a good deal of danger in the system, relying entirely on the generosity and sagacity (or, perhaps the naiveté and gullibility) of Washington would be the height of strategic irresponsibility. Indeed it is hard to think of a similar choice: When have any capable members of an alliance virtually disarmed and allowed another to protect their interests? It seems more logical to suggest that the other members of NATO and Japan just do not share the same perception of threat the United States does.[88] If dangers really exist, as so many in the U.S. national security community insist, then the grand strategies of the allies would be quite different. Even during the Cold War, allies of the United States were not always convinced that they could rely on its security commitments. Extended deterrence was never entirely comforting, since Europeans could never be completely sure the United States would indeed prove willing to sacrifice New York for Hamburg. In the absence of the unifying Soviet threat, their trust in

---

[87] For a review of the possible explanations for the current era of stability and peace, see John Mueller, "War Has Almost Ceased to Exist: An Assessment," *Political Science Quarterly*, Vol. 124, No. 2 (Summer 2009), pp. 297–321.

[88] See Christopher J. Fettweis, "Free Riding or Restraint? Examining European Grand Strategy," *Comparative Strategy*, Vol. 30, No. 4 (Fall 2011), pp. 316–32.

U.S. commitments for their defense would presumably be lower, if in fact that commitment was at all necessary outside of the most pessimistic works of fiction.

Furthermore, if hegemonic stability logic is to account for restrained allied behavior, it is not enough for these states to be convinced about the capability and benevolent intentions of the United States. They must also trust its judgment. As discussed earlier, the allies do not appear to believe that the United States consistently demonstrates the highest level of strategic wisdom. In fact, they often seem to look with confused eyes upon our behavior, unable to explain why Washington so often finds it necessary to go abroad in search of monsters to destroy. They will participate at times in its adventures, but minimally and reluctantly.

Finally, while proponents of hegemonic stability have articulated a logic that some find compelling, they are rarely able to cite much evidence to support their claims. In fact, the limited empirical data we have suggests that there is no connection between the relative level of U.S. activism and international stability. During the 1990s, the United States cut back on defense fairly substantially, spending $100 billion less in real terms in 1998 than it did in 1990, a 25 percent reduction.[89] To defense hawks and other believers in hegemonic stability, this irresponsible "peace dividend" endangered both national and global security. "No serious analyst of American military capabilities doubts that the defense budget has been cut much too far to meet America's responsibilities to itself and to world peace," argued Kristol and Kagan."[90] If global stability were unrelated to U.S. hegemony, however, the world would not have experienced an increase in conflict and violence.

The verdict from the last two decades is fairly plain: the empirical studies cited in Chapter 1 should be more than adequate to demonstrate that the world grew more peaceful while the United States cut its forces. No state appeared to believe that its security was endangered by a less capable U.S. military, or at least none took any action suggesting such a belief. No defense establishments outside of the Pacific rim

[89] Michael O'Hanlon, "America's Military, Cut to the Quick," *Washington Post*, August 9, 1998, p. C1.
[90] Kristol and Kagan, "Toward a Neo-Reaganite Foreign Policy," p. 24.

have been enhanced to address power vacuums, no security dilemmas drove insecurity or arms races, and no regional balancing occurred as the stabilizing presence of the U.S. military waned. The rest of the world acted as if the threat of international war was simply not a pressing concern, despite the reduction in U.S. capabilities. The incidence and magnitude of global conflict declined while the United States cut its military spending under President Clinton, and kept declining as the Bush administration ramped that spending back up. The two phenomena were unrelated.

These figures will not convince skeptics. One could presumably argue that military spending is not the only or even the best indication of hegemony, that it is instead U.S. foreign political and security commitments that maintain stability. Since neither was significantly altered during this period, instability should not have been expected. Alternately, advocates of hegemonic stability could believe that relative rather than absolute spending is decisive in bringing peace. Although the United States cut back on its spending during the 1990s, its relative advantage never wavered.

However, it is surely worth noting that if opposite trends had unfolded, if other states had reacted to news of cuts in U.S. defense spending with more aggressive or insecure behavior, then surely hegemonic stability theorists would note that their expectations had been fulfilled. If increases in conflict would have been interpreted as evidence for the wisdom of internationalist strategies, then logical consistency demands that the lack thereof should at least pose a problem. As it stands, the only evidence we have reveals no relationship between U.S. power and international stability, and suggests that the rest of the world can operate quite effectively without the presence of a global policeman. Those who think otherwise base their view on faith alone.

It requires a good deal of hubris for any actor to consider itself indispensable to world peace. Far from collapsing into a whirlwind of chaos, the chances are high that the world would look much like it does now if the United States were to cease regarding itself as God's gladiator on earth. Basic inertia affects calculations in this matter, as Jervis has said. While "it is very unlikely that pulling off the American security blanket would lead to thoughts of war," he argued, nonetheless he admits that he is "cautious enough not to want to run the experiment."[91] There is good reason to believe that such an experiment would not end badly, however, and at the very least it would certainly be cheaper than the status quo.

PATHOGENESIS

Like all American pathologies, hubris has complex roots. Since not all people have suffered from its effects to such a large degree, human nature cannot take all blame for its existence in the United States. A number of other conditions are necessary for the growth of hubris, all of which are present in America at the beginning of the twenty-first century. Hubristic societies are generally those that have a record of success, which seems to justify their inflated self-esteem; that have a narrative of exceptionalism; and that enjoy an advantage in relative power over potential rivals. In such circumstances, a segment of any population is likely to exhibit the symptoms of hubris. When that segment comes to influence the formulation of policy, the state cannot help but to believe pathologically and act counterproductively.

Individual Level: Overconfidence, Narcissism, and National Leadership

Some level of hubris might be helpful as a defense mechanism or even product of evolution. Dominic Johnson has suggested that overconfidence might be a natural, biological adaptation that leads to successful outcomes.[92] Human beings who maintain especially strong positive illusions about their charm and capabilities might enjoy greater levels of achievement, sexual and otherwise, in part because they tend to attempt more conquests. Even low batting averages produce many hits when confidence results in large numbers of trips to the plate.

There is a good deal of evidence to suggest that many, if not most, people harbor what might be thought of as a "positivity bias." While people tend to harbor overly negative impressions regarding the actions and intentions of others (the "negativity bias" discussed

---

[91] Robert Jervis, "Force in Our Times," *International Relations*, Vol. 25, No. 4 (December 2011), p. 415.

[92] Dominic Johnson, *Overconfidence and War: The Havoc and Glory of Positive Illusions* (Cambridge, MA: Harvard University Press, 2004), pp. 6–18.

in Chapter 1), they often feel quite optimistic regarding themselves. The currently fashionable "positive psychology" explains that it is perfectly normal for mentally healthy people to maintain exaggerated perceptions of their own capabilities, overestimations of their ability to control events, and excessive optimism in their projections of their own futures.[93] "This is not just a normative prescription for thinking positively," Dominic Johnson and Dominic Tierney argue, after examining the research. "Rather, people have deeply seated cognitive and motivated biases that make them overconfident by default."[94] Almost all people think they are above average drivers, for instance, and in a famous study 94 percent of professors reported believing themselves to be above average teachers.[95] The outcome of such biases is not necessarily neutral, especially in international relations, where a long literature exists linking overconfidence directly to aggression and war.[96] The result of the negativity bias, in which people tend to focus on the bad aspects of others, is fear; the positivity bias, which causes people to only see the good in themselves, leads to hubris.

Leaders are especially prone to excessive optimism by virtue of their successful, often unlikely rise to prominence. Whether that rise was within a democratic or authoritarian system, those who feel qualified and driven to lead nations tend to overflow with self-assurance and confidence. Hubris is common, if not ubiquitous, in staterooms. "If individuals with significant narcissistic characteristics were stripped from the ranks of public figures," notes Post, "the ranks would be perilously thinned."[97] The desire for reassurance, adulation, and applause exists to some degree in all of us, but for leaders it can be an obsession.

Evolutionary biology did not only affect people in the United States, and narcissism is present in all halls of government, not just those in Washington. Individual-level factors have limited utility to

93 Christopher Peterson, *A Primer in Positive Psychology* (New York: Oxford University Press, 2006).
94 Dominic Johnson and Dominic Tierney, "Bad World: The Negativity Bias and International Politics," Paper presented at the International Studies Association Conference, San Diego, CA, April 1–4, 2012, p. 42.
95 K. Patricia Cross, "Not Can, But *Will* College Teaching Be Improved?" *New Directions for Higher Education*, No. 17 (Spring 1977), pp. 1–15.
96 Johnson reviews this literature in *Overconfidence and War*.
97 Post, "Current Concepts of the Narcissistic Personality," p. 99.

help uncover the origins of specific American hubris. For variables with more specific explanatory power, one must look elsewhere.

State Level, Part I: Exceptionalism

Exceptionalism, or the feeling of moral and/or political superiority, is not unique to the United States. Dostoevsky argued that "every great people believes and must believe that in it, and it alone, lies the salvation of the world, and that it lives to lead all peoples into the new millennium."[98] There seems to be a human need to feel special or exceptional, and it appears natural to take pride in being even a small part of greatness. All people like to bask in the reflected glory of their country's (or culture's) unique, nonpareil stature; Americans, though, have long been exceptional in their exceptionalism.[99] Beginning with the first settlers to arrive on its shores, the United States has never considered itself a normal country. Its people left the Old World both physically and psychologically to create a wholly different place, and to the extent that they felt different, of course, they felt superior. A creation myth has grown regarding the beginnings of the country, making it seem less the result of natural *volkswanderung* and more divine intervention. The state was born under God's protection and has continued that way ever since, a "shining city on a hill" that towers above all others in any number of ways.

Success breeds exceptionalism. Their rather astonishing record of achievement and meteoric rise to prominence helped convince the American people of positive supernatural judgment. The first settlers discovered a new Garden of Eden and carved a perfect union out of its wilderness, guided by their secular saints, the founding fathers. From the rather unlikely revolution against the world's strongest power to the swift conquest of a continent, the people of the United States appear able to overcome even the longest odds. Anthropologist Margaret Mead observed that Americans like to imagine themselves

[98] Quoted in Wilber W. Caldwell, *American Narcissism: The Myth of National Superiority* (New York: Algora Publishing, 2006), p. 43.
[99] See Tami R. Davis and Sean M. Lynn-Jones, "Citty upon a Hill," *Foreign Policy*, No. 66 (Spring 1987), pp. 20–38; Seymour Martin Lipset, *American Exceptionalism: A Double-Edged Sword* (New York: W. W. Norton, 1996); and Deborah L. Madsen, *American Exceptionalism* (Oxford: University of Mississippi Press, 1998).

heirs of those who "virtually singlehanded – each man alone with an ax and a rifle – conquered a wilderness."[100] By the end of its first independent century, the United States had risen to be the largest industrial power in the world, one that was undefeated on the battlefield as well until the 1960s (as long as the War of 1812 could rather charitably be considered a draw). Its history contains many examples to support the belief that America can accomplish anything it puts its mind to, from putting men on the moon to finding treatments for AIDS. Survey data consistently indicate that Americans are significantly more patriotic than their counterparts elsewhere. In a 1999 poll, 72 percent of Americans professed pride in their country compared to 53 percent of Britons and only 35 percent of French, numbers that have been consistent for at least two decades.[101] The general trend is toward more patriotism, not less. A 2010 Gallup poll found the highest level ever recorded, with one-third of Americans reporting that they are "extremely patriotic."[102] Many in the United States hold the view that the rest of the world would be much better off if it were to adopt the American way, since God is clearly on their side.[103] Their country did not evolve; it is the result of intelligent design.

Americans have always combined this feeling of divine providence with a sense of mission to spread their ideals around the world and to battle evil wherever it lurks. Exceptionalism carries with it a strong evangelical impulse, the desire and at times obligation to remake the world in the U.S. image, or to make the world look more like Minnesota, to use the memorable formulation of George Quester.[104] As a result, those instances when other countries have not proven ready converts come as a shock. Exceptional societies believe that

---

[100] Margaret Mead, *And Keep Your Powder Dry: An Anthropologist Looks at America* (New York: William Morrow and Company, 1943), p. 159.

[101] Minxin Pei, "The Paradoxes of American Nationalism," *Foreign Policy*, No. 136 (May–June 2003), pp. 31–37. See also Anatol Lieven, *America Right or Wrong: An Anatomy of American Nationalism* (New York: Oxford University Press, 2004), p. 19.

[102] Gallup, "One in Three Americans 'Extremely Patriotic,'" July 2, 2010, available at http://www.gallup.com/poll/141110/one-three-americans-extremely-patriotic. aspx, accessed December 18, 2012.

[103] Samuel P. Huntington, *American Politics: The Promise of Disharmony* (Cambridge, MA: Harvard University Press, 1981), esp. chapter 2, "The American Creed and National Identity."

[104] George Quester, "Consensus Lost," *Foreign Policy*, No. 40 (Autumn, 1980), pp. 18–19.

deep down, whether they realize it or not, all people everywhere want
to be like them.[105]

It is this sense of a destiny, of being the object of history's call,
that most obviously separates the United States from other countries.
Only an American president would claim that by entering World War
I, "America had the infinite privilege of fulfilling her destiny and saving the world."[106] While many states are motivated by humanitarian
causes, no other seems to consider promoting its values a national
duty in quite the same way Americans do. "I believe that God wants
everybody to be free," said George W. Bush during the third presidential debate in 2004. "That's what I believe. And that's one part of my
foreign policy."[107] When Madeleine Albright called the United States
the "indispensable nation," she was reflecting a traditional, deeply
held belief of the American people. Exceptional nations, like exceptional people, have an obligation to assist the merely average.

Exceptionalism, like all symptoms of narcissism, is insecure and
fragile. Thus the various enforcers of patriotic correctness took serious umbrage in 2009 when President Obama responded to a rather
leading question from a journalist in Strasbourg by saying he believed
in American exceptionalism, "just as I suspect that the Brits believe in
British exceptionalism and the Greeks believe in Greek exceptionalism."[108] Charles Krauthammer was horrified that the president would
risk "the demolition of the moral foundation of American dominance" with insinuations of such abject equivalence.[109] He was not
alone. American exceptionalism was subsequently reaffirmed with
gusto by the 2012 GOP presidential candidates.[110] The president
committed what has become a sin in the United States: he seemed

[105] Trevor B. McCrisken, *American Exceptionalism and the Legacy of Vietnam: US Foreign Policy since 1974* (New York: Palgrave MacMillan, 2003).
[106] Woodrow Wilson, quoted in Anatol Lieven, *America Right or Wrong*, p. 33.
[107] Robert H. Swansbrough, *Test By Fire: The War Presidency of George W. Bush* (New York: Macmillan, 2008), p. 9.
[108] James Fallows, "Obama on Exceptionalism," *The Atlantic Online*, April 4, 2009, avail-able at http://www.theatlantic.com/technology/archive/2009/04/obama-on-exceptionalism/9874/, accessed December 18, 2012.
[109] Charles Krauthammer, "Decline Is a Choice: The New Liberalism and the End of American Ascendancy," *The Weekly Standard*, Vol. 15, No. 5 (October 19, 2009).
[110] The apotheosis, as usual, was Newt Gingrich, who pumped out a book-length response: *A Nation Like No Other: Why American Exceptionalism Matters* (Washington, DC: Regnery Publishing, 2011).

to denigrate the specialness of the United States. Andrew Bacevich notes that "paying homage to, and therefore renewing, this tradition of American exceptionalism has long been one of the presidency's primary extraconstitutional obligations."[111] Like a person of insecure religion – or a narcissist – many Americans are hypersensitive to the suggestion that their country just might be much like every other. Defense of their exceptionalism is an article of faith, not reason. It is a belief that often leads to outcomes that have often proven pathological to the host.

State Level, Part II: The Liberal Tradition

On his tour of the United States in the 1830s, de Tocqueville argued that one of the reasons its democratic experiment had succeeded where that of his homeland had failed was the great American advantage of not having had to endure a democratic revolution.[112] Democracy in the United States did not emerge following a violent class-based conflict that broke the political power of landed gentry. To Louis Hartz, the fact that this country was never feudal was a major factor in the development of its political culture and liberal tradition. America was "born equal," which has led it to display what he called a "colossal liberal absolutism," at least in comparison with countries with a history of internal struggle.[113] As a result, the people of the United States have a conception of politics – and what is possible – that is somewhat different from those in other countries. They cannot really relate to those who have had to win their freedom and establish democracy, and do not fully grasp the power the barriers to liberalism can wield. Those born free never understand the struggle others must undertake to get there. The different birth experiences help account for some of the most basic divergences of belief between the United States and other countries, even those to whom it is seemingly closest. For Hartz, the liberal tradition "hampers creative action

---

[111] Andrew J. Bacevich, *The Limits of Power: The End of American Exceptionalism* (New York: Metropolitan Books, 2008), p. 18.

[112] Discussed by Louis Hartz, *The Liberal Tradition in America: An Interpretation of American Political Thought since the Revolution* (New York: Harcourt, Brace and World, Inc., 1955), p. 35.

[113] Hartz, *The Liberal Tradition in America*, p. 285.

abroad by identifying the alien with the unintelligible, and inspires hysteria at home by generating the anxiety that unintelligible things produce."[114] That tradition is one of the sources of America's sense of exceptionalism, and of its hubris.

In modern foreign policy debates, liberalism is most passionately promoted by the profoundly misnamed neoconservatives. As discussed in Chapter 1, nothing is more central to the neoconservative world view than the belief that the United States is the strongest force for good in the world, without which evil would go on an unstoppable, chaotic march.[115] The extent to which the United States exhibits hubris in its foreign policy actions is directly related to the level of neoconservative influence on debates and actions. When neocons are ascendant, when decision makers become influenced by people who argue that the United States needs to "change the character of the Middle East," for example, the inner U.S. narcissist emerges prominently in its behavior.[116]

George W. Bush may have promised a "humble" foreign policy during his campaign in 2000, but once in office few administrations have proven more hubristic. Its first four years, when the influence of neoconservatives like Paul Wolfowitz and Douglas Feith was at its highest, exhibited all the symptoms of hubris: overestimation of capabilities, misjudgments of likely reactions of others, and unwillingness to listen to outside counsel. These symptoms waned in the second term following the departure of Wolfowitz and Feith and the diminution of the influence of the Office of the Vice President.[117] As the administration became more realist in orientation, in other words, it began to display

---

[114] Hartz, *The Liberal Tradition in* America, p. 285.

[115] Michael Williams has pointed out that the idea of "national greatness" has always been a key dimension of the neoconservative vision for the United States and its foreign policy. Michael C. Williams, "What is the National Interest? The Neoconservative Challenge in IR Theory," *European Journal of International Relations*, Vol. 11, No. 3 (September 2005), p. 318.

[116] William Kristol, remarks made on *Fox News Sunday*, September 11, 2011, available at http://www.foxnews.com/on-air/fox-news-sunday/2011/09/11/fox-news-sunday-911-then-and-now#ixzz1XlH1fYHa, accessed December 18, 2012.

[117] Vice President Cheney admits that although he argued vociferously for a strike on Syrian nuclear infrastructure and for the pardoning of Scooter Libby, he was unsuccessful both times. See his memoir, *In My Time: A Personal and Political Memoir* (New York: Simon and Schuster, 2011).

less influence of hubris. This was hardly a coincidence. In many ways, realism is the enemy of, and solution to, the hubris pathology.[118]

Neoconservatism is hardly the only home of liberalism – or narcissism – in U.S. foreign policy. It is worth remembering that the invasion of Iraq won support not only from those on the right but also from many scholars, strategists, and politicians normally thought to be denizens of the left, from Michael O'Hanlon to Hillary Clinton. No single book was more influential in the lead-up to the war than *The Threatening Storm* by Kenneth Pollack of the Brookings Institution, who by virtue of his service on the Clinton National Security Council appeared to have impeccable liberal credentials.[119] Pollack concluded that war to overthrow Saddam was the best in a set of bad choices. *New York Times* columnist Thomas Friedman also supported the invasion, telling Charlie Rose the United States had to invade in order to tell "the Arab world" to "suck on this."[120] These two men were instrumental in helping make the case that the invasion was not merely a crackpot idea cooked up by conservatives in the Bush administration but a necessary response to imminent threat, one likely to result in a cakewalk.

Princeton professor Anne-Marie Slaughter, later President Obama's first director of policy planning, went further. In a 2004 coauthored piece in *Foreign Affairs* she argued the biggest problem with the Bush policy of preemption was that "it does not go far enough." The United States should not stop with Iraq; it has a duty to prevent any autocrat from obtaining weapons of mass destruction. Although collective

---

[118] Bacevich, *The Limits of Power*, p. 7.
[119] Kenneth Pollack, *The Threatening Storm: The Case for Invading Iraq* (New York: Random House, 2002). Pollack has spent years trying to explain away that book, stating in 2007 that "I don't like to characterize myself as a supporter of the invasion," which is unsurprising, given how poorly it went. However, the longest chapter in his book (by far), is descriptively titled "The Case for an Invasion." See Michael Massing, "The War Expert," *Columbia Journalism Review*, Vol. 46, No. 4 (November–December 2007), pp. 18–20.
[120] Thomas Friedman, interview on PBS's *The Charlie Rose Show*, May 29, 2003. Friedman argued a "bubble" of immorality had built up in the Arab world, one that condoned terrorism and had to be burst: "What they needed to see is American boys and girls going house to house, from Basra to Baghdad, and basically saying 'which part of this sentence don't you understand? You don't think we don't care about our open society? You think this bubble fantasy, we're just going to let it grow? Well suck on this, OK?' That, Charlie, is what this war was about. We could have hit Saudi Arabia, it was part of that bubble. Could have hit Pakistan. We hit Iraq because we could."

responses are better, "given the Security Council's propensity for paralysis," unilateral intervention will sometimes prove necessary.[121] The United States, according to its liberals, must be prepared to punish evildoers preemptively on occasion, wherever they may be.

Historian Arthur Schlesinger, Jr. was criticizing communists when he wrote that "those who are convinced that they have a monopoly on The Truth always feel that they are saving the world when they slaughter heretics. Their objective remains that of making the world over in the image of their dogmatic ideology. The goal is a monolithic world, organized on the principle of infallibility."[122] Today's American liberals might benefit from asking themselves whether or not this also applies to them.

System Level: Power, Wealth, and Success

Finally, all of the possible origins of the hubris pathology are related to unipolarity, the background condition necessary but insufficient to explain the arrogance of power. The abundant wealth of the United States is hardly a mixed blessing – the benefits to the country far outweigh the costs – but hubris tends to follow success. In all great nations, Senator Fulbright wrote, "power tends to confuse itself with virtue," making the state "peculiarly susceptible to the idea that its power is a sign of God's favor, conferring on it a special responsibility for other nations – to make them richer and happier and wiser, to remake them, that is, in its own shining image."[123] The Romans sought to "Romanize"; the English, to "Anglicize"; the French, to "civilize."[124] Any state that rises to international prominence in as many categories as has the United States should be expected to display confidence in its abilities. It would be somewhat remarkable, therefore,

---

[121] Lee Feinstein and Anne-Marie Slaughter, "A Duty to Prevent," *Foreign Affairs*, Vol. 83, No. 1 (January–February 2004), pp. 136–50.

[122] Arthur M. Schlesinger, Jr., "One against the Many," in Arthur Schlesinger, Jr. and Morton White, eds., *Paths of American Thought* (Boston, MA: Houghton Mifflin, 1963), p. 538.

[123] J. William Fulbright, *The Arrogance of Power* (New York: Random House, 1966), p. 3.

[124] On the latter, see Alice L. Conklin, *A Mission to Civilize: The Republican Idea of Empire in France and West Africa, 1895–1930* (Palo Alto, CA: Stanford University Press, 1997).

if the current unipolar power had proven immune to its effects. The most obvious cause of hubris in the United States, therefore, is its relative power.

While there is nothing inherent in power that leads inexorably to pathological beliefs, power is their enabler and the reason the United States is able to engage in folly. Weak states occasionally display hubris, if often in the form of overcompensation, of national Napoleon complexes. Genuinely hubristic weak states are not terribly dangerous, however, since their possible actions are limited by their capabilities. Only strong states are dangers to themselves and to others, and only their pathological beliefs have external or systemic significance. Proponents of Albanian exceptionalism, for instance, are not likely to get involved in misadventures abroad. "Wealth shapes our international behavior, and our image," argued Derek Leebaert. "It brings with it the freedom to make wide-ranging choices well beyond common sense."[125]

The military strength of the United States has been a sine qua non for its hubris. Without enormous military capability, the actions of the United States would be much more circumscribed. While it may be comforting to think such capability brings a level of insurance against danger, that insurance does not come without a cost. More than a century ago, Speaker of the House Thomas Brackett Reed warned of "over insurance," which tends to create "what the insurance men call Moral Hazard," or an invitation to recklessness in the expectation of a bailout if things go wrong. Reed believed that great power invited conflict, "since leaders would either become complacent in the arrogance generated by seemingly overwhelming force or reckless in the cocky belief that no opponent could possibly triumph."[126] Capability creates security, but it also greases the gears of hubris.

One might think the financial crisis would have injected a bit of humility into U.S. society and foreign policy. An understanding of narcissistic personalities, though, would lead the sagacious observer to expect otherwise: when confronted by evidence of (or at least warnings about) unpleasant futures, the narcissist seeks out reassurance

[125] Leebaert, *Magic and Mayhem*, p. 237.
[126] Evan Thomas, *The War Lovers: Roosevelt, Lodge, Hearst, and the Rush to Empire, 1898* (New York: Little, Brown and Company, 2010), p. 188.

from those who argue that in fact the opposite is true. In times of relatively high anxiety, whether economic or otherwise, hubristic societies should be expected to retrench, to double down on their beliefs in greatness and power, if only to relieve those nagging doubts. It should therefore come as no surprise that exceptionalism was such a prominent issue during the 2012 election, and that challengers for the presidency made a contest of asserting it most forcefully. Reduced capabilities – to the extent that they are real – need not be accompanied by reduced hubris. In fact, anxious societies may instead seek out new opportunities to assert their power, to assure themselves and all others that perceptions of decline are illusions. The danger posed by hubris may well increase, in other words, if indeed relative U.S. power moves in the other direction. Pride might go before the fall, but it accompanies the slide downward as well.

On the other hand, faith in its ultimate success is part of the optimism that is one of the most attractive elements of the American character. The country for which failure is not an option has achieved a great deal and has contributed as much to the advancement of humanity as any other. But there are limits to its capabilities, the outline of which can become rapidly blurred if overconfidence is not kept in check. The United States is a superpower, not a superhero. In most cases it would behoove policy makers to recognize that hubris is probably warping their assessment of costs and benefits, and to presume that the execution of any particular foreign adventure is probably going to turn out to be somewhat more difficult than they initially expect. Minimization of the pathological beliefs that accompany hubris need not spell the end of American optimism, merely of the overestimation of what is possible to accomplish at a reasonable cost.

The line that separates confidence and arrogance is fine indeed; healthy positive attitudes are often hard to distinguish from pathological delusions of omnipotence. The task facing policy makers is to separate the two, to determine which ends are realistic and achievable with acceptable means. Those who fail to do so risk suffering the fate of Icarus or that of George W. Bush.

Conclusion

Pathology, Realism, and the Future

"There can be no solution to a problem," wrote Senator Fulbright a generation ago, "until it is first acknowledged that there is a problem."[1] One of the most basic purposes of any kind of psychological therapy is to investigate the causes of those hidden forces that cause counterproductive behavior, to bring pathology into the open. That initial goal, once achieved, soon gives way to the more important uses of analysis: treatment and cure. Awareness of pathological beliefs is of limited utility unless it is accompanied by a determination to minimize their effects.

Having identified pathologies in U.S. foreign policy, what is to be done? This concluding chapter turns the focus toward the future, reviewing the pathological beliefs identified in this volume and suggesting that treatment is indeed possible, at least over the long term. It then offers thoughts about how such treatment would proceed, and reasons why it is vitally important to begin implementing it as soon as possible. If in the future the United States is to avoid the kind of folly to which it has repeatedly proven susceptible, it will need to jettison some of its deeply held beliefs and turn toward those generated by rational, supportable, healthy realism and prudence.

[1] J. William Fulbright, *The Arrogance of Power* (New York: Random House, 1966), p. 38.

227

ALTERING POPULAR, PATHOLOGICAL BELIEFS

To review briefly, the United States displays the influence of a number of pathological beliefs in its foreign policy decisions, many of which have their roots in concepts that would have been familiar to the ancients. Because it fears more than other states, it believes the world is a dangerous place, full of enemies and threats that need to be addressed before they coalesce. Because they believe that credibility earned today will help in the crises of tomorrow, U.S. leaders are more belligerent than they otherwise would be. Because it is overly competitive, perhaps hypercompetitive, the United States puts undue importance on being the best across many categories. And because it sometimes seems to confuse its status as superpower with that of a superhero, the United States seems to believe that virtually no challenge is insurmountable. Taken together, these pathologies warp national debates, making a variety of unnecessary, unpleasant behaviors far more likely. The beliefs are summarized in the table below.

Category	Associated Beliefs
Fear	• The world is a very dangerous place. • The United States will always be the target of evil actors.
Honor	• Healthy credibility makes the achievement of foreign policy goals easier. Our actions today can shape the future actions of others. States can, through their actions, control the perceptions of others. • Cooperation is weakness that encourages challenges from other states.
Glory	• Competition, among people and states, is healthy and always leads to the best possible outcomes. • In international affairs, it is important to be the best.
Hubris	• The United States is a unique, exceptional country. • The people of the United States can accomplish almost anything they set their minds to.

Changing foreign policy beliefs is no small task. Once internalized, beliefs become stubborn by nature, part of an actor's very identity and therefore far more hardy and persistent than ideas or theories. Elaborate cognitive defenses protect fragile ideologies against potentially contradictory information. Since new evidence is interpreted according to extant belief systems, reevaluation of core assumptions is rarely even contemplated.[2] Changing one's mind takes a great deal more cognitive energy than merely ignoring troublesome facts or arguments, which places inertia on the side of the ideological status quo. Beliefs are, therefore, nearly immune to the impact of even irrefutable empirical data, much less academic argumentation such as that contained in this volume.

Nearly immune, however, is not immune. Even the most deeply held beliefs find it difficult to survive sustained, long-term assaults by contradictory information. Psychologists who have studied evolution in beliefs report that despite occasional epiphanies that instantly change minds, like that of Saul on the road to Damascus, generally speaking the process is very gradual and nearly imperceptible.[3] Individuals often recognize that a change in their beliefs has occurred only after the fact, and resist admitting even to themselves that their minds are evolving while it is happening. Young people are generally more susceptible to the possibility of change, while senior members of any generation are much less likely to admit that their long-held theories might be wrong. This is particularly true for senior scholars, as Thomas Kuhn has pointed out in his study of paradigms, because they rarely prove eager to adjust the belief systems that have served them well for so long.[4] Junior members of any field are much more likely to adopt new theories and beliefs, since they are not as invested in old ways and may gain a certain bit of pleasure in tearing down the old shibboleths.[5]

There are many examples of gradual, even generational evolution of beliefs that can give hope to those seeking to expunge pathology from U.S. foreign policy. Social Darwinism, for instance, poisoned international politics for decades. The belief that humanity was split into a number of distinct races in perpetual existential struggle where only the fittest survive shaped the world view of generations of

[2] Paul Slovic, *The Perception of Risk* (London: Earthscan, 2000), p. 222.
[3] Howard Gardner, *Changing Minds: The Art and Science of Changing Our Own and Other People's Minds* (Boston, MA: Harvard Business School Press, 2006).
[4] Thomas S. Kuhn, *The Structure of Scientific Revolutions* (Chicago, IL: University of Chicago Press, 1970).
[5] Gardner, *Changing Minds*, p. 117.

leaders.[6] Social Darwinism helped justify any number of pathological policies, from imperialism to the Holocaust, but over time it col-
lapsed under the weight of rational counterargument and evidence.
The identification of DNA and understanding of the genome allowed
science to put social Darwinism and its cousins, eugenics and phre-
nology, to rest once and for all.[7] Previously internalized beliefs about
the inevitability of competition among races were slowly changed by
the onslaught of evidence and reason, and the understanding that
differences among peoples were cultural, not genetic. The edifice
did not collapse all at once or with equal speed everywhere, but over
time arguments based on the foundation of social Darwinism stopped
winning popular debates on the "battlefield of beliefs," and foreign
policy behavior changed. There is precedent, then, for evolution in
fundamental beliefs, enough for one to hope a similar process could
eventually change popular perceptions toward modern, counterproductive irrationalities.

Precedent does not supply the only encouragement. Changing the
dominant U.S. foreign policy belief system is perhaps not as daunting
a challenge as it may at first seem, because only a small number of
opinions would have to be altered to have significant effect. As nice
as it is to imagine that the United States runs a democratic foreign
policy, in reality not all opinions are equally important. Altering the
beliefs of the masses may be quite difficult, but it is those of the elite
that are decisive in foreign policy; affecting elites, if only because they
are fewer in number, might not prove impossible. As influential as
NSC-68 was, for instance, it was an internal document read only by
senior government officials, and remained classified until 1975. The
various incarnations of the Committee on Present Danger concen-
trated their efforts solely on the upper echelons of the foreign policy
community, and were quite successful in affecting the marketplace of
ideas. Public opinion is heavily elite driven when it comes to foreign

---

[6] Richard Hofstadter, *Social Darwinism in American Thought* (Philadelphia: University
of Pennsylvania Press, 1944); and Mike Hawkins, *Social Darwinism in European and
American Thought, 1860–1945: Nature as Model and Nature as Threat* (New York:
Cambridge University Press, 1997).

[7] For an interesting discussion, see Peter K. Hatemi and Rose McDermott, "The
Normative Implications of Biological Research," *PS: Political Science and Politics*, Vol.
44, No. 2 (April 2011), pp. 325–29.

affairs.[8] Where the leaders go, the masses follow. Success in minimizing pathological foreign policy behavior can occur long before majorities alter their beliefs.

Some of the most important, influential minds may not prove the most resistant to change. Many modern American politicians know very little about foreign policy. The U.S. Congress is a wasteland of parochialism, where members can be punished for even appearing to know too much about the rest of the world.[9] Those at the top of the executive branch have been little better. No post–Cold War U.S. president has had any background in foreign affairs at all prior to coming into office. Bill Clinton even managed to turn his opponent's foreign policy expertise into a liability in 1992, claiming it demonstrated the elder Bush did not pay adequate attention to domestic concerns. Eight years later, voters were unfazed about George W. Bush's disinterest in the outside world, as manifest in a record of foreign travel stunningly low for a child of privilege, inability to name leaders of key countries, and devotion of only three pages in his campaign memoir to foreign affairs.[10] While Barack Obama spent large portions of his life abroad, he had no direct foreign policy experience prior to 2008, and his 2012 opponent had even less. So while twenty-first-century U.S. presidents have some predetermined beliefs about foreign policy, they are probably more malleable than those who came to office more seasoned in matters of state.

As a result of their inexperience, modern U.S. presidents rely even more than their predecessors on experts to guide them in their foreign policy decisions. It is worth noting that in a very real sense it is nearly impossible to be a "foreign policy expert," since the subject is too vast for any person to have extensive knowledge of all its facets. Advisors can have experience, wisdom, or knowledge about one aspect of the world, but not all of it; they can be skilled in diplomacy or operating the U.S. bureaucracy, but not in the minutiae of every decision. But for leaders, experts essentially become a heuristic, a device that aids

---

[8] See Adam J. Berinsky, *In Time of War: Understanding American Public Opinion from World War II to Iraq* (Chicago, IL: University of Chicago Press, 2009); and John R. Zaller, *The Nature and Origins of Mass Opinion* (New York: Cambridge University Press, 1992).

[9] See Jeremy D. Rosner, "The Know-Nothings Know Something," *Foreign Policy*, No. 101 (Winter 1995–96), pp. 116–29.

[10] David B. MacDonald, *Thinking History, Fighting Evil: Neoconservatives and the Perils of Analogy in American Politics* (Lanham, MD: Lexington Books, 2009), p. xvi.

decision making. "The canonization of an 'expert' can anesthetize reason," wryly summarizes Derek Leebaert. "The expert will settle the problem for us."[11] This small group of elite advisors, whether deserving of their status or not, are the most consequential participants in the marketplace of ideas, the ones whose beliefs are the true targets of any discussion such as this.

Finally, it is worth emphasizing that the target of this work is the arena of social debate, not the beliefs of every individual who contributes to it. The United States does not always act pathologically, after all. Rational forces are present in all its foreign policy discussions, and they often win the battle over its direction. It will not require an ideological revolution for the United States to minimize the pathologies that plague its foreign policy behavior. Planting the seeds of doubt in influential minds, seeds that can germinate and grow over time, may well prove enough to tilt the balance of national debate toward reason. The task of improving U.S. foreign policy performance, therefore, may not be as daunting as it at first seems.

There is reason to believe that rational beliefs may find future marketplaces friendlier than those of the current generation in power. Public opinion polling has suggested that the youngest generation of adults, the so-called millennials, is less concerned about terrorism and less supportive of an activist foreign policy than are its predecessors. Those between eighteen and twenty-nine years of age are also half as likely to be concerned about Islamic fundamentalism as those over sixty.[12] They also appear to be somewhat less patriotic.[13] Perhaps it will not be as necessary to change beliefs in the near future, when popular pressure might not be as pathological as it has proven to be in the past.

Thomas Jefferson once wrote that "If we think [the people] not enlightened enough to exercise control with a wholesome discretion, the remedy is not to take it from them, but to inform that discretion."[14]

---

[11] Derek Leebaert, *Magic and Mayhem: The Delusions of American Foreign Policy from Korea to Afghanistan* (New York: Simon & Schuster, 2010), p. 126.

[12] Dina Smeltz, *Foreign Policy in the New Millennium: Results of the 2012 Chicago Council Survey of American Public Opinion and U.S. Foreign Policy* (Chicago, IL: Chicago Council on Global Affairs, September 10, 2012).

[13] Gallup, "One in Three Americans 'Extremely Patriotic,'" July 2, 2010, available at http://www.gallup.com/poll/141110/one-three-americans-extremely-patriotic. aspx, accessed December 18, 2012.

[14] Quoted in Slovic, *The Perception of Risk*, p. 182.

One of the crucial tasks facing policy makers must be to inform the general public, however slowly and indirectly, of the evidence that might help it examine its foreign policy beliefs. Since an informed public is one of the central sine qua nons of a healthy, functioning democracy, U.S. leaders ought to repeat the facts about the decline of warfare, and of the real risks associated with terrorism, as many times as necessary for them to become accepted.[15] While correcting misinformation will not alter beliefs immediately, over time the constituency for reason will grow.[16] False beliefs, even false collective beliefs, cannot persist forever in the face of sustained, rational assault.

PATHOLOGY AND THE TWENTY-FIRST CENTURY

If its pathological beliefs are not addressed, if no progress is made in treatment, the United States will no doubt barrel headlong into folly again in the near future. In coming decades Washington is going to have to deal, at the very least, with economic and political ramifications of the ongoing global financial crisis; instability across the Arab world in the wake of the democratic revolutions, the outcomes of which are far from clear; growing authoritarianism in Russia; international organized crime; demographic dislocations caused by a warming globe; and so forth. Pathological beliefs are already evident in discussions regarding its policies toward two countries in particular: Iran and China.

Iran and the Hawk's Paradox

"There seems to be a curious American tendency," observed George Kennan toward the end of his life, "to search, at all times, for a single external center of evil, to which all our troubles can be attributed, rather than to recognize that there might be multiple sources of

[15] James H. Kuklinski, Paul J. Quirk, Jennifer Jerit, David Schwieder, and Robert F. Rich, "Misinformation and the Currency of Democratic Citizenship," *Journal of Politics*, Vol. 62, No. 3 (August 2000), pp. 790–816.
[16] See Stephan Lewandowsky, Ullrich K. H. Ecker, Colleen M. Seifert, Norbert Schwartz, and John Cook, "Misinformation and Its Correction: Continued Influence and Successful Debiasing," *Psychological Science in the Public Interest*, Vol. 13, No. 3 (September 2012), pp. 106–31.

resistance to our purposes and undertakings, and that these sources might be relatively independent of each other."[17] During the Cold War, the root of the world's ills was obvious; today it appears equally obvious for many observers of international affairs. Iran has become to the twenty-first century what the Soviet Union was for the second half of the twentieth: evil's epicenter, the origin and supporter of most of the world's problems. Iran is thought to finance and arm the world's Islamic fundamentalists, and is in general the anchor state of the enemy forces in the war on terror. "In a way strikingly similar to that of the Soviet threat that defined the Cold War," writes Iranian exile and Fox News analyst Alireza Jafarzadeh, "the Iranian regime wants global domination."[18] The road to victory in the war on terror, therefore, goes through Tehran. As a result, Iran periodically finds itself in the crosshairs of the United States, the target of its competitiveness, the state it most urgently needs to defeat.

In no other international relationship does the United States display its pathological beliefs more clearly. Although the Iranian regime might appear pathetically weak, barely able to control its own territory much less project power outward, many in U.S. foreign policy circles fear what Tehran might do. Ahmadinejad and the mullahs are not constrained by rational forces, we are told, so deterrence will not keep them from attacking. They are intent on bringing about the apocalypse and will use any nuclear weapons they develop, either on the United States or Israel.[19] Polls suggest Americans felt more threatened by Iran in 2012 than they did by the Soviet Union in 1985.[20] It was Iran that inspired Newt Gingrich to assert onstage at a Republican

---

[17] George Kennan, *At a Century's Ending: Reflections 1982–1995* (New York: W. W. Norton, 1996), p. 87.

[18] Alireza Jafarzadeh, *The Iran Threat: President Ahmadinejad and the Coming Nuclear Crisis* (New York: Palgrave-Macmillan, 2008), p. 209.

[19] One of the innumerable occasions during which Bernard Lewis explained this logic occurred at the Hay-Adams Hotel in Washington, DC in April 2006 ("Islam and the West: A Conversation with Bernard Lewis," Pew Forum on Religion and Public Life, April 27, 2006, transcript available at http://pewforum.org/politics-and-elections/islam-and-the-west-a-conversation-with-bernard-lewis.aspx, accessed December 18, 2012). Then again, Prof. Lewis suspected the ayatollahs would bring about the apocalypse in August of that year; see his "August 22: Does Iran Have Something in Store?" *Wall Street Journal,* August 8, 2006, p. A10.

[20] Max Fisher, "Fear Itself: Americans Believe Iran Threat on Par with 1980s Soviet Union," *The Atlantic Online,* April 19, 2012, available at http://www.theatlantic.

presidential debate that "all of us are more at risk today – men and women, boys and girls – than at any time in the history of this country."[21] Neoconservatives may have made the strongest case for bombing Iran, but they are not alone.[22] Alan Kuperman speaks for many in the mainstream of the American security debate when he writes that "the sooner the United States takes action, the better."[23]

According to these analysts, the United States is engaged in a competition with Iran over the future of the Middle East. The hawkish senators and neoconservative commentators who call for intervention in the Syrian crisis, for instance, rarely fail to put it in context of the regional geopolitical struggle with Iran.[24] To overthrow Assad would be to deal a blow to our regional enemy, to score points in the zero-sum game for influence over the region. The United States would win and Iran would lose, showering us with glory.

The telltale signs of hubris are present in the debate as well. Lest anyone be concerned about the ramifications of attacking Iran, many hawks assure us that it would be a cakewalk. Michael Ledeen leads the way, as usual, giving voice to what might be known as the Hawk's

[21] Republican Presidential Debate, Mesa, AZ, February 22, 2012.

[22] Two exemplary neoconservative recommendations for war are Norman Podhoretz, "The Case for Bombing Iran," *Commentary*, Vol. 123, No. 6 (June 2007), pp. 17–23; and William Kristol, "Speak Softly...and Fight Back," *The Weekly Standard*, Vol. 17, No. 6 (October 24, 2011), available at http://www.weeklystandard.com/articles/speak-softly-and-fight-back_595936.html (accessed December 18, 2012). See also Eric S. Edelman, Andrew F. Krepinevich, Jr., and Evan Braden Montgomery, "The Dangers of a Nuclear Iran: The Limits of Containment," *Foreign Affairs*, Vol. 90, No. 1 (January/February 2011), pp. 66–81, or their more direct, web update, "Why Obama Should Take Out Iran's Nuclear Program: The Case for Striking Before It's Too Late," *Foreign Affairs* online, November 9, 2011, available at http://www.foreignaffairs.com/articles/136655/eric-s-edelman-andrew-f-krepinevich-jr-and-evan-braden-montgomer/why-obama-should-take-out-irans-nuclear-program (accessed December 18, 2012); and Michael Ledeen, *Accomplice to Evil: Iran and the War against the West* (New York: St. Martin's Press, 2009).

[23] Alan J. Kuperman, "There's Only One Way to Stop Iran," *New York Times*, December 24, 2009, p. A23. See also David Broder, "How Obama Might Recover," *Washington Post*, October 31, 2010; and Matthew Kroenig, "Time to Attack Iran: Why a Strike is the Least Bad Option," *Foreign Affairs*, Vol. 91, No. 1 (January–February 2012), pp. 76–86.

[24] Alissa J. Rubin, "Two Senators Say U.S. Should Arm Syrian Rebels," *New York Times*, February 19, 2012, p. A7. The first of Michael Doran and Max Boot's "Five Reasons to Intervene in Syria Now" was to "diminish Iran's influence in the Arab world." *New York Times*, September 26, 2012, p. A29.

Paradox: *evil regimes are simultaneously terrifyingly powerful and essentially fragile.* "While Iran is a terrible threat to us," Ledeen argues, "it is also a very fragile regime," so much so that if we were ever serious about bringing it down, "we would almost certainly succeed."[25] "We've got three carriers in the region and a lot of submarines," Norman Podhoretz told *The Daily Telegraph.* "I would say it would take five minutes ... All the president has to do is say go."[26] William Kristol assured skeptics that although there might be repercussions to a U.S. strike on Iranian nuclear facilities, "they would be healthy ones, showing a strong American that has rejected further appeasement."[27] War, as usual, would bolster U.S. credibility, and teach lessons to those who would consider posing challenges in the future.

This is not the place for a detailed explanation of why war with Iran would be a mistake, yet another in a long string of self-inflicted wounds, especially since the case has been made so well many times already.[28] This brief discussion was just meant to demonstrate that the major pathological beliefs are present in this debate, and that if they are left unrecognized they threaten to overwhelm rational argument. As his term as secretary of defense drew to a conclusion, Robert Gates told the cadets at West Point that in his opinion, "any future defense secretary who advises the president to again send a big American land army into Asia or into the Middle East or Africa should have his head examined."[29] In fact without such an examination, an American land

---

[25] Ledeen, *Accomplice to Evil,* p. 189.

[26] Toby Harnden, "We Must Bomb Iran, Says US Republican Guru," *The Daily Telegraph,* October 27, 2007, available at http://www.telegraph.co.uk/news/worldnews/1567529/We-must-bomb-Iran-says-US-Republican-guru.html (accessed December 18, 2012).

[27] William Kristol, "It's Our War," *The Weekly Standard,* Vol. 11, No. 42 (July 24, 2006), available at http://www.weeklystandard.com/Content/Public/Articles/000/000/012/433fwbvs.asp (accessed December 18, 2012).

[28] The long list of such pieces includes Colin Kahl, "Not Time to Attack Iran," *Foreign Affairs,* Vol. 91, No. 2 (May/June 2012), pp. 166–73; James M. Lindsay and Ray Takeyh, "After Iran Gets the Bomb," *Foreign Affairs,* Vol. 89, No. 2 (March/April 2010), pp. 33–49; Vali Nasr and Ray Takeyh, "The Costs of Containing Iran," *Foreign Affairs,* Vol. 87, No. 1 (January/February 2008), pp. 85–94; and Barry R. Posen, "We Can Live with a Nuclear Iran," *New York Times,* February 27, 2006.

[29] Gates was paraphrasing General McArthur, who had made a similar remark to a reporter in 1949 regarding anyone who committed U.S. troops to a land war on the Asian mainland. Thom Shanker, "Warning against Wars Like Iraq and Afghanistan," *New York Times,* February 22, 2011, p. A7.

army may well be sent to the Middle East once again, depending on the result of future debates about the dangers posed by Iran, and the ease with which the regime could be replaced.

China

Pathology is also evident in the most important twenty-first-century international relationship, that between the United States and China. Since the end of the Cold War, no issue has been more widely discussed in U.S. security circles than the implications of China's rise. The economic recession of 2008 intensified both general U.S. anxiety over that rise and the determination on the part of many to shape its trajectory, to dissuade the Chinese from challenging U.S. dominance. Fear of China's rise is so pervasive it has been given its own name – the "China Threat Theory" – and its adherents are many.[30] Beijing's "ultimate goal," according to influential defense analyst Andrew Krepinevich, is to set "the conditions for a potential latter-day Chinese Greater East Asia Co-Prosperity Sphere of influence" (though, one suspects, the Chinese might not use that exact phrase).[31] Influential voices also warn that any compromise, no matter how beneficial (or inconsequential) will encourage further Chinese aggression. In other words, fear and the credibility imperative are misinforming decision makers in the Pacific, and will continue to do so, perhaps eventually convincing them to make pathological choices.

The formula is depressingly familiar. If U.S. credibility wanes because of excessive cooperation (read: appeasement), the Chinese will be encouraged to undertake further challenges. Its appetite will grow with the eating, and Beijing will grow more belligerent. On the other hand, if the United States maintains its commitments and demonstrates a willingness to fight, Chinese behavior might be more

---

[30] Representative works include Richard Bernstein and Ross H. Munro, *The Coming Conflict with China* (New York: Vintage, 1998); Bill Gertz, *The China Threat: How the People's Republic Targets America* (New York: Regnery Publishing, Inc., 2002); Constantine C. Menges, *China: The Gathering Threat* (Nashville, TN: Thomas Nelson, 2005); and Peter W. Navarro and Greg Autry, *Death by China: Confronting the Dragon – A Global Call to Action* (Upper Saddle River, NJ: Prentice Hall, 2011).

[31] Andrew F. Krepinevich, *Why AirSea Battle?* (Washington, DC: Center for Strategic and Budgetary Assessments, February 19, 2010), available at http://www.csbaonline.org/publications/2010/02/why-airsea-battle/.

moderate. The choice, according to one of the most prominent academic proponents of this position, Aaron Friedberg, is between confrontation and appeasement – and there is no need to guess which
course he recommends.[32] Only if China senses U.S. determination to
maintain its dominant position in the Pacific will it be dissuaded from
objectionable behavior.[33] The way to prevent cataclysmic war, therefore, is to be ready to fight at any time, over small issues.

Proponents of the credibility imperative have apparently learned
nothing from the Cold War. Conciliation, they warn, will cause U.S.
allies in the region to doubt its resolve, and perhaps even cast their
lot with Beijing. "Without strong tokens of its continuing commitment and resolve," Friedberg wrote in 2011, "America's friends may
grow fearful of abandonment, perhaps eventually losing heart and
succumbing to the temptations of appeasement. A serious response
to China's military buildup is therefore vital both for its own sake
and for its potentially spine-stiffening effects on others."[34] That no
allies ever tilted toward the Soviet Union because of perceptions of
U.S. resolve is apparently irrelevant; this time, "cascades of appeasement" are possible without sufficient U.S. belligerence.[35] And just
as so many analysts worried that various Soviet arms buildups would
upset the balance of power, today Friedberg urges the United States
to "strengthen deterrence by restoring a balance upset by China's
relentless buildup."[36] China's "relentless buildup" has brought its
spending up to about one-third of that of the United States. How
exactly that has upset a balance is something more easily asserted
than proven.

While this position is not yet dominant in security debates, it is present and growing, and is certainly the most prominent view in the U.S.
Congress, which for decades has been the epicenter of anti-China sentiment. Democratic Senator James Webb recently worried that "we are

[32] For two decades Friedberg has been discouraging appeasement of China from both
Princeton and Dick Cheney's Office of the Vice President. His most recent work is *A
Contest for Supremacy: China, America, and the Struggle for Mastery in Asia* (New York: W.
W. Norton, 2011), p. 252.
[33] John R. Bolton, "The West Needs to Stand Up to Beijing," *Financial Times*, January
18, 2011.
[34] Friedberg, *A Contest for Supremacy*, p. 275.
[35] Friedberg, *A Contest for Supremacy*, p. 263.
[36] Friedberg, *A Contest for Supremacy*, p. 277.

at a point in the South China Sea right now where we are approaching a Munich moment with China."[37] He may well be right, in the sense that a moment may be approaching when the specter of Munich will be dragged out yet again by those who, like Senator Webb, harbor deeply pathological foreign policy beliefs. Policy makers must be on guard against their effects to ensure that counterproductive actions do not follow and that the rise of China can be peaceful, and even beneficial to U.S. interests.

The prestige imperative is also shaping the U.S. image of China, alongside fear and honor. At some point in 2010, China seems to have overtaken Japan to become the second biggest economy in the world. According to a World Bank report, its total output might even reach the level of the United States by 2020.[38] The reaction to this event in the United States betrayed the depth of its anxiety for status: to listen to the tone of the analysis, if the People's Republic were to overtake the United States and move into the number one spot among economies, as many predict it will, disaster would ensue. "If current trends continue," argues Friedberg, "we are on track to lose our geopolitical contest with China," an outcome that would be damaging to our psyches as well as our security.[39] China is always imagined as the primary beneficiary of U.S. decline, the state most likely to take away its various championship belts.

As always, the United States is lagging behind its rival in depth of its strategic thinking. "The Sino-American competition has been underway for some time but has largely been one sided," writes former Defense Department official Thomas Mahnken. "As a result, the military balance in the Western Pacific has begun to shift dramatically in favor of China and against the United States and its allies."[40] He and his coauthors recommend the immediate adoption of a "competitive strategy" that focuses all our efforts on defeating the Chinese

---

[37] Remarks made on *Meet the Press*, June 26, 2011, available at http://www.msnbc.msn.com/id/43512460/ns/meet_the_press-transcripts/. See also James Webb, "The South China Sea's Gathering Storm," *Wall Street Journal*, August 20, 2012, p. A11.

[38] Louis Kuijs, *China through 2020 – A Macroeconomic Scenario* (Beijing: World Bank China Office, Research Working Paper Number Nine, June 2010).

[39] Friedberg, *A Contest for Supremacy*, p. 6.

[40] Thomas G. Mahnken, ed., *Competitive Strategies for the 21st Century: Theory, History and Practice* (Palo Alto, CA: Stanford University Press, 2012), p. 6.

in various measures of global power, on winning the global struggle for dominance. Though they may appear a bit vague on exactly how such a victory would benefit the United States, sophisticated strategists apparently understand that winning provides its own reward.

Many also seem to worry that the United States might soon be relegated to the number two spot in space exploration. China has announced plans to put men on the moon by 2025, which would apparently be a catastrophe despite the fact that it would happen (if it ever did) two full generations after the United States did so. "Nothing could better symbolize China overtaking America," laments Charles Krauthammer, "than its taking our place on the moon, walking over footprints first laid down, then casually abandoned, by us."[41] The *New York Times* reported that some "experts" in the United States were speaking ominously of a "Red Moon," or "the possibility that China might one day launch military astronauts into space with the aim of setting up a Communist lunar base."[42] While the practical effects of such an event would be hard to identify, sharing the glory of space travel with another state might prove an intolerable blow to the national prestige. Astrophysicist Neil DeGrasse Tyson and others with professional or romantic interest in NASA may be hopeful that competition with China will reinvigorate the space program, but it is not at all clear that such competition will be healthy for the relationship between the two powers here on the earth, which is significantly more important.[43]

Bradley Thayer worries that if the United States were to sink to second place in various world rankings, Chinese would become "the language of diplomacy, trade and commerce, transportation and navigation, the internet, world sport, and global culture," and that Beijing would come to "dominate science and technology, in all its forms" to the extent that soon the world would witness a Chinese astronaut who not only travels to the moon, but "plants the communist flag on Mars, and perhaps other planets in the future."[44] The material benefits that

41 Charles Krauthammer, "Farewell, the New Frontier," *Washington Post*, April 20, 2012.
42 Jim Yardley and William J. Broad, "Heading for the Stars, and Wondering if China Might Reach them First," *New York Times*, January 22, 2004.
43 Neil DeGrasse Tyson, "The Case for Space: Why We Should Keep Reaching for the Stars," *Foreign Affairs*, Vol. 91, No. 2 (March/April 2012), pp. 22–33.
44 Christopher Layne and Bradley A. Thayer, *American Empire: A Debate* (New York: Routledge, 2007), p. 117.

would accrue from having a Chinese flag on Venus are clearly not Thayer's concern. It is the status, the glory that would follow and the damage to the U.S. ego that worries him and those like him. And there are many.

Fear, honor, glory, and hubris will never be eliminated from U.S. foreign policy debates. However, better policy toward Iran, China, and every other state would surely result from an active attempt to remain vigilant against such pathologies, minimize their effects, and maybe even replace them with a more rational approach to decision making. The following section gives some initial thoughts about what such a replacement might look like.

MINIMIZING PATHOLOGY: SOME GENERAL RULES

In their discussion of U.S. foreign policy mistakes, Stephen Walker and Akan Malici point out that concluding chapters of books on foreign policy tend to contain recommendations that fall into four categories: accountability, or ones that seek to hold leaders responsible for mistakes through elections; generic design, or recommendations for adjusting the policy-making process; "actor-specific," or those that suggest that the solution lies in better leaders; and theoretical solutions, ones that outline general rules of thumb for policy makers.[45] This section falls into the latter category, but hopes to avoid the banality common to prior efforts ("think ahead" or "beware of historical analogies") by being somewhat specific in the beliefs that can be promoted to replace pathologies. Rational choices are not the norm for foreign policy makers, even if many analyses assume they are; instead they ought to be considered an ideal, the objective for which leaders should strive. Counterproductive beliefs are often the primary obstacle to rational choices and therefore to good policy.

The goal of those seeking to eliminate pathologies from U.S. foreign policy should be to replace them with competing, rational, beneficial notions that would actually promote, rather than undermine, U.S. interests. The ancients can again provide guidance. Those seeking the antidote to fear, honor, glory, and hubris should turn to other ideas that have their origins in Greece and Rome. Ancient

---

[45] Stephen G. Walker and Akan Malici, *U.S. Presidents and Foreign Policy Mistakes* (Palo Alto, CA: Stanford University Press, 2011), p. 176.

guidance regarding prudence, morality, power, and restraint would serve as better foundations for modern decision making. All of these, uncoincidentally, are drawn from the realist handbook. It is realism that contains the antidotes to pathology. In almost every instance, the United States would be well served if its leaders were to focus on its basic tenets while making decisions and make a conscious effort to internalize beliefs based on a realist foundation.

Psychologist Steven Pinker wrote recently that the "debunking of hogwash – such as ideas that gods demand sacrifices, witches cast spells, heretics go to hell, Jews poison wells, animals are insensate, children are possessed, Africans are brutish, and kings rule by divine right – is bound to undermine many rationales for violence." Furthermore, he believes, rationality "goes hand in hand with self-control."[46] Indeed there is good reason to believe that a United States run by realists would be a wiser, less belligerent, and ultimately happier country. The following sections outline what such a foreign policy might look like.

Prudence

Classical realists have long considered prudence, in Hans Morgenthau's words, "the supreme virtue in politics."[47] Their conception of the term, and how it has traditionally been used in U.S. foreign policy, is similar to the dictionary definition: wisdom, caution, circumspection, and "provident care in the management of resources."[48] Simply put, a prudent foreign policy would aim above all to minimize cost and maximize benefits.[49] It would strive to be rational, careful, and restrained, and it would not waste national resources pursuing low-priority goals or addressing minor threats.

Prudence is essentially the ability to weigh potential consequences of alternative political actions. It demands that the main criteria for

---

[46] Steven Pinker, *The Better Angels of Our Nature: Why Violence has Declined* (New York: Viking, 2011), p. 645.

[47] Hans J. Morgenthau, *Politics among Nations: The Struggle for Power and Peace*, 5th ed. (New York: Alfred A. Knopf, 1973), p. 11.

[48] Discussed by Robert Hariman in *Prudence: Classical Virtue, Postmodern Practice* (University Park: Pennsylvania State University Press, 2003), p. vii.

[49] Morgenthau, *Politics among Nations*, p. 8.

any decision be a cost-benefit analysis, or an honest attempt to assess the implications for the national interest. Although such calculations are by necessity uncertain in a world where rationality is bounded and values unquantifiable, if policy makers were to value prudence above all other virtues they would by force of habit explain and justify their decisions using a rational framework, with reference to reason and evidence rather than emotion. Were prudence the defining virtue in policy debates, the ideal for which policy makers strive, it would quickly silence the voices of fear, honor, glory, and hubris. The process of evaluation can never be foolproof, but by insisting that it be at the center of decision making at the very least prudence can make assumptions clear and offer a basis for evaluation absent in those decisions driven by pathology.

The evaluation of policy cannot be done without recognition of cost. Simply achieving a goal – or winning – does not justify action. To be considered rational, the other side of the ledger must be considered as well. This may sound obvious, but a surprising number of scholars and analysts judge foreign policies based solely on whether or not objectives are fulfilled.[50] Neoconservatives in particular tend to ignore costs, assuming that the United States is capable of paying virtually any price in the fight against evil. The war in Iraq, that exemplar of imprudence, was not preceded by extensive projections of the likely price tag. When pressed, Bush administration officials repeatedly deferred such discussions by denying such estimates were possible.[51] At best, they were of secondary relevance. In the war's aftermath, the same officials stress how much better the world is without Saddam rather than how much worse it is without those who gave their lives in removing him.

Like realism itself, prudence is hardly amoral. It merely demands a focus on the morality of *outcomes*, not *intentions*. Actions that produce bad results are imprudent, no matter how good the intent. On this, Morgenthau quotes Lincoln:

---

[50] David A. Baldwin makes this point in "Success and Failure in Foreign Policy," *Annual Review of Political Science*, Vol. 3 (2000), pp. 167–82. See also Walker and Malici, *U.S. Presidents and Foreign Policy Mistakes*, p. 14.

[51] James Fallows, *Blind into Baghdad: America's War in Iraq* (New York: Vintage Books, 2006), p. 81–83.

I do the very best I know, the very best I can, and I mean to keep doing so until the end. If the end brings me out all right, what is said against me won't amount to anything. If the end brings me out wrong, ten angels swearing I was right would make no difference.[52]

Although the central criteria for prudent cost-benefit analyses must be the national interest, no abnegation of national ideals or international responsibility need follow. Foreign humanitarian assistance is cheap, relatively speaking, and often carries benefits for donor and recipient alike. The entire operation in Somalia, during which as many as a quarter million lives were saved, cost U.S. taxpayers less than two billion dollars.[53] More was spent every week at the height of the Iraq war. Qaddafi was removed for half that.

A focus on the outcome makes it clear that the Iraq war was a blunder of the first order. Even if the intentions of the Bush administration were indeed good, it is hard to see how the outcome can be said to be worth the cost. Thomas Ricks quotes a senior intelligence official in Iraq as saying that the long-term American goal after the surge is "a stable Iraq that is unified, at peace with its neighbors, and is able to police its internal affairs, so it isn't a sanctuary for Al Qaeda. Preferably a friend to us, but it doesn't have to be."[54] Presumably one could add the absence of weapons of mass destruction to this rather scaled-back list of goals, and perhaps the continuation of the uninterrupted flow of oil from the Gulf. In other words, if all goes well over the course of the next few years – and there is obviously no guarantee it will – *Iraq might look quite a bit like it did in 2003*, only with a marginally more friendly dictator in charge. The cost of this restoration of the virtual status quo ante will be at least forty-five hundred American dead and some thirty thousand wounded, at least a hundred thousand Iraqis killed and millions more displaced, and up to as many as three trillion U.S. taxpayer dollars spent.[55] The war inspired many young Arabs, such as Ibrahim Hassan al-Asiri, to join the

---

[52] Morgenthau, *Politics among Nations*, p. 11.

[53] *Newsweek*, "The Final Cost of a Mission of Hope," April 4, 1994, p. 44.

[54] The official "pointedly noted that his list doesn't include democracy or the observation of human rights." Ricks points out that this is a "surprisingly common view among officials in Iraq, even if it hasn't quite sunk in with many Americans." Thomas E. Ricks, *The Gamble: General David Petraeus and the American Military Adventure in Iraq, 2006–2008* (New York: Penguin Press, 2009), p. 316.

[55] Three trillion is a rather conservative estimate once interest on the war debt and lifetime payments to disabled servicemen are taken into account. Joseph E. Stiglitz

ranks of *jihadi* terrorists, swelling the ranks of America's true enemies. Al-Asiri is currently the main bomb maker for "Al Qaeda in the Arabian Peninsula," the group that operates out of Yemen and continues to try to take down Western airliners, and he is considered the "most dangerous man in the world" according to many people who maintain such rankings.[56] The decision to invade Iraq may well turn out to be the most imprudent action this country has ever taken.

Another operation from the same year might serve as a counterexample to Iraq, a prudent foreign policy adventure where the benefits outweighed the costs. The July 2003 intervention in Liberia may be little remembered, but that is partially because it was such a success. The United States deployed around two thousand Marines to Monrovia and ended a siege during a particularly brutal civil war. Security returned to the capital and an unknowable number of lives were saved. Unlike in Somalia, the mission did not creep into nation building, proving that intervention need not be tainted by hubris. By October the civil war had effectively ended and the Marines withdrew, having suffered no casualties and incurring little cost to the U.S. taxpayer. In the years since, Charles Taylor, the paragon of the West African kleptocratic despot, was put on trial at The Hague and the security situation in Liberia has improved markedly. The Marines have not returned.

No assessment of costs and benefits can guarantee good decisions, of course. But by making assumptions clear, by inculcating and rewarding a systematic evaluation of alternatives, expectations can be assessed more rationally and decisions rescued from emotion. If leaders work actively to minimize pathologies and replace them with rational, fact-based beliefs, the odds of arriving at rational conclusions rise. If prudence is the goal, therefore, the following should form the core of the foreign policy conventional wisdom:

- The world is more peaceful than ever before.
- While no country is ever completely safe, the United States has few – if any – serious security threats.

and Linda J. Bilmes, *The Three Trillion Dollar War: The True Cost of the Iraq Conflict* (New York: W. W. Norton, 2008).

[56] Richard Engel of NBC News reported al-Asiri joined AQAP as a direct result of the U.S. invasion on the news program *Rock Center*, November 15, 2012, available at http://video.msnbc.msn.com/rock-center/49824445#49824445, accessed December 18, 2012.

- Credibility earned today does not help in avoiding or resolving the crises of tomorrow. It is never worth fighting for.
- Being "the best" has no real utility in a world where major war is all but obsolete. International politics is not a competition to be won or lost.
- There are limits to what even the strongest states can accomplish. Nation building in particular is very difficult under the best circumstances.

Before any major decision, the prudent policy maker should determine the extent to which his or her thinking on any issue has been affected by the common pathologies of foreign policy. History's final evaluation will occur after the action is over; however, leaders can take steps to maximize their chances for success.

By their nature pathological beliefs have more powerful effects on debates when there is no clear rational justification for action, filling the rhetorical gap where no tangible threats or interests exist. Framing debates from the outset in rational terms with national interest at the center can make their presence clear, and hopefully minimize their effects on the formation of broader societal opinion.

The Mirror of Our Own Vanity

A prudent foreign policy would hardly be an amoral one, as discussed earlier, but it certainly would approach issues of right and wrong in a fundamentally different way than a liberal would recommend. Realists are fundamentally uncomfortable with the assumption that any one state has a monopoly on morality, and they certainly bristle at the suggestion that U.S. foreign policy is essentially a crusade against evil. Moralism, or what George Kennan called "the projection of attitudes, poses and rhetoric that cause us to appear noble and altruistic in the mirror of our own vanity but lack substance when related to the realities of international life," is what concerns realists, not morality.[57] U.S. policy makers are especially vulnerable to moralism, which leads to misperception, Manichaeism, and war, outcomes that render even the best intended actions immoral. "In personal as in public life," to

---

[57] George F. Kennan, "Morality in Foreign Policy," *Foreign Affairs*, Vol. 64, No. 2 (Winter 1985), p. 213.

return again to Kennan, "whenever one has the agreeable sensation of being impressively moral, one probably is not. What one does without self-consciousness or self-admiration, as a matter of duty or common decency, is apt to be closer to the real thing."[58]

The belief in the existence of implacable evil also contributes directly to the formation of the enemy image. The pathological misperceptions that stem from that image could be minimized if U.S. leaders were to recognize its pathological foundations and ignore the tenets that accompany it, from the general ("they are evil") to the more specific ("they just don't value human life like we do"). Evil regimes have existed, of course, but in general state behavior becomes much more understandable and predictable once moral identifiers are removed from the analysis.

Overall, policy makers ought to be highly skeptical of any suggestion that *they* – whoever *they* are – are fundamentally different from *us*. Surface differences exist between states, of course, but when it comes to the most important, most basic aspects of governance, states tend to act in similar manners, pursuing their interests as they see fit. The number one goal of any person in power is to stay in power, for instance. Those who suggest that Iranian leaders are suicidal fanatics seeking to bring about Armageddon as a religious duty ask us to believe that they are fundamentally different from us. Such voices should be met with extreme skepticism.

Understanding Power: Patience, Necessity, and Restraint

The United States has no peer military competitors. No country or coalition can pose any real threat to U.S. security or prosperity, much less to its sovereignty. It is and will for the foreseeable future be without existential threats, which is a reality often lost on post–Cold War U.S. policy makers. Interpreting the meaning of that power is not a straightforward exercise, however. For too many analysts, unipolarity implies that the United States need not recognize limits on its actions, that it can flex its muscles whenever it wants without consequence. Power, to this way of thinking, is primarily the ability to never have to compromise, which often makes the United States its own worst

---

[58] Kennan, "Morality in Foreign Policy," p. 213.

enemy. Such pathological thinking leads rapidly to counterproductive policy choices. It need not be the case, however, that (in the words
of normative political theorist Stephen Holmes) "power unchecked is
power deranged."[59] Unipolarity does not have to lead to rogue actions.
Basic realist doctrine suggests that the quickest way to lose status is to
engage in excessive foreign adventurism, which wastes resources and
invites balancing by others. The primary goal of the United States
should not be to preserve *unipolarity* but the *security* it now enjoys. The
latter is perhaps related to, but it is not a direct result of, the former. A
number of implications for decision making should accompany overwhelming power for leaders hoping to make more sagacious choices
than did their predecessors.

First, the United States can afford to be patient when making its
foreign policy choices. Unlike small states, the unipolar power has
a large margin for error. Weak countries must employ worst-case
assumptions about their potential adversaries because misjudgments
may prove fatal. The United States, on the other hand, should have
no such fear, because there is no first blow it cannot absorb (barring
a suicidal, apocalyptic nuclear assault from Russia, which is far less
likely than it was a generation ago). Its foreign policy can therefore
be more deliberate and well considered than that of other states.
Power reduces, rather than expands, risk; it ought to *improve* decisions
because it provides the space and security for leaders to take their
time. Better decisions would come from leaders who ignore the pressures of politics and the twenty-four-hour news cycle, insisting instead
on patience and thought. The determination to act slowly might not
always improve decisions, but much of the time it will, without posing
any substantial risk to the United States.

Second, a more mature understanding of relative U.S. power
would lead policy makers to understand a basic rule for the unipolar
state: *necessity in foreign policy is always an illusion.* The perception of
necessity, of having no choice in any situation, is the ultimate salve for
the conscience of the policy maker; the terrible burden of decision
making is lifted when it appears no alternative exists. In reality, the
United States has a degree of freedom in its foreign policy choices

---

[59] Stephen Holmes, *The Matador's Cape: America's Reckless Response to Terrorism* (New
York: Cambridge University Press, 2007), p. 127.

that is greater than any other state in history, since it is inherently safe and will survive any decision, no matter how ill advised and counterproductive. Advisors who tell a future president that there is no choice in any given situation should be summarily dismissed, for they would be either trying to force the decision to their liking or betraying a fundamental misunderstanding of power (or, what is most likely, both). "The rhetorical strategy behind the argument from necessity," explained Gregory Raymond, "is to frame situations of limited options as situations where no options exist. How a situation is characterized can foreclose certain policy options without ever having them subjected to close scrutiny. When a situation is framed in terms of strategic necessity, political leaders appear compelled to act in a particular way."[60] Claims of necessity prevent the coherent analysis of options and make rational choices less likely. The United States has a set of options – which always includes the option to do nothing – in nearly every imaginable given situation.

The illusion of necessity helps policy makers sell decisions as well as make them. This is especially true for war, which is almost always justified as a last resort. National leaders, the public is told, simply had no choice. Even the 1983 U.S. intervention in Grenada was "forced on us by events," according to President Reagan, who claimed he "had no choice but to act strongly and decisively."[61] Thus it is not only decision makers who must guard against arguments of necessity; the public must beware as well, rejecting any suggestion that their leaders were compelled to act a certain way. Such justifications make for powerful rhetoric, but in an age of declining warfare, events never compel the unipole to do anything. The United States always has "the freedom of choice," as historian Barbara Tuchman noted, "to change or desist from a counter-productive course," if only its policy makers have the moral courage to exercise it. "Yet to recognize errors, to cut losses, to alter course, is the most repugnant option in government."[62] This is especially true for governments that hold pathological beliefs about honor and glory and war.

---

[60] Gregory A. Raymond, "Necessity in Foreign Policy," *Political Science Quarterly*, Vol. 113, No. 4 (Winter 1998–99), p. 679.
[61] Quoted in Raymond, "Necessity in Foreign Policy," pp. 684–85.
[62] Barbara Tuchman, *The March of Folly: From Troy to Vietnam* (New York: Ballantine Books, 1984, p. 383.

Finally, it is important to note that for the unipolar power, the dangers of inaction are rarely greater than those of action. When asked his opinion about a crisis with Britain over Venezuela in 1895, Speaker of the House Thomas Brackett Reed described what he called "a good rule" in politics: "When you don't know what to do," he said, "do nothing."[63] Since the basic security, prosperity, and independence of the United States will never be in serious danger, the default option for policy makers facing difficult decisions should be follow Reed's advice. For the unipolar power in what is by any reasonable definition a golden age of international peace, inaction is always an option. Action, in fact, ought to bear the burden of proof. In other words, to minimize the power of its pathological beliefs, the United States ought to follow a grand strategy based on what is known as *strategic restraint.*

It should not surprise even the most casual skimmer of this volume that the best grand strategy for the United States is likely to be one found on the end of the spectrum opposite that occupied by neoconservatism. Indeed while neoconservatives tend to recommend *primacy*, a grand strategy based on the establishment and maintenance of a benign (and illusory) hegemony as described in the previous chapter, the best course for the United States would be quite different. A restrained grand strategy would shape foreign policy decisions along three dimensions, as perhaps best described by Eric Nordlinger: "minimally effortful national strategy in the security realm; moderately activist policies to advance our liberal ideas among and within states; and a fully activist economic diplomacy on behalf of free trade."[64] Thus restraint is hardly isolationism.[65] No serious analyst of foreign affairs thinks the United States can or should cut itself off from the rest of the world, à la Tokugawa Japan. A restrained United States would continue to trade, participate in international organizations,

---

[63] Evan Thomas, *The War Lovers: Roosevelt, Lodge, Hearst, and the Rush to Empire, 1898* (New York: Little, Brown and Company, 2010), p. 111.

[64] Eric A. Nordlinger, *Isolationism Reconfigured: American Foreign Policy for a New Century* (Princeton, NJ: Princeton University Press, 1995), p. 4.

[65] Some of the best post–Cold War discussions include Eugene Gholz, Daryl G. Press, and Harvey M. Sapolsky, "Come Home America: The Strategy of Restraint in the Face of Temptation," *International Security*, Vol. 21, No. 4 (Spring 1997), pp. 5–48; Barry R. Posen, "The Case for Restraint," *The American Interest*, Vol. 3, No. 2 (November/December 2007), pp. 6–17; and Christopher A. Preble, *The Power Problem: How American Military Dominance Makes Us Less Safe, Less Prosperous and Less Free* (Ithaca, NY: Cornell University Press, 2009).

and play a role in humanitarian relief efforts. It would not, however, assume that maintenance of world security is the responsibility of the American taxpayer. It would cut back on commitments and military spending, defining threats, interests, and obligations far more narrowly and logically to ensure that catastrophic blunders like Iraq are never repeated. Strategic restraint is a logical and rational grand strategy for the strongest state in a world where threats to basic security are not terribly dire. And it contains the best chance of minimizing pathological choices in the years to come.

"Let us agree to overlook a great many things in those who are, as it were, our fellow-contestants," advised the great Roman stoic emperor Marcus Aurelius. "A simple avoidance ... is always open to us, without either suspicion or ill-will."[66] Today the United States can follow that advice without risk.

The United States is simultaneously the world's most optimistic country and its most paranoid, the most competitive and yet most magnanimous. It certainly does not always act on its pathological paranoia, narcissism, or hypercompetitiveness, but those elements win the battle of beliefs frequently enough to require a major national introspection. There is no doubt that America is a basically good country, but it is one that occasionally makes bad choices. At times the frightened, insecure, egomaniacal side of its national personality emerges, one that must be guarded against at all times lest it lead to disaster.

"Many of the tenets underlying American security policy are held with strong but unwarranted conviction," lamented Nancy Kanwisher as the Cold War drew to a conclusion. "Further, these dubious beliefs often persist even after their flaws have been widely exposed."[67] The preceding analysis of many such dubious beliefs was done in the (perhaps quixotic) hope that pathology will wilt once exposed to the sunlight of rational evaluation. If no such wilting takes place, then the rest of the century will contain more examples of the kind of foreign policy blunders that will puzzle future historians, who will struggle to understand why the strongest, safest country in the history of the world consistently refused to act that way.

---

[66] Marcus Aurelius, *Meditations* (New York: Penguin, 1964), p. 95.
[67] Nancy Kanwisher, "Cognitive Heuristics and American Security Policy," *Journal of Conflict Resolution*, Vol. 33, No. 4 (December 1989), p. 652.

Bibliography

Abadie, Alberto. 2006. "Poverty, Political Freedom, and the Roots of Terrorism." *American Economic Review*, Vol. 96, No. 2 (May), 50–56.

Abrams, Elliot, ed. 1998. *Honor among Nations: Intangible Interests and Foreign Policy*. Washington, DC: Ethics and Public Policy Center.

Adelman, Kenneth. 2002a. "Cakewalk in Iraq." *Washington Post*, February 13, A27.

   2002b. "Desert Storm II Would Be a Walk in the Park." *London Times*, August 29.

Aghion, Philippe and Rachel Griffith. 2005. *Competition and Growth: Reconciling Theory and Evidence*. Cambridge, MA: MIT Press.

Aguilar, Edwin Eloy, Benjamin O. Fordham, and G. Patrick Lynch. 1997. "The Foreign Policy Beliefs of Political Campaign Contributors." *International Studies Quarterly*, Vol. 41, No. 2 (June), 355–65.

Albright, Madeleine. 1993. "Yes, There Is a Reason to Be in Somalia." *New York Times*, August 10, A19.

   2003. *Madame Secretary*. New York: Miramax.

   2006. *The Mighty and the Almighty: Reflections on America, God, and World Affairs*. New York: Harper Collins.

Ali, Wajahat, Eli Clifton, Matthew Duss, Lee Fang, Scott Keyes, and Faiz Shakir. 2011. *Fear, Inc.: The Roots of the Islamophobia Network in America*. Washington, DC: Center for American Progress, August, available at http://www.americanprogress.org/issues/2011/08/pdf/islamophobia.pdf.

Allin, Dana H. 1994. *Cold War Illusions: America, Europe and Soviet Power, 1969–1989*. New York: St. Martin's Press.

Allison, Graham T. 2004. *Nuclear Terrorism: The Ultimate Preventable Catastrophe*. New York: Henry Holt.

Allison, Graham and Ernesto Zedillo. 2008. "The Fragility of the Global Nuclear Order." *Boston Globe*, September 30.

Altheide, David L. 2002. *Creating Fear: News and the Construction of Crisis.* New York: Aldine de Gruyter.

Anderson, Craig A., Mark R. Lepper, and Lee Ross. 1980. "Perseverance of Social Theories: The Role of Explanation in the Persistence of Discredited Information." *Journal of Personality and Social Psychology,* Vol. 39, No. 6 (December), 1037–49.

Angell, Norman. 1913. *The Great Illusion: A Study of the Relation of Military Power to National Advantage,* 2nd ed. London: William Heinemann.

Angrosino, Michael. 2002. "Civil Religion Redux." *Anthropological Quarterly,* Vol. 75, No. 2 (Spring), 239–67.

Aronson, Eliot. 1980. *The Social Animal,* 3rd ed. San Francisco, CA: W.H. Freeman.

Aurelius, Marcus. 1964. *Meditations.* New York: Penguin.

Avellar, J. and Spencer Kagan. 1976. "Development of Competitive Behaviors in Anglo-American and Mexican-American Children." *Psychological Reports,* Vol. 39, No. 1 (August), 191–98.

Bacevich, Andrew J. 2002. *American Empire: The Realities and Consequences of U.S. Diplomacy.* Cambridge, MA: Harvard University Press.

    2005. *The New American Militarism: How Americans are Seduced by War.* New York: Oxford University Press.

    2008a. "He Told Us to Go Shopping: Now the Bill is Due." *Washington Post,* October 5, B3.

    2008b. *The Limits of Power: The End of American Exceptionalism.* New York: Metropolitan Books.

Baker, Peter. 2006. "Cheney Back Delivering the Grim Campaign Speech." *Washington Post,* October 8.

Baker, William J. 1988. *Sports in the Western World.* Chicago: University of Illinois Press.

Baldwin, David. 1989. *Paradoxes of Power.* New York: Blackwell.

    2000. "Success and Failure in Foreign Policy." *Annual Review of Political Science,* Vol. 3, 167–82.

Ball, George W. 1969. "Slogans and Realities." *Foreign Affairs,* Vol. 47, No. 4 (July), 623–41.

Balzacq, Thierry and Robert Jervis. 2004. "Logics of Mind and International System: A Journey with Robert Jervis." *Review of International Studies,* Vol. 30, No. 4 (October), 559–82.

Barker, David C., Jon Hurwitz, and Traci L. Nelson. 2008. "Of Crusades and Culture Wars: 'Messianic' Militarism and Political Conflict in the United States." *Journal of Politics,* Vol. 70, No. 2 (April), 307–22.

Basler, Roy P., ed. 2001. *Abraham Lincoln: His Speeches and Writings.* Cambridge, MA: Da Capo Press.

Barash, David P. 1994. *Beloved Enemies: Our Need for Opponents.* Amherst, NY: Prometheus Books.

Barton, David. 2012. *The Jefferson Lies: Exposing the Myths You've Always Believed about Thomas Jefferson.* Nashville, TN: WallBuilder Press.

Baumeister, Roy F., Ellen Bratslavsky, Catrin Finkenauer, and Kathleen D. Vohs. 2001. "Bad is Stronger than Good." *Review of General Psychology,* Vol. 5, No. 4 (December), 323–70.

Baumol, William J., Robert E. Litan, and Carl J. Schramm. 2007. *Good Capitalism, Bad Capitalism and the Economics of Growth and Prosperity*. New Haven, CT: Yale University Press.

Bayles, Martha. 2005. "Goodwill Hunting." *The Wilson Quarterly*, Vol. 29, No. 3 (Summer), 46–56.

Beinart, Peter. 2010. *The Icarus Syndrome: A History of American Hubris*. New York: Harper Collins.

Bell, Coral. 1989. *The Reagan Paradox: American Foreign Policy in the 1980s*. New Brunswick, NJ: Rutgers University Press.

Bellah, Robert N. 1967. "Civil Religion in America." *Daedalus*, Vol. 96, No. 1 (Winter), 1–21.

1986. "Religious Influences on United States Foreign Policy." In Michael P. Hamilton, ed., *American Character and Foreign Policy*. Grand Rapids, MI: William B. Eerdmans Publishing, 50–59.

Bellah, Robert N., Richard Madsen, William M. Sullivan, Ann Swidler, and Steven M. Tipton. 1985. *Habits of the Heart: Individualism and Commitment in American Life*. Berkeley: University of California Press.

Bennett, William J. 2003. *Why We Fight: Moral Clarity and the War on Terrorism*. New York: Doubleday.

Berinsky, Adam J. 2009. *In Time of War: Understanding American Public Opinion from World War II to Iraq*. Chicago, IL: University of Chicago Press.

Berliner, David C. 2014. "Effects of Inequality and Poverty vs. Teachers and Schooling on America's Youth." *Teachers College Record*, Vol. 116, No. 1 (January 2014), forthcoming.

Berliner, David C. and Bruce J. Biddle. 1995. *The Manufactured Crisis: Myths, Fraud, and the Attack on America's Public Schools*. Boston, MA: Addison-Wesley.

Bernstein, George L. 2004. *The Myth of Decline: The Rise of Britain since 1945*. London: Pimlico.

Bernstein, Richard and Ross H. Munro. 1998. *The Coming Conflict with China*. New York: Vintage.

Beschloss, Michael R. 1991. *The Crisis Years: Kennedy and Khrushchev, 1960–1963*. New York: Edward Burlingame Books.

Best, Geoffrey. 1982. *Honour among Men and Nations: Transformation of an Idea*. Toronto: University of Toronto Press.

Betts, Richard K. 1982. *Surprise Attack: Lessons for Defense Planning*. Washington, DC: The Brookings Institution Press.

1991. "The Concept of Deterrence in the Postwar Era." *Security Studies*, Vol. 1, No. 1 (Autumn), 25–36.

Bin Laden, Usama. 1998. "American Soldiers are Paper Tigers." *Middle East Quarterly*, Vol. 5, No. 4 (December), 73–79.

Bittle, Scott and Jonathan Rochkind. 2007. "Anxious Public Pulling Back from Use of Force." *Confidence in U.S. Foreign Policy Index*, Vol. 4 (Spring), available at http://www.publicagenda.org/foreignpolicy/index.htm.

2008. "Energy, Economy New Focal Points for Anxiety over U.S. Foreign Policy." *Confidence in U.S. Foreign Policy Index*, Vol. 6 (Spring), available at http://www.publicagenda.org/foreignpolicy/index.htm.

Blair, Graeme, C. Christine Fair, Neil Malhotra, and Jacob N. Shapiro. 2013. "Poverty and Support for Militant Politics: Evidence from Pakistan." *American Journal of Political Science*, Vol. 57, No. 1 (January), 30–48.

Blake, Robert R. and Jane Srygley Mouton. 1961. "Reactions to Intergroup Competition under Win-Lose Conditions." *Management Science*, Vol. 7, No. 4 (July), 420–35.

Blang, Eugenie M. 2011. *Allies at Odds: America, Europe, and Vietnam, 1961–1968*. New York: Rowman and Littlefield.

Blechman, Barry M. and Robert Powell. 1992–93. "What in the Name of God is Strategic Superiority?" *Political Science Quarterly*, Vol. 97, No. 4 (Winter), 589–602.

Bloch-Elkon, Yaeli. 2011. "Public Perceptions and the Threat of International Terrorism after 9/11." *Public Opinion Quarterly*, Vol. 75, No. 2 (Summer), 366–92.

Blum, Douglas W. 1993. "The Soviet Foreign Policy Belief System: Beliefs, Politics, and Foreign Policy Outcomes." *International Studies Quarterly*, Vol. 37, No. 4 (December), 373–94.

Boettcher, William A. 2004. "The Prospects for Prospect Theory: An Empirical Evaluation of International Relations Applications of Framing and Loss Aversion." *Political Psychology*, Vol. 25, No. 3 (June), 331–62.

Bohlen, Charles E. 1973. *Witness to History 1929–1969*. New York: W. W. Norton and Co.

Bolton, John R. 2007. *Surrender is Not an Option: Defending America at the United Nations*. New York: Simon and Schuster.

2011. "The West Needs to Stand Up to Beijing." *Financial Times*, January 18.

Bonta, Bruce D. 1997. "Cooperation and Competition in Peaceful Societies." *Psychological Bulletin*, Vol. 121, No. 2 (March), 299–320.

Bourdie u, Pierre. 1965. "The Sentiment of Honour in Kabyle Society." In J. G. Peristiany, ed., *Honour and Shame: The Values of Mediterranean Society*. London: Weidenfeld and Nicolson 191–241.

Breslauer, George W. and Philip E. Tetlock, eds. 1991. *Learning in U.S. and Soviet Foreign Policy*. Boulder, CO: Westview Press.

Brewer, Paul R. and Marco R. Steenbergen. 2002. "All against All: How Beliefs about Human Nature Shape Foreign Policy Opinions." *Political Psychology*, Vol. 23, No. 1 (March), 39–58.

Broder, David. 2010. "How Obama Might Recover." *Washington Post*, October 31.

Broder, John M. 1993. "Clinton Orders 5,300 Troops to Somalia." *Los Angeles Times*, October 8, A1.

Bronner, Ethan. 2010. "Mood Is Dark As Israel Marks Its 62nd Year As a Nation." *New York Times*, April 20.

Brooks, David. 2004. "The Era of Distortion." *New York Times*, January 6.

Brooks, Risa A. 2011. "Muslim 'Homegrown' Terrorism in the United States: How Serious the Threat?" *International Security*, Vol. 36, No. 2 (Fall), 7–47.

Brooks, Stephen G. 2005. *Producing Security: Multinational Corporations, Globalization, and the Changing Calculus of Conflict.* Princeton, NJ: Princeton University Press.

Brooks, Stephen G. and William C. Wohlforth. 2002. "American Primacy in Perspective." *Foreign Affairs,* Vol. 81, No. 4 (July/August), 20–33.

2005. "Hard Times for Soft Balancing." *International Security,* Vol. 30, No. 1 (Summer), 72–108.

2008. *World out of Balance: International Relations and the Challenge of American Primacy.* Princeton, NJ: Princeton University Press.

Brown, Jerome, ed. 1995. *Social Pathology in Comparative Perspective: The Nature and Psychology of Civil Society.* Westport, CT: Praeger.

Brunt, P. A. 1990. *Roman Imperial Themes.* Oxford: Clarendon Press.

Brzezinski, Zbigniew. 1983. *Power and Principle.* New York: Farrar, Strauss and Giroux.

2004. *The Choice: Global Domination or Global Leadership.* New York: Basic Books.

2012a. "After America." *Foreign Policy,* No. 191 (January/February), pp. 1–4.

2012b. *Strategic Vision: America and the Crisis of Global Power.* New York: Basic Books.

Burnham, James. 1947. *The Struggle for the World.* New York: The John Day Company, Inc.

1967. *The War We Are In: The Last Decade and the Next.* New Rochelle, NY: Arlington House.

Bush, George W. 2002a. "Commencement Speech at the U.S. Military Academy." West Point, NY, June 1.

2002b. *The National Security Strategy of the United States of America.* Washington, DC: Government Printing Office.

2002c. "Remarks at the International Conference on Financing for Development." Monterrey, Mexico, March 22, available at http://www.un.org/ffd/statements/usaE.htm.

2010. *Decision Points.* New York: Crown Publishers.

Bushman, Brad J. 2002. "Does Venting Anger Feed or Extinguish the Flame? Catharsis, Rumination, Distraction, Anger and Aggressive Responding." *Personality and Social Psychology Bulletin,* Vol. 28, No. 6 (October), 724–31.

Butt, Dorcas Susan. 1987. *Psychology of Sport,* 2nd ed. New York: Van Nostrand Reinhold Co.

Buzan, Barry. 2004. *The United States and the Great Powers: World Politics in the Twenty-First Century.* Malden, MA: Polity.

Cahn, Anne Hessing. 1998. *Killing Détente: The Right Attacks the CIA.* University Park: Pennsylvania State University Press.

Cairns, Douglas L. 1996. "Hybris, Dishonour, and Thinking Big." *Journal of Hellenistic Studies,* Vol. 116, 1–32.

Caldwell, Wilber W. 2006. *American Narcissism: The Myth of National Superiority.* New York: Algora Publishing.

Callahan, David. 2004. *The Cheating Culture: Why More Americans Are Doing Wrong to Get Ahead.* New York: Harcourt, Inc.

Calleo, David. 1987. *Beyond American Hegemony: The Future of the Western Alliance.* New York: Basic Books.

Camerer, Colin F. 2004. "Prospect Theory in the Wild: Evidence from the Field." In Colin Camerer, ed., *Advances in Behavioral Economics.* Princeton, NJ: Princeton University Press, 148–61.

Campbell, J. K. 1964. *Honour, Family and Patronage.* Oxford: Clarendon Press.

Cannon, Lou and Don Oberdorfer. 1983. "Standing Fast: 'Vital Interests' of U.S. at Stake." *Washington Post,* October 25, A1.

Chandrasekaran, Rajiv. 2007. *Imperial Life in the Emerald City: Inside Iraq's Green Zone.* New York: Knopf.

Chace, James and Caleb Carr. 1988. *America Invulnerable: The Quest for Absolute Security from 1812 to Star Wars.* New York: Summit Books.

Cheney, Dick. 2009a. "Address to the Veterans of Foreign Wars, Nashville, TN, August 26, 2002." In John Ehrenberg, J. Patrice McSherry, Jose Ramon Sanchez and Caroleen Marji Sayej, eds., *The Iraq Papers.* New York: Oxford University Press, 2009, 75–80.

   2009b. "Concerns about America's Foreign Policy Drift," Center for Security Policy, October 22, available at http://www.realclearpolitics.com/articles/2009/10/22/concerns_about_americas_foreign_policy_drift.html.

   2011. *In My Time: A Personal and Political Memoir.* New York: Simon and Schuster.

Cheney, Liz. 2012. "Cairo, Benghazi and Obama Foreign Policy." *Wall Street Journal,* September 13, A15.

Chicago Tribune. 2007. "Chertoff's Gut." July 12.

Chittick, William O., Keith R. Billingsly, and Rick Travis. 1995. "A Three-Dimensional Model of American Foreign Policy Beliefs." *International Studies Quarterly,* Vol. 39, No. 3 (September), 313–31.

Clarke, Walter and Jeffrey Herbst. 1996. "Somalia and the Future of Humanitarian Intervention." *Foreign Affairs,* Vol. 75, No. 2 (March–April), 70–85.

Clymer, Adam. 2008. *Drawing the Line at the Big Ditch: The Panama Canal Treaties and the Rise of the Right.* Lawrence: University Press of Kansas.

Cohen, Eliot A. 1998. "Sound and Fury." *Washington Post,* December 19, A25.

Cohen, Roger. 2010. "Israeli Unassailable Might and Unyielding Angst." *New York Times,* April 23.

Coker, Christopher. 2008. "War, Memes and Memeplexes." *International Affairs,* Vol. 84, No. 5 (September), 903–14.

Converse, Philip E. 1964. "The Nature of Belief Systems in Mass Publics." In David E. Apter, ed., *Ideology and Discontent.* New York: Macmillan, 206–61.

Copeland, Dale C. 1997. "Do Reputations Matter?" *Security Studies,* Vol. 7, No. 1 (Autumn), 33–71.

Corn, Tony. 2006. "World War IV as Fourth-Generation Warfare." *Hoover Institution Policy Review* (January), available at http://www.hoover.org/publications/policy-review/article/6526.

Cox, Richard H. 2007. *Sport Psychology: Concepts and Applications*, 6th ed. New York: McGraw Hill.

Crawford, Neta C. 2000. "The Passion of World Politics: Propositions on Emotion and Emotional Relationships." *International Security*, Vol. 24, No. 4 (Spring), 116–56.

Crescenzi, Mark J. C. 2007. "Reputation and Interstate Conflict." *American Journal of Political Science*, Vol. 51, No. 2 (April), 382–96.

Crescenzi, Mark J. C., Jacob D. Kathman, Katja B. Kleinberg and Reed M. Wood. 2012. "Reliability, Reputation, and Alliance Formation." *International Studies Quarterly*, Vol. 56, No. 2 (June), 259–74.

Cross, K. Patricia. 1977. "Not Can, But Will College Teaching Be Improved?" *New Directions for Higher Education*, Vol. 1977, No. 17 (Spring), 1–15.

Danilovic, Vesna. 2001. "The Sources of Threat Credibility in Extended Deterrence." *Journal of Conflict Resolution*, Vol. 45, No. 3 (June), 341–69.

Davies, Richard O. 1994. *America's Obsession: Sports and Society Since 1945*. New York: Harcourt Brace & Co.

Davis, Tami R. and Sean M. Lynn-Jones. 1987. "Citty upon a Hill." *Foreign Policy*, No. 66 (Spring), 20–38.

Dawson, Paul A. 1979. "The Formation and Structure of Political Belief Systems." *Political Behavior*, Vol. 1, No. 2 (Summer), 99–122.

Decety, Jean, Philip L. Jackson, Jessica A. Sommerville, Thierry Chaminade, and Andrew N. Meltzoff. 2004. "The Neural Bases of Cooperation and Competition: An fMRI Investigation." *NeuroImage*, Vol. 23, No. 2 (October), 744–51.

Dempsey, Martin E. 2012. "Chairman's Remarks." John F. Kennedy Jr. Forum, Harvard University, Boston, MA, April 12, 2012, available at http://www.jcs.mil/speech.aspx?id=1690.

Department of Defense. 2000. *Joint Vision 2020*. Washington DC: U.S. Government Printing Office, June, available at http://www.fs.fed.us/fire/doctrine/genesis_and_evolution/source_materials/joint_vision_2020.pdf.

Desch, Michael C. 1998. "Culture Clash: Assessing the Importance of Ideas in Security Studies." *International Security*, Vol. 23, No. 1 (Summer), 141–70.

Deutsch, Karl W. 1968. *The Analysis of International Relations*. Englewood Cliffs, NJ: Prentice-Hall.

Deutsch, Morton. 1949. "A Theory of Cooperation and Competition." *Human Relations*, Vol. 2, No. 2 (May), 129–52.

    1973. *The Resolution of Conflict: Constructive and Destructive Processes*. New Haven, CT: Yale University Press.

    1985. *Distributive Justice: A Social Psychological Perspective*. New Haven, CT: Yale University Press.

Diamond, Sarah. 1998. *Not By Politics Alone: The Enduring Influence of the Christian Right.* New York: Guilford Press.

Dobbins, James. 2008. *After the Taliban: Nation-Building in Afghanistan.* Washington, DC: Potomac Books.

Dobbins, James, Seth G. Jones, Keith Crane, and Beth Cole DeGrasse. 2007. *The Beginner's Guide to Nation-Building.* Santa Monica, CA: RAND.

Dobrynin, Anatoly. 1995. *In Confidence.* New York: Random House.

Donelan, Michael. 2007. *Honor in Foreign Policy.* New York: Palgrave Macmillan.

Doran, Michael and Max Boot. 2012. "Five Reasons to Intervene in Syria Now." *New York Times*, September 26, A29.

Downes, Anthony. 1957. *An Economic Theory of Democracy.* New York: Harper and Row.

Drew, S. Nelson, ed. *NSC-68: Forging the Strategy of Containment.* Washington, DC: National Defense University.

Drezner, Daniel. 2011. *Theories of International Politics and Zombies.* Princeton, NJ: Princeton University Press.

Dudden, Alex. 2008. *Troubled Apologies among Japan, Korea and the United States.* New York: Columbia University Press.

Eagleburger, Lawrence S. 1999. "NATO, in a Corner," *New York Times*, April 4, D11.

Edelman, Eric S., Andrew F. Krepinevich, Jr., and Evan Braden Montgomery. 2011. "The Dangers of a Nuclear Iran: The Limits of Containment." *Foreign Affairs*, Vol. 90, No. 1 (January/February 2011), 66–81.

Egendorf, Laura, ed. 1999. *Terrorism: Opposing Viewpoints.* San Diego, CA: Greenhaven Press.

Eizenstat, Stuart, John Edward Porter, and Jeremy M. Weinstein. 2005. "Rebuilding Weak States." *Foreign Affairs*, Vol. 84, No. 1 (January/February), 134–46.

Elliott, J. H. 1991. "Managing Decline: Olivares and the Grand Strategy of Imperial Spain." In Paul Kennedy, ed., *Grand Strategies in War and Peace.* New Haven, CT: Yale University Press, 87–104.

Ellis, Richard J. and Michael Thompson, eds. 1997. *Culture Matters: Essays in Honor of Aaron Wildavsky.* Boulder, CO: Westview Press.

Elman, Colin and Miriam Fendius Elman, eds. 2001. *Bridges and Boundaries: Historians, Political Scientists, and the Study of International Relations.* Cambridge, MA: MIT Press.

Errington, Robert M. 1971. *The Dawn of Empire: Rome's Rise to Power.* London: Hamish Hamilton Ltd.

Europol. 2006–2011. *EU Terrorism Situation and Trend Report.* The Hague, Netherlands: European Police Office, available at https://www.europol.europa.eu/.

Evans, Richard. 1974. "A Conversation with Konrad Lorenz about Aggression, Homosexuality, Pornography, and the Need for a New Ethic." *Psychology Today*, Vol. 8, No. 6 (November), 82–93.

Everts, Steven. 2001. "Unilateral America, Lightweight Europe? Managing Divergence in Transatlantic Foreign Policy." Centre for European Reform Working Paper, No. 9 (February), available at http://www.cer.org.uk/pdf/cerwp9.pdf.

Evrigenis, Ioannis. 2008. *Fear of Enemies and Collective Action.* New York: Cambridge University Press.

Farrell, Theo. 1998. "Culture and Military Power." *Review of International Studies,* Vol. 24, No. 3 (July), 407–16.

Fallows, James. 2006. *Blind into Baghdad: America's War in Iraq.* New York: Vintage Books.

  2009. "Obama on Exceptionalism." *The Atlantic Online,* April 4, available at http://www.theatlantic.com/technology/archive/2009/04/obama-on-exceptionalism/9874/.

Fazal, Tanisha M. 2007. *State Death: The Politics and Geography of Conquest, Occupation, and Annexation.* Princeton, NJ: Princeton University Press.

Fearon, James D. 1994. "Signaling versus the Balance of Power and Interests: An Empirical Test of a Crisis Bargaining Model." *Journal of Conflict Resolution,* Vol. 38, No. 2 (June), 236–69.

Feinstein, Lee and Anne-Marie Slaughter. 2004. "A Duty to Prevent." *Foreign Affairs,* Vol. 83, No. 1 (January–February), 136–50.

Feith, Douglas J. 2008. *War and Decision: Inside the Pentagon at the Dawn of the War on Terrorism.* New York: HarperCollins.

Ferguson, Niall. 2004. *Colossus: The Price of America's Empire.* New York: Penguin.

Ferraro, Kathleen J. 2005. "The Culture of Social Problems: Observations of the Third Reich, the Cold War, and Vietnam." *Social Problems,* Vol. 52, No. 1 (February), 1–14.

Fettweis, Christopher J. 2008. *Losing Hurts Twice as Bad.* New York: W. W. Norton.

  2010. *Dangerous Times? The International Politics of Great Power Peace.* Washington, DC: Georgetown University Press.

  2011. "Free Riding or Restraint? Examining European Grand Strategy." *Comparative Strategy,* Vol. 30, No. 4 (Fall), 316–32.

Fineman, Howard. 2003. "Bush and God." *Newsweek,* March 10.

Finlay, David J., Ole R. Holsti, and Richard R. Fagen. 1967. *Enemies in Politics.* Chicago, IL: Rand McNally.

First, Michael B. and Allan Tasman, eds. 2004. *DSM-IV-TR Mental Disorders: Diagnosis, Etiology, and Treatment.* Hoboken, NJ: John Wiley & Sons.

Fishbein, Martin and Icek Ajzen. 1975. *Belief, Attitude, Intention and Behavior: An Introduction to Theory and Research.* Reading, MA: Addison-Wesley Publishing Co.

Fisher, Max. 2012. "Fear Itself: Americans Believe Iran Threat on Par with 1980s Soviet Union." *The Atlantic Online,* April 19, available at http://www.theatlantic.com/international/archive/2012/04/fear-itself-americans-believe-iran-threat-on-par-with-1980s-soviet-union/256135/.

Fischhoff, Baruch, Paul Slovic, and Sarah Lichtenstein. 1977. "Knowing with Certainty: The Appropriateness of Extreme Confidence." *Journal of Experimental Psychology*, Vol. 3, No. 4 (November), 552–64.

Frank, Robert H. 1985. *Choosing the Right Pond: Human Behavior and the Quest for Status*. New York: Oxford University Press.

Freedman, Lawrence. 1998. "Revolution in Strategic Affairs." *Adelphi Series*, Number 318. London: International Institute for Strategic Studies.

Friedberg, Aaron L. 2011. *A Contest for Supremacy: China, America, and the Struggle for Mastery in Asia*. New York: W. W. Norton.

Friedman, Benjamin and Harvey Sapolsky. 2006. "You Never Know(ism)." *Breakthroughs*, Vol. 15, No. 1 (Spring), 3–11.

Friedman, Thomas L. 2007. "9/11 Is Over." *New York Times*, September 30, 12.

Froese, Paul and F. Carson Mencken. 2009. "A U.S. Holy War? The Effects of Religion on Iraq War Attitudes." *Social Science Quarterly*, Vol. 90, No. 1 (March), 103–16.

Frum, David and Richard Perle. 2003. *An End to Evil: How to Win the War on Terror*. New York: Random House.

Fukuyama, Francis. 1981. *The Soviet Threat to the Persian Gulf*. Santa Monica, CA: RAND Corporation, No. 6596, March.

    2006. "Nation-Building and the Failure of Institutional Memory." In Francis Fukuyama, ed., *Nation-Building beyond Afghanistan and Iraq*. Baltimore, MD: Johns Hopkins University Press, 1–17.

Fulbright, J. William. 1966. *The Arrogance of Power*. New York: Random House.

Furedi, Frank. 1997. *Culture of Fear: Risk-Taking and the Morality of Low Expectation*. London: Cassell.

Gaddis, John Lewis. 1982. *Strategies of Containment: A Critical Appraisal of Postwar American Security Policy*. New York: Oxford University Press.

    1986. "The Long Peace: Elements of Stability in the Postwar International System." *International Security*, Vol. 10, No. 4 (Spring), 99–142.

    1998. "History, Grand Strategy and NATO Enlargement." *Survival*, Vol. 40, No. 1 (Spring), 145–51.

    2004. *Surprise, Security, and the American Experience*. Cambridge, MA: Harvard University Press.

Galbraith, John S. 1960. "The 'Turbulent Frontier' as a Factor in British Expansion." *Comparative Studies in Society and History*, Vol. 2, No. 2 (January), 150–68.

Galasso, Vittorio Nicholas. 2012. "Honor and the Performance of Roman State Identity." *Foreign Policy Analysis*, Vol. 8, No. 2 (April), 173–89.

Gallup. 2010a. "One in Three Americans 'Extremely Patriotic,'" July 2, available at http://www.gallup.com/poll/141110/one-three-americans-extremely-patriotic.aspx, accessed December 18, 2012.

    2010b. "U.S. Approval Gains Nearly Erased in Middle East/North Africa," September 30, available at http://www.gallup.com/poll/143294/

Approval-Gains-Nearly-Erased-Middle-East-North-Africa.aspx, accessed December 18, 2012.

Gardner, Daniel. 2008. *The Science of Fear: How the Culture of Fear Manipulates Your Brain.* New York: Plume.

Gardner, Howard. 2006. *Changing Minds: The Art and Science of Changing Our Own and Other People's Minds.* Boston, MA: Harvard Business School Press.

Gartzke, Erik. 2007. "The Capitalist Peace." *American Journal of Political Science,* Vol. 51, No. 1 (January), 166–91.

Gartzke, Erik and J. Joseph Hewitt. 2010. "International Crises and the Capitalist Peace." *International Interactions,* Vol. 36, No. 2 (April), 115–45.

Geither, H. Rowan, Jr. 1957. *Deterrence and Survival in the Nuclear Age.* Report of the Security Resources Panel of the Science Advisory Committee, November 7.

Geen, Russell G. and Michael B. Quanty. 1977. "The Catharsis of Aggression: An Evaluation of a Hypothesis." *Advances in Experimental Social Psychology,* Vol. 10, 1–37.

Gellman, Barton. 2008. *Angler: The Cheney Vice Presidency.* New York: Penguin.

Gelpi, Christopher, Peter D. Feaver, and Jason Reifler. 2009. *Paying the Human Costs of War: American Public Opinion and Casualties in Military Conflicts.* Princeton, NJ: Princeton University Press.

George, Alexander. 1993. *Bridging the Gap: Theory and Practice in Foreign Policy.* Washington, DC: U.S. Institute of Peace Press.

George, Alexander L. and Richard Smoke. 1974. *Deterrence in American Foreign Policy: Theory and Practice.* New York: Columbia University Press.

Gertz, Bill. 2002. *The China Threat: How the People's Republic Targets America.* New York: Regnery Publishing, Inc.

Gettleman, Jeffrey. 2010. "Africa's Forever Wars." *Foreign Policy,* No. 178 (March/April), 73–75.

Gigerenzer, Gerd and Reinhard Selten. 2002. *Bounded Rationality: The Adaptive Toolbox.* Cambridge, MA: MIT Press.

Gholz, Eugene, Daryl G. Press, and Harvey M. Sapolsky. 1997. "Come Home America: The Strategy of Restraint in the Face of Temptation," *International Security,* Vol. 21, No. 4 (Spring), 5–48.

Gilpin, Robert. 1981. *War and Change in International Politics.* New York: Cambridge University Press.

   1996. "No One Loves a Political Realist." *Security Studies,* Vol. 5, No. 3 (Spring), 3–26.

Gingrich, Newt. 1995. *To Renew America.* New York: Harper Collins.

   2005. *Winning the Future: A 21st Century Contract with America.* Washington, DC: Regnery Publishing.

   2011. *A Nation Like No Other: Why American Exceptionalism Matters.* Washington, DC: Regnery Publishing.

Glassner, Barry. 1999. *The Culture of Fear: Why Americans are Afraid of the Wrong Things.* New York: Basic Books.

Gleditsch, Nils Petter. 2008. "The Liberal Moment Fifteen Years On." *International Studies Quarterly*, Vol. 52, No. 4 (December), 691–712.

Gleijeses, Piero. 1995. "Ships in the Night: The CIA, the White House and the Bay of Pigs." *Journal of Latin America Studies*, Vol. 27, No. 1 (February), 1–42.

Goldberg, Jonah. 2000a. "A Continent Bleeds." *National Review Online*, May 3, available at http://www.nationalreview.com/articles/204646/continent-bleeds/jonah-goldberg.

2000b. "Goldberg's Africa Invasion." *National Review Online*, May 10, available at http://www.nationalreview.com/articles/204649/goldbergs-african-invasion/jonah-goldberg.

Goldgeier, James M. 1999. *Not Whether But When: The U.S. Decision to Enlarge NATO*. Washington, DC: Brookings Institution Press.

Goldstein, Joshua S. 2001. *War and Gender: How Gender Shapes the War System and Vice Versa*. New York: Cambridge University Press.

2011. *Winning the War on War: The Decline of Armed Conflict Worldwide*. New York: Penguin.

Goldstein, Judith and Robert O. Keohane, eds. 1993. *Ideas and Foreign Policy: Beliefs, Institutions, and Political Change*. Ithaca, NY: Cornell University Press.

Goldstone, Jack A., Ted Robert Gurr, Barbara Harff, Marc A. Levy, Monty G. Marshall, Robert H. Bates, David L. Epstein, Colin H. Kahl, Pamela T. Surko, John C. Ulfelder, Jr., and Alan N. Unger. 2000. *State Failure Task Force Report: Phase III Findings*. McLean, VA: Science Applications International Corporation [SAIC], September 30,), available at http://globalpolicy.gmu.edu/pitf/SFTF%20Phase%20III%20Report%20Final.pdf.

Gordon, Philip H. and Jeremy Shapiro. 2004. *Allies at War: America, Europe, and the Crisis over Iraq*. New York: McGraw Hill.

Grieco, Joseph, Robert Powell, and Duncan Snidal. 1993. "The Relative Gains Problem for International Cooperation." *American Political Science Review*, Vol. 87, No. 3. (September), 729–43.

Gruen, Erich S. 1986. *The Hellenistic World and the Coming of Rome*. Berkeley: University of California Press.

Gurr, Ted Robert. 2000. "Ethnic Warfare on the Wane." *Foreign Affairs*, Vol. 79, No. 3 (May/June), 52–64.

Gurr, Ted Robert and Monty G. Marshall. 2005. *Peace and Conflict 2005: A Global Survey of Armed Conflicts, Self-Determination Movements, and Democracy*. College Park, MD: Center for International Development and Conflict Management.

Guttman, Allen. 1994. *Games and Empires: Modern Sports and Cultural Imperialism*. New York: Columbia University Press.

Haaretz. 2010. "In its 62nd year, Israel Is in a Diplomatic, Security and Moral Limbo." April 19, available at http://www.haaretz.com/print-edition/opinion/in-its-62nd-year-israel-is-in-a-diplomatic-security-and-moral-limbo-1.284517.

Halper, Stefan and Jonathan Clarke. 2005. *America Alone: The Neoconservatives and the Global Order*. New York: Cambridge University Press.
2007. *The Silence of the Rational Center: Why American Foreign Policy is Failing.* New York: Basic Books.

Hanif, Mohammed. 2011. "Survival State." *New York Times*, June 26, BR29.

Hanson, Victor Davis. 2005. *A War Like No Other: How the Athenians and Spartans Fought the Peloponnesian War*. New York: Random House.

Harbom, Lotta, Stina Högbladh, and Peter Wallensteen. 2006. "Armed Conflict and Peace Agreements." *Journal of Peace Research*, Vol. 43, No. 5 (September), 617–31.

Hariman, Robert. 2003. *Prudence: Classical Virtue, Postmodern Practice*. University Park: Pennsylvania State University Press.

Harnden, Toby. 2007. "We Must Bomb Iran, Says US Republican Guru." *The Daily Telegraph*, October 27, available at http://www.telegraph.co.uk/news/worldnews/1567529/We-must-bomb-Iran-says-US-Republican-guru.html.

Harries, Owen. 1994. "An Anti-Interventionist No More: America's Credibility is Now at Stake." *Washington Post*, April 21, A31.

Harris, William V. 1985. *War and Imperialism in Republican Rome, 327–70 B.C.* Oxford: Clarendon Press.

Hartz, Louis. 1955. *The Liberal Tradition in America: An Interpretation of American Political Thought since the Revolution*. New York: Harcourt, Brace and World, Inc.

Hatemi, Peter K. and Rose McDermott. 2011. "The Normative Implications of Biological Research." *PS: Political Science and Politics*, Vol. 44, No. 2 (April), 325–29.

Hattie, John. 2009. *Visible Learning: A Synthesis of over 800 Meta-Analyses Relating to Achievement*. Routledge: New York.

Hawkins, Mike. 1997. *Social Darwinism in European and American Thought, 1860–1945: Nature as Model and Nature as Threat*. New York: Cambridge University Press.

Hayduk, Leslie A., Pamela A. Ratner, Joy L. Johnson, and Joan L. Bottorff. 1995. "Attitudes, Idealogy and the Factor Model." *Political Psychology*, Vol. 16, No. 3 (September), 479–507.

Heilbrunn, Jacob. 2008. *They Knew They Were Right: The Rise of the Neocons*. New York: Doubleday.

Helprin, Mark. 2012. "The Mortal Threat from Iran." *Wall Street Journal*, January 18.

Herman, Arthur. 1997. *The Idea of Decline in Western History*. New York: Free Press.

Herring, George C. 1979. *America's Longest War: The United States and Vietnam, 1950–1975*. New York: Knopf.

Herrmann, Richard K., Philip E. Tetlock, and Penny S. Visser. 1999. "Mass Public Decisions to Go to War: A Cognitive-Interactionist Framework." *American Political Science Review*, Vol. 93, No. 3 (September), 553–73.

Hewitt, J. Joseph, Jonathan Wilkenfeld, and Ted Robert Gurr, eds. 2010. *Peace and Conflict, 2010: Executive Summary.* College Park, MD: Center for International Development and Conflict Management.

Hines, John G., Ellis M. Mishulovich, and John F. Shull. 1995. *Soviet Intentions 1965–1985, Volume I: An Analytical Comparison of U.S.-Soviet Assessments during the Cold War.* McLean, VA: BDM Federal, Inc., September 22.

Hoberman, Harry M. 1990. "Study Group Report on the Impact of Television Violence on Adolescents." *Journal of Adolescent Health Care,* Vol. 11, No. 1 (January), 45–49.

Hofstadter, Richard. 1944. *Social Darwinism in American Thought.* Philadelphia: University of Pennsylvania Press.

  1964. "The Paranoid Style in American Politics." *Harper's Magazine,* Vol. 229, No. 1374 (November), 77–86.

Hofstede, Geert. 2001. *Culture's Consequences: Comparing Values, Behaviors, Institutions, and Organizations across Nations.* Thousand Oaks, CA: Sage Publications.

Holmes, Stephen. 2007. *The Matador's Cape: America's Reckless Response to Terrorism.* New York: Cambridge University Press.

Holsti, Ole R. and James N. Rosenau. 1979. "Vietnam, Consensus, and the Belief Systems of American Leaders," *World Politics,* Vol. 32, No. 1 (October), 1–56.

  1988. "The Domestic and Foreign Policy Beliefs of American Leaders." *Journal of Conflict Resolution,* Vol. 32, No. 2 (June), 248–94.

  1996. "Liberals, Populists, Libertarians, and Conservatives: The Link between Domestic and International Affairs." *International Political Science Review,* Vol. 17, No. 1 (January), 29–54.

Homer-Dixon, Thomas F. 1999. *Environment, Scarcity and Conflict.* Princeton, NJ: Princeton University Press.

Hopf, Ted. 1991. "Soviet Inferences from their Victories in the Periphery: Visions of Resistance or Cumulating Gains?" In Robert Jervis and Jack Snyder, eds., *Dominoes and Bandwagons: Strategic Beliefs and Great Power Competition in the Eurasian Rimland.* New York: Oxford University Press, 145–79.

  1994. *Peripheral Visions: Deterrence Theory and American Foreign Policy in the Third World, 1965–1990.* Ann Arbor: University of Michigan Press.

  2010. "The Logic of Habit in International Relations." *European Journal of International Relations,* Vol. 16, No. 4 (December), 539–61.

Hornblower, Simon and Antony Spawforth, eds. 1996. *Oxford Classical Dictionary,* 3rd ed. New York: Oxford University Press.

Horney, Karen. 1936. "Culture and Neurosis." *American Sociological Review,* Vol. 1, No. 2 (April), 221–30.

  1937. *The Neurotic Personality of Our Time.* New York: W. W. Norton.

Howard, Nigel. 1971. *Paradoxes of Rationality: Games, Metagames, and Political Behavior.* Cambridge, MA: MIT Press.

Hsu, Francis L. K. 1983. *Rugged Individualism Reconsidered: Essays in Psychological Anthropology.* Knoxville: University of Tennessee Press.

Huddy, Leonie, Stanley Feldman, Theresa Capelos, and Colin Provost. 2002. "The Consequences of Terrorism: Disentangling the Effects of Personal and National Threat." *Political Psychology*, Vol. 23, No. 3 (September), 485–509.

Huddy, Leonie, Stanley Feldman, Charles Taber, and Gallya Lahav. 2005. "Threat, Anxiety, and Support of Antiterrorism Policies." *American Journal of Political Science*, Vol. 49, No. 3 (July), 593–608.

Human Security Center. 2008. *Human Security Brief 2007*. Vancouver: Human Security Report Project, 2008.

Human Security Centre. 2005. *Human Security Report 2005*. New York: Oxford University Press.

 2010. *Human Security Report 2009/2010: The Causes of Peace and the Shrinking Costs of War*. New York: Oxford University Press.

Huntington, Samuel. 1981. *American Politics: The Promise of Disharmony*. Cambridge, MA: Harvard University Press.

 1988. "The U.S.: Decline or Renewal?" *Foreign Affairs*, Vol. 67, No. 2 (Winter), 76–96.

 1993. "Why International Primacy Matters." *International Security*, Vol. 17, No. 4 (Spring), 68–83.

 1999. "The Lonely Superpower." *Foreign Affairs*, Vol. 78, No. 2 (March/April), 35–49.

Huth, Paul K. 1988. "Extended Deterrence and the Outbreak of War." *American Political Science Review*, Vol. 82, No. 2 (June), 423–43.

Huth, Paul K., Christopher Gelpi, and D. Scott Bennett. 1993. "The Escalation of Great Power Militarized Disputes: Testing Rational Deterrence Theory and Structural Realism." *American Political Science Review*, Vol. 87, No. 3 (September), 609–23.

Huth, Paul K. and Bruce Russett. 1984. "What Makes Deterrence Work? Cases from 1900 to 1980." *World Politics*, Vol. 36, No. 4 (July), 496–526.

Ikenberry, G. John. 2011. *Liberal Leviathan: The Origins, Crisis, and Transformation of the American World Order*. Princeton, NJ: Princeton University Press.

Iklé, Fred Charles. 2005. *Every War Must End*, 2nd ed. New York: Columbia University Press.

Isikoff, Michael and David Corn. 2006. *Hubris: The Inside Story of Spin, Scandal, and the Selling of the Iraq War*. New York: Three Rivers Press.

Jafarzadeh, Alireza. 2008. *The Iran Threat: President Ahmadinejad and the Coming Nuclear Crisis*. New York: Palgrave-Macmillan.

Jaffe, Greg. 2012. "The World is Safer, But No One Will Say So." *Washington Post*, November 4, B1.

James, Harold. 2006. *The Roman Predicament: How the Rules of International Order Create the Politics of Empire*. Princeton, NJ: Princeton University Press.

Jay, Kathryn. 2004. *More than Just a Game: Sports in American Life since 1945*. New York: Columbia University Press.

Jehl, Douglas. 1993. "C.I.A. Nominee Wary of Budget Cuts." *New York Times*, February 3.

Jelen, Ted G. 1994. "Religion and Foreign Policy Attitudes." *American Politics Research*, Vol. 22, No. 3 (July), 382–400.

Jenkins, Brian Michael. 2010. *Would-Be Warriors: Incidents of Jihadist Terrorist Radicalization in the United States since September 11, 2001*. Santa Monica, CA: RAND.

Jentleson, Bruce W. 1987. "American Commitments in the Third World: Theory vs. Practice." *International Organization*, Vol. 41, No. 4 (Autumn), 667–704.

    1992. "The Pretty Prudent Public: Post-Vietnam American Opinion on the Use of Force." *International Studies Quarterly*, Vol. 36, No. 1 (March), 49–74.

    2002. "The Need for Praxis: Bringing Policy Relevance Back In." *International Security*, Vol. 26, No. 4 (Spring), 169–83.

Jervis, Robert. 1976. *Perception and Misperception in International Politics*. Princeton, NJ: Princeton University Press.

    1982–83. "Deterrence and Perception." *International Security*, Vol. 7, No. 3 (Winter), 3–20.

    1985. "Perceiving and Coping with Threat." In Robert Jervis, Richard Ned Lebow, and Janice Stein, eds., *Psychology and Deterrence*. Baltimore, MD: Johns Hopkins University Press, 13–33.

    1989. "Political Psychology: Some Challenges and Opportunities," *Political Psychology*, Vol. 10, No. 3 (September), 481–93.

    1991. "Domino Beliefs and Strategic Behavior." In Robert Jervis and Jack Snyder, eds., *Dominoes and Bandwagons: Strategic Beliefs and Great Power Competition in the Eurasian Rimland*. New York: Oxford University Press, 20–50.

    1993. "International Primacy: Is the Game Worth the Candle?" *International Security*, Vol. 17, No. 4 (Spring), 52–67.

    1994. "Political Implications of Loss Aversion." In Barbara Farnham, ed., *Avoiding Losses/Taking Risks: Prospect Theory and International Conflict*. Ann Arbor: University of Michigan Press, 23–40.

    2002. "Theories of War in an Era of Leading Power Peace." *American Political Science Review*, Vol. 96, No. 1 (March), 1–14.

    2005. *American Foreign Policy in a New Era*. New York: Routledge.

    2006. "Understanding Beliefs." *Political Psychology*, Vol. 27, No. 5 (October), 641–63.

    2009. "Understanding Beliefs and Threat Inflation." In A. Trevor Thrall and Jane K. Cramer, *American Foreign Policy and the Politics of Fear: Threat Inflation Since 9/11*. New York: Routledge, 16–39.

    2009. "Unipolarity: A Structural Perspective." *World Politics*, Vol. 61, No. 1 (January), 188–213.

    2011. "Force in Our Times." *International Relations*, Vol. 25, No. 4 (December), 403–25.

Jervis, Robert, Richard Ned Lebow, and Janice Stein, eds. 1985. *Psychology and Deterrence*. Baltimore, MD: Johns Hopkins University Press.

Johnson, David W., Geoffrey Maruyama, Roger Johnson, Deborah Nelson, and Linda Skon. 1981. "Effects of Cooperative, Competitive and Individualistic Goal Structures on Achievement: A Meta-Analysis." *Psychological Bulletin*, Vol. 89, No. 1 (January), 47–62.

Johnson, David W. and Roger T. Johnson. 1987. "Research Shows the Benefits of Adult Cooperation." *Educational Leadership*, Vol. 45, No. 3 (November), 27–30.

   2005. "New Developments in Social Interdependence Theory." *Genetic, Social and General Psychology Monographs*, Vol. 131, No. 4 (November), 285–358.

   2009. "An Educational Psychology Success Story: Social Interdependence Theory and Cooperative Learning." *Educational Researcher*, Vol. 38, No. 5 (June/July), 365–79.

Johnson, Dominic D. P. 2004. *Overconfidence and War: The Havoc and Glory of Positive Illusions*. Cambridge, MA: Harvard University Press.

Johnson, Dominic D. P. and Dominic Tierney. 2006. *Failing to Win: Perceptions of Victory and Defeat in International Politics*. Cambridge, MA: Harvard University Press.

Johnson, Lyndon Baines. 1971. *The Vantage Point*. New York: Holt, Rinehart and Winston.

Johnson, Robert H. 1983. "Periods of Peril: The Window of Vulnerability and Other Myths." *Foreign Affairs*, Vol. 61, No. 4 (Spring), 950–70.

   1994. *Improbable Dangers: U.S. Conceptions of Threat in the Cold War and After*. New York: St. Martin's Press.

Johnston, Alastair Iain. 1995. "Thinking about Strategic Culture." *International Security*, Vol. 19, No. 4 (Spring), 32–64.

Joll, James. 1992. *The Origins of the First World War*, 2nd ed. New York: Longman.

Jones, Graham. 1995. "More than Just a Game: Research Developments and Issues in Competitive Anxiety in Sport." *British Journal of Psychology*, Vol. 86, No. 4 (November), 449–78.

Jones, Howard. 2008. *The Bay of Pigs*. New York: Oxford University Press.

Kachalia, Allen, Samuel R. Kaufman, Richard Boothman, Susan Anderson, Kathleen Welch, Sanjay Saint, and Mary A. M. Rogers. 2010. "Liability Claims and Costs before and after Implementation of a Medical Error Disclosure Program." *Annals of Internal Medicine*, Vol. 153, No. 4 (August 17), 213–21.

Kagan, Donald. 1995. *On the Origins of War and the Preservation of Peace*. New York: Doubleday.

   1998. "Honor, Interest, and the Nation-State." In Elliott Abrams, ed., *Honor among Nations: Intangible Interests and Foreign Policy*. Washington, DC: Ethics and Public Policy Center, 1–16.

Kagan, Donald and Frederick W. Kagan. 2000. *While America Sleeps: Self-Delusion, Military Weakness, and the Threat to Peace Today*. New York: St. Martin's Press.

Kagan, Frederick W. 1999. "Back to the Future: NSC-68 and the Right Course for America Today." *SAIS Review*, Vol. 19, No. 1 (Winter–Spring), 55–71.

   2008. "Grand Strategy for the United States." In Michelle A. Flournoy and Shawn Brimley, eds, *Finding Our Way: Debating American Grand Strategy.* Washington, DC: Center for a New American Security, 63–80.

Kagan, Frederick W. and Kimberly Kagan. 2011. "Out of Iraq." *Los Angeles Times*, October 27, 29.

Kagan, Frederick W., Kimberly Kagan, and Marisa Cochrane Sullivan. 2011. "Defeat in Iraq." *The Weekly Standard*, Vol. 17, No. 8 (November 7).

Kagan, Frederick W. and Michael O'Hanlon. 2007. "The Case for Larger Ground Forces." The Stanley Foundation, Bridging the Foreign Policy Divide Project (April), available at http://www.stanleyfdn.org/publications/other/Kagan_OHanlon_07.pdf.

Kagan, Robert. 1998. "The Benevolent Empire." *Foreign Policy*, No. 111 (Summer), 24–35.

   2003. *Of Paradise and Power: America and Europe in the New World Order.* New York: Knopf.

   2008a. "Neocon Nation: Neoconservatism, c. 1776." *World Affairs*, Vol. 170, No. 4 (Spring), 13–35.

   2008b. *The Return of History and the End of Dreams.* New York: Knopf.

   2008c. "The September 12 Paradigm: America, the World, and George W. Bush," *Foreign Affairs*, Vol. 87, No. 5 (September–October), 25–39.

   2012. *The World America Made.* New York: Knopf.

Kagan, Robert and William Kristol. 2000. "National Interest and Global Responsibility." In Robert Kagan and William Kristol, eds., *Present Dangers: Crisis and Opportunity in American Foreign and Defense Policy.* San Francisco, CA: Encounter Books, 3–24.

Kagan, Robert and William Kristol, eds. 2000. *Present Dangers: Crisis and Opportunity in American Foreign and Defense Policy.* San Francisco, CA: Encounter Books.

Kagan, Robert and William Kristol. 2001. "We Lost." *Washington Post*, April 13, A23.

Kagan, Robert A. 2001. *Adversarial Legalism: The American Way of Law.* Cambridge, MA: Harvard University Press.

Kagan, Spencer and Millard C. Madsen. 1971. "Cooperation and Competition of Mexican, Mexican-American, and Anglo-American Children of Two Ages under Four Instructional Sets." *Developmental Psychology*, Vol. 5, No. 1 (July), 32–39.

Kagan, Spencer, G. Lawrence Zahm, and Jennifer Gealy. 1977. "Competition and School Achievement among Anglo-American and Mexican-American Children." *Journal of Educational Psychology*, Vol. 69, No. 4 (August), 432–41.

Kahl, Colin H. 2006. *States, Scarcity, and Civil Strife in the Developing World.* Princeton, NJ: Princeton University Press.

   2012. "Not Time to Attack Iran." *Foreign Affairs*, Vol. 91, No. 2 (May–June), 166–73.

Kahneman, Daniel and Jonathan Renshon. 2009. "Hawkish Biases." In A. Trevor Thrall and Jane K. Cramer, *American Foreign Policy and the Politics of Fear: Threat Inflation Since 9/11.* New York: Routledge, 79–96.

Kahneman, Daniel and Amos Tversky. 1979. "Prospect Theory: An Analysis of Decision under Risk." *Econometrica*, Vol. 47, No. 2 (March), 263–91.

Kaldor, Mary. 2001. "Beyond Militarism, Arms Races and Arms Control." Social Science Research Council, December 8, available at http://www.ssrc.org/sept11/essays/kaldor_text_only.htm.

Kamen, Henry. 1978. "The Decline of Spain: A Historical Myth?" *Past and Present*, No. 81 (November), 24–50.

Kanwisher, Nancy. 1989. "Cognitive Heuristics and American Security Policy." *Journal of Conflict Resolution*, Vol. 33, No. 4 (December 1989), 652–75.

Kaplan, Lawrence F. and William Kristol. 2003. *The War over Iraq: Saddam's Tyranny and America's Mission.* San Francisco, CA: Encounter Books.

Kaplan, Robert D. 2000. *The Coming Anarchy: Shattering the Dreams of the Post Cold War.* New York: Random House.

Kapuscinski, Ryszard. 1992. *The Soccer War.* New York: Vintage Books.

Kasper, Wolfgang. 2007. "Competition." In David R. Henderson, ed., *The Concise Encyclopedia of Economics*, 2nd, ed. Indianapolis, IN: The Liberty Fund, 73–75.

Katzenstein, Peter J. 1996. *Cultural Norms and National Security.* Ithaca, NY: Cornell University Press.

Katzenstein, Peter J. and Robert O. Keohane, eds. 2006. *Anti-Americanism and World Politics.* Ithaca, NY: Cornell University Press.

Kaufmann, Chaim. 2004. "Threat Inflation and the Failure of the Marketplace of Ideas: The Selling of the Iraq War." *International Security*, Vol. 29, No. 1 (Summer), 5–48.

Kaysen, Carl. 1990. "Is War Obsolete? A Review Essay." *International Security*, Vol. 14, No. 4 (Spring), 42–64.

Keegan, John. 1998. *War and Our World.* New York: Vintage Books.

Kegley, Jr., Charles W. 1986. "Assumptions and Dilemmas in the Study of Americans' Foreign Policy Beliefs: A Caveat." *International Studies Quarterly*, Vol. 30, No. 4 (December), 447–71.

Kennan, George F. 1951. *American Diplomacy, 1900–1950.* New York: Mentor.
  1977. *The Cloud of Danger: Current Realities of American Foreign Policy.* Boston, MA: Little, Brown & Co.
  1985. "Morality and Foreign Policy." *Foreign Affairs*, Vol. 64, No. 2 (Winter), 205–18.
  1996. *At a Century's Ending: Reflections 1982–1995.* New York: W. W. Norton.

Kennedy, Paul. 1987. *The Rise and Fall of the Great Powers: Economic Change and Military Conflict from 1500 to 2000.* New York: Random House.
  1999. "The Next American Century?" *World Policy Journal*, Vol. 16, No. 1 (Spring), 52–58.
  2010. "A Time to Appease." *The National Interest*, No. 108 (July–August), 7–17.

Keohane, Robert O. 1984. *After Hegemony: Cooperation and Discord in the World Political Economy.* Princeton, NJ: Princeton University Press.

Kessler, Glenn. 2011. "Obama's 'Apology Tour'," *Washington Post Online,* February 22, available at http://voices.washingtonpost.com/fact-checker/2011/02/obamas_apology_tour.html.

Khan, Ali S. 2011. "Preparedness 101: Zombie Apocalypse." Atlanta, GA: Centers for Disease Control and Prevention, May 16, available at http://blogs.cdc.gov/publichealthmatters/2011/05/preparedness-101-zombie-apocalypse/.

Khong, Yuen Foong. 1992. *Analogies at War: Korea, Munich, Dien Bien Phu and the Vietnam Decisions of 1965.* Princeton, NJ: Princeton University Press.

Kindleberger, Charles. 1974. *The World in Depression, 1929–1939.* Berkeley: University of California Press.

Kissinger, Henry A. 1962. *The Necessity for Choice: Prospects of American Foreign Policy.* Garden City, NY: Anchor Books.

    1979. *White House Years.* Boston, MA: Little, Brown & Co.

    2003. *Ending the Vietnam War: A History of America's Involvement in and Extrication from the Vietnam War.* New York: Simon and Schuster.

    2005. "How to Exit Iraq." *Washington Post,* December 19.

Klare, Michael T. 2001. *Resource Wars: The New Landscape of Global Conflict.* New York: Metropolitan Books.

Kohn, Alfie. 1992. *No Contest: The Case against Competition.* Boston, MA: Houghton-Mifflin.

Kohut, Heinz. 2009. *The Analysis of the Self: A Systemic Approach to the Psychoanalytic Treatment of Narcissistic Personality Disorders.* Chicago. IL: University of Chicago Press.

Krauthammer, Charles. 1991–92. "The Unipolar Moment." *Foreign Affairs,* Vol. 70, No. 1 (1991/92), 23–33.

    1998. "Saddam: Round 3." *Washington Post,* November 13, A23.

    2003a. "Korea Follies." *Washington Post,* January 17, A23.

    2003b. "No Turning Back Now." *Washington Post,* January 24, A27.

    2004. "In Defense of Democratic Realism." *The National Interest,* No. 77 (Fal), 15–25.

    2009. "Decline Is a Choice: The New Liberalism and the End of American Ascendancy." *The Weekly Standard,* Vol. 15, No. 5 (October 19).

    2011a. "Farewell, the New Frontier." *Washington Post,* April 20.

    2011b. "The Wages of Appeasement." *Washington Post,* December 15.

    2011c. "Who Lost Iraq?" *Washington Post,* November 4, A19.

Krebs, Ronald R. 2008. "Rethinking the Battle of Ideas: How the United States Can Help Muslim Moderates." *Orbis,* Vol.52, No. 2 (Spring), 332–46.

Krepinevich, Andrew F. 2010. *Why Air Sea Battle?* Washington, DC: Center for Strategic and Budgetary Assessments, February 19, available at http://www.csbaonline.org/publications/2010/02/why-airsea-battle/.

Kristol, Irving. 1995. *Neoconservatism: The Autobiography of an Idea.* New York: Simon and Schuster.

    2003. "The Neoconservative Persuasion: What It Was, and What It Is." *The Weekly Standard,* Vol. 8, No. 47 (August 25).

Kristol, William. 2002. "The Axis of Appeasement." *Weekly Standard*, Vol. 7, No. 47 (August 26).

2006. "It's Our War." *The Weekly Standard*, Vol. 11, No. 42 (July 24), available at http://www.weeklystandard.com/Content/Public/Articles/000/000/012/433fwbvs.asp.

2009. "A World Without Nukes – Just Like 1939." *Washington Post*, April 7, A23.

2011. "Speak Softly...and Fight Back." *The Weekly Standard*, Vol. 17, No. 6 (October 24), available at http://www.weeklystandard.com/articles/speak-softly-and-fight-back_595936.html.

Kristol, William and Robert Kagan. 1996. "Toward a Neo-Reaganite Foreign Policy." *Foreign Affairs*, Vol. 75, No. 4 (July/August), 18–33.

2001. "A National Humiliation." *The Weekly Standard*, April 16–23, 11–16.

Kroenig, Matthew. 2012. "Time to Attack Iran: Why a Strike is the Least Bad Option." *Foreign Affairs*, Vol. 91, No. 1 (January–February), 76–86.

Krueger, Alan B. and Jitka Malečková. 2003. "Education, Poverty and Terrorism: Is there a Casual Connection?" *Journal of Economic Perspectives*, Vol. 17, No. 4 (Fall), 119–44.

Krugman, Paul. 1994a. "Competitiveness: A Dangerous Obsession," *Foreign Affairs*, Vol. 73, No. 2 (March–April), 28–44.

1994b. *Peddling Prosperity: Economic Sense and Nonsense in the Age of Diminished Expectations*. New York: W. W. Norton & Co.

Kuhn, Thomas S. 1970. *The Structure of Scientific Revolutions*. Chicago, IL: University of Chicago Press.

Kuijs, Louis. 2010. *China Through 2020 – A Macroeconomic Scenario*. Beijing: World Bank China Office, Research Working Paper Number Nine, June.

Kuklick, Bruce. 2006. *Blind Oracles: Intellectuals and War from Kennan to Kissinger*. Princeton, NJ: Princeton University Press.

Kuklinski, James H., Paul J. Quirk, Jennifer Jerit, David Schwieder, and Robert F. Rich. 2000. "Misinformation and the Currency of Democratic Citizenship." *Journal of Politics*, Vol. 62, No. 3 (August), 790–816.

Kupchan, Charles. 2002. *The End of the American Era: U.S. Foreign Policy and the Geopolitics of the Twenty-First Century*. New York: Knopf.

Kuperman, Alan J. 2009. "There's Only One Way to Stop Iran." *New York Times*, December 24, A23.

Lacina, Bethany, Nils Peter Gleditsch, and Bruce Russett. 2006. "The Declining Risk of Death in Battle." *International Studies Quarterly*, Vol. 50, No. 3 (September), 673–80.

LaFeber, Walter. 1981. "The Last War, the Next War, and the New Revisionists." *Democracy*, Vol. 1, No. 1 (January), 93–103.

Laird, Melvin. 2005. "Iraq: Learning the Lessons of Vietnam." *Foreign Affairs*, Vol. 84, No. 6 (November/December), 22–43.

Lake, David A. 1993. "Leadership, Hegemony, and the International Economy: Naked Emperor or Tattered Monarch with Potential?" *International Studies Quarterly*, Vol. 37, No. 4 (December), 459–89.

Lamb, Christopher Jon. 1989. *Belief Systems and Decision Making in the Mayaguez Crisis*. Gainesville: University of Florida Press.

Lane, Robert E. 1969. *Political Thinking and Consciousness: The Private Life of the Political Mind.* Chicago, IL: Markham Publishing.

Larson, Deborah Welch and Alexei Shevchenko. 2010. "Status Seekers: Chinese and Russian Responses to U.S. Primacy." *International Security*, Vol. 34, No. 4 (Spring), 63–95.

Lasswell, Harold D. 1960. *Psychopathology and Politics*, new ed. New York: Viking Press.

Layne, Christopher. 2012. "This Time It's Real: The End of Unipolarity and the Pax Americana." *International Studies Quarterly*, Vol. 56, No. 1 (March), 202–13.

Layne, Christopher and Bradley A. Thayer. 2007. *American Empire: A Debate.* New York: Routledge.

Lazare, Aaron. 1995. "Go Ahead: Say You're Sorry." *Psychology Today*, Vol. 28, No. 1 (January), 40–45.

Lebow, Richard Ned. 1981. *Between Peace and War.* Baltimore, MD: Johns Hopkins University Press.

　　1984. "Windows of Opportunity: Do States Jump Through Them?" *International Security*, Vol. 9, No. 1 (Summer), 147–86.

　　1994. "The Long Peace, the End of the Cold War, and the Failure of Realism." *International Organization*, Vol. 48, No. 2 (Spring), 249–77.

　　2007. "Thucydides and Deterrence." *Security Studies*, Vol. 16, No. 2 (April–June), 163–88.

　　2008. *A Cultural Theory of International Relations.* New York: Cambridge University Press.

　　2010. *Why Nations Fight: Past and Future Motives for War.* New York: Cambridge University Press.

Lebow, Richard Ned and Janice Stein. 1993. "Afghanistan, Carter and Foreign Policy Change: The Limits of Cognitive Models." In Dan Caldwell and Timothy J. McKeown, eds., *Diplomacy, Force, and Leadership: Essays in Honor of Alexander L. George.* Boulder, CO: Westview Press, 95–128.

　　1994. *We All Lost the Cold War.* Princeton, NJ: Princeton University Press.

Ledeen, Michael. 1984. "The Lessons of Lebanon." *Commentary*, Vol. 77, No. 5 (May), 15–22.

　　2001. "Handling China." *National Review Online*, April 19, available at http://www.aei.org/news/newsID.12741,filter.all/news_detail.asp.

　　2002. *The War against the Terror Masters.* New York: St. Martin's Press.

　　2009. *Accomplice to Evil: Iran and the War against the West.* New York: St. Martin's Press.

Leebaert, Derek. 2010. *Magic and Mayhem: The Delusions of American Foreign Policy from Korea to Afghanistan.* New York: Simon and Schuster.

Leibovich, Mark. 2010. "Being Glenn Beck." *New York Times Magazine* (October 3), 35–**41**, 53–57.

LeoGrande, William M. 1981. "A Splendid Little War: Drawing the Line in El Salvador." *International Security*, Vol. 6, No. 1 (Summer), 27–52.

Lester, Will. 2005. "Poll: Americans Say World War III Likely." Washington Post, July 24.

Lettow, Paul. 2012. "A Romney-Ryan Foreign Policy." *National Review Online*, November 5, 2012, available at http://www.nationalreview.com/articles/332488/romney-ryan-foreign-policy-paul-lettow.

Levy, Jack S. 1983. "Misperception and the Causes of War: Theoretical Linkages and Analytical Problems." *World Politics*, Vol. 36, No. 1 (October), 76–99.

1994. "Learning and Foreign Policy: Sweeping a Conceptual Minefield." *International Organization*, Vol. 48, No. 2 (Spring), 279–312.

Lewandowsky, Stephan, Ullrich K. H. Ecker, Colleen M. Seifert, Norbert Schwartz, and John Cook. 2012. "Misinformation and Its Correction: Continued Influence and Successful Debiasing." *Psychological Science in the Public Interest*, Vol. 13, No. 3 (September), 106–31.

Lewis, Bernard. 1990. "The Roots of Muslim Rage." *The Atlantic Monthly*, Vol. 266, No. 3 (September), 47–60.

2006. "August 22: Does Iran have Something in Store?" *Wall Street Journal*, August 8, A10.

Levi, Michael A. 2007. *On Nuclear Terrorism*. Cambridge, MA: Harvard University Press.

Lieber, Robert J. 2005. *The American Era: Power and Strategy for the 21st Century*. New York: Cambridge University Press.

Lieven, Anatol. 2004. *America Right or Wrong: An Anatomy of American Nationalism*. New York: Oxford University Press.

2011. *Pakistan: A Hard Country*. New York: Public Affairs, 2011.

Lifton, Robert J. 1999. *Destroying the World In Order to Save It: Aum Shinrikyo, Apocalyptic Violence, and the New Global Terrorism*. New York: Henry Holt.

Lind, Jennifer. 2008. *Sorry States: Apologies in International Relations*. Ithaca, NY: Cornell University Press.

Lind, Michael. 1999. *Vietnam: The Necessary War*. New York: Free Press.

Lindsay, James M. and Ray Takeyh. 2010. "After Iran Gets the Bomb." *Foreign Affairs*, Vol. 89, No. 2 (March/April), 33–49.

Lipset, Seymour Martin. 1996. *American Exceptionalism: A Double-Edged Sword*. New York: W. W. Norton.

Logevall, Fredrik. 1999. *Choosing War: The Lost Chance for Peace and the Escalation of the War in Vietnam*. Berkeley: University of California Press.

2003. "America Isolated: The Western Powers and the Escalation of the War." In Andreas W. Daum, Lloyd C. Gardner, and Wilfried Mausbach, eds., *America, the Vietnam War, and the World*. New York: Cambridge University Press, 175–96.

Lopez, Anthony C., Rose McDermott, and Michael Bang Petersen. 2011. "States in Mind: Evolution, Coalitional Psychology, and International Politics." *International Security*, Vol. 36, No. 2 (Fall), 48–83.

Lord, Charles G., Lee Ross, and Mark. R. Lepper. 1979. "Biased Assimilation and Attitude Polarization: The Effects of Prior Theories on Subsequently Considered Evidence." *Journal of Personality and Social Psychology*, Vol. 37, No. 11 (November), 2098–109.

Lorenz, Konrad. 1966. *On Aggression*. New York: Harcourt.

Löwenheim, Oded. 2003. "'Do Ourselves Credit and Render a Lasting Service to Mankind': British Moral Prestige, Humanitarian Intervention, and the Barbary Pirates." *International Studies Quarterly*, Vol. 47, No. 1 (March), 23–48.

Luard, Evan. 1986. *War in International Society: A Study in International Sociology.* London: I. B. Taurus.

   1989. *The Blunted Sword: The Erosion of Military Power in Modern World Politics.* New York: New Amsterdam Books.

Luttwak, Edward N. 1976. *The Grand Strategy of the Roman Empire: From the First Century A.D. to the Third.* Baltimore, MD: Johns Hopkins University Press.

   1986. *On the Meaning of Victory: Essays on Strategy.* New York: Simon and Schuster.

   1993. *The Endangered American Dream: How to Stop the United States from Becoming a Third World Country and How to Win the Geo-Economic Struggle for Industrial Supremacy.* New York: Simon and Schuster.

   1995. "Toward Post-Heroic Warfare." *Foreign Affairs*, Vol. 74, No. 3 (May/June), 109–22.

Lyakhovskiy, Aleksandr Antonovich. 2007. *Inside the Soviet Invasion of Afghanistan and the Seizure of Kabul, December 1979.* Washington, DC: Woodrow Wilson Center, Cold War International History Project, Working Paper #51, January.

MacDonald, David B. 2009. *Thinking History, Fighting Evil: Neoconservatives and the Perils of Analogy in American Politics.* Lanham, MD: Lexington Books.

MacDonald, Paul K. and Joseph M. Parent. 2011. "Graceful Decline? The Surprising Success of Great Power Retrenchment." *International Security*, Vol. 35, No. 4 (Spring), 7–44.

Mack, Andrew. 2007. "Global Political Violence: Explaining the Post-Cold War Decline." Coping with Crisis Working Paper Series, International Peace Academy (March).

Mackay, Charles. 1932. *Extraordinary Popular Delusions and the Madness of Crowds.* Boston, MA: L. C. Page and Company.

Madsen, Deborah L. 1998. *American Exceptionalism.* Oxford: University of Mississippi Press.

Mandel, Robert. 1984. "The Desirability of Irrationality in Foreign Policy Making: A Preliminary Theoretical Analysis." *Political Psychology*, Vol. 5, No. 4 (December), 643–60.

   2006. *The Meaning of Military Victory.* Boulder, CO: Lynne Rienner.

Mandelbaum, Michael. 1981. *The Nuclear Revolution: International Politics before and after Hiroshima.* Cambridge: Cambridge University Press.

   2002. *The Ideas that Conquered the World: Peace Democracy and Free Markets in the Twenty-First Century.* New York: Public Affairs.

   2004. *The Meaning of Sports: Why Americans Watch Baseball, Football, and Basketball and What They See When They Do.* New York: Public Affairs.

   2005. *The Case for Goliath: How America Acts as the World's Government in the 21st Century.* New York: Public Affairs.

Markey, Daniel. 1999. "Prestige and the Origins of War: Returning to Realism's Roots." *Security Studies*, Vol. 8, No. 4 (Summer), 126–73.

Marsh, Elizabeth J. and Lisa K. Fazio. 2006. "Learning Errors from Fiction: Difficulties in Reducing Reliance on Fictional Stories." *Memory & Cognition*, Vol. 34, No. 5 (July), 1140–49.

Marsh, Elizabeth J., Michelle L. Meade, and Henry L. Roediger. 2003. "Learning Facts from Fiction." *Journal of Memory and Language*, Vol. 49, No. 4 (November), 519–36.

Marshall, Monty G. 2010. "Major Episodes of Political Violence, 1946–2009." Center for Systemic Peace, available at http://www.systemicpeace.org/warlist.htm.

Marshall, Monty G. and Benjamin R. Cole. 2011. *Global Report 2011: Conflict, Governance, and State Fragility.* Vienna, VA: Center for Systemic Peace, December.

Massing, Michael. 2007. "The War Expert." *Columbia Journalism Review*, Vol. 46, No. 4 (November–December), 18–20.

Matray, James I. 1979. "Truman's Plan for Victory: National Self-Determination and the Thirty-Eighth Parallel Decision in Korea." *Journal of American History*, Vol. 66, No. 2 (September), 314–33.

May, Mark A. and Leonard W. Doob. 1937. "Cooperation and Competition: An Experimental Study in Motivation." *Social Science Research Council Bulletin*, No. 25 (April), 1–191.

McAleer, Kevin. 1994. *Dueling: The Cult of Honor in Fin-de-Siècle Germany.* Princeton, NJ: Princeton University Press.

McCain, John. 1994. "The Nuclear Ambitions of North Korea." Remarks on the Senate Floor, October 7, available at http://www.fas.org/spp/starwars/congress/1994/s941007-dprk.htm.

2002. "No Time to Sleep." *Washington Post*, October 24, A35.

McCain, John, Joseph I. Lieberman, and Lindsey Graham. 2012. "Sustaining Success in Afghanistan." *Washington Post*, March 21.

McClintock, Charles. 1974. "Development of Social Motives in Anglo-American and Mexican Children." *Journal of Personality and Social Psychology*, Vol. 29, No 3 (March), 348–54.

McDermott, Rose, James H. Fowler, and Oleg Smirnoff. 2008. "On the Evolutionary Origin of Prospect Theory Preferences." *Journal of Politics*, Vol. 70, No. 2 (April), 335–50.

McMahon, Robert J. 1991. "Credibility and World Power: Exploring the Psychological Dimension in Postwar American Diplomacy." *Diplomatic History*, Vol. 15, No. 4 (Fall), 455–71.

Mead, Margaret, ed. 1937. *Cooperation and Competition among Primitive Peoples.* New York: McGraw Hill.

Mead, Margaret. 1943. *And Keep Your Powder Dry: An Anthropologist Looks at America.* New York: William Morrow and Company.

Mead, Walter Russell. 1988. *Mortal Splendor: The American Empire in Transition.* Boston, MA: Houghton-Mifflin.

2006. "God's Country?" *Foreign Affairs*, Vol. 85, No. 5 (September–October), 24–43.

Mearsheimer, John J. 2001. *The Tragedy of Great Power Politics*. New York: W. W. Norton.

Mencken, H. L. 1958. *Prejudices: A Selection*. New York: Vintage Books.

Mendelson, Sarah E. 1993. "Internal Battles and External Wars: Politics, Learning, and the Soviet Withdrawal from Afghanistan." *World Politics*, Vol. 45, No. 3 (April), 327–60.

Menges, Constantine C. 2005. *China: The Gathering Threat*. Nashville, TN: Thomas Nelson.

Mercer, Jonathan. 1996. *Reputation and International Politics*. Ithaca, NY: Cornell University Press.

2005. "Rationality and Psychology in International Politics." *International Organization*, Vol. 59, No. 1 (Winter), 77–106.

Michener, James A. 1976. *Sports in America*. New York: Random House.

Milad, Mohammed R. and Gregory J. Quirk. 2012. "Fear Extinction as a Model for Translational Neuroscience: Ten Years of Progress." *Annual Review of Psychology*, Vol. 63, 129–51.

Mill, John Stuart. 1989. *On Liberty*. New York: Cambridge University Press.

Miller, Gregory D. 2012. *The Shadow of the Past: Reputation and Military Alliances before the First World War*. Ithaca, NY: Cornell University Press.

Miller, Stephen E., ed. 1985. *Military Strategy and the Origins of the First World War*. Princeton, NJ: Princeton University Press.

Miller, William Ian. 1990. *Bloodtaking and Peacemaking: Feud, Law and Society in Saga Iceland*. Chicago, IL: University of Chicago Press.

Minorities at Risk Project. 2010. *Minorities at Risk Dataset*. College Park, MD: Center for International Development and Conflict Management, available at http://www.cidcm.umd.edu/mar/.

Mitchell, Alison. 1999. "McCain Keeps Pressing Case for Troops." *New York Times*, April 4, 7.

Mitzen, Jennifer. 2006. "Ontological Security in World Politics: State Identity and the Security Dilemma." *European Journal of International Relations*, Vol. 12, No. 3 (September), 341–70.

Modelski, George. 1990. "Is World Politics Evolutionary Learning?" *International Organization*, Vol. 44, No. 1 (Winter), 1–24.

Moody, Kenton J., Ian D. Hutcheon, and Patrick M. Grant. 2005. *Nuclear Forensic Analysis*. New York: Taylor & Francis.

Morgan, Patrick M. 1985. "Saving Face for the Sake of Deterrence." In Robert Jervis, Richard Ned Lebow, and Janice Stein, *Psychology and Deterrence*. Baltimore, MD: Johns Hopkins University Press, 125–52.

Morgenthau, Hans J. 1973. *Politics among Nations: The Struggle for Power and Peace*, 5th ed. New York: Knopf.

Morris, Dick and Eileen McGann. 2012. *Here Come the Black Helicopters! UN Global Governance and the Loss of Freedom*. New York: Broadside Books.

Mueller, John. 1970. "Presidential Popularity from Truman to Johnson." *American Political Science Review*, Vol. 64, No. 1 (March), 18–34.

1989. *Retreat from Doomsday: The Obsolescence of Major War.* New York: Basic Books.

1994. *Policy and Opinion in the Gulf War.* Chicago, IL: University of Chicago Press.

2004. *The Remnants of War.* Ithaca, NY: Cornell University Press.

2006. *Overblown: How Politicians and the Terrorism Industry Inflate National Security Threats, and Why We Believe Them.* New York: Free Press.

2009a. *Atomic Obsession: Nuclear Alarmism from Hiroshima to Al-Qaeda.* New York: Oxford University Press.

2009b. "War Has Almost Ceased to Exist: An Assessment." *Political Science Quarterly,* Vol. 124, No. 2 (Summer), 297–321.

Mueller, John and Mark G. Stewart. 2011. *Terror, Security, and Money : Balancing the Risks, Benefits, and Costs of Homeland Security.* New York: Oxford University Press.

2012. "The Terrorism Delusion: America's Overwrought Response to September 11." *International Security,* Vol. 37, No. 1 (Summer), 81–110.

Murphy, Gardner, Lois Barclay Murphy, and Theodore M. Newcomb. 1937. *Experimental Social Psychology: An Interpretation of Research upon the Socialization of the Individual.* New York: Harper & Brothers.

Murray, Shoon Kathleen and Jason Meyers. 1999. "Do People Need Foreign Enemies? American Leaders' Beliefs after the Soviet Demise." *Journal of Conflict Resolution,* Vol. 43, No. 5 (October), 555–69.

Nacos, Brigitte Lebens. 2007. *Mass-Mediated Terrorism: The Central Role of the Media in Terrorism and Counterterrorism.* New York: Rowman and Littlefield.

Nasr, Vali and Ray Takeyh. 2008. "The Costs of Containing Iran." *Foreign Affairs,* Vol. 87, No. 1 (January/February), 85–94.

Navarro, Peter W. and Greg Autry. 2011. *Death by China: Confronting the Dragon – A Global Call to Action.* Upper Saddle River, NJ: Prentice Hall.

Newport, Frank. 2007. "Americans More Likely to Believe in God Than the Devil, Heaven More Than Hell." Gallup News Service, June, available at http://www.gallup.com/poll/27877/americans-more-likely-believe-god-than-devil-heaven-more-than-hell.aspx.

New York Times. 2004. "Nourishing the Muslim World." October 25, 20.

New York Times. 2006. "The Sound of One Domino Falling." August 4, 16.

Newsweek. 1994. "The Final Cost of a Mission of Hope." April 4, 44.

Nisbett, Richard E. and Dov Cohen. 1996. *Culture of Honor: The Psychology of Violence in the South.* Boulder, CO: Westview Press.

Nisbett, Richard E. and Lee Ross. 1980. *Human Inference: Strategies and Shortcomings of Social Judgment.* Englewood Cliffs, NJ: Prentice-Hall.

Nitze, Paul H. 1974–75. "The Strategic Balance between Hope and Skepticism." *Foreign Policy,* No. 17 (Winter), 136–56.

Nixon, Richard M. 1985. *No More Vietnams.* New York: Arbor House.

Nordlinger, Eric A. 1995. *Isolationism Reconfigured: American Foreign Policy for a New Century.* Princeton, NJ: Princeton University Press.

Norris, Pippa and Ronald Inglehart. 2009. *Sacred and Secular: Religion and Politics Worldwide.* New York: Cambridge University Press.

Nozick, Robert. 1993. *The Nature of Rationality.* Princeton, NJ: Princeton University Press.

Nye, Joseph. 2004. *Soft Power: The Means to Success in World Politics.* New York: Public Affairs.

Oates, Sarah, Lynda Lee Kaid and Mike Berry. 2009. *Terrorism, Elections, and Democracy: Political Campaigns in the United States, Great Britain, and Russia.* New York: Palgrave Macmillan.

O'Hanlon, Michael. 1998. "America's Military, Cut to the Quick." *Washington Post,* August 9, C1.

O'Neill, Barry. 1999. *Honor, Symbols, and War.* Ann Arbor: University of Michigan Press.

Orme, John. 1987. "Deterrence Failures: A Second Look." *International Security,* Vol. 11, No. 4 (Spring), 97–124.

    1997–98. "The Utility of Force in a World of Scarcity." *International Security,* Vol. 22, No. 3 (Winter), 138–67.

Owen, David. 2007. *The Hubris Syndrome: Bush, Blair and the Intoxication of Power.* London: Politico's.

Owens, Mackubin Thomas. 2009. "The Bush Doctrine: The Foreign Policy of Republican Empire." *Orbis,* Vol. 53, No. 1 (Winter), 23–40.

Pape, Robert A. 2005. "Soft Balancing Against the United States." *International Security,* Vol. 30, No. 1 (Summer), 7–45.

    2009. "Empire Falls." *The National Interest,* No. 99 (January–February), 21–34.

Parisi, Francesco. 2002. "Rent-Seeking through Litigation: Adversarial and Inquisitorial Systems Compared." *International Review of Law and Economics,* Vol. 22, No. 2 (August), 193–216.

Parker, Charles F. and Eric K. Stern. 2002. "Blindsided? September 11 and the Origins of Strategic Surprise." *Political Psychology,* Vol. 23, No. 3 (September), 601–30.

Parker, Geoffrey. 1979. *Spain and the Netherlands, 1559–1659: Ten Studies.* Short Hills, NJ: Enslow Publishers.

    1994. "The Making of Strategy in Hapsburg Spain: Philip II's 'Bid for Mastery,' 1559–1598." In Williamson Murray, MacGregor Knox and Alvin Bernstein, eds., *The Making of Strategy: Rulers, States, and War.* New York: Cambridge University Press, 115–50.

    2004. *The Army of Flanders and the Spanish Road, 1567–1659,* 2nd ed. New York: Cambridge University Press.

Parkinson, Cyril Northcote. 1958. *Parkinson's Law: The Pursuit of Progress.* London: John Murray.

Payne, Richard J. 1995. *The Clash with Distant Cultures: Values, Interests, and Force in American Foreign Policy.* Albany: State University of New York Press.

Peffley, Mark and Jon Hurwitz. 1992. "International Events and Foreign Policy Beliefs: Public Response to Changing Soviet-U.S. Relations." *American Journal of Political Science,* Vol. 36, No. 2 (May), 431–61.

Pei, Minxin. 2003. "The Paradoxes of American Nationalism." *Foreign Policy*, No. 136 (May–June), 31–37.

Peristiany, J. G., ed. 1965. *Honour and Shame: The Values of Mediterranean Society.* London: Weidenfeld and Nicolson.

Peterson, Christopher. 2006. *A Primer in Positive Psychology.* New York: Oxford University Press.

Peterson, Peter G. 2002. "Public Diplomacy and the War on Terrorism." *Foreign Affairs*, Vol. 81, No. 5 (September–October), 74–94.

Pew Center for People and the Press. 2002. "Among Wealthy Nations: U.S. Stands Alone in its Embrace of Religion." Pew Center for People and the Press, December 19, available at http://pewglobal.org/2002/12/19/among-wealthy-nations/.

2006. "Islam and the West: A Conversation with Bernard Lewis." Pew Forum on Religion and Public Life, April 27, transcript available at http://pewforum.org/politics-and-elections/islam-and-the-west-a-conversation-with-bernard-lewis.aspx.

2009. "America's Place in the World in 2009: An Investigation of Public and Leadership Opinion about International Affairs." December 2009, available at http://www.people-press.org/files/legacy-pdf/569.pdf.

Pew Research Center for People and the Press. 2010. "Public Sees a Future Full of Promise and Peril." Pew Center for People and the Press, June 22, available at http://people-press.org/2010/06/22/public-sees-a-future-full-of-promise-and-peril/.

2013. "Majority Says the Federal Government Threatens Their Personal Rights." Pew Center for People and the Press, January 31, available at http://www.people-press.org/2013/01/31/majority-says-the-federal-government-threatens-their-personal-rights/.

Piazza, James A. 2006. "Rooted in Poverty? Terrorism, Poor Economic Development, and Social Cleavages." *Terrorism and Political Violence*, Vol. 18, No. 1 (March), 159–77.

Pinker, Steven. 2011. *The Better Angels of Our Nature: Why Violence has Declined.* New York: Viking.

Pipes, Richard. 1977. "Why the Soviet Union Thinks It Could Fight and Win a Nuclear War." *Commentary*, Vol. 64, No. 1 (July), 21–34.

Pippa Norris and Ronald Inglehart. 2009. *Sacred and Secular: Religion and Politics Worldwide.* New York: Cambridge University Press.

Pitt-Rivers, Julian. 1965. "Honour and Social Status." In J. G. Peristiany, ed., *Honour and Shame: The Values of Mediterranean Society.* London: Weidenfeld and Nicolson, 21–77.

Podhoretz, Norman. 1977. "A Culture of Appeasement." *Harper's*, Vol. 255, No. 1529 (October), 25–32.

1980. *The Present Danger.* New York: Simon and Schuster.

1982. *Why We Were in Vietnam.* New York: Simon and Schuster.

2007a. "The Case for Bombing Iran." *Commentary*, Vol. 123, No. 6 (June), 17–23.

2007b. *World War IV: The Long Struggle against Islamofascism.* New York: Doubleday.

Pollack, Kenneth. 2002. *The Threatening Storm: The Case for Invading Iraq.* New York: Random House.

Posen, Barry R. 2007. "The Case for Restraint." *The American Interest*, Vol. 3, No. 2 (November/December), 6–17.

2006. "We Can Live with a Nuclear Iran." *New York Times*, February 27.

Post, Jerrold M. 1993. "Current Concepts of the Narcissistic Personality: Implications for Political Psychology." *Political Psychology*, Vol. 14, No. 1 (March), 99–121.

Powell, Colin. 1992. *National Military Strategy of the United States.* Washington, DC: U.S. Government Printing Office, January.

Powell, Robert. 1991. "Absolute and Relative Gains in International Relations Theory." *American Political Science Review*, Vol. 85, No. 4. (December), 1303–20.

Preble, Christopher A. 2009. *The Power Problem: How American Military Dominance Makes Us Less Safe, Less Prosperous and Less Free.* Ithaca, NY: Cornell University Press.

Press, Daryl G. 2006. *Calculating Credibility: How Leaders Assess Military Threats.* Ithaca, NY: Cornell University Press.

Program on International Policy Attitudes. 2006. "Large and Growing Numbers of Muslims Reject Terrorism, Bin Laden." College Park, MD: Center for International and Security Studies, University of Maryland, June 30, available at http://www.worldpublicopinion.org/pipa/articles/international_security_bt/221.php?nid=&id=&pnt=221&lb=btis.

Pye, Lucian W. 1991. "Political Culture Revisited." *Political Psychology*, Vol. 12, No. 3 (September), 487–508.

Rabasa, Angel, Cheryl Benard, Lowell H. Schwartz, and Peter Sickle. 2007. *Building Moderate Muslim Networks.* Santa Monica, CA: RAND.

Rabbie, Jacob M. and Murray Horwitz. 1969. "Arousal of Ingroup-Outgroup Bias by a Chance Win or Loss." *Journal of Personality and Social Psychology*, Vol. 13, No. 3 (November), 269–77.

Rachman, Gideon. 2011. "Think Again: American Decline." *Foreign Policy*, No. 184 (January/February), 59–63.

Rauchhaus, Robert. 2009. "Evaluating the Nuclear Peace Hypothesis: A Quantitative Approach." *Journal of Conflict Resolution*, Vol. 53, No. 2 (April), 258–77.

Ravenal, Earl C. 1982. "Counterforce and Alliance: The Ultimate Connection." *International Security*, Vol. 6, No. 4 (Spring), 26–43.

Ravitch, Diane. 2010. *The Death and Life of the Great American School System: How Testing and Choice are Undermining Education.* New York: Basic Books.

Ray, James Lee. 1989. "The Abolition of Slavery and the End of International War." *International Organization*, Vol. 43, No. 3 (Summer), 405–39.

Raymond, Gregory A. 1998/99. "Necessity in Foreign Policy." *Political Science Quarterly*, Vol. 113, No. 4 (Winter), 673–88.

Record, Jeffrey. 2002. *Making War, Thinking History: Munich, Vietnam, and Presidential Uses of Force from Korea to Kosovo.* Annapolis, MD: Naval Institute Press.

2007. *The Specter of Munich: Reconsidering the Lessons of Appeasing Hitler.* Washington, DC: Potomac Books.

Reid, T. R. 2004. *The United States of Europe: The New Superpower and the End of American Supremacy.* New York: Penguin.

Reiter, Dan. 1996. *Crucible of Beliefs: Learning, Alliance, and World Wars.* Ithaca, NY: Cornell University Press.

Reveron, Derek S. 2008. "Military Diplomacy and the Engagement Activities of Combatant Commanders." In Derek S. Reveron and Judith Stiehm, eds., *Inside Defense: Understanding the U.S. Military in the 21st Century.* New York: Macmillan, 2008, 43–54.

Richardson, J. L. 1988. "New Perspectives on Appeasement: Some Implications for International Relations." *World Politics,* Vol. 40, No. 3 (April), 289–316.

Ricks, Thomas E. 2006. *Fiasco: The American Military Adventure in Iraq.* New York: Penguin.

2009. *The Gamble: General David Petraeus and the American Military Adventure in Iraq, 2006–2008.* New York: Penguin Press.

Robin, Corey. 2004. *Fear: The History of a Political Idea.* New York: Oxford University Press.

Robins, Robert S. and Jerrold M. Post. 1997. *Political Paranoia: The Psychopolitics of Hatred.* New Haven, CT: Yale University Press.

Robinson, Ronald and John Gallagher. 1961. *Africa and the Victorians: The Official Mind of Imperialism.* London: Page.

Rock, Stephen R. 2000. *Appeasement in International Politics.* Lexington: University Press of Kentucky.

2011. *Faith and Foreign Policy: The Views and Influence of U.S. Christians and Christian Organizations.* New York: Continuum.

Rojahn, Krystyna and Thomas F. Pettigrew. 1992. "Memory for Schema-Relevant Information: A Meta-Analytic Resolution." *British Journal of Social Psychology,* Vol. 31, No. 2 (June), 81–109.

Rokeach, Milton. 1960. *The Open and Closed Mind: Investigations into the Nature of Belief Systems and Personality Systems.* New York: Basic Books.

Romney, Mitt. 2010. *No Apology: The Case for American Greatness.* New York: St. Martin's Press.

Rose, David. 2008. "The Gaza Bombshell." *Vanity Fair,* April.

Rosecrance, Richard. 1986. *The Rise of the Trading State: Commerce and Conquest in the Modern World.* New York: Basic Books.

1999. *The Rise of the Virtual State: Wealth and Power in the Coming Century.* New York: Basic Books.

Rosen, Stephen Peter. 2009. "Blood Brothers: The Dual Origins of American Bellicosity." *The American Interest,* Vol. 4, No. 6 (July/August), 20–28.

Rosenau, Pauline Vaillancourt. 2003. *The Competition Paradigm: America's Romance with Conflict, Contest, and Commerce.* Lanham, MD: Rowman and Littlefield.

Rosner, Jeremy D. 1995–96. "The Know-Nothings Know Something." *Foreign Policy,* No. 101 (Winter), 116–29.

Ross, Dennis. 1981. "Considering Soviet Threats to the Persian Gulf." *International Security,* Vol. 6, No. 2 (Fall), 159–80.

Ross, Michael and Fiore Sicoly. 1979. "Egocentric Bias in Availability and Attribution." *Journal of Personality and Social Psychology*, Vol. 37, No. 3 (March), 322–26.

Rove, Karl. 2009. "The President's Apology Tour." *Wall Street Journal*, April 23.

Rozin, Paul and Edward B. Roysman. 2001. "Negativity Bias, Negativity Dominance, and Contagion." *Personality and Social Psychology Review*, Vol. 5, No. 4 (November), 296–320.

Rubin, Alissa J. 2012. "Two Senators Say U.S. Should Arm Syrian Rebels." *New York Times*, February 19, A7.

Rumsfeld, Donald. 2002. "DoD News Briefing." February 12, 2002, available at www.defenselink.mil/transcripts/transcript.aspx?transcriptid=2636.

Rutherford, Brent M. 1966. "Psychopathology, Decision-Making, and Political Involvement." *Journal of Conflict Resolution*, Vol. 10, No. 4 (December), 387–407.

Ryckman, Richard M., Bill Thornton, and J. Corey Butler. 1994. "Personality Correlates of the Hypercompetitive Attitude Scale: Validity Tests of Horney's Theory of Neurosis." *Journal of Personality Assessment*, Vol. 62, No. 1 (Winter), 84–94.

Sagan, Scott and Jeremi Suri. 2003. "The Madman Nuclear Alert: Secrecy, Signaling and Safety in October 1969." *International Security*, Vol. 27, No. 4 (Spring), 150–83.

Schatz, Edward and Renan Levine. 2010. "Framing, Public Diplomacy, and Anti-Americanism in Central Asia." *International Studies Quarterly*, Vol. 54, No. 3 (September), 855–69.

Schelling, Thomas C. 1960. *The Strategy of Conflict*. Cambridge, MA: Harvard University Press.

1966. *Arms and Influence*. New Haven, CT: Yale University Press.

Schlesinger, Arthur M. Jr. 1963. "One Against the Many." In Arthur Schlesinger Jr. and Morton White, eds., *Paths of American Thought*. Boston: Houghton Mifflin, 531–38.

Schuman, Howard and Michael P. Johnson. 1976. "Attitudes and Behavior." *Annual Review of Sociology*, Vol. 2, 161–207.

Schumpeter, Joseph A. 1951. "The Sociology of Imperialisms." In Joseph A. Schumpeter, *Imperialism and Social Classes*. Oxford: Basil Blackwell, 3–130.

Schuster, Mark A., Bradley D. Stein, Lisa H. Jaycox, Rebecca L. Collins, Grant N. Marshall, Marc N. Elliott, Annie Jie Zhou, David E. Kanouse, Janina L. Morrison and Sandra H. Berry. 2001. "A National Survey of Stress Reactions after the September 11, 2001, Terrorist Attacks." *New England Journal of Medicine*, Vol. 345, No. 20 (November 15), 1507–12.

Schwartz, Barry. 2004. *The Paradox of Choice: Why More is Less*. New York: Harper Collins.

Schweller, Randall L. 1999. "Realism and the Present Great Power System: Growth and Positional Conflict over Scarce Resources." In Ethan B.

Kapstein and Michael Mastanduno, eds., *Unipolar Politics: Realism and State Strategies after the Cold War.* New York: Columbia University Press, 28–68.

Scoblic, J. Peter. 2008. *U.S. vs. Them: Conservatism in the Age of Nuclear Terror.* New York: Penguin Books.

Seliktar, Ofira. 1986. "Identifying a Society's Belief Systems." In Margaret G. Hermann, ed., *Political Psychology: Contemporary Problems and Issues.* San Francisco, CA: Jossey-Bass Publishers, 320–354.

Sen, Amartya. 1999. *Development as Freedom.* New York: Knopf.

Shackleford, Todd K. 2005. "An Evolutionary Psychological Perspective on Cultures of Honor." *Evolutionary Psychology,* Vol. 3, 381–91.

Shanker, Thom. 2011. "Warning against Wars Like Iraq and Afghanistan." *New York Times,* February 22, A7.

Shannon, Vaughn P. and Michael Dennis. 2007. "Militant Islam and the Futile Fight for Reputation." *Security Studies,* Vol. 16, No. 2 (April–June), 287–317.

Sherif, Muzafer, O. J. Harvey, Jack White, William R. Hood, and Carolyn W. Sherif. 1988. *The Robbers Cave Experiment.* Middletown, CT: Wesleyan University Press.

Simons, Anna. 2003. "The Death of Conquest." *The National Interest,* No. 71 (Spring), 41–49.

Simon, Herbert A. 1983. *Reason in Human Affairs.* Stanford, CA: Stanford University Press.

1957. *Models of Man: Social and Rational.* New York: John Wiley & Sons.

1995. "Rationality in Political Behavior." *Political Psychology,* Vol. 16, No. 1 (March), 45–61.

Sinclair, Upton, Jr. 1935. *I, Candidate for Governor: And How I Got Licked.* Berkeley: University of California Press.

Singer, J. David and Melvin Small. 1972. *The Wages of War, 1816–1965: A Statistical Handbook.* New York: John Wiley & Sons.

Sipes, Richard. 1973. "War, Sports and Aggression: An Empirical Test of Two Rival Theories." *American Anthropologist,* Vol. 75, No. 1 (February), 64–86.

Slater, Jerome. 1993/94. "The Domino Theory and International Politics: The Case of Vietnam." *Security Studies,* Vol. 3, No. 2 (Winter), 186–224.

Slovic, Paul. 2000. *The Perception of Risk.* London: Earthscan.

Smeltz, Dina. 2012. *Foreign Policy in the New Millennium: Results of the 2012 Chicago Council Survey of American Public Opinion and U.S. Foreign Policy.* Chicago, IL: Chicago Council on Global Affairs, September 10.

Smidt, Corwin E. 2005. "Religion and American Attitudes toward Islam and an Invasion of Iraq." *Sociology of Religion,* Vol. 66, No. 3 (Autumn), 243–61.

Smith, Anthony. 1981. "States and Homelands: The Social and Geopolitical Implications of National Territory." *Millennium,* Vol. 10, No. 3 (September), 187–202.

Snegirev, Vladimir and Valery Samunin. 2012. *The Dead End: The Road to Afghanistan,* National Security Archive Electronic Briefing Book No.

396, October 13, available at http://www.gwu.edu/~nsarchiv/NSAEBB/
    NSAEBB396/Full%20Text%20Virus%20A.pdf.

Snidal, Duncan. 1991. "Relative Gains and the Pattern of International
    Cooperation." *American Political Science Review*, Vol. 85, No. 3
    (September), 701–26.

Snyder, Glenn H. 1961. *Deterrence and Defense: Toward a New Theory of National
    Security*. Princeton, NJ: Princeton University Press.

Snyder, Glenn H. and Paul Diesing. 1977. *Conflict among Nations: Bargaining
    Decision Making and System Structure in International Crisis*. Princeton, NJ:
    Princeton University Press.

Snyder, Jack L. 1984. *The Ideology of the Offensive: Military Decision Making and
    the Disasters of 1914*. Ithaca, NY: Cornell University Press.

    1991a. "Introduction." In Robert Jervis and Jack Snyder, eds., *Dominoes and
    Bandwagons: Strategic Beliefs and Great Power Competition in the Eurasian
    Rimland*. New York: Oxford University Press, 3–19.

    1991. *Myths of Empire: Domestic Politics and International Ambition*. Ithaca, NY:
    Cornell University Press.

    2009. "Imperial Myths and Threat Inflation." In A. Trevor Thrall and
    Jane K. Cramer, eds., *American Foreign Policy and the Politics of Fear: Threat
    Inflation since 9/11*. New York: Routledge, 40–53.

Snyder, Jack L. and Karen Ballentine. 1996. "Nationalism and the Marketplace
    of Ideas." *International Security*, Vol. 21, No. 2 (Autumn), 5–40.

Snyder, Thomas D., ed. 1993. *120 Years of American Education: A Statistical
    Portrait*. Washington, DC: Department of Education, National Center for
    Education Statistics.

Sparks, Glenn G. and Cheri W. Sparks. 2002. "The Effects of Media Violence."
    In Jennings Bryant and Dolf Zillmann, eds., *Media Effects: Advances in
    Theory and Research*. London: Routledge, 269–86.

Spengler, Joseph J. 1972. "Social Science and the Collectivization of Hubris."
    Political Science Quarterly, Vol. 87, No. 1 (March), 1–21.

Spengler, Oswald. 1926–28. *The Decline of the West*. New York: Knopf.

Sprout, Harold and Margaret Sprout. 1965. *The Ecological Perspective on Human
    Affairs*. Princeton, NJ: Princeton University Press.

Sorley, Lewis. 1999. *A Better War: The Unexamined Victories and Final Tragedy of
    America's Last Years in Vietnam*. New York: Harcourt Brace.

Stanne, Mary Beth, David W. Johnson, and Roger T. Johnson. 1999. "Does
    Competition Enhance or Inhibit Motor Performance: A Meta-Analysis."
    Psychological Bulletin, Vol. 125, No. 1 (January), 133–54.

Stein, Janice. 1988. "Building Politics into Psychology: The Misperception of
    Threat." *Political Psychology*, Vol. 9, No. 2 (June), 245–71.

    1996. "Deterrence and Learning in an Enduring Rivalry." *Security Studies*,
    Vol. 6, No. 1 (Autumn), 104–52.

Stelzer, Irwin, ed. 2004. *The Neocon Reader*. New York: Grove Press.

Stephan, Alexander. 2000. *Communazis: FBI Surveillance of German Émigré
    Writers*. New Haven, CT: Yale University Press.

Steward, Dick. 2000. *Duels and the Roots of Violence in Missouri.* Columbia: University of Missouri Press.

Stewart, Frank Henderson. 1994. *Honor.* Chicago, IL: University of Chicago Press.

Stiglitz, Joseph E. and Linda J. Bilmes. 2008. *The Three Trillion Dollar War: The True Cost of the Iraq Conflict.* New York: W. W. Norton.

Suri, Jeremi. 2011. *Liberty's Surest Guardian: American Nation-Building from the Founders to Obama.* New York: Free Press.

Swansbrough, Robert H. 2008. *Test by Fire: The War Presidency of George W. Bush.* New York: Macmillan.

Tang, Shiping. 2005. "Reputation, the Cult of Reputation, and International Conflict." *Security Studies,* Vol. 14, No 1 (January–March), 34–62.

   2008. "Fear in International Politics: Two Positions." *International Studies Review,* Vol. 10, No. 3 (September), 451–71.

Tavuchis, Nicholas. 1991. *Mea Culpa: A Sociology of Apology and Reconciliation.* Stanford, CA: Stanford University Press.

Telhami, Shibley. 2005. "What Arab Public Opinion Thinks of U.S. Policy." Brookings Institution Forum, December 12, transcript available at http://www.brook.edu/fp/saban/events/20051212.pdf.

   2011. *"2011 Arab Public Opinion Poll."* College Park: University of Maryland, November 21, available at http://www.brookings.edu/research/reports/2011/11/21-arab-public-opinion-telhami.

Themnér, Lotta and Peter Wallensteen. 2012. "Armed Conflict, 1946–2011." *Journal of Peace Research,* Vol. 49, No. 4 (July 2012), pp. 565–75.

Thomas, Evan. 2010. *The War Lovers: Roosevelt, Lodge, Hearst, and the Rush to Empire, 1898.* New York: Little, Brown and Company.

Thompson, John A. 1992. "The Exaggeration of American Vulnerability: The Anatomy of a Tradition." *Diplomatic History,* Vol. 16, No. 1 (Winter), 23–43.

Thompson, Nicholas. 2009. *The Hawk and the Dove: Paul Nitze, George Kennan, and the History of the Cold War.* New York: Henry Holt and Co.

de Tocqueville, Alexis. 2003. *Democracy in America.* New York: Penguin.

Tolstoy, Leo. 1904. *What is Art?* New York: Funk and Wagnalls Company.

Triandis, Harry C. 1995. *Individualism and Collectivism.* Boulder, CO: Westview Press.

Triandis, Harry C., Robert Bontempo, Marcelo J. Villareal, Masaaki Asai, and Nydia Lucca. 1988. "Individualism and Collectivism: Cross-Cultural Perspectives on Self-Ingroup Relationships." *Journal of Personality and Social Psychology,* Vol. 54, No. 2 (February), 323–38.

Tuchman, Barbara. 1984. *The March of Folly: From Try to Vietnam.* New York: Ballantine Books.

   1978. *A Distant Mirror: The Calamitous 14th Century.* New York: Knopf.

Tucker, Robert C. 1965. "The Dictator and Totalitarianism." *World Politics,* Vol. 17, No. 4 (July), 555–83.

Tucker, Robert W. 1979. "America in Decline: The Foreign Policy of 'Maturity.'" *Foreign Affairs,* Vol. 58, No. 3, 449–84.

Tutko, Thomas and William Bruns. 1976. *Winning is Everything and other American Myths.* New York: MacMillan Publishing Co.

Tyler, Patrick E. 1992. "U.S. Strategy Plan Calls for Insuring No Rivals Develop." *New York Times*, March 8.

Tyson, Neil DeGrasse. 2012. "The Case for Space: Why We Should Keep Reaching for the Stars." *Foreign Affairs*, Vol. 91, No. 2 (March/April), 22–33.

U.S Department of Commerce. 2009. *Educational Attainment in the United States: 2009.* Washington, DC: U.S. Census Bureau, February, available at http://www.census.gov/prod/2012pubs/p20-566.pdf.

Väyrynen, Raimo. 2006. *The Waning of Major War: Theories and Debates.* New York: Routledge.

Volkan, Vamik D. 1988. *The Need to Have Enemies and Allies: From Clinical Practice to International Relationships.* Northvale, NJ: Jason Aronson, Inc.

Wachtel, Paul L. 1983. *The Poverty of Affluence: A Psychological Portrait of the American Way of Life.* New York: Free Press.

Wallensteen, Peter and Mikael Eriksson. 2004. "Armed Conflict, 1989–2003." *Journal of Peace Research*, Vol. 41, No. 5 (September), 625–36.

Walling, Kurtl. 1998. "Alexander Hamilton on Honor and American Foreign Policy." In Elliot Abrams, ed., *Honor among Nations: Intangible Interests and Foreign Policy.* Washington, DC: Ethics and Public Policy Center, 75–96.

Walliser, Bernard. 1989. "Instrumental Rationality and Cognitive Rationality." *Theory and Decision*, Vol. 27, Nos. 1–2 (July), 7–36.

Walker, Stephen G. and Akan Malici. 2011. *U.S. Presidents and Foreign Policy Mistakes.* Palo Alto, CA: Stanford University Press.

Walt, Stephen M. 2012. "Why are U.S. Leaders so Obsessed with Credibility?" *Foreign Policy* Blog, September 11, available at http://walt.foreignpolicy.com/posts/2012/09/11/the_credibility_fetish.

Waltz, Kenneth N. 1959. *Man, the State, and War: A Theoretical Analysis.* New York: Columbia University Press.

1990. "Nuclear Myths and Political Realities." *American Political Science Review*, Vol. 84, No. 3 (September), 731–45.

Webb, James. 2012. "The South China Sea's Gathering Storm." *Wall Street Journal*, August 20, A11.

Weinstein, Franklin B. 1969. "The Concept of a Commitment in International Relations." *Journal of Conflict Resolution*, Vol. 13, No. 1 (March), 39–56.

Wells, Samuel F., Jr. 1979. "Sounding the Tocsin: NSC 68 and the Soviet Threat." *International Security*, Vol. 4, No. 2 (Autumn), 116–28.

Wendt, Alexander. 1992. "Anarchy is What States Make of It: The Social Construction of Power Politics." *International Organization*, Volume 46, No. 2 (Spring), 391–425.

1999. *Social Theory of International Relations.* New York: Cambridge University Press.

2004. "The State as Person in International Theory." *Review of International Studies*, Vol. 30, No. 2 (April), 289–316.

White, Ralph K. 1968. *Nobody Wanted War.* New York: Doubleday.

White, Theodore H. 2010. *The Making of the President 1968.* New York: Harper Collins.

Wiggins, David Kenneth, ed. 1995. *Sport in America: From Wicked Amusement to National Obsession.* Champaign, IL: Human Kinetics.

Wiesman, Steven R. 1993. "President Appeals before Congress for Aid to Latins." *New York Times,* April 28, A1.

Wilcox, Clyde and Carin Robinson. 2010. *Onward Christian Soldiers? The Religious Right in American Politics,* 4th ed. Boulder, CO: Westview Press.

Williams, Dan and Ann Devroy. 1994. "U.S. Policy Lacks Focus, Critics Say: Bosnia Cited as Prime Case." *Washington Post,* April 24, A1.

Williams, Michael C. 2005. "What is the National Interest? The Neoconservative Challenge in IR Theory." *European Journal of International Relations,* Vol. 11, No. 3 (September), 307–37.

Wilson, Timothy D. 2002. *Strangers to Ourselves: Discovering the Adaptive Unconscious.* Cambridge, MA: Harvard University Press.

Wirls, Daniel. 2010. *Irrational Security: The Politics of Defense from Reagan to Obama.* Baltimore, MD: Johns Hopkins University Press.

Wohlforth, William. 1998. "Honor as Interest in Russian Decisions for War, 1600–1995." In Elliott Abrams, ed., *Honor Among Nations: Intangible Interests and Foreign Policy.* Washington, DC: Ethics and Public Policy Center, 21–43.

2009. "Unipolarity, Status Competition, and Great Power War." *World Politics,* Vol. 61, No. 1 (January), 28–57.

Wohlstetter, Albert. 1959. "The Delicate Balance of Terror." *Foreign Affairs,* Vol. 27, No. 2 (January), 211–35.

Wolfowitz, Paul. 2000. "Statesmanship in the New Century." In Robert Kagan and William Kristol, eds., *Present Dangers: Crisis and Opportunity in American Foreign and Defense Policy.* San Francisco, CA: Encounter Books, 307–36.

2011. "Shaping the Future: Planning at the Pentagon, 1989–93." In Melvyn P. Leffler and Jeffrey W. Legro, *In Uncertain Times: American Foreign Policy after the Berlin Wall and 9/11.* Ithaca, NY: Cornell University Press, 44–62.

Wolfers, Arnold. 1962. *Discord and Collaboration: Essays on International Politics.* Baltimore, MD: Johns Hopkins University Press.

Woodward, Bob. 2002. *Bush at War.* New York: Simon and Schuster.

2004. *Plan of Attack.* New York: Simon and Schuster.

Woodward, C. Vann. 1960. "The Age of Reinterpretation." *American Historical Review,* Vol. 66, No. 1 (October), 1–19.

Wright, Quincy. 1965. *A Study of War.* Chicago, IL: University of Chicago Press.

Wright, Robin. 2007. "From the Desk of Donald Rumsfeld…" *Washington Post,* November 1.

Wyatt-Brown, Bertram. 1982. *Southern Honor: Ethics and Behavior in the Old South.* New York: Oxford University Press.

Wyden, Peter. 1979. *Bay of Pigs: The Untold Story.* New York: Simon and Schuster.

Yardley, Jim and William J. Broad. 2004. "Heading for the Stars, and Wondering if China Might Reach Them First." *New York Times*, January 22.

Younger, Stephen M. 2009. *The Bomb: A New History*. New York: Echo.

Zacher, Mark W. 2001. "The Territorial Integrity Norm: International Boundaries and the Use of Force." *International Organization*, Vol. 55, No. 2 (Spring), 215–50.

Zakaria, Fareed. 2002. "Time to Take on America's Haters." *Newsweek*, October 21.

2008. *The Post-American World*. New York: W. W. Norton.

Zaller John R. 1992. *The Nature and Origins of Mass Opinion*. New York: Cambridge University Press.

Zarate, Michael A., Bernice Garcia, Azenett A. Garza, and Robert T. Hitlan. 2004. "Cultural Threat and Perceived Realistic Group Conflict as Dual Predictors of Prejudice." *Journal of Experimental Social Psychology*, Vol. 40, No. 1 (January), 99–105.

Zenko, Micah and Michael A. Cohen. 2012. "Clear and Present Safety: The United States is More Secure than Washington Thinks." *Foreign Affairs*, Vol. 91, No. 2 (March/April), 79–93.

Index